Florida A&M University, Tallahassee
Florida Atlantic University, Boca Raton
Florida Gulf Coast University, Ft. Myers
Florida International University, Miami
Florida State University, Tallahassee
New College of Florida, Sarasota
University of Central Florida, Orlando
University of Florida, Gainesville
University of North Florida, Jacksonville
University of South Florida, Tampa
University of West Florida, Pensacola

Democracy and U.S. Policy in Latin America during the Truman Years

Steven Schwartzberg

University Press of Florida
Gainesville/Tallahassee/Tampa/Boca Raton
Pensacola/Orlando/Miami/Jacksonville/Ft. Myers/Sarasota

Copyright 2003 by Steven Schwartzberg
Printed in the United States of America on acid-free paper
All rights reserved

First cloth printing, 2003
First paperback printing, 2008

Library of Congress Cataloging-in-Publication Data
Schwartzberg, Steven, 1962–
Democracy and U.S. policy in Latin America during the Truman years /
Steven Schwartzberg.
p. cm.
Includes bibliographical references and index.
ISBN 978-0-8130-2664-0 (cloth)(alk. paper)
ISBN 978-0-8130-3342-6 (pbk.)
1. Latin America—Foreign relations—United States. 2. United States—Foreign
relations—Latin America. 3. United States—Foreign relations—1945–53. 4. Latin
America—Foreign relations. I. Title.
F1418.S395 2003
327.7308'09'044—dc21   2003056422

The University Press of Florida is the scholarly publishing agency for the State
University System of Florida, comprising Florida A&M University, Florida Atlantic
University, Florida Gulf Coast University, Florida International University, Florida
State University, New College of Florida, University of Central Florida, University
of Florida, University of North Florida, University of South Florida, and University
of West Florida.

University Press of Florida
15 Northwest 15th Street
Gainesville, FL 32611–2079
http://www.upf.com

To the memory of
Elie Kedourie
John Roche
Edward Shils,

each of whom embraced the commandment of Leviticus 25:10,
without letting his faith cloud his vision.

This country has won the good fight, and has been fortunate enough to maintain its gains as far as its domestic affairs are concerned. Whatever may be said about the national situation here today, it is undeniable that the highest spiritual, economic, and political values are placed on the individual in this nation. No other land has achieved so much for so many. It is natural to inquire whether this phenomenon is peculiar and unique, or whether it would be possible to extend these advantages to the rest of humanity. The pilgrim strain in the population, with its generous missionary spirit, yearns to share with all the world. Others do not believe it either feasible or desirable. The history of the United States for some time back reveals a special propensity of the American people, which certain factions have used for their own ends, and this is the fear of being taken in by strangers who would take advantage of their inexperience. Among a people that prides itself on its practicality and business acumen, although at heart it is definitely mystical and generous, the awakening of suspicion is a very effective device. And so we find the paradox of the most outstanding exponents of missionary zeal warmly defending the position that it is good business to assist less fortunate peoples. And of course, in the last analysis, so it is. . . . But the question as I see it is not whether this policy is good business, but rather whether or not it is possible to evade the supreme law of our times: the oneness of the human family.

Alberto Lleras Camargo

Contents

Preface

Getting ready for bed one night in El Salvador in the summer of 1982, I noticed that one of my new acquaintances was putting on a pair of bullet-proof pink underwear. The house in which we were guests belonged to a representative of the AFL-CIO's American Institute for Free Labor Development (AIFLD), so there was some reason for concern. Two AIFLD representatives, Mike Hammer and Mark Pearlman, had been murdered the year before along with José Viera, the head of El Salvador's land reform program. Of the four hundred or so activists who were explaining the land reform to the peasant families it affected, roughly 10 percent had been killed by then. At a closet door, I had been shown a small arsenal which included a grenade with a "long" delay—seven seconds. If anyone tried to break in during the night, I was to throw it into the garage and then run around two corners before it went off. However, the most disturbing thing I saw was a double bill of *Mommie Dearest* and *The Postman Always Rings Twice.*

Books have obscure origins. The one you are holding began in a sense in El Salvador that summer, or at least in the political outlook that led me there—a faith in the Cold War liberalism best exemplified by the likes of George Meany and Lane Kirkland. The eloquence of these labor leaders, and their combination of patriotism, anticommunism, and liberal democratic internationalism, was profoundly appealing to the high school political activist I was in the late 1970s. At Meany's funeral in January 1980, Kirkland prophesied that better days lay ahead for the working people of America and of the world, "because George Meany is up there, negotiating the matter with God."[1] Arriving at Reed College as a freshman that fall, I was inclined to view the strikes in Poland as evidence that Kirkland was right. Here were ten million people, the vast majority of the country's workforce, repudiating communism and championing democratic self-government and free trade unions. The United States must have seemed to many of them, as Lincoln had described it, the last best hope of mankind.[2]

A member of the national committee of the Young Peoples Socialist League in the early 1980s, I considered myself heir to the anticommunist tradition of Bayard Rustin and Norman Thomas.[3] Historical interpretations that attributed a malevolent character to American policy simply because it was anticommunist seemed utterly unpersuasive. Nor did the charge of "imperialism" seem grounds to deny American policy a capacity for benevolence. Arguing that "the greatest first step our world could take towards peace would be the nonnuclear dismantling of the Soviet Empire," I had my sights set on the malevolence of another imperialism.[4]

The postwar American "empire" in Western Europe and Japan was obviously more successful and enjoyed more elite support and popular legitimacy than the postwar American empire in Latin America. I was interested in the reasons for this difference and whether there were any lessons that might be drawn from past successes and failures.[5] By the time I began serious research for this book, I was inclined to suspect that the motives behind postwar American policy toward Latin America were of a piece with the motives behind postwar American policy toward Western Europe and Japan.[6] I believe I have now proven that suspicion correct. The primary political advice I would offer is to have a greater measure of confidence in the legitimacy and viability of an American international leadership that genuinely holds itself accountable to the twin principles of democratic solidarity and respect for the national sovereignty of other peoples. A leadership that seeks to practice the virtue of civility can make mistakes, but it can also advance the general welfare by the coherence and decency of its endeavor.[7]

The civility of American liberals has tended to shade off into an arrogance that cares little for the views local allies hold of their own situation and the strategies they consider appropriate for pursuing their own rights and interests. The civility of American conservatives has tended to shade off into an indifference to the sufferings of others and the complicity of the United States in the continuation of remediable evils. Yet the historical record shows that at times American officials have succeeded in avoiding these extremes and have contributed to the strengthening of the international moral consensus at the foundation of our emerging planetary society. They have successfully participated with others in the struggle for the realization of common human values and have done so in Latin America as well as in Europe and Asia.

This book is about the transmission of impulse across borders. It is about the dynamic interaction between the hopes of American officials and the aspirations of political leaders in Latin America. It shows how a concern with the common good helped shape American policy and how ideas for pursuing it varied with the course of ongoing political struggles in Latin America as well as with the convictions of individual American officials. It shows a much greater autonomy to Latin American politics than diplomatic historians have previously recognized and a far greater role for political leaders and developments in the region in shaping American policy than Latin Americanists have previously perceived. It also shows that competing conceptions of the ways in which the rights and interests of others should be defined and taken into account were much more important to American policy than political scientists have previously appreciated.

The liberal impulse in American policy is concisely expressed in the conviction that "we cannot build our future without helping others build theirs."[8] It is an impulse that sustains concern with the domestic welfare and liberties of other countries and promotes a shared belief in progress and reform as a foundation for cooperation. The conservative impulse in American policy is manifest in the sentiment of "the neighbor who resolutely respects himself and, because he does so, respects the rights of others."[9] It is an impulse that sustains a reluctance to intervene in the internal affairs of the rest of the world and promotes recognition of the diversity and autonomy of other countries as a foundation for cooperation. The rivalry between these two impulses is a permanent part of American policy and of the interaction between the United States and other countries.

The end of the Second World War saw a wave of democratic openings in Latin America. It was a time, as the great Venezuelan social democrat Rómulo Betancourt later recalled, when, "with ballots or with bullets, the peoples were bringing democrats to power."[10] These victories encouraged American liberals and were encouraged by them. American policy actively contributed to democratic openings in Cuba and Brazil and welcomed democratic openings in Guatemala, Peru, and Venezuela. "The peoples of the Americas," President Harry Truman declared in April 1946, "have a right to expect of the Pan American system that it show its validity by promoting those liberties and principles which the word 'democracy' implies to them." Whatever their differences, he suggested, they could all agree that certain political rights were fundamental, including free speech, a free press, freedom of assembly, and freedom of conscience.

If we dedicate ourselves to this objective, we shall make the fullest contribution to the welfare of our own people and of the world at large. By giving tangible expression to the meaning of democracy, we shall widen and strengthen its hold upon the imagination of the world. In that way we can revitalize, through our Pan American cooperation, the faith of peoples everywhere in their ability to build a peaceful world upon a firm foundation.[11]

Speaking before a meeting of the Pan American Women's Association in February 1948, the Peruvian social democrat Víctor Raúl Haya de la Torre offered a strikingly similar exposition of the aspirations of Latin America's democrats. He began by noting that while diplomatic efforts to maintain peace and friendly relations among the countries of North and South America were welcome, they were not enough. Genuine good neighborliness would require popular involvement and support. A strong foundation for progress would be laid when the working men and women of the United States became familiar with the economic realities and conditions of life of their fellow workers in Latin America. The formation of a vigorous public opinion on inter-American problems, rooted in their friendship and solidarity, would help encourage and safeguard both political and economic democracy throughout the New World. Such a consolidated democratic hemisphere, Haya de la Torre suggested, could have a great impact on the rest of the world.

Then we will be able to tell the Old World—"Here you have a system for getting along together. Here you have an example of democratic good neighborliness which not only guarantees civil equality but also social justice. Here you have a method to achieve material welfare without the need of 'blessings' from class dictatorships or the chance benevolence of despotic and intolerant political parties." This, I believe, is the manner in which the Americas can contribute to the peace of the world. This is the manner in which our countries can best serve the ideals of the United Nations. Despite the hatred and clashes between races and religious groups in other parts of the world, it is possible that we three hundred million Americans of North and South can perform the historic feat of showing the rest of the world how one can live and enjoy spiritual and economic liberty under a government "of the people, by the people and for the people." It is toward this goal that many men and women of Latin America are working. The history of our republics is the story of the struggle of their peoples for democracy.[12]

The success of democracy in Latin America and the acceptability of the American empire in the region were primarily dependent upon the strength and skill and luck of local democratic forces. While these forces were at a historic zenith in the early Truman years, they were still weak and poorly organized in many countries. Even where they enjoyed strong and cohesive organizations that succeeded in winning solid majority support in successive free elections—as in Cuba, Peru, and Venezuela—they faced formidable obstacles. These included traditionally unprofessional and politicized military forces, civilian opponents of democracy on both the right and the left of the political spectrum, and an inconsistently supportive American policy. It is to such obstacles, and especially to the strategic and tactical mistakes made by the leadership of the democratic forces, that one should look for an understanding of the wave of democratic breakdowns of the late 1940s and early 1950s. Without the corruption tolerated by the Cuban Auténticos, and with greater attention to the maintenance of inter-elite consensus on the part of Peruvian Apristas and Venezuelan Adecos, the democratic openings in each of these countries could have continued.

Had the liberals maintained their ascendancy among American officials, one can easily imagine alternative American policies that might have succeeded in giving Venezuelan and Cuban democrats a second chance. As it was, growing conservative influence meant that democrats like Haya and Betancourt would become increasingly critical of American policy as American officials pursued cordial relations with dictatorial regimes in their countries. Although the defeat of democratic forces in Peru and Venezuela was at the heart of the shift toward conservatism in American policy, conservative officials had already begun to draw strength from the failure of a liberal policy toward Argentina led by Assistant Secretary of State Spruille Braden. Still, it was only after military coups in Caracas and Lima, and after the repudiation of an inefficacious antidictatorial effort in Panama, that the conservatives gained the ascendancy. Their growing influence before this time did not prevent American officials from assisting democratic forces in Ecuador and Costa Rica.

Where the liberals sought to advance American interests by encouraging democratic victories, conservatives did not attempt to pursue an analogous policy in the opposite direction. They did not seek to encourage dictatorial victories but rather to remain neutral in the struggle between democratic and dictatorial forces as long as they were confident that American security would not be greatly and adversely affected by the outcome. There was an abortive and dubiously authorized covert operation against the elected government of Guatemala during the later Truman years under the code name PBFORTUNE. However, it must be stressed that no such operation was directed against the Adecos in Venezuela or the Apristas in Peru. On the contrary, American officials recognized that these social democratic movements were capable of combating communism in ways that right-wing dictatorships were not, and that they were therefore superior allies. Interpretations that suggest that the postwar wave of democratic political openings "collapsed on the advent of the Cold War" do not hold chronological water.[13] The Cold War did not play a significant role in the breakdown and overthrow of democracy in Peru and Venezuela in 1948. Anticommunism and Cold War considerations exercised a predominantly prodemocratic influence on American policy from before the end of the Second World War until after the military coups in Lima and Caracas.

Acknowledgments

I am grateful to Gaddis Smith, Donald Fleming, Akira Iriye, Ernest May, Jonathan Spence, Paul Kennedy, Gil Joseph, Fred Logevall, Kurk Dorsey, David Frisk, Sheri Berman, Gideon Rose, Elizabeth White, Kathy Newman, Max Bell, Jean Bell, Kevin Bell, Hugh Schwartzberg, Joanne Schwartzberg, Jenny Schwartzberg, Elizabeth McPike, and Richard Wilson. I am especially grateful to Diane Bell, my wife of many years, and to our children, Thalia Bell and Galen Schwartzberg.

The author and publisher appreciate permission from Cambridge University Press to reprint chapter 5 on Rómulo Betancourt, originally published in the *Journal of Latin American Studies*, volume 29, part 3, October 1997, pp. 613–65.

1

The Rise of Cold War Liberalism
in Latin America

The Cold War came early to Latin America. Well before the end of the Second World War, American officials were seeking to support reformist and democratic movements in the region as the best possible bulwark against the threat that they thought communist forces loyal to Stalinist Russia posed to American security. The single most important figure in the struggle of these Cold War liberals for ascendancy in American policy was the American ambassador to Cuba, Spruille Braden. Almost since setting foot on the island in 1942, he had been warning of the strength of a local communist party that was supporting Cuban strongman Fulgencio Batista and receiving support from him in return. Although the Cuban Communist Party (CP) was one of the youngest and smallest of the Cuban parties, Braden reported in August 1943, it was also the only party that had its own radio station, a sizable newspaper, a publishing house, and bookstore and would soon have its own movie theater. Batista, Braden warned, was increasingly coming under the influence of international communism and was grooming himself, or was being groomed, to play a major role not only in Cuba but throughout Latin America.[1]

Concerned over Batista's cordial relations with the Cuban CP, Braden was also repulsed by the corruption that Batista's regime encouraged. This corruption, Braden suggested, affected practically every citizen of the republic from the humblest gambler placing a five-cent bet on the numbers racket to the industrialist who found it cheaper to settle his taxes personally with the inspector. Batista was shrewd and ruthless and probably determined to retain control after the expiration of his term in office. Should he succeed, his profound dislike of the United States and everything it stood for would be an unending source of trouble.[2]

Attempting to advance American security interests, to promote the democratic cause in Cuba, and to defend private American economic interests, Braden publicly insisted that American citizens and corporations on the island not contribute to any of the candidates running in the elections scheduled for 1 June 1944. This officially neutral stance was correctly interpreted as hostile by Batista (Braden later estimated that it had cost Batista on the order of $2,000,000) and led Batista to ask, without success, for Braden's recall.[3] Defending his policy in a letter to Assistant Secretary of State Adolf Berle, Braden summarized the problem confronting the United States.

> The question for us to decide is broader than whether or not we think we could stomach a second Trujillo in the Caribbean area. Personally I think we could not, having in mind that Cuba is vastly more important than the Dominican Republic, and the huge tangible stake of American citizens in Cuba. More important than whether we can tolerate a cunning and ambitious creole trouble-maker, such as Batista, on our doorstep, who, if he thinks he can get away with it, will kick American interests all over the lot are our pledges to democracy and our freedoms. Certainly these pledges would be seriously distorted in the light of conditions which are rapidly developing in Cuba.[4]

As the 1944 elections drew near it became apparent that the social democratic opposition, the Partido Revolucionario Cubano Auténtico, might make a good showing. Ramón Grau San Martín, the leader of the Auténticos, was a hero of the 1933 revolution against the dictatorship of Gerardo Machado and enjoyed considerable popular backing. The indirect support of an American ambassador was doubtless welcome to Grau, but it was perhaps a source of some bittersweet reflection as well. In 1933, another of Franklin Roosevelt's ambassadors, Sumner Welles, had contributed to Grau's downfall and to the strengthening of Batista's position within Cuban politics. Recognition had been denied to Grau's revolutionary government, and Batista had been encouraged to think that recognition might be forthcoming in the event that Grau and his allies were removed from office. The only obstacle to a political settlement in Cuba, Welles told Batista at one point, "was the unpatriotic and futile obstinacy of a small group of young men, who should be studying in the university instead of playing politics."[5]

From 1934 to 1944, Batista was the most important political figure in

Cuba. Although opposition leaders were sometimes harassed by his thugs, there was greater freedom of association and expression on the island than there had been under Machado. Elections were held in 1936—in which women voted for the first time—but progress toward democracy was limited: Batista had the victor impeached a year later when he had the temerity to veto a bill on his own initiative. Beginning in the late 1930s, Batista moved to establish cordial relations with the Cuban CP and to support a number of reforms including the establishment of workmen's compensation and minimum wages and the provision of pensions to workers. Communist domination of the Cuban trade union movement was actively promoted by the Cuban Ministry of Labor, and by 1944 members of the central committee of the CP were serving in Batista's cabinet.[6]

Grau had run against Batista in the 1940 elections and lost, and this may have contributed to an underestimation of his prospects in 1944. Confronting Batista's handpicked successor, Carlos Saladrigas, Grau defeated him easily. In a report to the national executive committee of the Communist Party, Secretary-General Blas Roca (later a prominent figure in Fidel Castro's regime) attempted to put a favorable spin on the upset. Although Saladrigas lost, Roca declared, his stature had grown in public opinion. "Batista, who became president of the republic four years ago, with our enthusiastic support, now prepares to abandon office as one of the firmest and most sincere democrats of the Americas."[7]

A note of 29 August 1944 from Adolf Berle's diary indicates that there was more to Braden's efforts on behalf of the integrity of the 1944 elections than was commonly known at the time. Just back in Washington for a visit, Berle wrote, Braden told of an incident that he had not previously reported to the State Department.

> The Army junta behind Batista had been so convinced that [Batista's candidate] would win and that they would be in power that they were not set for this [defeat]; they promptly held a meeting designed to take over the power and set up a government. Braden was dining with a prominent American resident of Havana, Johnson the drug man. One of Grau's men burst into the garden where they were seated and told them of this, asking Braden to intervene at once. He said he would not touch it until the facts were verified; but an hour or so later they were verified, and Braden in the meantime had gone over to where a number of these Army officers were. He stated to one of them that he would not intervene in the situation at all except by

nonintervention. Specifically, the United States recognized the existing government and would recognize Grau as soon as he was inaugurated; and would not recognize anybody else nor any group that
seized the government by force; and there ought to be no misunderstanding about it at all. According to Braden, he made it pretty solid
and added that anybody could figure out exactly what that would
mean when taken in all its implications. The Army junta thereupon
thought better of the idea and abandoned the plan.[8]

From the first months of the new government onward, Braden expressed doubts about Grau's administrative ability and concern over his
"Messianic complex." But at least Grau was "honest and inspired with the
best intentions for the good of his people." That his reform program
threatened established interests in the army, in business, in Congress, and
in the media was all the more reason not to undercut his position. The
support, in every legitimate way, of the United States government and of
this embassy, Braden observed, "is not only of material assistance but is a
powerful psychological influence in favor of the Grau administration. It is
encouraging to those who desire peace and order and discouraging to possible conspirators."[9]

While the Auténticos would move to take control of the Cuban labor
movement away from the CP in 1947, a short-lived détente was arranged
after Grau's victory. During this period Senator Juan Marinello, one of the
party's leaders, held an interesting conversation with Allan Dawson, a
close friend of Braden's and the American chargé in Caracas:

> Comparing the Grau and Batista regimes, Sr. Marinello commented
> that Batista and his Government were completely venal and that
> Grau had cleaned things up as well as the Cuban character and his
> own unworldliness permitted. Sr. Marinello went on to say that a
> combination of Grau's honesty and straightforwardness with Batis-
> ta's political sense would be ideal but that one could not expect per-
> fection in Chiefs of State. He then remarked, "I guess we will have to
> wait until we are in power." When I asked him jokingly when he
> thought that would be, he replied, "That depends on how quickly the
> world evolves; we cannot do much in Cuba until events elsewhere
> make you pull in your horns."[10]

Pleased that Cuba seemed to be moving in the right direction, and convinced that an assertively prodemocratic American policy had helped, in

January 1945 Braden argued for the extension of this policy to Latin America as a whole. He remained concerned over the strength of the Cuban CP, particularly in the Cuban labor movement, and warned that "should the United States Government appear to Stalin to be too intrusive in European affairs, it would be possible through agitation, such as a general strike, to give us a headache practically on our own doorstep which might induce us to abandon our activities abroad."[11]

Presenting his ideas to Nelson Rockefeller, who had replaced Berle as assistant secretary of state, Braden argued that another cycle of revolution had begun in the region and the continued survival of the remaining dictatorships was not in America's political or economic interest. Any indication of American approval would help the dictators to retain power. It would be counter to the Good Neighbor policy and to the very principles for which the war was being fought. Such a continuance of dictatorial rule might ultimately lead to the triumph of extreme rightist or leftist forces. Higher living standards would help to reduce this danger as would educational programs that might be greatly assisted by American labor unions. Exaggerated nationalism was a threat both to American investments and to the long-term development of the region, but aside from arguing its case on the merits, the United States had no right to intervene in matters essentially within the domestic jurisdiction of the other American republics. Rockefeller's response, according to Braden, was "one hundred per cent approval" and a request that he further develop his ideas about policy toward dictatorships in another memorandum.[12]

In dispatch 9103 of 5 April 1945 from Havana—the Braden Memorandum—Braden made his case for a redirection of American policy. Dictatorial and disreputable regimes, he argued, were not merely noxious in themselves, they were a breeding ground for what might prove to be "the most dangerous and insidious threat of all to the American mode of life and to democracy—Communism." The mass of the people living under dictatorships in Latin America aspired to democracy, but they might come to adopt or acquiesce in an extremist position out of desperation. It is extraordinary, he wrote, "that those who have suffered under the rule of Martinez, Ubico, Trujillo, etc., should be so understanding as they are." This was no cause for complacency. If the United States failed to sustain and augment an enthusiasm for the practice of democracy throughout the continent, the void would be filled by pernicious and threatening "isms." Braden had no patience for the arguments of those who claimed that Latin America was not ready for democracy. Colombia, with a literacy rate below

50 percent and extremely low sanitary and living standards, was a functioning democracy, in contrast to Argentina with its far better economic conditions. Guatemala was traveling the road to democracy in spite of the arguments of those who said that this was impossible with an Indian majority. Referring to the claim that true Pan-Americanism would have to wait until the peoples of Latin America caught up with their constitutions, Braden declared: "There is no time to wait, when the enemies of democracy are not merely at the door but are already energetically at work from within."[13]

American policy in the past, Braden argued, particularly as American citizens abroad often catered to the local martinet, had left itself open to the misinterpretation that the United States was more interested in authority and order than in liberty and human rights. American economic and other aid had been distributed on a more or less evenhanded basis, and this had been presented by the despots as evidence of American support for their regimes. "As a result, the most genuine friends and supporters we have in the Latin American countries—the liberals and educated classes of modest means, who comprehend the issues involved—are baffled and sometimes discouraged."[14]

What was necessary, Braden concluded, was a modification of past practices. In particular, he offered seven specific recommendations that may be summarized briefly as follows:

1. Treat dictatorships in the region with "aloof formality," at least "until such time as by inter-American agreement some other procedure is jointly established."
2. Deny dictatorships any economic assistance, military cooperation, visits to Washington, or other honors.
3. Avoid public statements in praise of dictatorships. "Even to applaud their constructive endeavors may be capitalized by them and generally misunderstood, thus placing us in a false light."
4. Encourage "honesty in government."
5. Instruct the members of the foreign service to maintain and develop as "wide contacts as may be possible with the people, of all classes, in the country to which they are accredited."
6. Grant diplomatic recognition "with deliberation and only when we are so sure as possible that our decision is accurate and in keeping with the will of the people concerned."

7. Be "tolerant, patient, and generous" with democratic governments and "exacting" with dictatorships in regard to their "fulfillment of their agreements with and commitments to our government."[15]

Distributed among the American ambassadors to Latin America by Acting Secretary of State Joseph Grew, Braden's proposed policy soon won the
support of a solid majority of its readers.[16] A particularly enthusiastic reply came from Claude Bowers, the American ambassador to Chile, who
offered a memorandum of his own in response. Seconding Braden's suggestion that American diplomats develop contacts with people of all classes
in the countries to which they were assigned, Bowers particularly stressed
labor leaders "since one of our duties is to win them to democracy and
divorce them from the extremism of communism." At all times, he concluded, "but especially in these days when the world struggle revolves
around ideologies, no man should be sent here who is not a convinced and
militant democrat."[17] Raising Bowers's memorandum at a meeting of the
secretary of state's staff committee, Acting Secretary of State Grew observed that it "corresponded exactly to his own thinking."[18]

Without underestimating the importance of a clearly articulated program and powerful support within the foreign service, it should be stressed
that the Cold War liberals also benefited greatly from the vigor of Braden's
personality and the increasingly public aura of success that accompanied
his missions in Latin America. He was, as his friend and colleague Ellis
Briggs later described him, an indefatigable toiler capable of putting in successive fifteen-hour days while looking around for more terrain to conquer: "He had been a Yale water polo player and later an amateur heavy-
weight pugilist, a dancer whose tango belied his two hundred and sixty
pounds, a mining engineer turned highly successful businessman, a diplomat who singlehandedly and against the sustained hostility of an Argentine Foreign Minister had achieved in the 1930s a peace treaty between
Bolivia and Paraguay, after a bitter and frustrated struggle."[19]

As ambassador to Colombia in the late 1930s and early 1940s, Braden
helped to eliminate German military control of a local airline and helped to
make sure that private American businesses stayed out of Colombian politics.[20] Formerly, Colombian president Eduardo Santos told Braden,
"American interests endeavored to coerce our governments by threatening appeals to Washington—now we warn them that we will protest to

Washington."[21] But Braden was best known for his missions to Cuba and Argentina, and, as we shall see in another chapter, it was in the light of these that he was appointed assistant secretary of state in August 1945.[22] "You have done a magnificent job, with wisdom and great courage," Grew wrote to him on his return from Buenos Aires, "and the country appreciates it and knows that you have added laurels to American diplomacy."[23] "I am delighted that you are coming back to give us your help and the benefit of your wise and experienced counsel," was Under Secretary of State Dean Acheson's comment.[24]

The contribution of the Cold War itself to the ascendancy of the Cold War liberals should not be overlooked. By the end of 1945, a marked shift in the policy of communist movements in Latin America was exacerbating official concern about the loyalty of these movements to the Soviet Union. Among American officials the Cold War liberals were the best informed observers of these movements, and this strengthened their own sense of the urgency and legitimacy of their position. It probably also affected the willingness of others to defer to their knowledge and conviction.[25] In a letter to Braden of 19 November 1945, Ambassador Bowers summarized the recent history of the CP line in Chile:

> Before Russia was attacked, the Communist party here was militantly and offensively against us. After that and throughout the war, they were completely with us and cooperated as a party more perfectly than any other party as a whole. Now they are back where they began, propagandizing against us, attacking us on all points where our policy does not run along with Russia's. This is manifest in their paper. Also in an occasional speech in Congress. Their line of attack is the old classic one—that we are imperialistic—that our plutocratic element dictates our policy toward South America. American interests here are attacked for their alleged mistreatment of Chilean labor, though of course no Chilean industry remotely approaches us in the matter of wages or treatment. Along with this goes wild laudation of Russia and their paper implies that Russia alone won the war in Europe.[26]

In his reply, Braden noted that the same shift in the party line had taken place throughout the hemisphere.[27] Even where the communists praised his actions in Argentina, he observed, they characterized them as part and parcel of the same policy of intervention that prevented acceptance of the governments in Bulgaria and Rumania. "In keeping with this whole Communist situation," he told Bowers, "it is my feeling that democracy as we know it in this country is not merely on trial or at the crossroads but is approaching a precipice, and that the only way it can be saved is by fighting [for] it tooth and nail, and this is the policy that I have tried to initiate here in the Office of American Republic Affairs." It was precisely for this reason, he continued, "that the Communists who fear a genuine liberal more than they ever do the dictator or Fascist-Nazi have attacked me."[28]

Having watched the Fascists triumph in the Spanish civil war, at a time when the government he represented was unwilling to do anything for the Spanish Republic, Bowers shared Braden's conviction of the need for democratic militancy in the face of antidemocratic forces.[29] In a letter to Secretary of State James Byrnes of 3 December 1945, he stressed how enormously costly halfheartedness had been in the past. In the international struggles of the day, he insisted, it was vital that American diplomats be thoroughly democratic in their political ideology.

> I have observed that no German was tolerated in the foreign service of his country who was not a militant supporter of the Nazi view; and no Italian who did not flamboyantly wear the black shirt of Fascism; and no Russian who did not ardently battle for the Russian view; but that the foreign services of most of the European Democracies were crowded with men who at heart were antidemocratic and who looked with cynical contempt on democracy and scarcely concealed their admiration for the totalitarian systems. That, I am convinced, is the reason the Democracies lost the diplomatic battles to the totalitarians during the five or six years before the war—thus making war inevitable. It is impossible to win a battle with an army secretly in sympathy with the enemy.[30]

The position of the Cold War liberals was greatly strengthened by the existence of democratic governments in Chile, Costa Rica, Colombia, and Uruguay and especially by the democratic openings in Cuba, Guatemala, Peru, Venezuela, and Brazil. While these developments were primarily the product of independent political struggles within each of these countries, they had an international resonance. Visiting Guatemala in July of 1946, Venezuela's Rómulo Betancourt spoke of recent changes there and in his own country as two parallel revolutions that had broken the classical pattern of Latin American coups: military involvement had been a prelude not to a consolidation of power in the hands of the military but to a military withdrawal from politics and the holding of free elections.[31]

The rising democratic movements of the hemisphere and the cordial relations their leaders soon established with the United States seemed the best possible evidence for the propriety of the Cold War liberals' position. This optimism seems to have been shared by much of the intelligence community. Championing the Venezuelan social democratic political party Acción Democrática as "pro-US and anti-USSR," the Central Intelligence Agency hailed its landslide victory in the 1947 elections: "In fact, the great popular support won by the party in the December elections is another indication that, in the special conditions of Latin American politics, an active non-Communist progressive party constitutes one of the best guarantees against a strong Communist movement."[32] Looking back on those years in the mid-1970s, at a time when there were only three democratic governments in all of Latin America, Ellis Briggs stressed the remarkable optimism of the early postwar period:

> It was a period when democratic self-government, while not exactly enjoying universal acclaim among the politicians of the Good Neighborhood was nevertheless doing better than it has since—or seems likely to do in the predictable future. In 1946–47, notwithstanding the stench of the late Juan Vicente Gomez still contaminating Venezuelan air or the activities of a Perón in Argentina or a Trujillo in the Dominican Republic, both Braden and I were more hopeful of the future of free institutions than we would be thirty years later.[33]

By the end of 1945, the Cold War liberalism of Braden, Briggs, Bowers, Berle and many others was dominant in American policy toward Latin America. Those who held this outlook—like all those who held a Cold War perspective—were determined to avoid a hot war and were convinced that there was a serious risk of one. They did not necessarily place all of the blame for this danger on the Soviet Union. In a letter of August 1946 to Ambassador Walter Thurston in Mexico, Braden suggested that the battles that had been fought over Russian territory in the twentieth century— and the obvious hopes of some in the West that the Germans and Russians would exterminate one another like Kilkenney cats—had contributed to Soviet suspicions. In this whole ominous situation, he observed, Soviet rhetoric was reminiscent of Bolivian and Paraguayan rhetoric during the years of negotiations involved in settling the Chaco War. "The cries regarding sovereignty, the xenophobia, the harsh insults, inability to understand the real attitude of the other powers, in general and frequently in detail, are very similar."[34]

To the question of how a hot war should be avoided, a renewed and reinvigorated commitment to political democracy was obviously an insufficient answer. Nevertheless it was held to be—at least among the Cold War liberals—an essential part of the answer. As far as policy toward Latin America was concerned, their outlook was twofold in its influence. In the first place, it put a premium on support for democratic and reformist movements and governments in the region as the best and the only really effective response to communism. In the second, it continued the strategic emphasis on Europe and Asia that had relegated Latin America to a secondary status among American concerns. It was, after all, in Europe and Asia that military forces capable of seriously threatening the American people had been mobilized by the Axis dictators, and it was there that the resources that had made those forces possible might fall into the hands of either revanchist regimes or the Soviet Union. The postwar success of the economies of Western Europe and Japan was of vital importance to the future of the global economy and that of the United States, and to political developments throughout the world. The economies of Latin America were much smaller and correspondingly less important. Those in charge of day-to-day policy toward Latin America understood that the basic issue in world politics was whether or not a favorable international environment could be established for the survival and success of liberal civilization. They realized that Latin America's contribution to this larger issue could hardly determine the outcome and accepted its lesser strategic importance and its limited claim on scarce resources.[35] On the other hand, they also appear to have recognized that at a time when European and East Asian politics were in a fluid and unsettled condition, developments in the global periphery could have an unusually large impact on developments at a greatly weakened global center.

While Cold War liberalism contributed to a more assertively prodemocratic American policy, the experience and commitments of previous decades were not forgotten. There was even a conservative tendency within the State Department, most articulately represented by Louis Halle of the Division of Analysis and Liaison, that argued forcefully against the new direction. In contrast with their liberal rivals, conservatives like Halle did not mention American Cold War interests in the mid-1940s. When they did so in the early 1950s, the political environment in Latin America was more conducive to their position.

In the summer of 1945, the conservative position still had enough strength that those who were concerned that American aid was being wasted in a country like Paraguay, where the military took up half the national budget, or the Dominican Republic, where it added to the wealth of a corrupt elite, had to argue why ending or conditioning economic assistance to these countries did not constitute a form of intervention in their internal affairs.[36] On the other side, Halle and his allies insisted that the basic requirement of American policy in Latin America was self-restraint, that this had been the great contribution of the Good Neighbor policy, and that it was being threatened by the new approach. Self-restraint was, Halle admitted, a reversal of the traditional problem in foreign policy of applying the maximum potential power to the point at which particular issues were awaiting solution. But despite this divergence with conventional conceptions of foreign policy, the United States had a long-term interest in "maintaining a respectfully chivalrous attitude toward its much weaker neighbors." Halle wrote,

> The other American republics today are clearly in a position of economic dependence on the United States. By using its economic power freely for political ends, the United States could to a considerable degree reduce them to a state resembling peonage. This is especially true at the present moment, when other powers are in a poor position to give them such economic support as the United States might withhold. In requiring Ecuador, for example, to put its economy on a sound basis as a condition of receiving economic assistance, the United States might, if it failed to exercise due restraint, find itself approaching a position in which Ecuador would have to obtain United States approval for almost any exercise of its national sovereignty. Ecuador's military budget, labor legislation, trade agreements, financial controls, and eventually domestic political arrangements, might be submitted for "clearance" in Washington. In other words, if the United States put no check at all on its policy, Ecuador would probably become a colonial dependency in all but name. What applies to Ecuador applies as well to the majority of other American republics. It would not be long, under such circumstances, before they were looking to one another and to the non-American powers for support in their "liberation." This is the eventual extreme that could result from a lack of restraint by the United States in the use of its economic power. It would represent an abandonment of the Good Neighbor Policy.[37]

Braden and the other Cold War liberals had no desire to abandon the Good Neighbor policy. On the contrary, they believed that self-interest and principle together required restraint in the exercise of American power in Latin America. Their position was that good intentions and self-restraint were not enough to absolve the United States of responsibility for the influence it would inevitably continue to exercise. A sense of democratic solidarity had to guide that influence. That the struggle for democracy in Latin America was primarily a Latin American struggle Braden and his allies did not deny. But they wished to help and to leave no doubt as to where the United States stood.

> The views and actions of the United States Government and its representatives exert a tremendous influence, particularly in some of the smaller Latin American Republics. We could not divest ourselves of this influence even if we wished to; it will be at work whether we consciously direct it in a way which will be helpful to our neighbors, or make decisions without taking into consideration their effect on the internal affairs of other American states. It is our duty to see that it is exerted in a way which does good rather than harm. This does not mean that we shall attempt to dictate forms of government or courses of political action. It does mean that decisions which the United States has a right to make, and must make, will be shaped by our desire to promote progress toward human freedom and self-government throughout the hemisphere.[38]

In a memorandum of late September 1945, Dana Munro sought to reconcile the newly ascendant perspective of the Cold War liberals with more traditional views. Having been personally involved in shaping the policy that President Roosevelt had repudiated in 1933, he suggested that there were few thinking people with similar experience who would wish to see the old policy revived. The use of actual force, as exemplified by the American military control over Haiti and the maintenance of American marines in Nicaragua, was something to be avoided.

> There is a vast difference, however, between such intervention and the use of moral and economic influence in ways which affect internal political conditions, and there has been a long series of incidents since our non-intervention pledge where the United States has in fact taken non-military action which had a great effect on internal political conditions. It would probably not be profitable to attempt to spell out the exact meaning of the non-intervention commitment, but it

might be advisable to make clear in some appropriate way the fact that we consider that the proper use of a friendly influence in behalf of democracy is not intervention.[39]

The intrusion of foreign ideologies into Latin America during the previous decade, Munro stressed, had been the chief threat to inter-American solidarity—and with it to continued American leadership in the hemisphere. The situation in Argentina showed that fascism continued to be a menace, and recent developments indicated that communism might become an even more serious danger. This was the unsentimental reason for the American interest in the promotion of democracy: "The events of the past few years have shown that the essential basis of inter-American solidarity is a common interest in democratic ideals, as they relate to internal political development and as they find expression in the conduct of international relations."[40]

While the Cold War liberals generally believed that their emphasis on democratic solidarity was compatible with a policy of nonintervention, a number of them recognized that others might not view matters in the same light and saw the desirability of being able to take action covertly. In a memorandum of early November 1945, John Wiley, the American ambassador to Colombia, pointed out that the Soviet legation in Bogotá was in the unusually advantageous position of being able to maintain a friendly attitude toward the United States while the Colombian Communist Party pursued a policy of hostility.

> No one is in a position successfully to blame either the Soviet Union or its Legation in Bogotá. One of the great problems in the future for the United States is somehow to find an antidote for Communist penetration in Latin America. Such an antidote, which, with ingenuity it might be feasible to devise, should be constituted of some means for action for which the American Government would at no time be responsible. In any event, there should be in Latin America a powerful, Left Liberal-pro-Labor movement that would respond wisely to the aspirations of the masses and repudiate any direction from without the Western Hemisphere. One fights fire with fire.[41]

Until all governmental records from the Truman years are fully declassified, the extent to which a policy of covert support for the democratic left in Latin America was adopted will remain unclear. The financial assistance that the Central Intelligence Agency (CIA) would provide to Costa Rica's

José Figueres and others in his circle in the late 1950s and early 1960s is fairly common knowledge, but when this assistance began remains obscure.[42] Covert assistance was certainly provided to the democratic left in Europe during the Truman years, in part though private American organizations such as the American Federation of Labor. Socialists and people on the left in Europe were often, as a former head of the CIA's International Organization Division once put it, "the only people who gave a damn about fighting communism."[43] This was largely true in Latin America as well, and it would hardly be surprising to find that an analogous policy had been pursued there.

Although it is unclear whether Cold War liberalism led to significant covert action in Latin America during the Truman years, there are indications, as we will see in future chapters, that covert efforts to support democratic forces were contemplated with regard to Argentina in 1945, attempted with regard to the Dominican Republic in 1947, and successfully undertaken in Costa Rica in 1948.[44] Rear Admiral Roscoe Hillenkoetter, the first director of the CIA, certainly saw himself and his agency as heavily indebted to Braden for his "splendid support" in establishing what would become the various CIA stations in Latin America. Braden's help, Hillenkoetter informed him, "has rendered our task much less difficult, and we feel that any success we may attain has been, to a large extent, due to you."[45]

Regardless of what may or may not have been done covertly, there can be no doubt that overt American policy sought to support democratic and reformist forces in the fight against communism. "I have always maintained," Braden warned after a year and a half in office as assistant secretary of state, "that to join with Fascists and ultra-reactionaries in 'common cause' against Communism is against principle, foolhardy and will greatly weaken us in the struggle to defeat totalitarianism of every variety."[46] When the great Peruvian social democrat Víctor Raúl Haya de la Torre visited the United States in March 1947, Braden hosted a dinner in his honor.[47]

The emergence of an anticommunist inter-American labor federation in January 1948, at a conference in Lima hosted by Haya de la Torre, was greeted enthusiastically by American officials. Addressing the need for anticommunist measures in Latin America, the State Department's policy planning staff noted that the Confederation of Latin American Workers (CTAL) was "the most effective and well organized force at the disposal of the Communists" in much of Latin America, and it argued that support should be given "by every practicable means" to the CTAL's new rival, the Confederation of Inter-American Workers (CIT).[48] Secretary of State George Marshall then sent the planning staff's paper to the American ambassadors in Latin America along with a note indicating that it should be used for their information and guidance as he had approved its conclusions and recommendations.[49] This left no doubt that the secretary of state saw the national security of the United States as requiring a serious effort to win the support of social democratic forces in Latin America and requiring also great wariness in dealing with their reactionary rivals:

> There are strong and extreme reactionary forces in Latin America which, through selfishness and lack of any sense of social responsibility, impose a minority will through military or other dictatorial governments and so alienate large segments of their populations which otherwise probably would be anti-Communist. These reactionary forces often adopt a strong anti-Communist line, but frequently apply repressive measures to all political opponents, alleging that the latter are Communists whether or not that is the fact. These reactionary forces also work with Communists against Liberal and Socialist elements for reasons of pure political opportunism. Consequently, cooperation of the United States with these reactionary elements, even in anti-Communist measures, should be very carefully considered in the light of our long-range national interests. . . . It is extremely important, always with our own national security in mind, to concentrate upon the defeat of international Communism. As a corollary, it is essential to follow policies and to adopt measures calculated not only to command the very valuable support of anti-Communist labor, liberal and Socialist elements, but also to persuade sufferers from reactionary forces in the American Republics that the United States is a better and more promising hope than Communism or the Soviet Union.[50]

A New Dealer and Cold Warrior in Brazil

For the liberal Cold Warriors, opposition to communism (and to a potential Soviet bid for global hegemony) was in part a reflection of a more general democratic philosophy, a liberal vision of world order, and a conviction that the only legitimate model for a modern empire was something analogous to the American sphere of influence in Latin America. Adolf Berle's Cold War liberalism was unusually articulate and influenced the evolution of American global strategy; an examination of his views is worth a brief digression. The evolution of Berle's thinking was generally similar to that of State Department Soviet specialist Charles Bohlen and lends support to the interpretation advanced by Eduard Mark as to the importance of the closed character of the Soviet sphere of influence in Eastern Europe for the origins of the Cold War.[1]

Berle was not the only American official who believed that the United States had come to a mutually beneficial set of relations with Latin America during the Roosevelt years. He was, however, the most articulate advocate of the proposition that this set of relations should serve as a standard for Soviet relations with the countries of Eastern Europe and British relations with the countries of the Near East. He helped to define the initial postwar American objectives for these regions and, as his hoped-for world of good neighbors failed to emerge, he was increasingly inclined to hold the Soviet Union responsible for the failure. His view of Soviet intentions was decisively shaped by what he considered as their unwillingness to meet the minimum requirements for any Great Power seeking to maintain a modern sphere of influence. He argued, in effect, that because the Soviets were unwilling to pursue a good neighbor policy in Eastern Europe, they could not be trusted not to be seeking global hegemony. In this, he was an early representative of what would become a major current in the mainstream of American strategic thinking.

In 1945, as Gaddis Smith has shown, Berle and other American officials were concerned over the possibility of international arrangements that would seriously weaken the traditional position of the United States in the Western Hemisphere. In defense of that position, they attacked the proposal to give to what would become the Security Council of the United Nations the sole authority to sanction the use of force internationally. Such an arrangement, Berle argued, "would mean that the United States and others could not prevent Argentina from seizing Uruguay without the consent of Britain and Russia—who at that moment might be backing Argentina."[2] The premises of this kind of criticism were fundamentally at odds with those of Secretary of State Cordell Hull's hoped-for postwar world—a world where there would no longer be a need "for spheres of influence, for alliances, for balance of power, or any other of the special arrangements through which, in the unhappy past, the nations strove to safeguard their security or to promote their interest."[3] In rejecting this vision of the future as unrealistic and defending a sphere of influence for the United States in Latin America, Berle and the others inevitably raised what Smith refers to as a "sauce-for-the-gander-problem."[4]

As far as Berle was concerned, this problem was not particularly troubling. He was perfectly willing for the Soviets to have a sphere of influence in Eastern Europe as long as it was analogous to the American sphere of influence in Latin America: "I'd like to see a whole group of contented little states, friendly to the Soviet Union as the states of Central America are friendly to us," he told a *Time* reporter in early 1943. "They would not be buffer states any more than Guatemala is a buffer. But they would be in Russia's orbit and they would know that they were and they would learn to welcome a Soviet desire to establish a base at some convenient point as Latin Americans have learned to welcome the establishment of a U.S. base in their territory. A base means a lot of soldiers spending money; it's good for trade; they don't think any more about it."[5]

Berle's mistake was not in failing to see an analogy between American and Soviet spheres of influence, but in imagining that the Soviets could be closely held to such a compromise's requirements—that they could see it as in their interest, and within their ability, to operate their sphere of influence "in somewhat the same fashion as we have operated the good neighbor policy in Mexico and the Caribbean."[6] Over the course of 1944 and 1945, as Soviet actions raised doubts that they had any such "open" sphere in mind, Berle's concern over their capabilities was combined with an increasingly dim view of their intentions. By the summer of 1945, he was already drawing explicit parallels between the postwar conduct of Soviet Russia and the prewar conduct of Nazi Germany.

Berle firmly believed that the United States had set the standard for what a modern Great Power's policy should be in its sphere of influence. His conviction was rooted in a strongly favorable appreciation of a policy he had personally helped to implement and in the basic beliefs that had led him to become a New Dealer in the first place. Great Powers were, for him, like great corporations, entities obliged to serve the interests of the people they affected or face social protest. A constant warfare has always existed, he insisted in *The Modern Corporation and Private Property*, between the individuals wielding power, in whatever form, and the subjects of that power. "Just as there is a continuous desire for power, so there is a continuous desire to make that power the servant of the bulk of the individuals it affects."[7] For Berle, this desire to make power more socially responsible was part of what the Good Neighbor policy was all about and, after 1938, was part of his own contribution to the Roosevelt administration as the assistant secretary of state responsible for Latin America.

Addressing the Academy of Political Science in the spring of 1939, Berle argued that the United States had learned from such earlier major mistakes in its relations with Latin America as the occupations of the Dominican Republic, Nicaragua, and Haiti. It had learned the lesson of self-restraint and the advantages of cooperative relations. The final result had been the firmer establishment of independent nations who owed their safety not to their military force but to the strength of the Pan-American idea. That these more cooperative relations with Latin America were also in the interest of the United States, Berle did not deny.

> In sordid fact, it is more advantageous to live at peace, to cooperate in international relations, and to open trade channels, than it is to conquer, to seize territory, and to govern an unwilling population. It so happens—and I am glad of it—that the method of our American relations was not worked out on a basis of sordid self-interest; but we have learned that self-interest is served by the processes of ordinary morality.[8]

On the eve of the Second World War—as on the eve of the Cold War—it was Berle's naive hope that a cooperative peace like the one brought about under the Good Neighbor policy could somehow be extended to Europe. "At all events, the Eastern European States and the Baltic States are talking about it," he told a friend.[9] Even after the deluge of conquest and massacre that followed the Hitler-Stalin Pact, he continued to articulate a vision of the cooperation that had been achieved in the hemisphere as the brightest hope for the future: an intelligent method of dealing with international affairs in "the common interest of peoples."[10]

Berle's concern for the interests of other peoples did not prevent him from adopting the language of imperialism—and recognizing the prerogatives of imperial powers—but it was a distinctly modern imperialism that he had in mind. The United States, he suggested in an early wartime memorandum, was being asked to assume a position, in the sphere of economics, that was roughly analogous to the position exercised by Great Britain in the previous century in the sphere of politics. Having helped to establish a cooperative group of nations in the Western Hemisphere, it was now finding that vast portions of the world, chiefly constituents of the British Empire, were being driven to join this grouping. Canadian membership was perhaps a matter of geography, but Australia and New Zealand were also increasingly being supported economically and militarily by the United States.

> In any other period of history a situation of this kind would be accompanied by sweeping changes of sovereignty. We should, on the Nineteenth Century model, find ourselves engaged in taking over, wholly or partly, various Latin American countries, Australia, New Zealand, etc. The experience of the Nineteenth Century has indicated that empires do not pay and likewise in many free governing units, changes in sovereignty are relatively unimportant. A cooperative relationship in the New World is literally more advantageous to us (aside from being more theoretical internationally) than would be an imperialist conquest.[11]

Any political relationship that was needed with Australia, for example, could be worked out by its assimilation into a cooperative grouping analogous to the inter-American grouping. It did not matter whether or not it remained under the British Crown. A more serious difficulty was the fact that most of the areas being discussed were not economic complements but competitors. Australia, Argentina, and Canada were all in competition with each other and also with American agriculture. Given American manufacturing capacity, Berle thought that it would be possible for the United States—at least in the immediate postwar period—to simply print the money necessary to buy the normal exports of Argentina, Brazil, Australia, and the rest of the group. As long as they promptly used their dollars to buy their requirements in manufactured goods in the United States, it would be possible to meet every order without materially inconveniencing the domestic American economy. The problem would be what to do with the huge supplies of goods that the United States would accumulate. Ultimately, European demand would be the real balancing item, but it might not turn up for a number of years. In the meantime, the United States would have to function as "the financial and economic pumping station, shock absorber, and general supply station for the whole unit."[12]

Rather than the "Anglo-American" or "English-speaking" hegemony that certain enthusiasts were advocating, Berle argued in another memorandum, the real question for the future was the "contribution which Britain and America can make to other peoples who are equal not only in theory and in international law, but actually and tangibly." Britain's world position, he suggested, rested less on its navy and its imperial control than on its moral and intellectual ability to bring about common action among a great number of countries. This would be essential to the future cooperative grouping of independent nations. Whether London or Washington would become the center of this grouping perhaps did not make a great deal of difference: "Eventually the center will have to be the point at which there is the greatest confidence, the most flexible mentality, the greatest generosity, and the greatest ability to give tangible assistance."[13]

In the past the American people had been among the worst sinners in obstructing the free flow of commerce. It would be necessary for American opinion to change in order to get rid of protective tariff legislation. But if there was widespread agreement on free transport and free flow of commerce, then the private exchange of goods and services could be counted on to do most of the work in the postwar world economy. There would still be significant areas of continuing governmental responsibility, particularly in finance. Great Britain could hardly be expected to face the prospect of an "open world" unless the better-supplied countries, and especially the United States, made sure that Great Britain did not find itself short of supplies because it was short of exchange.[14]

A favorable international environment for democracy was a central part of Berle's conception of an open world. He thought the very survival of democratic politics was at stake in the Second World War. Addressing the Association of American Universities in late 1940, he reminded his audience that democracy as a world system was a revolutionary development in human history and one that rested on intellectual forces that had only begun to flower relatively recently.

Now there is in progress a counter-revolution, whose avowed object is to drive democracy out of existence. In historical rhythm, this is precisely what we should expect. Rarely has a new force gained ascendancy without having to struggle for its very life against the reformed battalions of the ideas which it had displaced. At present the struggle takes the form of a world war, carried on by the methods of revolution quite as much as by those of military science. We are in the midst of a crucial phase of that war. The difference between this and most wars lies in the fact that a challenge has been thrown out not merely to the force of the resisting nations, but also to the ideas and intellectual structure of those nations. As a result, the conflict is fought not only on land and sea and air, but in the mind of every thinking man.[15]

If the populations of the enemy countries were not convinced that their leaders had taken them along a sterile and deadly line of thinking, Berle argued during the war, "we shall merely have another armistice, followed by another explosion."[16] Not only was the war being fought in the minds of every thinking person, the peace would have to be won there as well. Among those involved in planning for the postwar period, this would increasingly be seen to require American support for the kinds of social and economic reforms that could help to change broader political orientations.[17] But, as Berle noted at one point in regard to Japan, ultimately emphasis would have to be placed on local liberal ideas and forces capable of "altering the direction of the emotion and thought of the Japanese people."[18]

In a memorandum of early September 1943, Berle examined possible postwar threats to American and global security. A renaissance of militarism in Japan and Germany could take place only after a generation had passed, and the maintenance of American security against such a threat would be a major responsibility of postwar policy. Although there were some indications that Charles de Gaulle wished to pursue a militaristic and expansionist policy, France would probably not be capable of such a venture. The Soviet Union would certainly have the capability of taking in much of the territory envisaged in the Haushofer theories of "world island." But a capability, Berle cautioned, "does not by any means imply the will."[19]

So far as diplomatic claims were concerned, the Soviet Union had already indicated that it expected to be dominant in the entire Balkan area east of the Adriatic, to have the 1939 line with Poland, and to have the Baltic republics. Its expectations with regard to Finland and Norway were unclear, but it had given evidence of interest in the Dardanelles and in northern Iran. It was possible that southern Iran and ports on the Persian Gulf were also desired. No claims had been stated in the East, but they might be expected to include an intensification of interest in Outer Mongolia and Manchuria, perhaps including warm-water ports on the Yellow Sea or the Sea of Japan, and southern Sakhalin.

> If these claims in substance are realized, and if everything else in terms of her guerrilla organization be regarded as merely necessary warfare and not for permanent purposes, this would still give her a foundation for substantial domination of pretty much everything in Europe east of the Rhine. If she attains far less than this, she would still have the capability of becoming a world aggressor should her will take that turn, which must not be assumed.[20]

In fact, Berle argued, even if there were a desire to do so, there was no possibility of depriving Russia of the capacity of undertaking a war of world conquest after a period of recovery from the current war. This did not mean that it could or would be victorious in such a war, provided that substantially all the rest of the world again united in opposition to the aggression. But the capacity could not be denied and a "mere alliance" with the British Empire group of nations would not by itself provide adequate insurance. This is as far as Berle went in this memorandum down the path of that contingency. He appears to have sincerely hoped that the postwar Soviet leadership would be primarily concerned with internal reconstruction and development and that this concern would occupy their energies and ambitions. To maintain the security of the United States, he concluded, American policy "should be such as to create the greatest possible stability on the continent of Europe, accompanied by the greatest attainable degree of comfort and satisfaction within Soviet Russia."[21]

Over the course of 1944 Berle became more pessimistic about Soviet intentions.[22] The Soviet response to the Warsaw uprising reinforced both the trend of his concern and his belief that the United States had a positive role to play in Eastern Europe. He was not prepared to conclude, at least not in late August of that year, that the Soviet armies had deliberately left the Polish underground to be murdered by the Germans. Perhaps it was by design, but perhaps the Russian advance had spent itself to a point where it could be checked by the Germans. There was no question, however, that

Soviet propaganda had been "condemning these people to death with a gusto which does not make pleasant reading."[23] A month later he was both more pessimistic about Soviet intentions and encouraged by the results of American pressure:

> For the moment matters go a little better at Warsaw. I think the Eastern European Division of the State Department there did a really good job. After the Soviets denounced the Warsaw Poles and General Bor for fighting, after they had prevented use of our bases in Soviet Russia as a place from which aid could be sent to Warsaw, and after they had forbidden certain bombing operations against the Germans lest incidentally they might be used to give aid to the Poles (this a report from Harriman), certain steps were taken. First, our boys suggested that the Polish army be recognized as a belligerent and notice of this be given the Germans—which, of course, also was notice to the Soviets. Second, general public opinion only understood one thing: namely, that General Bor and his men were putting up a superhumanly brave fight and did not "take" the Soviet denunciations. This got to be bad medicine; and the Soviets finally acquiesced in sending aid, which they are now doing.[24]

Since 1940, Berle's responsibilities had included problems of counterespionage and the interpretation of intelligence. At first through an interdepartmental intelligence committee and later through the Joint Intelligence Committee of the Joint Chiefs of Staff, he helped coordinate work among the Federal Bureau of Investigation, the Military Intelligence Division of the War Department, the Office of Naval Intelligence, and the State Department.[25] Within the State Department, his assistant, Fletcher Warren, ran the intelligence division known as the Foreign Activities Correlation (FC).[26] Thanking Berle for his advice and good wishes when he became the director of the CIA in 1953, Allen Dulles promised to turn to him "for help and guidance as you are one of the few who really understand the problems of this job."[27] In 1944, intelligence reports Berle received played an important role in shaping his growing concern with Soviet intentions and in leading him to attempt to define postwar American policy toward Eastern Europe and the Near East.

The principal instrumentalities within the State Department for formulating foreign policy at this time were the Policy Committee and the Postwar Programs Committee, the former concentrating on more immediate problems and the latter more on planning for the postwar period. On

26 September 1944, Berle presented a memorandum to the Policy Committee suggesting that if a third world war was being generated, the breeding ground lay in Eastern Europe, the eastern Mediterranean, and the Middle East.[28] All the way from the Adriatic to Iran, he informed the committee, Great Britain and the Soviet Union were clashing dangerously. The intelligence reports he had been receiving showed "more and more intense conflict throughout these regions with armed clashes between groups backed by the two powers already taking place in Greece and Albania."[29]

The Soviet Union was seeking to extend its sphere of influence to the Adriatic through Rumania, Bulgaria, and Yugoslavia and probably to secure some method of entry into the Aegean Sea through either Turkish territory or Thrace. Soviet policy toward Saudi Arabia was unclear, but the available data suggested that they proposed to extend their influence south to the Persian Gulf along its length and westward as far as Cairo. The Soviet doctrine that countries within their sphere of influence must have "friendly" governments was still obscure. "If it is meant that these governments could not engage in intrigue against the Soviet Union there could be no possible objection; if it is meant that, by subsidizing guerrilla or other movements, virtual puppet governments are to be established, a different situation would prevail." In the latter case, the British would be cut off from their Far Eastern interests including India and reduced from the status of a world power to the status of a strong Atlantic power. Taken in connection with the British economic situation, many Englishmen would see this as a life-or-death issue. Hence the antagonism between British and Soviet aspirations and the potential for a conflict of global significance.[30]

Among the possible responses, the solution Berle preferred "would be for us to persuade the British and Soviets to abandon their exclusionist and domination policies in the Near East and Eastern Europe and to apply a good-neighbor policy in those areas."[31] A Soviet sphere of influence—operated in somewhat the same fashion as the United States had operated the Good Neighbor policy in Mexico and the Caribbean—would be no threat to anyone. The same could be said of a British sphere similarly operated. There were two key principles involved: the removal of the countries in these areas from the field of power politics and a concern for the rights and situations of their populations. The application of these principles would provide a ground on which the contending forces could meet in friendship. This would, however, require "a modification of the ruthlessness of British commercialism and the ruthlessness of Soviet nationalism."[32]

In the immediate future, the United States would become something of a battleground for sympathy and influence between contending international propaganda machines. In the absence of impartial reporting the public would be unable to form an intelligent opinion capable of supporting any policy. The only corrective would be a free flow of information, and American representatives should be given standing instructions to press for it. American policy in general should be one of continuous opposition to closed zones whether closed to commercial intercourse, to travel, to information, or to any other aspect. There were interests of the United States that had to be defended and advanced.

> These are the essential interests of a free access by communications, by air landing and transit rights, by the rights of our shipping to call at ports. These rights, if maintained with vigor, can, in my judgement, be obtained and held. It will need all of the influence of the Department to do this. But our representatives in all of these countries can and should take the position that it is inadmissible for any ally to deny to us in any area peaceful access for peaceable communications and transport. This is not primarily a commercial interest, though in the United States it is commonly so conceived. These thin lines are likely to be the only real lines through which we can maintain contact with and exert some influence over the underlying situation.[33]

Claiming to accept "without discussion" the decision not to engage American troops east of Italy or east of the American zone of occupation in Germany, Berle stressed its deleterious consequences. "We have not, by manipulating our troop movements, created a status quo representing our ideas, and others, by their troop movements, are creating situations along the lines of their national interest."[34] Fortunately, he believed, this situation would not last. Demobilization was inevitable and could be expected to diminish the importance of positions resting exclusively on force. In the longer term, Great Britain's hope for survival as a Great Power and the Soviet Union's hope for economic reconstruction both rested largely on the assumption that the United States would support them. This would provide some leverage. Nevertheless, in presenting his ideas to the Policy Committee, Berle suggested that it would be well to consider what should be done in the event that Britain and Russia "persisted in playing power politics."[35]

In the absence of Secretary of State Cordell Hull, Under Secretary of State Edward Stettinius chaired the Policy Committee. His initial response to Berle's presentation was to note that President Roosevelt had been "rather cheered by the progress achieved so far in the Stalin-Churchill talks at Moscow." James Dunn, the director of the European office, declared that he had been out of touch with developments while engaged in the Dumbarton Oaks Conference. There was no doubt that the facts described in the memorandum were correct, observed Charles Bohlen. The United States, moreover, was to some extent at fault for failing to indicate what it would do and how much responsibility it would assume. Leo Pasvolsky suggested that before attempting to mediate between Britain and Russia, the United States should first define its own policy. Bohlen agreed. Because of its traditional stand as an observer in these parts of the world, he remarked, the United States usually waited to support or oppose a position that Russia or Britain had taken. A positive stance would be preferable. Stettinius inquired whether a public statement of policy should not be made within the next few weeks. Berle replied that Anglo-Soviet friction would probably not come to a head before the fall of Germany and suggested the appointment of a subcommittee to recommend policy. The directors of the four geographic offices were appointed to this subcommittee, and Berle was named its chairman. Their task was, Pasvolsky concluded, "the most fundamental question of policy with which we have at present to deal."[36]

Berle's subcommittee reported back in late October and within a few days had a revised statement of general principles and a series of short papers containing recommendations on policy toward Poland, Hungary, Rumania, Bulgaria, Yugoslavia, Albania, Greece, Turkey, Iran, the Near East, Afghanistan, and India.[37] In general, these recommendations were designed to strengthen the individual countries' positions. With the exception of the paper on India, they were adopted by the Policy Committee on 8 November 1944. The general principles read as follows:

1. The right of peoples to choose and maintain for themselves without outside interference the type of political, social, and economic systems they desire, so long as they conduct their affairs in such a way as not to menace the peace and security of others.

2. Equality of opportunity, as against the setting up of a policy of exclusion, in commerce, transit and trade; and freedom to negotiate, either through government agencies or private enterprise, irrespective of the type of economic system in operation.

3. The right of access to all countries on an equal and unrestricted basis of bona fide representatives of the recognized press, radio, newsreel and information agencies of other nations engaged in gathering news and other forms of public information for dissemination to the public in their own countries; and the right to transmit information gathered by them to points outside such territories without hindrance or discrimination.

4. Freedom for American philanthropic and educational organizations to carry on their activities in the respective countries on the basis of most-favored nation treatment.

5. General protection of American citizens and the protection and furtherance of legitimate American economic rights, existing or potential.[38]

Sincere in their civility—if misguided as to how others would define their own rights and interests—the authors of this wish list appear to have believed that it could form the basis of some sort of mutually acceptable accommodation with the Soviet Union and Great Britain. It was time, they argued, for the United States to assert its independent interest in the situation—"which is also believed to be in the general interest"—and by so doing help to bring about equitable arrangements designed to attain general peace and security on a basis of good neighborship.[39] As this position was approved by the Policy Committee, it would appear to represent something of a consensus within the State Department at this time. What Berle would have tried to do with these general principles if he had stayed in Washington will never be known.[40] By the time Stettinius forwarded them to Roosevelt, Berle was already in Chicago as the chairman of the International Conference on Civil Aviation.[41] In December, Stettinius replaced Hull as secretary of state and Berle was asked to resign.[42] By January 1945, he was in Brazil as the American ambassador.

Talking about international affairs with the president of Brazil in June 1945, Berle was asked for the American view of Soviet Russia. "I answered that President Roosevelt had believed the Soviet Union was merely seeking security for her frontiers; but recent developments had been somewhat disturbing and we were still endeavoring to make up our minds whether this was her real policy, or whether she was entering an imperialist phase on a large scale."[43] A month before, Berle had already written in his diary of a Soviet Union that had "taken, and is governing, by force, and unilaterally, Poland, Bulgaria, Rumania, Hungary, substantially also Yugoslavia and now Austria."[44] By mid-July, he was convinced that the Soviets sought virtual control of Turkey and Iran and a dominant position in Arabia as well. The power politics by which they were forcing their position violated "any process by which we might hope to get freedom from fear, let alone freedom of information, in this world."[45]

Telegraphing his views to President Harry Truman on 13 July 1945, and to newly appointed Secretary of State James Byrnes, Berle described his memo to the Policy Committee as "foreseeing substantially this situation" and asked if the time had not come to defend the British Empire. The British position in the Middle and Far East was capable of evolution along the lines of a group of cooperative nations. In contrast, the net result to date of Soviet expansion had been "warfare, cruelty and misery." Soviet moves through Iran and Turkey, and such things as its reported request for Aleppo, suggested that it was hoping to gain control of the traditional oil supply of Western Europe. Should it manage to absorb the British position from the Mediterranean eastward, it would have in its hands much of the military and economic resources of which the Nazi geostrategists had dreamed.

> In addition, moral aspects of present situation closely approximate moral aspects German policy from 1933 until defeat of Hitler. Same tactics are used: violent propaganda, smear accusations, portrayal of other people's patriotism as criminal or reactionary, financing of fifth columns, stimulated disorders, street terrorism, ultimately direct territorial and occupation demands. Such tactics give no present prospect development of eventual good neighbor policy enabling us to realize world of good neighbors pledged to mutual respect, mutual cooperation and mutual maintenance of peace, which is our principal national interest. Nothing has been gained and much may have been lost if we are merely going into another cycle like that between 1919 and 1939.[46]

Opposition to a potential Soviet bid for global hegemony thus became one of the basic components of postwar American grand strategy as far as Berle was concerned, joining the prevention of a renaissance of militarism in Germany and Japan, the encouragement of global economic reconstruction and growth, the internationalization of the Good Neighbor policy, and the defense and promotion of democracy. There were significant differences of emphasis among American officials on the relative importance of these objectives, and over time and in different contexts serious disagreements emerged over the ways they should be combined and pursued, but by and large Berle's definition of American strategic goals would become widespread over the course of the Truman years.

Helping to Oust a Pro-American Dictator

Arriving at Rio de Janeiro in January 1945, Berle defined in liberal terms the basic problem American policy confronted in Brazil. His definition of the situation was very similar to the one that Braden would offer a few months later with regard to Argentina, but with an important difference. Where Brazil could have flirted with the fascists—and conceivably even have provided Nazi U-boats with a decisive advantage in their campaign to cut allied supply lines—it had in fact been a close ally of the United States. It had sent twenty-five thousand soldiers to the European theater and cooperated in the establishment of bases that were important to the invasion of North Africa and to Allied supply lines as far as the Far East. It had been an effective regional counterweight to Argentina and a source of valuable resources ranging from manganese to rubber. It had also been ruled by a populistic dictator named Getúlio Vargas.[47]

Within a week of his arrival, Berle was summarizing the dilemma he faced in his diary:

> I must say that the more I get into this, the tougher the assignment looks. For the young intellectuals who are all for democracy are against the Government and want the United States to do something about that; the entrenched Government group knows that they have cooperated with the United States during the war up to the limit; and I am afraid neither side will be particularly happy at a merely "neutral" or "hands off" attitude. The problem is to find and hold a moral position capable of comprehending all elements.[48]

Despite the different contexts, the position Berle adopted as his solution to this problem was of a piece with the stance Braden took in Argentina. Where Braden carried out most of his campaign in public, Berle conducted most of his in private. Where Braden's criticisms of the Argentine regime were easily read in his analogies, Berle tended to restrict his advocacy of Brazilian democratization to championing commitments the Brazilian government itself had already undertaken. But they shared a common underlying conviction. In a letter to the State Department of 9 May 1945,

Berle stated it succinctly: "Both our short and long-range interest, as well as our moral integrity, requires continuance of the classic policy of non-intervention, accompanied by encouragement of the steady development of democratic institutions."[49]

With the noteworthy exception of a public speech he gave in late September of 1945, Berle's tenure as ambassador was much less controversial than Braden's. In the end it was also more successful. The reasons for this lie primarily in the differences between Argentine and Brazilian politics during this period. The democratic opposition in Brazil was not all that much better organized than its Argentine counterpart. Brigadier General Eduardo Gomes, the candidate most closely associated with this opposition, was defeated in the elections of early December 1945. But in contrast with the Argentine military's attitude toward Perón, most of the Brazilian military appears to have been firmly opposed to a continuance of Vargas's rule. While this would prove decisive to the outcome, American policy would also help to push a pro-American dictator from power.

By language, population, geographic extent, and above all by its history, Brazil is set apart from the other countries of Latin America. For a brief period during and after the Napoleonic wars, it was the seat of the Portuguese monarchy. Alone among the countries of the region it maintained a monarchical form of government for some sixty years after independence—Dom Pedro's declaration "I will stay" becoming famous as the first step toward Brazilian independence. The transition to a republican form of government in 1889 involved remarkably little bloodshed, and the same may be said of the revolution of 1930 that first brought Getúlio Vargas to power.

Elections under the Old Republic were dominated by rivalries between state governments—particularly those of Minas Gerais and São Paulo—and often marred by fraud. As the 1930 elections approached, the outgoing president, Washington Luiz, broke an unwritten agreement to alternate political leadership by choosing a fellow Paulista as his successor. With the support of the Mineiros, Getúlio Vargas, the governor of Rio Grande do Sul, ran as the opposition candidate. Defeated in the elections, Vargas protested the fraud inherent in the system but appeared resigned to the result, until the assassination of his running mate crystallized opposition to the regime. On 3 October 1930 Vargas's forces launched a revolt. Before they could reach Rio de Janeiro, however, elements in the military had already stepped in to overthrow the government. Turning power over to Vargas in early November, General Tasso Fragoso declared that the military had

been unwilling to continue spilling blood in a cause that the national conscience did not endorse.[50]

Although threatened briefly by a Paulista revolt in 1932, a communist
revolt in 1935, a constitutional prohibition on reelection in 1937, and fascist subversion in 1938, Vargas would remain the dominant figure in Brazilian politics for the next fifteen years. Elections for a constituent assembly were held in May of 1933 that were widely acclaimed as the freest in
Brazil's history. The new constitution extended suffrage to women and
offered new guarantees of an impartial judiciary. It also gave the government the power to establish minimum wages, guaranteed the eight-hour
workday, and prohibited child labor. Vargas was named by the Assembly to
a four-year presidential term.[51]

In the new political environment the Brazilian Communist Party and
its popular front organization, the Aliança Nacional Libertadora (ANL),
grew spectacularly. Luís Carlos Prestes, the head of the ANL, was already
famous nationally. For two and a half years in the mid-1920s, he and his
fellow military rebels, or *tenentes*, had fought skirmishes with the regular
army in the Brazilian interior. By the early 1930s he had moved to the
Soviet Union and become a member of the executive committee of the
Communist International. Not long after his clandestine return to Brazil,
Comintern observers were imagining that a million Brazilians would support him in a successful revolution. In the event, poorly coordinated barracks revolts in late November of 1935 were easily quashed and the Communist Party soon driven underground. Arrested in March of 1936,
Prestes would spend the next nine years in jail. His wife—deported to Germany—would die in a concentration camp. In the meanwhile, the threat of
communist subversion would be used to justify the imposition of new and
expanded emergency powers for the federal government.[52]

On 10 November 1937, with the backing of the army, Vargas cut short
the electoral campaign to choose his successor. Claiming that a democracy
of parties was threatening Brazilian unity, he promulgated a new constitution giving himself sweeping powers and promising the establishment of
an *Estado Nôvo* with a strong government of peace, justice, and work. By
the end of the year all political parties had been dissolved, although the
fascist green shirts, or Integralistas, were allowed to maintain most of their
previous organization in the form of civic associations. When they overreached and launched a revolt of their own in May of 1938, they were
swiftly crushed.[53]

Like Batista in Cuba, at roughly the same time, and Perón in Argentina slightly later, Vargas sought to build a base of popular support in the working class and at the same time to bring about governmental domination of the labor movement. As part of this endeavor the Ministry of Labor claimed the right to "intervene" in any union, seizing its offices and funds and installing a new leadership. Dues were deducted from every worker's paycheck and then distributed by the Ministry of Labor to government-recognized unions. A system of labor courts was set up to approve all contracts and resolve grievances. But while basic political freedoms were denied, Vargas did not attempt to create a totalitarian political party. In practice, his dictatorship was a good deal less repressive than, for example, that of Rafael Trujillo in the Dominican Republic.[54]

During the Second World War the United States had a compelling and narrowly defined national security interest in the maintenance of cordial relations with Brazil. Brazil received more than 70 percent of all American lend-lease assistance to Latin America and considerable economic assistance as well. This assistance arguably made the United States complicit in the maintenance of the Vargas dictatorship. It would be most unfortunate for the United States, Under Secretary of State Sumner Welles observed in the spring of 1942, "if anything should happen to President Vargas at this time."[55] But Vargas's hold on power was well established before significant American economic and military assistance began, and in the end such assistance did not constitute an obstacle to his overthrow. From the perspective of American officials who sympathized with the cause of Brazilian democracy, during most of the war there were simply no readily apparent and politically preferable alternatives to Vargas's dictatorship. When such alternatives began to appear, American policy moved to embrace them.

In early September of 1945 Berle wrote to President Truman outlining the situation in Brazil and the course he had been following. Responding to the suggestion of some Brazilians that he attack Vargas as Braden had attacked Perón, Berle insisted on the differences in the two situations. Where Vargas had been America's most active ally in the hemisphere and had kept his obligations, Perón and Argentina had done the opposite. Vargas was a dictator, but under "quiet encouragement" from the embassy he had lifted restrictions on the press, pledged free elections, amnestied all political prisoners, set 2 December 1945 as the date for elections, and stated that he would not be a candidate. The registration of voters was going forward honestly, and any Brazilian who wanted to could form a committee, hire a hall, organize a party, start a newspaper, and campaign against the government in safety. As long as Vargas kept going in the same direction, a continuation of quiet encouragement was the best policy. If he were to change course or do something violent, then a change of policy might be in order. But Vargas, Berle reminded Truman, enjoyed considerable popularity.

> All hands agree that if Vargas were to run, all lower classes and some of the upper would vote for him. His government is almost as corrupt as Pennsylvania. It is inadequate economically, but has done more for the masses than its predecessors. Brazilian people may be misplacing their confidence; but he has it.[56]

What Vargas did not have was the confidence of the Brazilian military. For many officers and soldiers, particularly those serving in Italy, there was an uncomfortable dissonance between participation in the struggle against dictatorship abroad and the continued existence of dictatorial rule at home. Moreover, there were some grounds for anticipating that without a democratic government in Rio de Janeiro, a high level of cooperation with the United States and its military could not be maintained once the war was over. Among those who had fought alongside the Allies, most had become staunchly pro-American. In the fall of 1944, two of the chief architects of Vargas's 1937 coup—Minister of War Eurico Gaspar Dutra and former Army chief of staff Pedro de Góes Monteiro—stressed to him the need to restore civil liberties and reestablish democratic institutions. In Frank McCann's formulation, "Dutra and Góes Monteiro gave Getúlio dictatorial powers in 1937, when such powers were fashionable, and took them away when the mode changed."[57]

In mid-February of 1945, Berle left Brazil briefly to attend the inter-American conference being held in Mexico City. While he was advocating, among other things, a resolution calling for the abolition of wartime censorship, the counselor of the American embassy in Rio was writing to him of a Brazilian opening that was just becoming visible.

Vargas's real desires remain a subject for debate. On the one side are those who argue that he was sincere in his many public and private statements that he wished to preside over free elections and then leave office.[58] On the other are those who suggest that he was secretly hoping to find some means of remaining in power.[59] Whatever his intentions, there is no doubt that his room for maneuver was greatly restricted by the Brazilian military. At one point an American military attaché reported a conversation with a Brazilian major who asserted that at least 80 percent of the officers in the Brazilian Expeditionary Force were opposed to the present government. It was for this reason that units returning from Europe were being so rapidly demobilized.[60] It is by no means clear, Berle concluded in mid-September of 1945, "that any solution which continued Vargas in power would not also result in Army rising against him."[61]

From the beginning of his tenure, Berle sought to maintain cordial relations with Vargas's opposition. When Vargas seized dictatorial powers in 1937, Juracy Magalhães was one of only two state governors who resigned in protest.[62] A few weeks after Berle had arrived in Brazil, Magalhães arrived unannounced at the American embassy and asked if Berle wished to see him. He was invited in and the two talked for a while before parting with expressions of mutual esteem. The United States, Berle explained, had no quarrel in the world with Vargas, who had cooperated faithfully and wholeheartedly. Equally, it had no reason to believe that any other line of policy would be taken by any government that might come in later. The rumor that the United States would intervene to prevent a change in government was absolutely untrue. The nonintervention policy of the United States would be scrupulously adhered to. As a democratic country, the United States naturally trusted democratic processes, "and we had full and complete confidence that the Brazilian people would find their own way towards democracy and a sound government."[63]

The first striking sign that censorship was ending in Brazil was the publication on 22 February 1945 of a lengthy interview in *Correio da Manhã* with José Américo de Almeida, one of the presidential candidates from 1937. New presidential elections were necessary, Almeida insisted, and it would be "inappropriate" for Vargas to be a candidate. Before long, the young leftist journalist who had conducted the interview, Carlos Lacerda, was invited to the American embassy. Highly active in antiadministration politics, Lacerda impressed Berle as honest but a bit on the poetic side.[64]

A group of young people calling itself Resistência Democrática did in fact meet with Berle over the course of his tenure as ambassador. This presented him with the problem, as he noted rather awkwardly in his diary, of "how to do this sort of thing and still keep out of local politics."[65] Firmly convinced that the reforms that the agrarian and labor movements in the United States had forced upon industry were of lasting benefit to American economic development, Berle urged at least some variant of them upon the Brazilians. Members of the embassy staff were directed to the study of Brazilian social and economic problems, and Berle advocated the general cause of economic reform in public speeches.[66] "Today the chief duty of a state is to increase the economic well-being of its masses," Berle told a group of Brazilian lawyers, adding that "perhaps it would be better to say that the chief concern of the state is to make it possible for the masses to better their own condition, and to assure that they have opportunity and means to do this."[67]

In the Brazilian political atmosphere of 1945, Berle's implicit call for a program of economic and social reform found relatively little resonance. In his words, Brazilian intellectuals were simply "not showing very much in the way of dead-weight lift for the masses."[68] By February much of the opposition to Vargas had already coalesced around Brigadier General Eduardo Gomes, a *tenente* in the 1920s and one of the few opponents within the military of Vargas's coup in 1937.[69] Politically, Gomes and his supporters in the newly formed União Democrática Nacional (UDN) were liberal constitutionalists; economically, they were opponents of protective tariffs who looked to the dismantling of wartime controls and warned against the dangers of using the Bank of Brazil for the creation and financing of unviable industries.[70] Minister of War Eurico Dutra, the candidate of the government-sponsored Partido Social Democrático (PSD), was even less desirable from Berle's perspective. Gomes, at least, enjoyed the confidence of most liberals, intellectuals, artists, and businessmen and the bulk of the upper classes. Dutra simply represented "one branch of the conservative forces in the country." Neither one was really addressing what Berle considered the major economic and social issues in a country with more than 70 percent illiteracy, a population of more than 45 million people, and a national income of less than 3 billion dollars.[71]

On matters of economic policy, Berle was more sympathetic to Vargas than to either Gomes or Dutra. At least Getúlio had been really interested in the little people, he told his daughter: "He had done a great many good things; and too often governments don't do anything."[72] The result of the election, he suggested to the State Department, would probably be a government more reactionary in economic matters than its predecessor.[73] But Vargas was dictatorial, and his political fortunes appeared increasingly tied to unsavory elements. In April, Luís Carlos Prestes was one of those released in the political amnesty, and the Communist Party soon reemerged as a significant political force. While avoiding direct attacks on the United States, the party had attacked the American stand on Poland and was trying to create the impression that the Soviet Union alone had won the war.[74] Before long, Berle was worrying that the Party could "tie up several cities" if Russian policy called for it.[75] "USSR espionage, propaganda and organization in South America," he warned the State Department, "are following lines very similar to German lines in 1936 and 1937."[76]

Sharing Berle's disenchantment with the candidacies of Dutra and Gomes, Prestes worked to organize support for Vargas. He was not alone. Over the course of the summer a *"Queremos Getúlio"* movement took shape, supported by Minister of Labor Alexandre Marcondes Filho and Minister of Justice Agamenon Magalhães, and by the recently organized Partido Trabalhista Brasileiro (PTB), with its base in the government-dominated unions. By the end of the summer these forces had joined the Communists in calling for elections for a *"Constituinte com Getúlio"*—a constituent assembly to write a new constitution before presidential elections took place. Aside from their personal interest in their own sinecures, Berle observed, many of the Queremistas had been among those "most active in opposing the United States and cheering Italian Fascism in 1937."[77]

In mid-September, Berle informed the State Department that he thought Vargas still wanted to fulfill his pledge to preside over presidential elections and then retire, but he cautioned that Vargas was subject to "great temptation" to remain in power. This was in spite of the fact that any effort on his part to do so, such as a decree suspending the presidential elections, might well provoke a coup.[78] As the demonstrations scheduled for the fifteenth anniversary of the revolt that had first brought Vargas to power approached, Berle grew increasingly apprehensive and increasingly convinced of the desirability of stating clearly where the United States stood.[79] The idea of making a speech on internal Brazilian politics initially generated skepticism within the State Department, but Braden approved it while passing through Rio on his way to take up his new position as assistant secretary of state in Washington. As far as the State Department was concerned, it was largely Braden's decision to take.[80]

On the evening of 28 September 1945, a Friday night, the American ambassador to Brazil met with the Brazilian president at the Guanabara Palace. He took the opportunity to praise Vargas for his statesmanship in guiding Brazil back onto a democratic path and to stress that the United States took no stock in the statements of those groups claiming that he was secretly plotting a coup d'état. Vargas replied that he had given his word that he would not be a candidate and besides was tired and wished to leave office while he still had the affection and applause of his people. At this point Berle told him that he had thought of saying something himself on the subject and showed Vargas the text of his remarks. Vargas would later claim that Berle had read him the speech in such "badly masticated Portuguese" that he was unsure whether the speech Berle later gave was the same one he had approved or not.[81] This assertion, however, is at odds with Berle's contemporary record of their meeting:

> He read it and asked one question: whether this meant we were op-posed to a Constituinte. I told him certainly not, though speaking as an individual I did not recall any case where a constituent assembly had been able to take over executive power; that of course was a mat-ter which the Brazilians themselves would decide. Our fear was lest the hotheads would defeat the policy he had so wisely and brilliantly worked out during the last year.[82]

Assuming that Vargas was sincere in wishing to preside over free elec-tions and then retire, he could perhaps have seen some utility in a public assertion by the American ambassador of confidence in the political pro-cess that was under way. Such a statement might conceivably help to dis-courage military plotting against the government. Berle would later de-scribe the speech in his diary as "designed if possible to head off violent moves in either direction."[83] Alternatively, if Vargas secretly hoped to re-main in power, Berle's speech might have some utility as a means of delay-ing his enemies until he had found a mechanism for forcing the army to back down. Such considerations may help to explain Vargas's acquiescence. But if he was seeking to overcome the army's opposition, his plans would necessarily rest upon the mobilization of popular pressure. For this, the idea of a constituent assembly was essential as both a rallying call and a claim to democratic legitimacy. His one question thus bore directly on his own political options. Berle's answer, in the light of his text, was rather disingenuous. If the timing and propriety of a *constituinte* was a matter for Brazilians to decide, it was also a matter on which the American ambassa-dor intended to offer some unmistakable advice.

The following day, in plenty of time for the Sunday papers, Berle ad-dressed a group of journalists at the Hotel Quitandinha in Petrópolis. Be-ginning with the long friendship between the United States and Brazil, a friendship strengthened by recent and common sacrifice, Berle went on to praise the steps Brazil had taken toward the development of constitutional democracy. Millions of American friends of Brazil had rejoiced over the establishment and safeguarding of a free press, the free organization of political parties, and the political amnesty. The pledge of free elections, set for a definite date, by a government whose word the United States had found inviolable, had been hailed with great satisfaction. That constitu-tional democracy was emerging by political discussions and the democratic institution of elections was the happiest omen for Brazil's future. No true friend of Brazil or of the Brazilian people would interrupt that process. Democratic processes, like other processes, might make mistakes. But democratic institutions, unlike other institutions, contained within themselves the possibility of correcting their mistakes.[84]

To that point in his speech Berle had perhaps succeeded in offering something to almost everyone. It was with his next paragraph that he really took sides. It would be tragic, he warned, if the essential task of constitution writing was allowed to interrupt or prevent the process of democratic self-government by the popular choice of executive power.

> History once taught the world a grim lesson in this regard. During the French Revolution, a convention was set up to draw a constitution; but because the orderly choice of executive government was delayed, the political road led straight to the Terror, and to military dictatorship—we should call it Fascist today—from which the convention could not protect the French people, and from which France took a generation to emerge.

Brazilian leadership was wiser and had arranged for elections without impeding whatever constitutional reorganization might be desired. Brazil, the United States, and the other great nations, Berle concluded, were engaged in a titanic effort to unify the world. To succeed, such unity would have to be based upon respect for the rights of peoples. Some of these rights were increasingly recognized internationally: a right to be freely informed; a right to be free from invasion; a right to access to economic resources; a right to religious freedom. These and other domestic freedoms could only be guarded by each country for itself, but it was this safeguarding of liberty that established a nation's grandeur. Admiring the progress Brazil had made, and convinced that the Brazilian nation would not falter in its steady march on the democratic path, the United States looked forward to deepening friendship and increased common understanding: "Together we can serve each other, and the entire world."

Berle's speech was favorably received by most of the Brazilian press and even referred to as the "atomic bomb that ended *Queremismo.*"[85] This it was not. All Berle had really done, as he later told his father, was to establish "the moral position of the United States."[86] The demonstrations of 3 October 1945 came and went without great incident. Vargas repeated that he would not be a candidate, but at the same time he told the crowd that they had a right to demand a *constituinte.*[87] Demonstrations on Vargas's behalf continued. The financing and organization of the Queremistas reached such proportions, Berle later told the State Department, that the pretense that they were entirely independent of the Palace was impossible to maintain.[88] By late October, an embassy observer could speculate that what Vargas was really hoping for were popular demonstrations and strikes of such magnitude that the army would be unable to put them down without bloodshed and considerable loss of prestige. Perhaps the police could be persuaded to declare that they would not cooperate with the army in the event of a threatened crackdown.[89] Such suspicions received a tremendous boost on 29 October when Vargas replaced João Alberto, the federal chief of police, with his brother, Benjamin Vargas. For those in the military who were already looking for an excuse to overthrow Vargas, and for those who sincerely thought that he was planning a coup d'état, this was the time for action. The leadership of the army met with Gomes and Dutra, and it was agreed that the president of the Supreme Court should replace Vargas and preside over the elections. By the evening of that day, Vargas had resigned under duress.[90]

"As these things go," Berle wrote to his daughter, "it was as quiet a party as I have ever seen."[91] In fact, the tranquillity of the transition, and the speed and thoroughness with which Queremismo vanished, were taken by Berle as proof that the movement had been almost completely artificial. A few top officials had created the appearance of agitation by spreading money around and by compelling attendance at demonstrations through government-controlled unions.[92] Berle had more respect for the Communists, who he thought had decided to break with the Queremistas at the last moment once Benjamin Vargas was named to head up the police.[93]

Berle's attitude toward the Brazilian Communist Party was complex. Although hostile to the Party as a result of its loyalty to Moscow, he thought that its steady pressure to "do something for the masses" could be a constructive element in Brazilian politics.[94] He hoped that the party would be fought by argument and action rather than by banning.[95] A number of Communists had been arrested during Vargas's ouster, and both their headquarters and the offices of their paper, *Tribuna Popular*, had been raided. On the evening of 30 October 1945, Berle took up their cause with Pedro Leão Velloso, who was remaining in office as foreign minister. As long as the Communists kept to peaceful methods, he suggested, it was better to respect their rights. The arrests gave the new government the appearance of weakness whereas in fact it was in excellent shape. Moreover, the arrests raised a lot of unjustified noise in the outside world.[96] The following day, a forceful defense of the Communist Party's rights was made by the president of the UDN, Otávio Mangabeira: "Since the UDN is one hundred percent democratic, it will, consequently, be one hundred percent anticommunist. But, at the same time, because it is one hundred percent democratic, it believes that the Communist Party should have absolute liberty. We are adversaries, but we respect the freedom of thought and conscience of others."[97] In the elections that December, Yeddo Daudt Fiuza, the Communist candidate, won 10 percent of the vote, and Prestes was elected a senator from the federal district.[98]

The elections of 2 December 1945 involved the broadest popular participation in Brazilian history. Suffrage was still limited by a literacy requirement but no longer limited by gender. In the end, more than 80 percent of the electorate and a third of the entire adult population voted, roughly 6.2 million people.[99] Contrary to expectation, Gomes and the UDN lost, and Dutra and the PSD won. A few days before the election Vargas had endorsed Dutra. In addition to Vargas loyalists in general, this had brought the state directors of the PTB out on Dutra's behalf. Although his margin of victory was more than a million votes, Dutra himself credited Vargas with his triumph.[100] Particularly in industrial São Paulo, Vargas's popularity was enormous. He was elected senator from two states and congressman from six and from the federal district as well. His political career was hardly over.

Reviewing the election results as they were coming in, Berle suggested that while Dutra would pursue less enlightened policies than Gomes, there was no reason to think that Brazilian-American relations would suffer as a result. Dutra would be considerably rougher with the Communists than Gomes would have been, but he would probably continue Vargas's social legislation. There was even reason to believe that he would work out a cooperative arrangement with the UDN so that the Gomes group would have some influence in government.[101]

A few days later, Berle reiterated the importance of maintaining democratic processes. Although he did not believe it was a "serious sounding," Gomes's private secretary had asked him during the course of a visit how the United States would view a coup, noting that a number of the army men were very unhappy about the election results and wanted to take some action. "I said Brazilian politics was of course a Brazilian affair, but my own opinion was that such [a] movement would emphatically not be well received," wrote Berle later.[102]

Despite Berle's genuine admiration for Getúlio and the sincerity of his democratic convictions, Berle's speech at Petrópolis placed him on the anti-Vargas side of Brazilian politics. In the spring of 1946, Vargas himself charged that Berle's speech had been a signal to his enemies in the military to overthrow him; he repeated this charge while campaigning successfully for the presidency in 1950.[103] Vargas did not present any evidence to support his charges, and none has come to light from either State Department records or from Berle's private papers. There is in fact no good reason to doubt that Berle sought to encourage a peaceful electoral transition to democracy. In doing so, however, he helped to significantly limit Vargas's room for maneuver by placing the moral support and prestige of the United States behind the idea of holding presidential elections before elections for a constituent assembly. This idea already had strong and widespread support in Brazilian politics before Berle endorsed it, but his endorsement seems to have helped consolidate the consensus behind this position. In effect, holding presidential elections first came to be regarded as the primary mechanism for insuring the transition to democracy that everyone professed to want. While many different agendas were involved in Vargas's overthrow, and his own long tenure as a dictator had certainly helped to mobilize opposition to his continuing in office, it was only after he appeared to have decided to try to circumvent the consensus path to democracy that he was overthrown.

Although the consensus in support of Brazilian democracy would break down in the early 1960s, the political freedoms of the intervening years are indicative of the strength of this consensus and constitute a substantial historical victory.[104] It is hardly surprising that there should have been a distinct undercurrent of satisfaction in the letter Berle drafted on the eve of the elections offering his resignation: "We have got Brazil onto a democratic basis without violence or bloodshed and she has peace, freedom and a clear opportunity to solve her own problems by men of her choice."[105] When Truman's reluctant letter of acceptance came a few months later, it spoke of Berle's having done "a grand job."[106] The tributes in the Brazilian press were also glowing. A column in *Diario de Noticias* insisted that the American ambassador was taking with him "the *simpatia*, respect, and admiration of all free-thinking people in this country." In *A Manhã* a professor at the University of Brazil described him as having performed a greater labor than any previous American ambassador and having earned "the admiration of all men of culture in Brazil." The distrust that might have been produced by his Petrópolis speech, *Folha Carioca* observed, was swept away by the struggle "in favor of democracy in which we found ourselves, in which the Ambassador became a powerful ally and in the triumph of which he personally participated." One writer in *O Jornal* stressed the opening of the American embassy to include a wide range of visitors beyond the traditional *granfinos*. Another, in *Correio da Manhã*, suggested that a street should be named after Mrs. Berle: "When children in their natural curiosity ask who Beatriz Berle was, we shall answer: 'She was an American Ambassadress, a medical doctor, who spent more time in a doctor's gown in our hospitals than in an evening dress in our ballrooms!'"[107]

After he left office, Berle maintained a network of personal contacts with American officials and Latin American friends and worked closely with the Inter-American Association for Democracy and Freedom. The IADF might not be rich or powerful, he remarked at one point, but its good opinion was important everywhere, and it had "the best information about Latin America currently available."[108] When the second postwar wave of democratic openings swept over Latin America in the late 1950s, he could boast in his diary of "a fairly good galaxy of governments composed of exiles who at one time had few friends except Beatrice and me."[109]

In November 1960 Berle was asked by Senator John Kennedy's friend and adviser Theodore Sorensen to head a task force on American policy toward Latin America for the incoming administration. "We are agreed," the members of this group reported to the president-elect—in the spirit of Cold War liberalism—"that the greatest single task of American diplomacy in Latin America is to divorce the inevitable and necessary Latin American social transformation from connection with and prevent its capture by overseas Communist power politics." Toward that end they urged the United States to encourage social and economic reform including agrarian reform throughout Latin America; to mobilize public as well as private capital for investment; to promote greater and freer trade; to provide technical assistance in setting development targets; and generally to seek a New Deal for the region—an "Alliance for Progress." Democratic and reformist movements, such as Acción Democrática in Venezuela and the Partido de Liberación Nacional in Costa Rica, would be essential to the Alliance's success and the United States should seek to aid them directly.

To do this, the task force suggested, it should encourage and covertly finance a "democratic internationale" that would support "movements and governments in other countries adhering to the democratic-progressive view."[110] While Berle and his fellow liberal Cold Warriors were not advocating a democratic version of the Comintern in the early Truman years, they were calling for democratic solidarity in ways that resonated within the politics of many Latin American countries. Perhaps the strongest such resonance was in Argentina.

3

The Yankee Cowboy and Argentina

For almost eighty years following adoption of the Constitution of 1853, Argentina enjoyed a fairly stable political order with considerable respect for the political rights and civil liberties of its citizens. Citizenship, however, was highly restricted and did not include vast numbers of recent immigrants to the country. Elections were marred by fraud the extent of which was sometimes, as Robert Dahl puts it, "not far from those famous elections in Spain in the nineteenth century when the outcome of the vote was announced in advance."[1] Public contestation and debate did play a role in political decision making, although a limited one. It was in this context that the major Argentine political parties emerged. Of these the Radical Party was the largest, but the Socialist Party and the Conservative Party also commanded substantial loyalties. Traditionally, the Conservatives—based in the landed elite linked to Argentina's highly successful export sector—had been dominant in Argentine politics. Argentina in the early twentieth century was one of the wealthiest countries in the world. Real wages were higher in Buenos Aires than in Paris, and the oligarchy took both its dominance and the propriety of its economic policy largely for granted.[2]

With the extension of suffrage in the early 1910s, the Conservatives began to lose their ascendancy. Although women and the large immigrant sector of the working class remained disenfranchised, the more middle-class Radical Party consistently won national elections. Unfortunately, even in victory, the Radicals maintained something of an oppositionist mentality. Seeking to redress years of deprivation in which their followers had been excluded from patronage and governmental favor, the Radicals overreached and began to politicize traditionally professional institutions such as the army by placing a high value on party loyalty in making promotions, and they frequently used the power of the national government to "intervene" and take over hostile provincial governments that were still in Conservative hands. Such violations of the traditional rules of the game helped to bring about a military coup d'état in 1930.[3] While this coup partially restored Conservative influence, it left the country without an adequate institutional mechanism for changing political leadership. Congress functioned in the 1930s, but elections were again marred by fraud and limits on participation and by frequent "interventions" against provincial governments. It was against this background, when it looked as though the next Conservative president would be a strongly pro-British member of the oligarchy, a man reputed to own "all that was worth owning in Salta province," that a group of military officers pulled off a coup in June of 1943.[4]

By the end of 1943 political parties were officially abolished, press censorship intensified, and the provinces placed under military intervenors. The new regime sought to build a base of popular support by decreeing a freeze on rents in urban areas and a 20 percent reduction in the rents paid by tenant farmers. Tramway fares in Buenos Aires were reduced and a British-owned gas company was nationalized. Juan Perón, the new secretary of labor and social welfare, proclaimed that he knew the true needs of Argentina's workers and urged them to seek the same cohesiveness and strength that the army had attained. Argentina's businesses, he suggested, should offer their workers a month's salary as a Christmas bonus.[5]

Initially, the new regime was recognized by the United States. Privately confronted with evidence that it had attempted to purchase arms from Nazi Germany, the Argentine government even broke diplomatic relations with the Axis. This provoked another coup in February 1944 and brought Edelmiro Farrell to the presidency and soon brought Perón to the ministry of war and the vice presidency. In response, the United States broke diplomatic relations with Argentina and persuaded most of the rest of the American republics to do likewise. As long as the "military-Fascist group" was in control, insisted Secretary of State Cordell Hull, American recognition would be denied.[6]

The secret Grupo Obra de Unificación (GOU) to which both Farrell and Perón belonged certainly resonated with the rhetoric of European fascism.[7] But Perón's views were more than simply an adoption of abstract fascist notions of legitimacy. They were an attempt to grapple with the problems of Argentine economic and political development, and they foreshadowed views that would become more common in Latin America in the postwar period. Perón had been in Europe from 1939 to 1941 and was clearly impressed with the appearance of lasting integration and strength presented by the Axis powers. The sudden collapse of France was for him a stark demonstration of the dangers of "profound internal disorganization." Presenting his views in a speech at the University of La Plata in June 1944, he argued that national defense was a work of long years of constant and conscientious effort; a work that could not be done by the armed forces alone but one that would require "the harmonious and integrated labor of the diverse organs of government, of distinct institutions, and of every Argentine, whatever their sphere of action." Taking the sphere of industry as one of his examples, Perón argued that foreign capital had shown little interest in developing Argentine natural resources in ways that would bring Argentine industrial products into competition with the products of foreign industry. The absence of various Argentine industries—such as an arms-manufacturing industry—had imposed a great burden on the national defense of the country. A number of new industries had emerged under the impact of the First World War, but many of them had disappeared after the war.

> The state did not possess the foresight to know that it ought to guide and protect them, directing the national utilization of energy; facilitating the training of labor and management; harmonizing the exploration and extraction of primary materials with the necessities and possibilities for their development; directing and protecting their placement in national and foreign markets, from all of which the national economy would have benefited considerably.[8]

As secretary of labor, Perón sought to contribute to his vision of state-directed national integration by encouraging unionization in previously unorganized industries and by seeking to bring unions under governmental domination through the selective provision of legal status, governmental assistance, and coercion. To encourage general support among the working class, the Christmas bonus that had been voluntary in 1943 was made mandatory in the winter of 1944. In many ways, this endeavor appeared to be working. Aside from popular demonstrations celebrating the liberation of Paris, the regime's opposition had been fairly quiescent. With the defeat of the Axis powers in sight, however, an accommodation with the United States and the other American republics seemed desirable.

In February and March of 1945 an inter-American conference of foreign ministers was held in Mexico City, with Argentina's representatives excluded. Looking toward the establishment of a mutual security agreement at the next inter-American gathering, the foreign ministers indicated that they hoped to see a restoration of hemispheric solidarity before then. An invitation was extended to Argentina to declare war on the Axis, to express its conformity with the principles and resolutions of the Mexico City Conference, and to sign the Act of Chapultepec.[9] On 28 March 1945 Argentina accepted this invitation. The extent to which the Argentine regime saw itself as obliged, under this arrangement, to eliminate Axis agents and influence in Argentina is unclear. Its formal note indicated only that it would take "all emergency measures incident to the state of belligerency, as well as those that may be necessary to prevent and repress activities that may endanger the war effort of the United Nations or threaten the peace, welfare or security of the American Nations."[10] By apparently agreeing to comply with anti-Axis Resolutions 7 and 19 of the Mexico City Conference, and by taking such preliminary steps as the registration of enemy nationals, the suspension of pro-Axis newspapers, and the issuance of a decree taking over the assets of Axis firms, the Argentine regime won both diplomatic recognition and the visit of an unexpectedly assertive American ambassador.[11]

Shortly before arriving as ambassador in Argentina, Spruille Braden was assigned to serve as the American representative to the inauguration of Juan Arévalo in Guatemala. While the United States had not played an important role in the overthrow of the Ubico dictatorship the previous June, American officials had refused Ubico's last-minute appeals for American support and similar appeals from his successor, General Ponce, when the latter sought to perpetuate himself in power. They had allowed the Guatemalan revolutionaries to use the American embassy as a place for negotiating Ponce's surrender, in October 1944, and had welcomed the revolutionary government's commitment to preside over free elections, elections that Arévalo had won handily.[12] The appointment provided Braden with an additional opportunity to develop the antidictatorial position and reputation that he would bring to Buenos Aires. It is something one does not often see, Braden told a reporter from *El Imparcial* on his arrival. "Major Arana, Captain Arbenz and Mr. Toriello, resisting the temptation to perpetuate themselves in office, as is so often done, have surrendered power and have given with it a demonstration of the highest civic and democratic spirit; a demonstration that is comparable only to that given by Washington, San Martín and Máximo Gómez."[13] Such public praise, Braden later explained to the State Department, might help to fortify the Guatemalans in their determination to continue on a democratic course.[14]

"We are carrying on a war in favor of democracy throughout the world," said Braden in his first public statement as ambassador in Buenos Aires, "and when we say that we are fighting for democracy we mean just that. We propose to support democracy and we should like to see democratic governments in all parts of the world."[15] It was through statements of principle such as this that Braden sought to encourage Argentina's democrats. The closest he came to directly criticizing the Argentine regime was probably a story he told in late August about a European satellite of the Axis in which a stone-throwing demonstration had been organized against the embassy of one of the Allied powers. The minister behind this "spontaneous" demonstration, Braden told his audience, had, presumably for the sake of appearances, sent some police along with several hundred "patriotic defenders of the national sovereignty." When the ambassador, knowing who was responsible, called the minister to protest, the latter offered to send more police. "You don't have to send me more police," replied the ambassador, "just send fewer 'nationalists.'"[16]

Widely reported in the Argentine media, such indirect attacks and general statements of principle helped to turn Braden into a rallying point for opposition to the regime. From May to September, as Félix Luna puts it, Braden became "the virtual leader of the opposition."[17] An Argentine friend later described him as having been "the backbone of a sane reaction."[18] This was a source of tremendous irritation to the Peronistas. On the night of 19 July 1945 handbills critical of the American ambassador flooded the streets of Buenos Aires. One of the more colorful read, "Do you know that cowboy Braden told the entire Diplomatic Corps that he was going to 'tame' in one month the country of the Argentines putting it in his pocket like the swarthy Batista? Look out for flying hoofs, boys."[19] If anything, such attacks only served to increase Braden's stature and influence. In a letter of early August to Ambassador Claude Bowers in neighboring Santiago, Braden observed that there had been some real progress since his arrival. Roughly three hundred political prisoners had been freed, press restrictions had been somewhat loosened, and efforts were beginning to be made to control Nazi elements and make relevant archives about them available. "However, as I have pressed in on these various fronts, Perón et al. naturally realize that they are being pushed into a corner from which there will be no escape excepting into democracy. Hence they are fighting like cornered wild animals and it promises to be a knock-down drag-out from here on."[20]

It was at this point that Braden was prematurely recalled to assume responsibilities for policy toward Latin America as a whole. In early July, President Truman had asked former South Carolina senator James F. Byrnes to become his secretary of state, and with Japan's surrender in hand, Byrnes was now selecting his own team.[21] The decision to include Argentina at the founding conference of the United Nations in San Francisco had been widely criticized, and Assistant Secretary of State Nelson Rockefeller had been blamed for that decision. Braden's forceful stand in Argentina, in contrast, had generally been reported favorably in the American media.[22] In fact, as is evident in Rockefeller's support for Braden's basic policy memoranda in January and April, there was much less disagreement between the two than was commonly assumed. As far as Braden was concerned, he had never had the "slightest difference" with Rockefeller.[23] As far as Rockefeller was concerned, Braden had done a "brilliant job" as ambassador in Argentina.[24] But Byrnes was determined to make the change, and while Braden had some reservations he was in the end "most anxious to accept."[25]

In his letter to Byrnes accepting the promotion, Braden cautioned that since he had become something of a symbol for the Argentine people, it would be fatal if they were to feel abandoned as a result of his transfer. He suggested that the new appointment be publicized as a promotion made in recognition of his policies in Argentina and in order to give those policies even greater effect. He also suggested that the ambassadorship be left temporarily open so that he could direct affairs from Washington and that his departure be delayed for several weeks. All of these suggestions were adopted.[26]

On 14 September 1945 Braden gave one of his last public speeches in Argentina. Directing his audience's attention toward Germany, he argued that totalitarian systems by their nature wrought not only economic devastation but tremendous moral destruction as well. In earlier times, Germany had been a country with a great and powerfully abundant spiritual life, and what had happened?

> A country that had produced some of the greatest spiritual figures that the world has known; the country of Kant and Hegel; of Bach and Wagner; of Goethe, Heine and Schiller, of Dürer and Holbein; a country, in sum, that had given the world some of its greatest philosophers, poets, architects, scientists, engineers, musicians, etc., had ended by converting itself into a spiritual wasteland in which such ideas perished at birth, in which the citizenry submitted abjectly to crime and degradation and in which the only individual or collective

initiatives that could prosper were those directly applied to the service of the so-called art of war. Three weeks before the contest in Europe ended, a journalist asked General Eisenhower if he had found any trace, however small, of effective resistance against nazism. "Absolutely none," was the reply. No one, absolutely no one, was capable of active resistance against the barbarism and savagery represented by the sinister concentration camps of Dachau and Büchenwald. How could they have been able to resist? The best Germans had been brutally annihilated or had fled abroad. In reality, we all have a part of the responsibility for what has happened. Without the so-called policy of appeasement—deaf and blind to the pain and anguish of others—surely the dictators would not have been able to perpetrate their monstrous crimes.[27]

Five days later, several hundred thousand Argentines gathered in a great antigovernment March of the Constitution and of Freedom. Braden would later claim that half a million people had turned out.[28] Arthur Whitaker puts the crowd at only a quarter of a million, but writes that it was so successful "that it was taken as marking the beginning of the end for Perón."[29] In the words of the British ambassador to Argentina, Sir David Kelly, "Long before Mr. Braden left the country, and especially at the moment of his leaving, he had become a national hero and temporarily made the United States popular in Argentina for the first time in living memory."[30]

Until the March of the Constitution, the concessions the Argentine regime had made in the interest of accommodation with the United States could perhaps be justified. The beginnings of a united front of all the major political parties, including even the small Argentine Communist Party, and with the cooperation and support of both business and labor elements, was a threat requiring response—a threat intensified by an abortive revolt within the military in sympathy with the civilian demonstrators. On 26 September 1945, a week after the March of the Constitution had taken place, and three days after Braden had left Buenos Aires for his new job, the state of siege that had been lifted in early August was reimposed and hundreds of opposition figures were rounded up and arrested, although many were released within a day or two.[31]

When Braden arrived in Washington, his first recommendation was that the United States ask the Brazilian government to postpone the inter-American conference scheduled to begin in late October in Rio de Janeiro.[32] The United States, he argued, could not in dignity and self-respect sit down and negotiate a treaty of military alliance with the present Argentine regime. Acheson and Truman agreed.[33] By postponing the conference for this reason, moreover, Braden hoped to give "a well-merited slap to the Perón regime which would be helpful in that whole situation in Argentina."[34] In Argentina, meanwhile, a wave of student strikes swept the country's universities and the Supreme Court ruled that the government had exceeded its authority in dismissing a federal judge in Córdoba. On 9 October 1945, an uprising in the Campo de Mayo garrison led President Farrell to dismiss Perón from his offices and have him imprisoned on the island of Martín García.[35]

Victory was to be short-lived. The opposition, overestimating both its own strength and the weakness of its adversaries, insisted that Perón's ouster was not enough and that all executive authority had to be turned over to the Supreme Court. Promises that the next Argentine government would be chosen in free elections were greeted with complaints about the political parties statute and repeated demands that the military go back to the barracks. The Radicals refused to enter the cabinet or to collaborate in any way with the military, and the Conservatives waited many days before agreeing to do so.[36]

During more than a week of political uncertainty and confusion following Perón's ouster, Eva Duarte helped to organize Perón's considerable support among Argentine workers into demonstrations on his behalf. On 17 October 1945, in the face of a general strike that paralyzed Buenos Aires, Perón was released and presented to a crowd of several hundred thousand cheering Argentines. To them he announced that he had resigned from his offices in order to run for the presidency. From them he asked the creation of "a bond of union that will make indestructible the brotherhood between the people, the army and the police—an eternal and infinite union within which the people can grow in the spiritual unity of the true and authentic forces of nationality and order."[37]

Aside from the failure of the opposition to seize the opportunity presented to them by Perón's ouster, there was a wide variety of reasons for his comeback. In power, perhaps even those who had been helped by his policies might have been indifferent to his continuance in office. Imprisoned on an island in the middle of the Río de la Plata, he became for many a martyr who had promised and delivered benefits that were now at risk. There seem to have been significant elements in the army who were unwilling to impose Perón on the country by force but who nonetheless favored his candidacy for the presidency. Many American corporations in

Argentina, Braden noted at one point in late October, had provided "an object lesson in how American companies abroad should *not* handle their labor problems." They had "stubbornly and stupidly refused to permit unionization" and were now reaping the harvest of their errors.[38]

Braden's own errors also contributed to Perón's comeback. Aside from his premature departure, his decision to postpone the Rio Conference had earned him considerable enmity among a group of American senators who were irked that the sudden postponement had been decided upon without consultation with either the other American republics or with them. Their delay in approving Braden's appointment as assistant secretary of state appears to have been of some significance to the course of events. On 19 October 1945, the American chargé d'affaires in Argentina, John Moors Cabot, wrote to the State Department that "opinion is widespread in Buenos Aires both in Government circles and opposition that delay regarding Braden's nomination by Senate Committee had important influence in most recent overturn. Pro-Perón *La Epoca* recently claimed that failure of Senate to act showed that Braden did not represent American opinion while opposition elements were disconcerted and disheartened."[39]

During the Senate Foreign Relations Committee hearings on his nomination—in sessions closed to the public on 3 and 10 October 1945—Braden was repeatedly attacked for having pursued a "big stick" policy and for having intervened in the internal affairs of Argentina. "It is their country," insisted Senator Tom Connally, the chairman of the committee, "and if they want a dictator, let them have a dictator. They aren't worth a damn if they don't rise up and throw him out, if they don't want him."[40] Rather than fight the issue out, Braden simply denied that he had ever engaged in intervention. He made no effort to defend his conviction that the promotion of democracy in Latin America was in America's interest or that it was something the United States could do without violating its commitment to nonintervention. He took, as he told his friend Ambassador Frank Corrigan in Caracas, "the more diplomatic course of limiting myself strictly to answering the questions put to me."[41] Since the questions the senators asked were often rather hostile, this in itself was no easy matter. "Argentina signed the Act of Chapultepec," Connally reminded Braden, "she signed at the Conference in San Francisco. We took her in, we were brothers to her. Regardless of that, are we going to say to her, 'We are not going to let you sign anything else, because you haven't got the kind of government within Argentina that we like?'"[42]

At this point Under Secretary of State Dean Acheson intervened in the discussion. During the period when Ambassador Braden was in the country, Acheson observed, he had been making progress. "The moment he leaves they take advantage of a phony revolution in Argentina in order to go back on every one of these promises which they have taken. They do nothing about enemy personnel, they backslide on the control of enemy property, they slap on the censorship . . . and we are right back to where we were before Mexico City, nothing being done at all."[43]

For Braden and Acheson, Argentina was being run by a fascist dictatorship that was a potential threat to the peace of the hemisphere; a dictatorship that had been and still was collaborating with the enemy and appeared to have been involved in efforts to subvert the governments of its immediate neighbors. In days gone by, Braden told the committee, the United States would have responded to such a situation by going in and intervening. "Now, because of our commitment of non-intervention, we cannot; we have got to sit back and hope and pray that the Argentine people will be able to cure their own situation."[44]

For Connally and other senators, concerns with Argentine internal politics that had been legitimate during the war were no longer valid. What was important now was inter-American unity and Latin American support for the United States in world affairs. This could hardly be obtained, they assumed, if the State Department was pursuing a "big stick" policy against Argentina. "I have a very deep feeling," Senator Arthur Vandenberg told Braden, "that as affairs in this world are developing it becomes of increasing importance that we should maintain inter-American solidarity, that we should have the good faith, support, sympathy, respect, and fidelity of our Pan American neighbors."[45] The great unasked question was how to obtain this result. Vandenberg and Connally both appear to have assumed that it could be obtained simply by pursuing a policy of respect for state sovereignty and inter-American consultations. More complex answers—in which democratic solidarity was also considered essential to the maintenance and strengthening of hemispheric solidarity—were not heard.

On the first day of his confirmation hearings, Braden had observed that communist forces in Latin America, although small, were under intelligent leadership, well disciplined, well organized, and well supplied with funds that were always conjectured to come from Russia.[46] At his next appearance, Vandenberg asked him if the communist menace north of the Argentine was not in fact "a greater menace from our point of view than what is left of the fascist menace in the Argentine." To this Braden was unwilling to give a clear answer. Arguing that they were both threats to be taken seriously, he made no effort to explain to the committee his broader strategy for dealing with them. He did express his hope that the news they had just received of Perón's ouster was "a first step on the part of the Argentine people."[47]

It is difficult to weigh the value of speculations like those of the British ambassador in Buenos Aires that Braden "might just possibly have brought it off if he had stayed to see it through."[48] Or the speculations of J. D. Murray, of the British Foreign Office, who wrote that if Braden had stayed in Argentina a few weeks longer "his dynamic personality might have produced—or at least hastened—the formation of a Govt. strong enough to have prevented the return to power of the Peronistas."[49] What is clear is that the failure of the Argentine opposition in October of 1945 was to weigh heavily on Braden's broader policy from the beginning of his term as assistant secretary.

As early as 7 June 1945, in the first response to the State Department's circular conveying the Braden memorandum, the American ambassador to Peru had suggested that Argentina might provide a test case. "Whatever criticisms may be made of Mr. Braden's seven points," Ambassador John White observed, "it seems probable that he himself will have an excellent opportunity of testing their effectiveness."[50] After the events of October, it could be argued that the test had been failed and, worse, that the effort had strengthened the dictator's hand. Even among Braden's supporters in the embassy in Buenos Aires, such as John Cabot, the events of 17 October prompted rethinking. In an insightful analysis of Perón's comeback, written within twenty-four hours of the event, Cabot cautioned that unless the course of developments was immediately reversed, the United States might find its crackdown policy effectively portrayed as merely another show of gringo imperialism.

> General impression seems to be that unless opposition forces react promptly, Perón public support will snowball with Perón making a better showing than heretofore appeared possible as people's candidate. One observer suggests that this is end of Radical and Socialistic Parties in favor of Perón organized Labor Party. Others feel that knell of oligarchy has been sounded. Obviously much can happen before these are more than guesses.[51]

Denouncing the fatuous and selfish character of Argentina's democrats in a letter to Braden of 22 October 1945, Cabot suggested that their conduct was analogous to an American policy that would have let Nazi Ger-

many win rather than fight alongside the Russians. The Radicals and Socialists were ineffective. To have the Conservatives return to power would
be a tragedy. "They don't know what democracy is," he observed. By starting immediately to undo some of Perón's measures, the Conservatives had
undoubtedly antagonized labor. There were some democrats with guts
among the students, but further American diplomatic pressure was not
likely to have favorable results. The army was hardly going to hand itself
over to democratic civilians to be punished for its misdeeds. Without a
military organization of their own, any democratic elements that came to
office would not even have the force to maintain themselves in power.
Here Cabot came to the nub of his argument. The United States had often
been accused by democratic and allegedly democratic elements of furnish-
ing arms to dictatorial governments. "Why then should it be so immoral to
furnish arms to a democratic opposition when our own national safety is at
stake?" Admittedly, there were risks that such military support would be
discovered, that it would probably succeed only after hard fighting, and
that it might even provoke a civil war, chaos, and communism. But if action
had to be taken against the forces now in control in Argentina, "the most
effective way to do so would probably be to furnish arms to such members
of the opposition forces as show that they have sufficient organization to
move against the existing forces."[52]

Cabot had discussed this possibility only with Colonel King, who would
later head up the CIA's Western Hemisphere division, and King's assessment had been encouraging.[53]

A few thousand men who really knew what they intended to do—
catch Peron and his rabble unawares—might readily turn the trick.
Colonel King believes that a group of such men could probably be
assembled by the opposition, including enough men trained in the
Spanish Civil War, to make such a force effective. If demoralization
has spread as far as there is reason to believe in the Army, I question
whether it would react very strongly and whether such reaction
would have any effect whatsoever. Colonel King doubts that it would
be necessary even to have planes and tanks; rather that lighter arms
would be all that would be necessary if the surprise were sufficient.
He is convinced, moreover, that only one or two people in this country would have to know where the arms actually came from. To most
people they could be made to appear bargain sale purchases made
with money provided by wealthy Argentines.[54]

At this point, the criticism of the Braden memorandum that was offered by the American ambassador to Bolivia should be mentioned. If Braden's proposed policy was pursued unilaterally, Ambassador Walter Thurston warned, the progression would be "aloof formality," "annoyance," "admonition," "controversy," and finally "conflict."[55] Although a reasonable prediction, the conflict Thurston had anticipated did not materialize. Cabot's argument would be all right, wrote George Butler, the deputy director of the Office of American Republic Affairs, "if we were not committed to non-intervention." Ellis Briggs, the director of the office, was more forceful in his minute: "We would be violating our own pledges if we did this—and that would be the worst step possible for real inter-Am. relationship."[56] Intervention, if it came, would have to be collective, Braden told Cabot, although he did keep open the possibility that "something far enough removed from us could be done along the lines you suggest."[57]

From the idea of covert intervention against Perón, discussion among American officials soon turned to whether the United States should attempt to do anything at all. The Argentine opposition managed to form a Unión Democrática and to agree on a common presidential candidate for the elections scheduled for February 1946—José P. Tamborini—but they hardly shared a common program. Aside from the top of the ticket, the separate parties in the coalition ran their own candidates. Unable to take the initiative and campaign on what should be done in the future, they were effectively presented by Perón as advocates of an ancien régime—an image that was strengthened by staunch conservative opposition to the Peronista decree obliging businesses to grant their workers a month's salary as a Christmas bonus. The opposition was, in fact, in the unenviable position of trying to attack as fascist a government that was allowing a competitive election and to portray as a totalitarian threat a man who was out of office.[58] Where attacks on the fascism of the Peronistas had often been well received before Perón's comeback on 17 October 1945, they did not work as well thereafter. Thrown out by an army coup and restored under civilian pressure, Perón had escaped from much of the burden of association with the Farrell regime and acquired both the appearance and the substance of considerable and increasing popular support.[59]

In a letter to Ellis Briggs of 17 November 1945, Cabot laid out his fear that a continuation of diplomatic pressure might prove counterproductive and his concern that Perón might have sufficient popular support to win a free election. Although he was using largely fascist methods, and although his social reforms were of dubious wisdom, Perón was at least beginning to make social reforms of some kind. Argentine society was marked by immense discrepancies in wealth. Landholding was notoriously concentrated in the hands of a few landlords, and industrialists had used war scarcities to gouge the public. By at least doing something, Perón was steadily gaining support among the lower classes. "In short," Cabot warned, "while I have no desire to play into Perón's hands, I can see danger that we shall not only be accused of blocking social reform but, worse, that we shall be charged with the worst sort of dollar diplomacy to protect our capital from the legitimate demands of Argentine labor." Ongoing inter-American consultations were doubtless a restraining influence on the regime, but the case that it was inherently Nazi-Fascist in nature was not one that could easily be made. In the absence of documents from Germany that would damn the government beyond retrieval, it would be hard to justify the pressure that would be needed to bring the other American republics into line in support of an effective crackdown on Argentina. In a postscript, Cabot added that Enrique Gil, a friend of Braden's and the editor of *La Semana Financiera*, was suggesting that the United States quietly withdraw from the political picture: "We could do little good and might do much harm."[60]

Briggs shared this letter with Braden, and Braden expressed considerable agreement in his response to Cabot of 11 December 1945. Additional diplomatic pressure was to be avoided as it "might only assist the Argentine Government in preparing its case, specious though it be." The earlier policy had been vindicated by Perón's ouster, but the combination of senatorial delay and the "utter ineptitude" on the part of the Argentine opposition that had brought about Perón's comeback had created a new situation requiring new tactics. On the fundamental issue of principle, however, there could be no compromise.

> Expediency might lead us now to the easier path of compromising with Perón, et al. Yet we know positively from our own experience and from everything that Perón and his group have said and done that they are evil to the roots. He is a Fascist megalomaniac and we cannot, in decency, dignity, and self-respect, or in terms of our own security, compromise with him and his followers. Admittedly to stand on this principle may result in much disagreeableness for us. We may be attacked from both the right and the left, and it may be alleged by some of our critics that we are breaking down hemisphere solidarity—a solidarity, incidentally, which has never really existed in the full.[61]

Rather than stubbornly reiterating principle, Braden told Cabot, "the best defense may be to attack." To develop an effective attack, the highest priority in the State Department had been given to gathering ammunition from the German archives. Once the case as a whole was assembled, it would be made public. In any event, Braden had to argue intensively to obtain publication of this information. More intensively, he told a friend, than at any time during all of the negotiations to settle the Chaco War between Paraguay and Bolivia.[62] Officially titled "Consultation among the American Republics with Respect to the Argentine Situation: Memorandum of the United States Government," it soon became universally known as the "Blue Book."[63] Although released on 12 February 1946, less than two weeks before the Argentine elections, Braden would later claim that it was not put out "with the remotest intention in the world" of influencing them.[64] In the light of his comments to Cabot on the value of taking the offensive and his struggle to obtain publication, this appears rather disingenuous. Yet there are good reasons for thinking that his claim was sincere. Braden took it for granted that Perón would probably win the Argentine presidency through electoral fraud, and he was preoccupied with the host of problems that this would generate. In a letter to Claude Bowers in late December 1945, he predicted a fraudulent Peronista victory and observed that Argentina might have to be excluded from what would become the Rio Treaty. Failure to do so would make a mockery of the treaty's purposes. While recognizing that this position would not easily win inter-American support, he suggested that, in the end, "the other republics will wish to sign the treaty with us even though Argentina is excluded."[65] It was primarily to mobilize support for this position—and to justify postponing the Rio Conference—that the Blue Book was written.

Above all else, the Blue Book was an effort to win inter-American support for U.S. claims that those in charge of Argentina had collaborated with the enemy during the Second World War, that they had repeatedly broken their commitments to the inter-American community, and that they were a potential threat to the peace and security of the hemisphere. Perhaps Braden hoped that it would also have a positive influence on the Argentine elections, but there is no evidence that he sought to have it written with that end in mind. On the contrary, it is obvious to anyone who has plodded through its dull prose that it was not written for the Argentine electorate. The possible responses of that electorate were not considered in the drafting, and the final version would have looked different if they had been. As political propaganda, it violates one of the elementary rules of the game by failing to consistently distinguish between the Argentine people and the Argentine regime: Even the headings of major sections are in the form "Argentine-Nazi Complicity," "Argentine-Nazi Efforts to Subvert the Governments of Neighboring Countries," "Argentine-Nazi Political and Social Collaboration," and so on. In part, this may have been the product of a simple lack of sophistication among the authors, but it seems mostly to have been a consequence of addressing a non-Argentine audience.

Shortly after the Blue Book's release, Secretary of State Byrnes wrote to the American ambassador in Brazil of his expectation that once the other American republics had had the opportunity to analyze the information it contained, they would agree with the United States and would jointly refuse to conclude a mutual assistance pact with the Farrell-Perón regime or with any regime controlled by the same elements. Even if Perón were to win the upcoming elections, the ambassador was to tell the Brazilian foreign minister, "such an event certainly would not remove grounds for distrust which are foundation of our case."[66]

In the fall of 1945, after the state of siege had been reimposed in Argentina, and particularly after Perón's comeback, there had been considerable discussion in the hemisphere about the possibility of collective intervention on behalf of democracy and human rights. The foreign minister of Uruguay had formally proposed that such collective intervention be accepted by the inter-American community as part of inter-American law, and his argument had strongly implied that the first application of the principle should be in Argentina.[67] It was soon clear, however, that this was a minority position among the states of the region. By February of 1946, and particularly after Perón's victory in what were widely conceded to have been fair elections, even the idea of excluding Argentina from a mutual security pact was criticized by a number of states in the region. Many of the replies to the Blue Book urged that the new Argentine government be given a chance to prove its character. With the defeat of nazism and fascism at their centers of irradiation, observed the Brazilian foreign minister, it did not seem likely that they would encounter a propitious climate for new adventures in the Western Hemisphere.[68]

In the face of Perón's electoral victory and critical opinion among many of the states in the region toward the idea of once again isolating Argentina, the United States retreated to its old position that the new Argentine government would have to comply with its commitments. In January of

1946, Braden had written to Cabot that "the time is long past for us to even suggest that compliance with obligations would change our attitude toward Perón, et al."[69] But by 1 April, it was evident that the time for negotiation was not past. In a circular telegram to American ambassadors in Latin America, it was observed that the Argentine people had surely not intended to approve the continuance of conditions that would threaten the safety of the inter-American system. Were there to be unequivocal compliance on the part of the new Argentine government, the road would then be open to the negotiation and signature of a mutual assistance pact. A week later, this telegram was released to the press under Secretary of State Byrnes's name as a statement of American policy.[70] On the same day—without publicity and without a single concession from the Argentine government—the State Department informed the Commerce Department that "with respect to economic controls Argentina should now be placed on an equal footing with the other American republics."[71]

Within Argentina, the release of the Blue Book had touched off an immediate controversy. Earlier in January, the release of German telegrams documenting Axis support for various Argentine newspapers had been well received by the opposition and not seriously challenged by any of the generally embarrassed papers in question. The only criticism so far heard in democratic circles, Cabot observed on 18 January 1946, "is that it is not enough. . . . [T]here is great expectancy of and anxiety for further releases."[72] It would be unfair to keep from the Argentine people pertinent information regarding Nazi penetration, Cabot argued a week later. "Delay in making facts known is bound to discourage democratic forces and lessen their chances of getting rid of totalitarianism in this country."[73]

Aside from its length and its lack of easily quotable and persuasive documentation, the Blue Book may have had an unintended effect on Argentine politics in part because the Peronistas were already braced for additional American revelations and the opposition simply assumed that such revelations would work to their advantage. By early February, however, Cabot had come to think better of his earlier request for additional ammunition. The tide of public opinion already seemed to be running against Perón, he observed, and in the highly charged atmosphere that had emerged, the consequences of a direct attack on the Argentine government were incalculable. "Opinion will be universal that we are trying to influence election results. Some Argentines will warmly applaud attack, others bitterly resent it; relative size of groups cannot be determined."[74] The considerations Cabot had offered, he was informed, had been weighed carefully, and, on balance, publication was held to be the course of action least vulnerable to criticism as a matter of both principle and long-range policy.[75] The reasoning behind this decision remains obscure. More than half a year before, Braden had explicitly recognized the danger that the Argentine opposition would place its hopes "on a foreign [U.S.] intervention which they themselves would be the first to resent."[76] In December 1945, he had admitted to Claude Bowers that while he had been able to provide the opposition with a certain amount of indirect leadership during the time when he was in Buenos Aires, it was impossible to do so from the distance of Washington.[77] His position on releasing the Blue Book is most intelligible given two assumptions: first, that he saw no real chance of a free election in Argentina, and, second, that he thought it would be much easier to begin to mobilize inter-American sentiment against Perón before he managed to win a fraudulent electoral victory.

For Perón, publication of the Blue Book came at a moment of internal dissension within his recently formed Labor Party and provided a great opportunity to rally his supporters. "The choice of this transcendental hour," he told enthusiastic crowds, "is this: Braden or Perón!"[78] It would become the most famous slogan of the campaign. Among the opposition, Cabot suggested that the initial reaction was one of stunned surprise at the extent of Argentine complicity with the enemy.[79] "Most democratically minded Argentines are deeply pleased at publication," he reported on 14 February 1946, "but enthusiasm is dampened by sense of humiliation."[80] A week later he observed that opinion among Argentina's democrats appeared to be "swinging against timing of publication of Blue Book."[81] Perón, in contrast, was publicly delighted: "I am much obliged to Braden for the votes he has given me. If I win two thirds of the electorate, I will owe a third to Braden's propaganda."[82]

By the time the votes were finally counted, Perón had won roughly 55 percent of the total in an election that his opposition described as fair.[83] Dean Acheson's judgement in his memoirs was classic:

> Not that I did not join the crusade willingly enough. Perón was a fascist and a dictator detested by all good men—except Argentines. But I still had to learn the hard way what Woodrow Wilson's experience with Huerta in Mexico should have taught me—that dictators, in Latin America or elsewhere, are not overthrown by withholding recognition and dollars or even by harsh verbal disapproval. In fact, such treatment may well make them national heroes.[84]

The elegance of retrospective verdicts is often misleading. While Acheson's general point is sound, the measures he disparaged have in fact sometimes helped to overthrow authoritarian governments. In Cuba, in 1944, the mere threat of a denial of recognition appears to have prevented a military coup d'état. In Ecuador, in 1947, a denial of recognition helped to prevent a would-be dictator from consolidating power. The vital question in all such cases is what impact external influences will have on the interplay of local forces. Much as nationalistic dictators might wish it to be true, there is no law of inevitable backlash to guarantee that American hostility will make them popular. In the summer of 1945, great numbers of Argentines responded favorably to Braden's implicit criticisms of Perón as a puppet of fascist European powers. But lasting failures are more memorable than temporary successes. Whatever the intention behind the Blue Book, and whatever the reasons behind the timing of its release, its publication did Argentina's democrats more harm than good. This, in turn, together with the memory of Perón's campaign slogan, left a legacy of considerable doubt among American officials about the extent to which the United States could directly contribute to the struggle for democracy in Latin America. Claude Bowers was almost alone in offering a more favorable assessment. "The democratic element across the border became active and articulate six months too late," he told Braden. "The fact that it did so well was due mostly to your work."[85]

Regardless of whether or not Braden had intended for the Blue Book to influence internal Argentine politics, he had failed to foresee the influence that its release would have, and he was held responsible for that failure. Although he would continue in office until June of 1947 and attempt to apply his assertively antidictatorial policy on a hemispheric basis, Perón's victory was both the beginning of the end and the most lasting symbol of the defeat of his endeavor.

The more general lesson to be drawn from the course of American policy toward Argentina in this period is not that failure is inevitable, but that the outcome of any prodemocratic policy the United States may adopt, however skillfully it is conducted, will be determined by factors over which the United States has no control and limited influence. All American efforts to promote democracy in other countries are dependent for their success on the strength and skill and luck of local democratic forces and their opponents. If the leadership of the Unión Democrática had been able to present a program that a majority of their fellow Argentines thought preferable to the program offered by Perón, then Perón would have lost the elections. The contribution of the Blue Book to their difficulties in this regard should not be exaggerated.

Even if the Unión Democrática had won, this would hardly have meant that Argentina had made a transition to stable democratic politics. The military would have remained politicized, and the Peronistas would have constituted a mass-based party actively hostile to the new government. Decades of antidemocratic practices and assumptions on the part of all of the major parties would still have to have been overcome. Differences of outlook and interest among and within each of the major political parties would somehow have to have been at least partially composed to mutual advantage if effective policies were to be fashioned and implemented. Difficult as this might have been, it would have been easier for democracy to develop under such a scenario than it was under Perón.[86]

The Debate over Sovereignty and Democracy

According to the classical legal positivists, humanity is divided by law into states, and recognition of the sovereignty of states is the beginning of political wisdom. States are juristic persons consisting of a government exercising effective control over a population and a territory.[87] Neither political democracy nor national self-determination have any sort of exclusive or privileged legal claim on sovereignty. On the contrary, sovereignty is a "fact," and aspirants to sovereign power have no legal personality. The only partial exception to this rule is for those would-be powers that are capable of mobilizing and deploying sufficient military force to deserve recognition as a belligerent. For nationalists, in contrast, humanity is divided by nature into nations, and national self-government is the only legitimate form of government.[88] Only the nation is sovereign, and all other authority is a foreign usurpation. For democrats, sovereignty resides with the people, and their exercise of self-government requires an institutional and cultural framework in which basic political rights and civil liberties are respected and political leaders are chosen in periodic and free elections.[89]

The positivist ideal of a world in which each state would recognize other states exclusively on the basis of their effective control over population and territory, and would refrain from intervening in the internal affairs of other states as long as its own national safety was not at stake, is at odds with the experience of most of humanity over most of human history. So is the nationalist ideal of a world in which the boundaries of sovereign states would coincide with the boundaries of nationalities and the democratic ideal of a world in which every state would be governed democratically.

Struggles over positivist, nationalist, and democratic ideals, and over the particular interests with which they have been combined, have formed an important part of international politics for several centuries. At times, nationalist movements have been able to persuade the governments of states to intervene in the internal affairs of other states on their behalf.[90] On other occasions, the governments of states have been able to blunt the appeal of nationalist movements by championing the principle of nonintervention. In still other cases, nationalist governments have pursued a similar course with regard to democratic movements bent on their overthrow. Depending on the circumstances, positivists have found allies among democrats and nationalists, nationalists have found allies among democrats and positivists, and democrats have found allies among nationalists and positivists. There are no inevitable antagonisms among these claims to legitimacy and no inevitable affinities. Some combinations are, however, more attractive than others.

In a 1941 "Plan for the Affirmation of Democracy," Haya de la Torre argued that national sovereignty could only have a valid meaning within a democratic political context. To suppress the freedom of a people, he insisted, was to attack the juridical equilibrium upon which a nation's rights also rested. Violations of democratic rights demanded a common response. Making inter-American obligations out of all of the articles in each of the American constitutions would be a good first step. It would permit international demands for their fulfillment. The next step would be to establish "the right of any state in the Americas to demand the aid of the rest when governments are proven to exist which, violating democratic freedoms, use their powers to impose un-American procedures tending towards totalitarianism." To monitor adherence to democratic obligations—and to resolve disputes through arbitration—a permanent intercontinental institution should be established with branches in every state.[91]

A plan like Haya de la Torre's could hardly win effective support in an inter-American environment in which the overwhelming majority of states were governed dictatorially and in which a decidedly different conception of national sovereignty was predominant. By late 1945, however, the prospects for something recognizably similar had improved. The wave of democratic openings that had taken place had changed the political balance and left most of the remaining undemocratic regimes vulnerable.

The Braden memorandum had looked forward to the establishment of an inter-American procedure for dealing with dictatorial regimes, and American officials were particularly hopeful of winning the active cooperation of a solid majority of the other states in the region in dealing with what they saw as the threat of a fascist dictatorship in Argentina.[92] It was with this hope in mind, in early October 1945, that the United States informed the other American republics that it would soon send them a review of the available evidence on Argentina's compliance with its obligations concerning the elimination of Axis interests and influence. These governments were asked for their opinion as to whether the establishment of a totalitarian-type government in the hemisphere would constitute a serious threat to inter-American welfare and security. This was the origin of what would come to be known as the Blue Book.[93]

Two days after Perón's comeback in Buenos Aires, the foreign minister of Uruguay, Eduardo Rodríguez Larreta, responded to this inquiry. The principle of nonintervention could not be indefinitely extended to cover notorious and repeated violations of essential human rights, he told the American ambassador. There was a parallelism between democracy and peace and therefore a limit beyond which—in the interests of both peace and democracy—the inter-American community would have to act.[94] Greatly encouraged, Secretary of State Byrnes urged his ambassador to convey American support for this thesis. The U.S. government, Byrnes noted, was satisfied that the majority of the American republics, their peoples and governments, would accept the foreign minister's proposition.

> A unique opportunity is now presented to carry forward and implement a principle of public law *(derecho de gentes)* which would be of enduring significance to the Americas. We would gladly follow the leadership of the Foreign Minister should he urge its acceptance by all of the governments as a basis for joint action in relation to the Farrell Government. We believe that an inter-American declaration at this time which asserted a joint concern with the protection of elementary human and civil rights by governments of this Hemisphere in relation to the Argentine situation would not only have an immediate impact on that situation, but would have significant implications outside the Hemisphere.[95]

On 22 November 1945, Larreta handed a note to the ambassadors to Uruguay of each of the twenty other American republics. In this note, he observed that the American republics had often affirmed—as they had at the 1939 conference in Panama and the 1945 conference in Mexico City—"their adherence to the democratic ideal." Indeed, at Chapultepec they had affirmed not only their support for human rights but also declared "their support of a system of international protection of these rights." Repeated violations of human rights and of the democratic ideal not only affected the American sense of justice, they sooner or later produced international repercussions: "A Nazi-Fascist regime is a system which, prompted by the instinct of self-preservation in an environment which is hostile to it, must spread out in order to survive."[96]

If this threat to peace was to be dealt with at its source, Larreta argued, then the principle of nonintervention had to be reconciled with the principle that human rights should be defended, that peace was indivisible, and that there was a parallelism between democracy and peace.

> It is not difficult to harmonize such principles. "Nonintervention" cannot be converted into a right to invoke one principle in order to be able to violate all other principles with immunity. Therefore a multilateral collective action, exercised with complete unselfishness by all the other republics of the continent, aimed at achieving in a spirit of brotherly prudence the mere reestablishment of essential rights, and directed toward the fulfillment of freely contracted juridical obligations, must not be held to injure the government affected, but rather it must be recognized as being taken for the benefit of all, including the country which has been suffering under such a harsh regime.[97]

Less than a week after Larreta's note was distributed, Byrnes expressed his government's "unqualified adherence."[98] This adherence was "to the principles enunciated," since at the operational level the Larreta doctrine was remarkably vague. The Uruguayan note contained no definition of democracy or human rights; no suggestion as to an inter-American mechanism for ascertaining when either democracy or human rights had been sufficiently violated as to justify collective action; no guidelines as to the courses of action that might be taken in the event of such violation; and no procedures whereby a particular course of action might be selected. These matters Larreta left to be dealt with in a collective multilateral pronouncement after the basic idea of collective action on behalf of democracy had garnered sufficient support. Such a pronouncement, he suggested, could be developed by an advisory committee, a separate consultation, or by inclusion of the subject in the agenda of the inter-American conference scheduled to meet at Rio de Janeiro.[99]

In addition to concern over the means to be employed, there was also some initial concern in liberal circles that the practical application of the Uruguayan note would be restricted solely to Argentina. The Colombian paper *El Tiempo* pointedly raised the matter in its endorsement: "It would be enough to summon up the names of the Dominican Republic, Honduras and Nicaragua, to see that the Uruguayan suggestion will have to be extended to those nations as a general thesis—as an authentic doctrine—and not partisanly limited to the case for which it appears to have been promulgated with exclusive intention."[100] There is little doubt, however, that the American supporters of the Larreta doctrine anticipated and desired a broad application. Where Larreta had written of a Nazi-Fascist regime that must spread out in order to survive—a description that might apply only to Argentina—Byrnes attributed this expansionist tendency to dictatorial regimes in general and argued that, for this reason, "if they are to preserve the peace, the American republics cannot permit oppressive regimes to exist in their midst."[101]

On the same day that Byrnes was endorsing Larreta's position in Washington, the new Venezuelan foreign minister, Carlos Morales, was offering the Uruguayan foreign minister his strong support.[102] Venezuelan officials appear to have believed that a solid majority of the American republics would soon follow the Uruguayan lead. Mariano Picón Lares, director of international policy in the Venezuelan foreign ministry, certainly conveyed that expectation to the American ambassador, Frank Corrigan, in a conversation of 27 November 1945. Picón Lares, who had just been named the senior Venezuelan delegate to the General Assembly, observed that most countries would be favorable and when asked which would be opposed replied: "those at which it is aimed, Argentina, the Dominican Republic, Nicaragua, Honduras and Paraguay." To which Corrigan added in reporting to the State Department, "He did not mention Bolivia but this may have been oversight."[103]

In the first formal replies to Larreta's note, both Guatemala and Panama endorsed the doctrine. "Collective intervention," wrote the Panamanian foreign minister, "that has for its object the fulfillment of inter-American agreements and obligations acquired in accordance with the Charter of the United Nations, is licit intervention and is the logical consequence of said agreements and said Charter."[104] The Guatemalan foreign minister, after noting that his government had unsuccessfully urged the establishment of an inter-American policy of nonrecognition of "antidemocratic regimes" at the Chapultepec conference, wrote that it was still firmly convinced of

the need for joint action among the democracies. The doctrine Uruguay
had presented, therefore, had "the unqualified support of the Government
of Guatemala."

> My government considers that this doctrine, apparently in conflict
> with the principle of nonintervention, is perfectly acceptable and
> logical, and is entirely in agreement with the modern principle of
> international interdependence which is replacing the archaic concept
> of the absolute sovereignty of states; this being the only possible
> manner to protect internationally the rights of man, and to attain a
> genuine democracy throughout the world.[105]

On 7 December 1945, Ellis Briggs, the director of the State Department's Office of American Republics Affairs, wrote a letter to Senator
Warren Austin summarizing the information the State Department then
had as to the reception of the Uruguayan note among the other American
republics. In this summary, a solid majority appeared to be leaning toward
approval.[106] Slightly more than a week later, the prospect of majority support had vanished. Chile, Ecuador, El Salvador, Haiti, Mexico, and the Dominican Republic had all come out against the Larreta doctrine, and Brazil
had adopted a position the American ambassador described as neither rejection nor acceptance.[107] Asked by the press how the Uruguayan proposal
was going, Braden replied: "Not at all well. A few countries including the
U.S.A. are for it, but the majority are not favorable to it. However, I think
it is sound and that over the years this conviction will spread and the principle will eventually be accepted."[108]

Braden's and Briggs's vision, like Haya's and Larreta's, was a vision of
an inter-American community constituted by democratic societies. In pursuing this vision they did not dwell on its conflict with most of Latin
American political history. Nor did they give much indication of recognizing the incongruity in appealing to all of the states in the region—dictatorships and democracies alike—to join in establishing an inter-American legal order that could include dictatorships only as lawbreakers subject to
sanction. While their vision had better prospects of being realized at the
end of 1945 than at any previous period in the history of the Americas, its
prospects were still far from good.

Because the Uruguayan proposal was in part a response to the situation
in Argentina and because it was so rapidly embraced by American officials,
there was a widespread belief that the United States was putting pressure
on the other American republics to support it. In fact, Braden desired a

"real reaction" and had issued instructions to American diplomatic representatives to avoid exercising their influence on the question.[109] But a potentially dangerous Great Power does not so easily counter impressions of being overbearing. The *New York Times*, in its editorial endorsing the Larreta doctrine, made a point of criticizing the State Department for supporting the proposal "before the Governments of the other American countries have had an opportunity to study it or even, in some cases perhaps, to receive the official text."[110] By February 1947, if not sooner, this was a view Braden had come to share. He had come to see the American position as one that encouraged counterproductive attitudes in the region and put many states "on guard against any proposal that would appear to limit their respective sovereignties, whether that limitation was imposed by individual powers or by the organized inter-American community."[111]

In the larger debate over sovereignty and democracy, the Farrell-Perón dictatorship in Argentina provided a practical test of whether or not a solid majority of Latin American states could be persuaded to join with the United States in taking action against another Latin American state on behalf of democracy. Had such a group been formed—and had the measures it undertook somehow been successful in contributing to the emergence of a more democratic political order in Argentina—it is not hard to imagine similar measures being undertaken with regard to dictatorships such as those in the Dominican Republic, Honduras, and Nicaragua. These measures would then doubtless have been described by this group of states as collective action and not as intervention: as legal sanctions designed to uphold the principle that peoples rather than states were sovereign. In the 1990s, under Organization of American States (OAS) Resolution 1080 and associated state practice, just such a transformation of inter-American law appears to have taken place.[112] In the 1940s, majority opposition to the Larreta doctrine instead strengthened the position of those who advanced more traditional conceptions of national sovereignty and nonintervention.

Among the critics of the Larreta doctrine, Colombia's representatives offered some of the most articulate arguments and, given the country's long-standing reputation as a democracy, some of the most telling. Was it possible to affirm, they asked, that democracies—as conceived by the Uruguayan or Colombian governments—were serious majorities in the organized group of nations? If they were now, would they always be? The inhabitants of Colombia, having established their own laws and practices, would not look favorably on a request to change them even though a majority of the nations of the continent or the world should find them at fault. What sort of harmony could exist in the hemisphere with inter-American policy subject to the intrigues and agitations of every party and faction that could consider, justly or unjustly, its rights to have been abused?[113]

Cold War Liberalism versus Cold War Conservatism

Within the American government, the defeat of the Larreta doctrine combined with Perón's electoral victory to produce strong criticism of Braden's policy. Secretary of State Byrnes's statement of 8 April 1946, insisting upon "deeds and not merely promises" and offering the Argentine government collaboration after it had fulfilled its commitments, was in part a response to this criticism.[114] For these critics, it was Braden's policy, rather than political circumstances in Argentina and Latin America, that stood in the way of a collective security pact for the hemisphere. They showed no sign of sharing Braden's concern over the potential dangers to long-term American security interests of entering into a mutual defense agreement with a government like Perón's. Nor did they appreciate his conviction that American interests would be best served—assuming Argentina was to be included in such an agreement—by insisting that the Argentine government first demonstrate its good faith. On the contrary, as the Joint Chiefs of Staff (JCS) soon suggested, they believed that an agreement that included Argentina was highly desirable and that the primary obstacle standing in the way of this agreement was a continued effort to alter the principle of nonintervention:

> Should the Argentine people, apart from their present fascist-type government, be deeply antagonized by our efforts to press this policy, the attainment of true hemispheric solidarity might be dangerously jeopardized. Further, since many of the Latin American countries have signified their disagreement with the Uruguayan position, untimely pressure for modification of the non-intervention principle may jeopardize the early and successful negotiation of the treaty proposed by the Act of Chapultepec for the settlement of disputes arising in the Western Hemisphere. . . . The full and free participation of Argentina in the Latin American Security organization, and the preservation of peace among the nations of South America, are believed to be of sufficient importance to warrant the suggestion by the Joint Chiefs of Staff that our policy toward Argentina be directed in such a

manner that the willing partnership of the Argentine people is both established and made capable of early and complete realization.[115]

What the JCS meant by the willing partnership of the Argentine people, as against that of "their present fascist-type government," was not specified. Nor did the JCS offer any suggestions as to how such a partnership might be established. This did not prevent their position from winning strong support from Ambassador George Messersmith, Braden's successor at Buenos Aires. This was one of two major factors behind Braden's decision to resign in June of 1947. While he remained in office, however, his views held sway, and the Rio Conference was delayed pending changes in the Argentine government or at least Argentine compliance with its inter-American obligations concerning the elimination of Axis influence in Argentina.

Braden's position was spelled out in a forty-six-page memorandum endorsed by Truman on 22 July 1946.[116] There were two related Argentine problems, Braden explained: a long-term problem and a short-term problem. The long-term problem was the traditional aspiration of Argentine governments to try to build up an anti-U.S. bloc of Latin American states; a danger that was increased by Perón's aim of establishing a totalitarian-type state with almost absolute power concentrated in his hands. The short-term problem was whether or not to sign a military pact with Argentina and furnish that country with arms before it had complied with its obligations to liquidate key German business enterprises and repatriate dangerous German nationals. The two problems were related because a failure to insist on compliance would demoralize the liberal and democratic elements in Argentina and the other American republics. These elements were potentially the only true friends the United States could count on for the long term. A failure to insist on compliance would provide encouragement to military and reactionary leaders who were innately inimical to the American way of life. It would encourage both traditional Argentine ambitions and the traditional Argentine strategy of attempting to play off a non-American power against the United States. In insisting on compliance, the United States was not intervening in Argentina's internal affairs any more than it was intervening in the Soviet Union's internal affairs when it insisted on Soviet compliance with the Soviet Union's obligations under the UN Charter. This was not to suggest that a firm stand would be enough by itself to achieve long-term American objectives but rather "that the realization of those objectives will become infinitely more difficult and may be set back for years to come if our weakness gives new strength to Perón and leaders like him in the other republics."[117]

For more than a century, Braden observed, Argentine history had been characterized by clashes between democratic and autocratic forces with control of the government alternating between them. It had been almost twenty years since the last genuine elections, and during this period—although there had recently been a growing demand for democracy—autocratic forces had effectively dominated the country. Perón's electoral victory had taken place after a three-and-a-half-year state of siege in which freedom of assembly, habeas corpus, and other basic rights had been denied; after a government-enforced "bonus" for all workers of a month's salary had been decreed; and after a campaign in which opposition meetings were repeatedly broken up, the opposition's press was censored, and their candidates were almost completely denied radio access.[118]

Not only in Argentina but throughout the Americas, there was an ongoing political struggle between democratic and dictatorial forces. In this struggle almost every political program—whether of the extreme left, the center, or the extreme right—was built around the theme of improving economic and social conditions for the people. It was this theme that Perón had successfully exploited through demagoguery. The key question was how the broader struggle would go. With its technical genius and know-how, the United States was in a position to contribute substantially to progress in industrial development, health, sanitation, and agriculture—to help do what Perón and the Communists would be merely talking about for years to come—and it was very much in the interest of the United States to do so.

> In the continuing struggle in this Hemisphere between the democratic and totalitarian ideologies our long-range interest requires that we continue to be identified with economic progress, liberalism and liberty rather than with opportunism or totalitarianism. Only by thus aligning ourselves can a solid basis be laid for an enduring friendship among the peoples of the Hemisphere.[119]

This was Braden's basic reason for resisting pressures to forgive and forget; "forgive our enemies and forget our friends," as he later put it.[120] He was deeply unwilling to be generous to Perón and his regime at the expense—at least in prestige—of those governments that had stood by the United States during the war and particularly of the democratic governments and movements on which he pinned his hopes for the future. Those who claimed that a policy of appeasement was required by the American interest in a mutual security pact, he suggested to Truman, were panicky and unfamiliar with the inter-American agreements that already protected this interest. The Act of Chapultepec and all of its provisions would remain binding until the Second World War was formally terminated. All of the signatories to the Declaration of Havana of 1940, moreover, were already bound to consider an attack by a non-American power against any one of them as an act of aggression against themselves. Yet it was a measure of what the Argentine government's signature had been worth in the recent past that—immediately after Pearl Harbor—Argentina had not only failed to act on the Declaration of Havana but had urged Peru, Bolivia, Paraguay, and Chile to stand together as a "neutral bloc." If the United States was to have any confidence that this would not happen again, the Argentine government would have to provide evidence of its good faith by complying with its previous commitments. A secondary American interest in the proposed pact, Braden noted, was to induce the other American republics to standardize their military equipment with that of the United States and so facilitate the establishment of American military missions and the exclusion of the missions of non-American powers. Without waiting for the treaty, this objective could be pursued immediately upon congressional authorization with every country except Argentina. Agreements with Great Britain, Canada, and Sweden already prevented the export of armaments to that country and effectively prevented non-American military missions as well.[121]

Braden was also pragmatic in his outlook and was willing to compromise on such things as the extent of Argentine compliance. "No responsible official of our Government," he stressed in another memo, "has taken an extreme view of this question; that is to say, we neither expect nor require perfect performance nor will we accept mere token acts coupled with promises of future acts." The real issue was whether the United States should settle for 20 to 40 percent compliance or press instead for 60 to 80 percent. Entering into a military pact with Argentina would bring an end to the international agreements controlling arms sales to it. Before doing this, Braden argued, it should be ascertained "whether Argentina will accept the principle of standardization which cannot but imply a certain dependence on our military establishment as well as affect its program for building a large armament industry."[122]

The American ambassador in Buenos Aires had different ideas about what would constitute sufficient Argentine compliance.[123] "The performance of the American Republics with respect to enemy aliens," George Messersmith argued, "has been rather sketchy, and if we get from the Argentine a measure of performance which is relatively as good as that of the other American Republics, we cannot ask for more. Any other procedure we could not defend and would serve no useful purpose."[124] The same principle would apply to the liquidation of enemy property.

Messersmith differed starkly from Braden in his views of the nature of the political struggle going on in Argentina, the interest of the United States in the outcome of that struggle, and the proper role of American policy. Braden's attempt to insure that the United States not abandon liberal and democratic elements in Argentina, Messersmith commented, was a violation of the established principle "that we do not interfere in the internal affairs of other countries and we do not deliberately aid any particular parties or groups in other countries." This criticism was perhaps something of a surprise in Washington since Messersmith had been one of the supporters of the Braden memorandum the year before, but Messersmith had a ready answer for any charge of inconsistency: the Argentine government had been constitutionally elected—there was "no basis for our not carrying along our relations with that government in a cordial and collaborative manner."[125]

As far as Messersmith was concerned, Perón was neither dictatorial nor disreputable. Ninety-nine out of a hundred of Perón's most ardent opponents, he maintained, had become convinced that anything that could replace him would be infinitely worse: "There is no doubt that they are right, for it would mean that any government which would succeed Perón would come about through a 'palace' revolution and would be either an army dictatorship or a dictatorship of the most irresponsible elements in the Argentine."

> Whether Perón will be able to carry through in an adequate way a program of social reform in this country, I am not able to say, but one thing is certain and that is that he has started to do it, and it was time it was started. Whether he will be able to carry it through wisely, it is still too early to say. One thing is certain, however, and that is whether he carries through the program or someone else, a program will be carried forward.[126]

Braden saw Perón as a demagogue and a dictator; one who, in addition to the damage that he would do directly, would provide the Argentine communists with a long-term opportunity and perhaps even offer them a cooperative relationship. Addressing a group of intelligence personnel from the War Department in January 1946, he stressed the extraordinary tactical flexibility of communist movements and the dangers this presented in Argentina and Latin America generally.

> In fact, we may now be in a position similar to that of August 1939 when Germany and Russia signed their non-aggression pact. There are signs of this alliance already. The Russian Communist Party organ Trud took the trouble recently of publishing the full text of an anti-U.S. article which appeared in *El Debate,* a pro-Nazi newspaper of Montevideo. Such an alliance would constitute the most dangerous threat encountered by our country in the Western Hemisphere since the days of the Holy Alliance and the adoption of the Monroe Doctrine.[127]

Messersmith, while sharing Braden's concern over the threat to American interests posed by movements loyal to the Soviet Union, was nevertheless convinced that Perón would be helpful in combating such movements.[128] The debate between them was the beginning of a larger debate among Cold Warriors over the terms on which the United States should attempt to deal with unsavory governments that alleged that they were willing to cooperate in the Cold War. Braden was the first advocate in this debate on the side of Cold War liberalism. He believed that sooner or later all of the dictatorships in Latin America would be replaced by democratic governments, that this transformation would benefit the United States in many ways—not least in its struggle with communism—and that American policy could and should help to bring this transformation about by treating dictatorial and disreputable regimes with "aloof formality." Messersmith, although he did not attempt to articulate his underlying assumptions, became in Argentina one of the first advocates of Cold War conservatism. He came to believe, in short, that Perón was the best or perhaps the only alternative in sight and that he should be treated cordially if this would help to bring about a cooperative relationship.

For the Cold War conservatives, the United States would best protect its own rights and interests in Latin America—and at the same time respect the rights and interests of others—if it followed a policy of nonintervention in the internal affairs of the countries of Latin America as long as developments in those countries did not threaten American security. Democratic governments in Latin America would certainly be preferable, but it was not the responsibility of the United States to attempt to promote them. Direct efforts to promote democracy were unlikely to succeed and would probably be resented and prove counterproductive. The best thing that the United States could do for itself, and for Latin American democracy, was to provide a good example while cooperating with all of the governments of the region in the pursuit of common interests.[129]

One of the central difficulties of the Cold War liberals' approach was the difficulty of portraying the Perón regime as so far outside the mainstream of Latin American politics that it deserved to be held to a different standard. By 1947 Perón had purged Argentina's main labor federation, its universities, and some of its judiciary, but his worst abuses were still in the future.[130] Even his staunchest critics had to grant that in practice, whatever his intentions, his regime was far from totalitarian. An American Federation of Labor delegation, returning from Buenos Aires, announced that it would not collaborate with the Argentine Confederation of Labor because the latter was an arm of the Argentine government and as such was incapable of electing its own officers and determining its own policies. But the delegation explicitly recognized that the Argentine government was taking little formal action to suppress civil liberties:

> The fact that unions which are independent of the government can publish their newspapers without censorship and continue to meet indicates that the situation is considerably different from that which prevailed in Germany or Italy under dictatorship, which prevails currently in Russia and her satellite countries, or prevailed in Argentina itself from June, 1943, to the eve of the last presidential elections.[131]

If relative political openness in Argentina made it increasingly difficult for Braden to pursue his approach, the presence of an American ambassador with Messersmith's views made it impossible. The suggestion that Argentina would turn to the Soviet Union if it could not get what it wanted from the United States—a suggestion various Argentine officials had made—Braden viewed as both implausible and as offering insight into the true character of the Argentine regime. Braden conveyed this opinion directly to Messersmith in an effort to persuade him of the correctness of his approach:

> We cannot overlook the fact that Argentina is Catholic and conservative to an extent that a close, active alliance would be opposed domestically by forces so powerful that the existence of Perón's regime would be at stake; or the fact that such an alliance would alienate other American republics whose support Argentina needs; or the fact

that the Argentine economy is tied to those of the democracies; or the fact that a military alliance with the USSR would leave Argentina exposed and separated from the USSR in case of war. The more probable—certainly the most logical—conclusion is that the Argentine Government is aware of its own interests in this respect and is up to its old trick of attempting to use a European power as a counterpoise to us. In any event, there is nothing to suggest that, if we now pay tribute under this threat, Argentina's bargaining position will be any the weaker or that we will not in the future be asked for other payments. One doesn't discourage these tactics by paying blackmail.[132]

Messersmith was not persuaded. Frustrated with Braden's position and with what he considered as Braden's denigration of the best available Argentine government, Messersmith took to sending long letters to various journalists, to Braden's subordinates in the State Department, to Braden's opponents in Congress, and to Undersecretary of State Acheson, Secretary of State Byrnes, and President Truman.[133] In Acheson's judgement, Messersmith "behaved outrageously."[134] Arthur Krock of the *New York Times* told Braden that he had received a letter from Messersmith of 65,000 words whose meaning could have been conveyed in six.[135] These letters started in August 1946 and in general asserted that Braden was attempting to wage a personal vendetta against Perón and to place obstacles in Messersmith's way at a time when Argentina was on the verge of complying with its obligations. A letter from Messersmith to Byrnes of 23 October 1946 is representative of both the substance and tone of these complaints:

> There isn't any doubt that Spruille, in the last weeks, has been leaking out information to friends and to the press, and he has really been doing this ever since I came down here, or at least since a month after I came down. As soon as he saw that there was a probability and even a certainty of the Argentine complying with her commitments he became very unhappy and he has done nothing to help me in my task.[136]

Byrnes told Messersmith that his criticisms of Braden were a disappointment and unfair, that Braden had the full confidence of Byrnes and Truman, and that Messersmith was to cease writing such letters to members of the press. There was no foundation in fact, he was bluntly informed, for the claim in one of his letters that if he had not accepted the assignment to Argentina, Braden would have been unable to remain in office. Stressing the point, Byrnes added that neither he nor Truman had ever been under any pressure to ask for Braden's resignation and that neither of them had ever considered doing so. Hopefully, he suggested, "you can forget your suspicions about Mr. Braden." The final decision about whether or not Argentina had complied with its obligations, he reminded the ambassador, was a decision that Byrnes and the president—and not Braden—would make.[137] Hearing of Byrnes's letter from Acheson while it was still in draft, Braden told a friend that he hoped it would be enough to end Messersmith's insubordination, but he expressed doubt because Byrnes "is more tempted by the token compliance proposed by Messersmith than by my insistence that we stand on principle."[138]

For the better part of a year, Messersmith's dispatches routinely contained the claim that great progress would be had in just a few more weeks.[139] After visiting Argentina in the spring of 1947, Cecil Lyon concluded that in fact Messersmith would soon start "preparing us to accept the deportation of a relatively small group of Nazi agents."[140] Although Argentina's actions appear to have amounted to little more than token compliance, they were ultimately accepted by Truman and Marshall.[141] It would have been extraordinarily difficult to get more out of an Argentine government that had become used to an ambassador like Messersmith; an ambassador who had "gone local" to the extent that he felt the need to counter—rather than support—even a personal last-minute effort by Truman to obtain greater Argentine compliance.[142] In August 1947, Perón's Argentina was allowed to join with the other American republics in the Rio Treaty. By then, Braden had resigned and Messersmith had been fired.[143]

The Fight over Arms Sales

The immediate cause of Braden's resignation was not the change in policy toward Argentine compliance but rather a change in policy with regard to arms sales to Latin America in general.[144] Before becoming assistant secretary of state, Braden had already been engaged in skirmishes with the American military on this question.[145] By the end of 1946, these had escalated into a full-scale battle. A large program of arms sales and training, he argued, would have the same effect on the militaries of Latin America as the advertisement of a bargain sale would have on housewives: "It will invite everyone to rush in to be sure they get as much as possible in order not to be outdone by their neighbors."[146] The resulting increase in expenditure would perpetuate conditions favorable to the spread of communism by standing in the way of economic readjustment and growth.[147] Military expenditure in 1947 already averaged about 7.5 percent of national incomes in Latin America—more than double the 3.3 percent it had averaged in 1939.[148]

As with the issue of Argentine compliance, Braden was willing to compromise to some extent. During 1946, he supported limited arms sales under the Surplus Property Act after insuring that the governments of Argentina, the Dominican Republic, Honduras, and Nicaragua were excluded.[149] He also went along with the State Department's acquiescence in the presentation to Congress of the first version of the Inter-American Military Cooperation Act (IAMCA). This act would have authorized the president to determine the amounts of American arms and training to be furnished to the countries of Latin America and the terms on which they were to be provided. By the end of the year, however, it had become clear that the War and Navy Departments had in mind a program that would cost close to a billion dollars. This was, Braden protested, much more than most of the countries of Latin America could afford. It was ten times the payments due for Lend-Lease to the region during the Second World War and three times the total loans of the Eximbank over the twelve years of its operations. It would promote an arms race, strengthen reactionary forces antagonistic to the purposes and interests of the United States, increase the danger of communism by perpetuating conditions favorable to its spread, and aggravate the destructive effects of future upheavals in the region.[150]

For the first several months of 1947, opposition from Braden and his allies successfully blocked the program. Those opposed initially enjoyed Acheson's backing, but they lost his support—apparently on the judgement that the arms involved would be purchased from some supplier in any case—and were overruled.[151] On 26 May 1947, Truman transmitted the draft bill to Congress.[152] "For Spruille Braden, whose Latin American policy has been discredited and abandoned," *Time* magazine commented, "it was a pointed hint."[153] Taking the hint and resigning, Braden received a host of letters that suggested that his policy still had some support. John Dreier, the head of the Division of Special Inter-American Affairs in the State Department, wrote to him of his absolute certainty "that your position on the fundamental political issues regarding Latin America is sound and will be vindicated."

It has been a real pleasure for me to have fought one with you on the arms question. Even though we were overruled, it looks now as though a large body of opinion was seeing this problem in its true light. Likewise I shall not be surprised if all over Latin America people do not soon wake up and realize how foolish they were not to have supported your realistic policy when they had the chance.[154]

Caught between congressional liberals worried over the threat of reactionary forces in Latin America and congressional conservatives worried over the threat of increasing governmental expenditures, the program over which Braden resigned was never approved. For the remainder of the 1940s and into the 1950s, the scarcity of available resources for such purposes, and the far greater strategic importance of Europe and Asia, combined to keep American arms sales to Latin America at a relatively low level. The American military attempted to use surplus armaments to promote arms standardization for the region, but by mid-1948 even this option had effectively run out.[155] "The inability of Latin American governments to obtain desired US equipment for which they were willing to pay," a CIA estimate concluded at the end of the Truman years, "has caused considerable resentment and has led to some purchases of European materiel, to the detriment of arms standardization."[156] It was also clear by this time that American training—even when subsidized under the Mutual Security Act of 1951—was nowhere near as strongly desired by the states of Latin America as the American military had assumed. Mexico turned down the proffered program, and other states bargained hard for more generous terms. At the beginning of the Eisenhower years there were military assistance agreements with only seven countries in the region.[157]

Notwithstanding the failure of the IAMCA, there was an underlying philosophy behind the program that deserves to be examined. Although it seems mostly to have been a matter of unreflective institutional self-interest on the part of the military—a desire to promote military training missions and improve the prestige of military attachés—there was also an outlook involved that can be considered as forming part of Cold War conservatism. This centered on the belief that the militaries of Latin America were an established part of the region's societies and often a dominant factor in their politics, and it was therefore in the interest of the United States to cultivate cordial relations with them.[158] Braden was not opposed in principle to maintaining military-to-military relations, but he wanted to maintain them on terms that would not threaten more important

American interests. The American military, in contrast, had a very limited capacity for perceiving that their pursuit of cordial relations with the militaries of Latin America could in any way harm broader objectives of policy. On the contrary, they were inclined to grossly exaggerate the potential of such relations to advance American objectives.

Addressing the question of arms sales at a meeting with State Department officials in January 1946, one general asserted that "from his personal observation the prestige of the United States was definitely waning in the American Republics largely owing to our failure to live up to our commitments in supplying arms to those countries."[159] This was a common opinion among military officers who mistakenly believed that they had been authorized to make commitments in the staff talks that they had conducted with their counterparts in Latin America. In fact, the diplomatic notes given by the American ambassadors to the other American republics opening these talks had stated explicitly that they were to be "purely exploratory and preliminary."[160] But this counted for less than it might have with an American military accustomed to a wartime blurring of the hierarchy of political and military objectives—and lines of authority—and profoundly convinced of the value of the program.

Writing of the IAMCA's virtues, Secretary of War Robert Patterson engaged in what can charitably be referred to as self-deception. Secretary of State Byrnes, he claimed, had told the House Foreign Affairs Committee that the bill's implementation "would not only promote the peace and security of the Americas, but would also result in assistance to the other American nations in raising their living standards and achieving the political, economic and cultural objectives of democratic society."[161] In fact, as John Dreier soon pointed out, what Byrnes had actually said was that "any activities which we may recommend to the President in the event this bill is passed will be governed by the basic objectives of our policy toward the countries immediately concerned. These objectives include, along with the protection of the peace and security of the Americas, assistance to our sister American nations in the raising of living standards for their peoples and in the progressively greater achievement of the political, economic and cultural objectives of a democratic society."[162]

Patterson seems to have sincerely believed that there could be no conflict between the cultivation of good military-to-military relations and the promotion of broader American objectives. If arms purchases would constitute an excessive economic burden for any given country, the State Department could always reduce or deny military assistance to that country.

Yet it was ultimately the sovereign states of Latin America themselves, he insisted, that would decide what they required and what they thought they could afford. Thus the question was not whether they would purchase arms but whether they would purchase foreign or American arms.

> In the final analysis, I feel very strongly that this legislation is a preventive measure of the highest importance. It is designed to prevent the very type of crisis which has arisen in Turkey and Greece where we are now desperately trying to lock the stable door while the horse is almost in process of being stolen. In Latin America, we must lock the stable door before the danger ever arises. Prevention is relatively cheap; crises are exorbitantly expensive in money, in time, and often in blood.[163]

To Braden, this was absurd: the crisis in Turkey and Greece was in no way parallel with the situation in Latin America. No country in Latin America was faced with that kind of external military pressure, and there was no prospect that any of them would be.[164] Internal subversion was where communism presented a threat in the hemisphere, and this threat would be exacerbated, not reduced, by arms sales on the scale encouraged by the IAMCA.[165] But Braden and his allies lacked an effective reply to Patterson's claim that other countries would supply arms if the United States did not. The "gentlemen's agreement" not to sell arms to Argentina was breaking down in 1947, and this, more than anything else, appears to have led to the shift in American policy.

On notifying the Americans that they would no longer follow a parallel policy, the British initially indicated that they were only thinking of a "trivial program" of arms sales to Argentina. Braden's response was to suggest that an effort be made to persuade them to return to the policy they had abandoned and to maintain an American embargo in any case.[166] In spite of American expressions of concern, however, there were rumors that the British had a much larger program in mind.[167] By late May 1947, it was evident that this was the case. The British had signed a contract with Argentina for the sale of 100 Meteor jet fighter planes—a weapon no other Latin American country possessed—and were negotiating for the sale of 30 Lincoln bombers.[168] This was, Ellis Briggs protested, incompatible with British pledges not to arm Latin America unduly or to embarrass the American chiefs of staff in their arms standardization program. Impelled as the they were by a need for hard currency and for Argentine foodstuffs, the British were nevertheless threatening to provoke an arms race that would be disastrous both to hemispheric unity and to the economies of the region. This, in turn, would facilitate both communist penetration and the establishment of military dictatorships.[169] These arguments, Acheson noted, had already been presented to the British ambassador and to the British government "without result."[170] By late June, Marshall presented Truman with a memo urging that he approve an arms sale to Argentina for two paramount reasons:

1. The shipbuilding industry in this country is badly in need of work in order to maintain its existence.
2. Should the United States refuse the Argentine request, the Argentines will undoubtedly contract for the ships elsewhere.[171]

It became apparent that the reversal of Braden's policy on arms sales to Argentina was simply a response to the policy's perceived impracticability, without much effort to think about what would constitute a preferable alternative. This was evident from a statement that Acheson gave to the Policy Committee on Arms and Armaments. On 25 July 1947, he told this committee that henceforth Argentina's commercial purchases of arms, ammunition, and implements of war in the United States would no longer be limited.[172] In response, the committee suggested that the undersecretary of state reconsider the policy he had just set forth. "It was pointed out that, whereas prior to the enunciation of the said policy toward Argentina, that nation was in a more restricted position than the other American Republics (with the exception of the Dominican Republic, Nicaragua, and Honduras) insofar as the purchase of U.S. arms was concerned, under this new policy Argentina would be in a preferential position."[173] After discussion of the matter it was decided that arms sales to the other American republics would be approved only where they were deemed "reasonable and necessary for (1) maintaining internal order, (2) providing for self-defense, (3) fulfilling international obligations."[174]

In other words, even after Braden's departure, American officials still found that it was in the interest of the United States to decide what was "reasonable" in the way of arms sales to Latin America and to try to discourage sales beyond this.[175] As Marshall explained to the British foreign secretary in December 1947, "he had to decide, when issuing arms export licenses, how to maintain the balance between different Latin American countries so that one did not get more powerful than another." The delivery of the jet planes Britain had sold to Argentina, Marshall implied, would constitute an unacceptable escalation. For this reason, the British ambassador reported, while Marshall was willing to see if British manufacturing capacity could be used to contribute to the American arms standardization program, he "feared that it would be quite impracticable at the present time to agree to our proposal to send jet aircraft to Argentina."[176]

Bradenism in Retrospect

For the Cold War conservatives, treating friendly dictatorial regimes with aloof formality was by definition "unrealistic." A more objective assessment would require knowledge of what difference, if any, the maintenance of a course of policy informed by Cold War liberalism would have made. Subsequent chapters will suggest that for a handful of countries—at critical junctures in their histories—such a policy might well have made a substantial difference and that American and Latin American interests might both have been better served as a result. This is particularly evident in a careful examination of the situation in Venezuela in 1948 and in Cuba in 1952 where mild American interventions might have helped local democrats to maintain their hold on power and, given democratic "rules of the game," another chance to become more securely established. As against these potential positive contributions, the possibility of additional counterproductive endeavors must also be considered. If the avoidance of embarrassment is the standard by which policy is judged, then it is not surprising that Braden's contribution to failure in Argentina should overshadow his contributions to success in Cuba and Brazil and elsewhere. Braden's policy did Latin America's democrats and American interests more good than harm; it could have been expected to continue to do so if maintained, but at the cost of occasionally backfiring. The policy of the Cold War conservatives, in contrast, carried costs in terms of close association with disreputable regimes and missed opportunities to advance common American and Latin American interests through support for political democracy.

Despite the genuine divisions between them, the Cold War conservatives and the Cold War liberals were largely in agreement in the hopes that they placed in the Rio Treaty and the establishment of the OAS.[177] Both thought that these inter-American institutions would facilitate cooperative relations and the maintenance of peace among the states of the hemisphere and that they would strengthen the common defense. They appear to have viewed the establishment and maintenance of these institutions as among the most important objectives of American policy in the region. Their hopes as to what such institutions could accomplish were largely a matter of self-deception, and it is worth reviewing the foundations upon which these hopes rested to see why this was the case.

Under the Rio Treaty, signed at Rio de Janeiro in the summer of 1947, one or more of the participating states could call for an Organ of Consultation to meet and determine an appropriate response to any extracontinental or intracontinental threat to the peace. This Organ of Consultation was to be constituted by a meeting of foreign ministers or by any other procedure agreed upon by the states who had ratified the treaty. A two-thirds majority among this group was authorized to sanction a wide variety of measures up to and including the use of armed force.[178] An important exception to the principle of nonintervention was thereby established, or rather a wide range of specially sanctioned activities were set aside as not constituting intervention under inter-American positive law. This was explicitly recognized the following year when the OAS Charter was signed at Bogotá. Article 15 of the charter declared: "No State or group of States has the right to intervene, directly or indirectly, for any reason whatever, in the internal or external affairs of any other State." Article 17 declared "inviolable" the territory of every state. Article 19, however, left no doubt that "measures adopted for the maintenance of peace and security in accordance with existing treaties do not constitute a violation of the principles set forth in Articles 15 and 17."[179]

Cold War conservatives imagined that this exception to the principle of nonintervention would be important to the cause of hemispheric security. Cold War liberals imagined that it would also be important to the cause of political democracy. Both recognized that under traditional international law, and under the Charter of the United Nations, the United States had retained its right to self-defense. Both knew that the United States could always maintain that any action it undertook in Latin America was not an intervention but an act of self-defense. Article 19 of the OAS Charter added nothing to existing American rights in this regard. But actions that American officials might consider as self-defense, or as in the broader interests of hemispheric peace and security, could easily be seen by others as intervention—the publication of the Blue Book on the eve of the Argentine elections in 1946, for example. Within international law there is no mechanism for resolving such differences of interpretation beyond disputes among the states concerned. American officials wanted not only to win such disputes, they wanted their conduct to be lawful and to be seen as lawful by others. With the Rio Treaty and the OAS Charter, they could hope to win support for their position from a two-thirds majority of the

Organ of Consultation and thus avoid or greatly weaken any charges of intervention that might be raised.

During the negotiation of the Rio Treaty and the OAS Charter, a prominent American jurist wrote to Braden expressing concern that the draft charter's prohibition on intervention by "one or more" states would undermine the prospects for collective action on behalf of democracy and human rights.[180] A State Department official suggested in response that the most important thing was to formulate a comprehensive exception to the principle of nonintervention; an exception that would permit adequate scope for collective discussion and action and would allow for evolution in thinking as to the possible bases for action. "You will note in this connection that the exception to the principle of nonintervention in this [draft] article is much broader than the corresponding exception in Article 2 of the UN Charter, which limits the exception to enforcement action. The Rodriguez Larreta presumption that anti-democratic governments are per se a danger to the maintenance of peace and security could become a basis for action."[181]

The problem with all of this, a jaded Ellis Briggs would conclude by 1964, was that no matter what the treaties said, effective sanctions would "never be voted by the Latin American members against a wayward *latino* brother."[182] Briggs's formulation was extreme, but in general the OAS and the Rio Treaty had to that point exercised only a very minor influence on the politics of the region, and there is no reason to believe that they could have exercised a much more significant influence without a fundamental change in political regimes and prevailing attitudes in most of the countries of Latin America.[183] Without such a change, the hopes of both Cold War liberals and Cold War conservatives rested on a fundamentally unrealistic assessment of what could be achieved through interstate cooperation among a solid majority of the states of the Western hemisphere.

Assuming that Braden and his allies had had their way on arms sales and Argentine compliance—and that he had remained in office—American policy would, at least initially, probably not have been very different from the policy followed immediately after his resignation. Between the scarcity of arms available for sale in Latin America and the continuing American interest in discouraging an arms race, there were only a few arms sales that would not have taken place if Braden had remained. While these sales do not appear to have had any military significance for the dictatorships in question, a continued ban on them—and other indications of American disapproval of such regimes—might eventually have had some political impact. On the other hand, in the absence of practical alternatives, Braden would doubtless have settled for a Rio Treaty that included the likes of Trujillo, Carías, and, after a few more Axis agents had been deported, Perón as well. Much as he might have wished to leave the dictators out—or in some other way indicate that they were not full-fledged members of the inter-American system—he recognized that the Larreta doctrine had been rejected.

In the absence of a conviction among a solid majority of the states in Latin America that certain regimes in the region were beyond the pale, and above all in the absence of a willingness to act on that conviction, Braden favored the unilateral maintenance of a position of aloof formality toward those regimes that the United States deemed dictatorial and disreputable. Contrary to his reputation at the time and since, this meant that he favored largely normal relations with them—even with Perón's Argentina. "We shall continue to maintain normal political and commercial relations with the Argentine Government and to collaborate with it in fields of activity conducive to the creation of a better political, economic and social environment for democracy," was Braden's position.[184] Had he remained in office, this might have become more apparent. "I gathered the distinct impression that our policy is not generally understood and is considered by the average person as more drastic than it actually is," Cecil Lyon reported to Braden after a trip to Buenos Aires in the spring of 1947: "Few people realize that our relations with Argentina are completely normal short of selling arms."[185]

Aloof formality, as Braden formulated and practiced it, was almost compatible with "completely normal" political and economic relations. It did not involve any great intervention in the internal affairs of other states. On the contrary, more often than not it involved a creative use of "nonintervention," such as a ban on arms sales. It involved a withholding of fulsome and gratuitous praise—and economic and military assistance—but it did not involve economic or military sanctions. It could involve a strong insistence that international obligations be fulfilled and private advice and public statements of principle to which a dictator and his supporters might take exception, but this was the full extent of the diplomatic pressure by which Braden sought to encourage democratic openings in Latin America. These were the measures by which he hoped to demonstrate a greater American friendliness toward democracies and a decided lack of cordiality toward dictatorships.

Braden was not a utopian moralist following visions or vendettas far removed from practical politics.[186] On the contrary, he was willing to recognize and cooperate with every established government in the hemisphere. He did not favor quixotic efforts to break off political and economic relations with established dictatorial regimes. At the same time, he believed that the United States was in a position to insist that the cooperation it extended to Latin America's dictators be on terms more of its own choosing—and visibly less generous—than in the past. This, he believed, would ultimately help to improve the underlying political situation in the countries in question. He assumed that democratic government had excellent prospects throughout Latin America; that American policy could directly and significantly improve those prospects; and that all of America's basic interests would be best served by keeping a sense of democratic solidarity in mind in formulating short-term policy.

> If we but persevere and properly use our great influence in this hemisphere, there is more than a probability—almost a certainty—that eventually we shall succeed. It is a practicable policy. The trend towards democracy is already in motion. Brazil, Guatemala, Bolivia, Venezuela, Paraguay and Haiti have all recently achieved, or are in the process of achieving, constitutional democracy. Uruguay and Colombia, and in varying lesser degrees Mexico, Chile, Costa Rica, Ecuador, Cuba, and Peru, are traditionally democratic. An important fact, often completely overlooked, is that even in Argentina the democratic forces, disorganized and divided as they were, succeeded in forcing the election of a Congress and actually came within a relatively few votes (1,400,000 to 1,200,000) of defeating the government-backed candidate during a state of siege lifted for only twenty-four hours on election day.[187]

Over the rest of the Truman years, Braden's successors would increasingly come to differ with him on each of his crucial assumptions. As American assumptions changed—largely in response to changing political circumstances in Latin America and the perceived failure of Braden's policy—American policy changed with them. For the Cold War conservatives, democratic government had poor prospects in much of Latin America (at least in the short term); there was little that American policy could do to alter those prospects (again at least in the short term); and all of America's basic interests would be best served by keeping a respect for the national sovereignty of others in mind in formulating short-term policy.[188] This shift in underlying assumptions, it is worth reiterating, had next to nothing to do with the Cold War. Braden was as militant a Cold Warrior as ever occupied the office of assistant secretary of state for inter-American affairs.

The difference between Braden and his allies—figures such as Ellis Briggs, A. A. Berle, Claude Bowers, George Butler, Frank Corrigan, Allan Dawson, and many others—and some of their successors was the difference between liberalism and conservatism, or between optimism and pessimism. It was not a difference between those who were strongly opposed to the Soviet side in the Cold War and those who were not. Even during a hot war against the Axis—at a time when considerations of short-term advantage were at a premium—Braden was already articulating the central underlying assumption that he and the other liberal Cold Warriors would later share. Surely, he wrote to Briggs in August 1943, "we are not going to esteem and accord greater collaboration to a Trujillo who, because of the very reason that he is a dictator, may be better able to cooperate with us for a time than a Santos who is restrained in some measure by constitutional and legislative restrictions."[189] Expediency, in other words, was no substitute for a policy that recognized that the triumph of democracy was "the only sound basis for prosperity and peace."[190]

Braden's departure was regretted by his friends and admirers on the democratic left in Latin America and by prodemocratic American activists. It was widely recognized that during his tenure dictators in the region had received, as J. Lloyd Mecham later put it, "no White House visits, no favors, no decorations, no loans, [and] no military equipment."[191] If Braden did not succeed in identifying the United States with liberal and democratic forces in the hemisphere, he at least succeeded in identifying himself with them. The government of Guatemala, praising him for his "fervent efforts in defense of democracy," gave him its highest honor and made him a Grand Officer of the Order of the Quetzal.[192] Frances Grant, the chairman of the Latin American section of the International League for the Rights of Man, was equally convinced of Braden's dedication. "Those of us who have been working on behalf of human rights," she wrote to him, "have felt strengthened by your presence in our government. Despite the constant evidence of civil and political violations in various parts of the Hemisphere, we have been convinced that your leadership guaranteed a vigilant and uncompromising stand against these abrogations of human liberty."[193]

4

Coming to Terms with Yankee Imperialism

Aspirations for democracy, prosperity, and national sovereignty have been a part of Latin American politics since before the Wars of Independence.[1] Although triumphant in their military conflicts with Spain, the new states and societies that emerged in the 1810s and 1820s generally failed to satisfy these aspirations. Subsequent generations of Latin American reformers and revolutionaries have had to grapple both with this failure and with the extraordinary success and imperial ascendancy of the United States. Surveying the situation in the 1850s, Argentine liberal Juan Alberdi mourned the way almost everything in Spanish America had degenerated into anarchy and dictatorship. Guarantees of individual liberty, proclaimed by the new states, had become vain words and glaring lies, he observed. Yet in contrast with Bolívar, who late in life concluded that a revolutionary in Spanish America "plows the sea,"[2] Alberdi was unwilling to give up. Instead, he called for the transformation of governments and societies throughout the region:

> Today we search for the practical reality of what in another time we were content merely to write and proclaim. This is the purpose behind the constitutions of today: they should tend to organize and establish great practical measures for elevating emancipated America from the obscure and inferior position in which it finds itself. These measures should figure today at the forefront of our constitutions. Just as we previously placed independence, liberty, and religion in our constitutions, so we should now place free immigration, liberty of commerce, unfettered industry and railway lines, not in place of those great principles, but as essential means of insuring that they will cease to be mere words and become instead realities.[3]

Among the Argentine liberals who came to power in the 1850s and 1860s, there was a strong current of admiration for the United States.

Many of them sought to learn from its experience, and some explicitly hoped to play a role in their country's history analogous to the role that they saw America's Founding Fathers having played in the United States. Well before becoming president of Argentina in 1868, Domingo Sarmiento had given voice to this aspiration in his memoirs.

> Franklin's autobiography was for me what Plutarch's lives had been for him.... I felt myself to be Franklin; and why not? I was poor like him, I was studious like him, and disciplining myself, and following in his footsteps, a day could come when, like him, I would make myself a doctor *ad honorem* and establish a place for myself in American politics and letters. Franklin's autobiography should be a text in the primary schools. Inspired by his example, by his extraordinary career, there would not be a child, even a little well-inclined, who would not try to be a little Franklin through that beautiful tendency of the human spirit to imitate those models of perfection which it perceives.[4]

By the turn of the century, the program of emulation that had become associated with the names of Alberdi and Sarmiento, and which had met with a considerable measure of success in Argentina, had come under increasingly articulate attack.[5] The emulators, the Uruguayan writer José Rodó charged, were suffering from *nordomanía*—the "vision of an America *delatinized* by its own will, without the coercion of conquest, and then regenerated in the image and likeness of the northern archetype."[6] What was needed, Rodó argued, was a program that would seek to contribute to the genuine development of Latin American civilization; a program that prized the highest accomplishments of the spirit and that saw the crude and materialistic society of the United States without illusions:

> The religiosity of the Americans, an extract derived from that of the English, is nothing more than an auxiliary force to penal legislation. It would vacate its post on the day utilitarianism could be given the religious authority which Stuart Mill hoped to give it. The highest peak of this morality is the ethic of Franklin: a philosophy of conduct which finds its end in the mediocrity of honesty and the utility of prudence; an ethic in whose breast holiness and heroism never stir. It is suitable only for lending to the conscience, on the ordinary paths of life, the support of that applewood walking stick with which its

propagator habitually travelled. It is nothing more than a weak reed when it comes to climbing steep slopes.[7]

It was against the background of these two programs—the program of emulation and the program of defending the dignity and worth of Latin American identity—that Víctor Raúl Haya de la Torre formulated and championed his alternative. Other movements and programs might have better served the causes to which Haya and the Apristas were devoted. But a persuasive case that a more radical movement could have made a greater contribution to progress toward democracy and prosperity, or for that matter generated a more effective challenge to American hegemony, has yet to be made.[8]

Born in Peru in 1895, Haya gained fame in the late 1910s and early 1920s as a student leader who fought for university reforms and organized popular universities to provide adult education for Peruvian trade unionists. In 1924, he founded Apra as a continent-wide movement that he hoped would ultimately take power in every country in the region. Although Apra only became an effective political party in Peru, Haya's ideas exercised a strong influence on the leadership and programs of parties that came to power elsewhere.[9] Robert Alexander has written that Haya's ideas became "fundamental elements" in the programs of nearly a dozen parties; he has characterized Haya as "the most important political philosopher and ideologist of the democratic left" that Latin America had in the twentieth century.[10] After Haya's death, in August 1979, both Peru and Venezuela declared a national day of mourning. Some two million Peruvians, nearly 30 percent of the country's electorate, joined his funeral procession.[11]

Haya has had his share of critics over the years as well. He has been denounced for running Apra in a highly centralized and authoritarian fashion, for developing and relishing a cult of personality, and for pursuing political power with markedly opportunistic and self-centered tactics. He has been charged with having forsaken the radical politics of his youth, for propagating a political religion—complete with the slogan "Only *Aprismo* will save Peru"—and, more recently, for having a range of superstitious and spiritualist beliefs as well.[12]

There is a good deal of truth in both the praise and the criticism. The central issue to be examined here is Haya's role in articulating a view of the United States and its relationship to Latin American progress, which would later become widespread among the parties of the democratic left. While this did involve a break with his youthful enthusiasm for the Soviet Union, that break had been completed by the late 1920s.[13] From that point onward, Haya's basic conception of Yankee imperialism remained remarkably consistent. In his mature speeches and writings he continually distinguished between the underlying forces generating Yankee imperialism, which he saw as fundamentally economic in nature and potentially beneficial to Latin America, and their various political accompaniments that he more frequently saw as oppressive and potentially disastrous. He maintained that if Latin America—or, as he preferred to call it, Indoamerica—was to eliminate the negative aspects of Yankee imperialism, then Aprista or like-minded parties would have to triumph throughout the region. Only together, perhaps in a great federative republic, could they manage to deal with the United States on more equal terms.

Short of such unity, Haya was convinced that American capitalism could still be utilized to help promote the economic development of the countries of Latin America, provided that Aprista parties in those countries were in power and could limit its negative aspects. He believed that it was worth seeking allies in this cause among the anti-imperialist forces of the United States, and in his more optimistic moments he hoped that they would ultimately be capable of transforming the policy of the United States from one of intervention on behalf of reactionary local elites into one that would seek to develop a mutually beneficial and harmonious relationship with the peoples of Latin America.

Toward that end, during Haya's early visits to the United States in the 1920s, he went on a speaking tour for the League for Industrial Democracy, debated the meaning of the Monroe Doctrine at Harvard, and had discussions with Upton Sinclair, the editors of the *New Republic,* Senator William Borah, and such American socialist leaders as Norman Thomas and Harry Laidler.[14] In later decades, he would form close friendships with Serafino Romualdi, the Latin American representative of the American Federation of Labor, and Frances Grant, the secretary-general of the Inter-American Association for Democracy and Freedom.

In his writings in the 1920s, Haya frequently and favorably quoted the works of American anti-imperialists such as Scott Nearing and Samuel Guy Inman.[15] "Until now," he wrote in 1928, "the best books against North American imperialism—we say it frankly—have appeared in North America."[16] A quarter of a century later he went even further in his praise, reminding a close friend that "anti-imperialism—as a movement and as a term—was born in the United States between 1890 and 1900. The first anti-imperialists that were called such—that were under that banner, using that word and concept—were Bryan's Democrats in their struggle against Theodore Roosevelt and Henry Cabot Lodge. And that anti-imperialism can be likened to our own, taking account of differences in space and time, because it was in opposition to the economic and political intervention of the United States in the rest of the world."[17]

Intervention, as far as Haya was concerned, was a term that derived its meaning from its relation to popular sovereignty: If something was damaging to the cause of popular sovereignty, it was an intervention; if it aided the cause of popular sovereignty, it was not.[18] From this perspective, he could and did argue that what American officials sometimes claimed was nonintervention was in fact a form of support for dictatorship. Nevertheless, he ultimately came to see Franklin Roosevelt, and a portion of the Democratic Party, as sincere in their efforts and as legitimate heirs to the anti-imperialist tradition of William Jennings Bryan.[19] The Good Neighbor policy, he would come to argue, was a good starting point "for anti-imperialist cooperation in inter-American relations."[20]

Haya's view of imperialism was both original and complex. His most systematic treatment of the problem came in a book written in 1928—although not widely published until 1936—called *Anti-imperialism and Apra*.[21] The great danger, as he then saw it, was that the United States would not merely continue intervening militarily in Latin America but would ultimately absorb the entire region and make a giant Nicaragua of it. To a considerable extent, he suggested, it had done so already.

> Are we, in reality, free peoples? A hundred years after the overthrow of Spanish rule, after our festive commemorations of that victory, it is painful to think that we are again slaves—more or less slaves. Many are enraged at the suspicion; and there is no lack of Cuban or Nicaraguan officials, for example, capable of fighting a duel in the name of the sacred honor of their fatherland, against any who dare to doubt its absolute national liberty, having its own flag and presidents of the republic with ribbons and decorations.[22]

Defining his approach to the problem as within the Marxist tradition, Haya took issue with the conception of imperialism formulated by J. A. Hobson and modified somewhat by Lenin, in which imperialism is to be understood as the highest stage of capitalism; the stage characterized by the export of capital and the conquest of markets and zones of primary

material production.[23] That thesis was correct as far as the advanced countries were concerned, but the social and economic realities of Latin
America were different. In Latin America, imperialism was not the ultimate stage of capitalism but the first. "For our peoples," he argued, "immigrant or imported capital establishes the initial stage of the modern capitalist age."[24] "Our countries are in the first stages of capitalism or moving
toward them, searching for their liberation from feudalism, or attempting
to do so. That is their course. . . . What, then, is our alternative?"[25] "Our
economic time and space indicate to us a position and a path—while capitalism remains the dominant system in the most advanced countries, we
will have to deal with capitalism. How to deal with it?—that is the great
question."[26]

Those who wished to deal with capitalism by accepting foreign capital
unconditionally, in whatever manner and under whatever terms it wished
to come, were simply agents of imperialism—and Haya placed most Latin
American governments in this category. Mexico, with its great revolution,
was a significant exception.[27] The advanced countries exporting foreign
capital, he insisted, were responding to an economic law as imperious as
that which impelled the less-developed countries to receive it.[28] What was
necessary—especially given the weakness of the proletariat—was a movement uniting the middle classes with the workers and the peasantry in an
anti-imperialist and reformist state capable of utilizing foreign capital
without being absorbed by it.[29] The need of the United States to export
capital, and the need of Latin America to import American capital if it was
to develop, provided the economic foundation on which Haya hoped to
build a mutually advantageous relationship.[30]

Five years before writing *Anti-imperialism and Apra,* Haya had been
exiled by the Peruvian dictator Augusto Leguía. He had traveled first to
Cuba and then to Mexico, where Apra was founded in the spring of 1924.
That summer, he was invited to attend the Fifth Congress of the Third
International in Moscow as an observer. Staying on in the Soviet Union for
several months, he had the opportunity to discuss politics with Trotsky,
Lunacharsky, Frunze, and many others. He was impressed by the new Soviet state but also dismayed by his hosts' ignorance of Latin America and
their arrogance in seeking to dictate the proper course of policy for a revolutionary in Latin America to pursue.[31] Over the next few years, Apra's
resistance to communist efforts to dominate various anti-imperialist organizations would lead to a profound and permanent antagonism between
the two movements.[32]

During the late 1920s and early 1930s, Haya spent a considerable amount of time in Europe, including several years in England and Germany, which further helped to shape his mature outlook.[33] He was greatly disturbed by the rising strength of the Nazis and predicted in May of 1931 that they would eventually come to power. This prospect was, for him, an object lesson of the depths to which the leadership of the working class could sink.[34] In September 1930 Leguía was overthrown. By August 1931, Haya had returned to Peru and was campaigning for the presidency. "We must not forget," he warned one audience, "that communism and fascism are extremes that meet in a deformed, totalitarian, and tyrannical vision of the state. Our mission, the mission of America and of Peru, is to save our peoples from the disgrace of despotism as much as from misery and backwardness."[35]

In his campaign speeches, Haya at times took a remarkably broad historical view of the problems confronting Peru. The Peruvian Aprista Party, he declared, was a party of the democratic left. Its views were nourished by a tradition of liberty inspired by the ideals of the North American and the French revolutions.[36] It recognized the fundamental importance of the fact that while the thirteen colonies of North America had maintained their unity, Latin America had fragmented. It also recognized the importance of the great gap in Latin America between ideology and social reality. While the Wars of Independence had given the class of the great landowners control of the state, the ideology of that struggle—largely imported from France—was one of the destruction of feudalism and the formation of the bourgeoisie. This gap between system and reality was responsible for the oscillation of Latin American political life, for the continual alternation between tyranny and anarchy. Still, there had been a range of historical experiences, and other countries had done better than Peru. Argentina, under the leadership of figures such as Alberdi and Sarmiento, had made great progress. But progress from the feudal age to the industrial age required the technology that only foreign capital could provide, hence, the need to deal with imperialism. Imperialism, Haya insisted, was not a sinister term, dangerous and threatening. It was "an economic concept referring to the economic expansion of modern civilization."[37]

Stressing the fact that the underlying problems confronting Latin America were not caused by Yankee imperialism, although they could be exploited by it, Haya left little doubt that he was strongly sympathetic to cooperation with the United States as long as an Aprista party could limit or eliminate the threat an unrestrained Yankee imperialism would pose to

national sovereignty. Whether he wished to be understood as claiming
Alberdi and Sarmiento as precursors in this endeavor is uncertain, but that
is a reasonable inference.[38] As late as the 1950s, he would explicitly assign
such a role to Rodó.[39]

Initially, the American ambassador to Peru, Fred Dearing, was hostile to
Haya, considering him a subversive and perhaps even a Russian agent. But
after hearing reports of his speeches and meeting with him personally,
Dearing changed his mind. In a report to the State Department of early
September 1931, Dearing praised Haya's apparently sincere regard for the
United States and his desire for a cooperative relationship between the two
countries.

> While talking to me, Haya de la Torre gave me the impression of
> relaxation, and while I was conscious of his intensity of purpose and
> have the evidence of the last few months to show that he is a man of
> ability and has the respect of his fellow-citizens, I am still uncertain
> as to whether I should say that he is a man of destiny or not. From
> what I know up to this point, however, I should think that if he should
> become president of Peru, we should have nothing to fear and on the
> contrary might expect an excellent and beneficent administration of
> strongly liberal tendencies in which justice in the main would be
> done, and a period of confidence and well being be initiated.[40]

The original five-point platform with which Apra was established in
1924 was fairly vague and designed to apply to the continent as a whole.
Calling for action against Yankee imperialism, the political unity of Latin
America, the nationalization of land and industry, the internationalization
of the Panama Canal, and the solidarity of all oppressed peoples and
classes, it could hardly have appealed to an American ambassador.[41] The
Apra campaign platform of 1931, in contrast, was a reformist and social
democratic document. It stressed the need for such developments as a national department of statistics and a national census; the establishment of a
social security system; the guarantee of political rights to women, including legal rights within marriage; the establishment of the eight-hour
workday; the dedication of a high percentage of national income to education; the establishment of night schools, mobile public libraries, and rural
schools with instruction in both Spanish and indigenous languages; the
incorporation of the Indian into the life of the nation; the imposition of
limits on mining concessions; the progressive nationalization of insurance

and transportation; the creation of a ministry of hygiene and the organization of public health campaigns; the encouragement of agricultural cooperatives and collectives and the provision of technical and economic assistance to them; antitrust legislation; readjustment of the external debt; the maintenance of a stable currency; the maintenance of friendly relations with every country in the world; and, of course, an active and cooperative role for the state in the encouragement of agriculture, mining, industry, and commerce.[42]

For decades, the Apristas would claim that there was no conflict between what they termed their "maximum" and "minimum" programs—between the program of 1924 and those that followed. Even with regard to nationalization, which they would later interpret as a goal that could be satisfied by governmental oversight, they maintained that there was a continuity between their original purposes and the later means by which they sought to advance them.[43] "It is *false* to claim that we should return to our seminal ideas, or that we have abandoned a single one," Haya would insist in the early 1950s: "The analogy is inappropriate: a tree does not revert to being a seed in order to feel itself more treelike."[44] More than forty years later, his lifelong friend and colleague, Luis Alberto Sánchez, would make much the same point in a survey of Haya's ideological legacy. Sánchez observed that the title of Haya's first book was *For the Emancipation of Latin America;* that was also the underlying aim of his life's work. That he and his colleagues should have learned from their experience in the pursuit of this aim was hardly surprising. The idea that they could only have been faithful to their ideology by maintaining it in stasis was an absurdity.[45] Had Apra gained power in 1931, the Apristas might have been capable of demonstrating the kind of fundamental transformation that reformist and social democratic movements are capable of helping to bring about over time.[46] Unfortunately, this was not to be.

According to the official count, Haya lost the 1931 elections to Luis Sánchez Cerro, the military leader who had overthrown Leguía. The Apristas claimed that the election was stolen, but some historians have since suggested that the fraud to which they referred was not enough to swing the margin of around 25,000 votes.[47] In any case, as Luis Alberto Sánchez has observed, "The country was divided in such a way that no one could govern without dealing with the other side."[48] Instead of political cooperation, however, what followed was a period of increasing polarization, a police crackdown on Apra, an Aprista revolt in Trujillo—in which thousands were killed and relations between Apra and much of the military permanently embittered—and long years in which Apra operated as an underground movement.[49]

Particularly after the nationalization of the petroleum industry in Mexico in the spring of 1938, and the mild reaction of the United States to that nationalization, Haya took Roosevelt's Good Neighbor policy seriously. At the same time, he stressed that it was a policy and thus subject to change. He warned that elections in the United States might bring a Republican like Theodore Roosevelt to the presidency, or a Democrat like Woodrow Wilson, whose vague liberal-democratic rhetoric had led in practice to a similar Big Stick policy. The threat posed by international fascism required a united front between Indoamerica and North America, but this should be a genuine cooperative effort without the "complicit tolerance" by which the government of the United States supported dictators and petty tyrants and alienated the sympathies of oppressed peoples.[50]

There *was* a fundamental difference, Haya insisted in April 1941, between a nazi-fascist imperialism that was fundamentally racist as well as economic in nature and the more purely economic imperialism of the Anglo-Saxons. The former left far less room for maneuver and was more difficult to fight. The philofascists and philocommunists who spoke of a "democratic imperialism" were mistaken. In the first place, they were forgetting that as a norm and a principle democracy preceded capitalism. The two coincided in the United States and Great Britain, but they did not have to. Democracy also existed among poor peoples in countries that were not capitalist, such as Colombia and Costa Rica. In the second place, political liberty, even in capitalist and imperialist countries, left open the road to reform and progress.[51]

Haya's support for the United States was never uncritical. He was particularly opposed to its efforts to group together—professedly in order to defend democracy—both dictators and democrats. It was only for the oppressed peoples of the Old World, he protested, that Washington had eyes and ears; only for them that it offered antitotalitarian condemnations. In its dealings with Indoamerica, it had treated the brutal tyrannies of Guatemala and Peru as though they were equal to the effective democracies of Colombia, Costa Rica, and Chile.[52]

To the claim that the moral solidarity for which he was asking was a form of intervention, Haya had two answers. In the first place, sovereignty and democracy were inseparable: true national sovereignty and a right to be free from intervention could only exist within a larger moral and juridical democratic framework.[53] In the second, the United States was already intervening. There were many dictatorships that it recognized and that enjoyed its moral and economic support. "Very rarely," he claimed, "is public opinion in the United States ever made aware that a dictatorship has almost never existed in Latin America without some form of support from the outside."[54]

What was needed, Haya argued in late 1943, was a "democratic inter-Americanism without empire"—a genuine solidarity between the United States and a united Latin America freed from dictatorial regimes. This would involve the triumph of a spiritual force, one that France had lacked in its mistaken belief that it would be madness to die for Czechoslovakia or Danzig. It would also involve a right of "democratic intervention" within an association not only of states but also of peoples. The kind of intervention in which the United States had engaged in the past—and in which it was still engaged to some extent—was unacceptable. It was an intervention for the selfish benefits derived from the oppression of peoples. Intervention that would respect the interests of peoples would be a different matter. While stressing that such democratic intervention should take place within a juridical framework involving at least some of the states in the region, Haya strongly implied that leadership on the part of the United States would be welcome:

> When San Martín left Argentina for Chile and then Peru, he carried out a historic emancipatory intervention. When Bolívar left his homeland in order to give independence to five other countries, he also carried out a good intervention. . . . So did O'Higgins in aiding Peruvian independence. Neither San Martín nor Bolívar attempted to use their interventions, imperialistically, for strictly national benefits. Both returned to their countries and every Indoamerican people praises their *interventions*.[55]

For decades to come, these were the basic terms on which the Apristas argued that Latin America should seek to deal with the United States: (1) Indoamerican unity to strengthen Latin America's bargaining position; (2) the triumph of social democratic forces within each of the countries of Latin America capable of carrying out social democratic reforms and taking advantage of the benefits of American capitalism while limiting or eliminating its detrimental aspects; (3) the persuasion of the people and the government of the United States that American cooperation with and complacency toward dictatorial regimes was an unacceptable form of complicity in their survival; and (4) solidarity among all the democratic coun-tries of the New World—including the United States—against the threats posed by totalitarian and dictatorial powers. The extent to which mutually beneficial relations with the United States were possible short of success in each of these areas remained ambiguous for the Apristas and for many of the Latin American democrats whom they would influence as well.

The American Reaction to Haya and Apra

Already widely known and admired in Latin America by the time the Sec-ond World War drew to a close, Haya de la Torre was a figure of consider-able interest to American officials. This would have been the case even if he had not been the leader of the largest and most important political party in Peru. His organizational activities in Latin America in the early Truman years were impressive and generally welcome to American officials. This was particularly true of his strong support for the establishment of an an-ticommunist inter-American labor federation.[56] Haya's activities within Peruvian domestic politics, in contrast, initially drew criticism from the American embassy. The first two American ambassadors to Lima during Peru's democratic opening went so far as to question Apra's democratic credentials. This was not entirely without reason. As with Acción Demo-crática in Venezuela, there was a significant gap between Apra's democratic rhetoric and some of its actions.[57] On the other hand, the embassy's most strident criticism was aimed at a party discipline that differed little from that of, say, Germany's Sozialdemokratische Partei Deutschlands (SPD) before the First World War.[58] This sort of criticism was heavily discounted by officials in Washington, some of whom knew Haya personally. While American attitudes toward Haya were complex, the dominant sentiment was one of sympathetic appreciation.

Writing to the American ambassador to Lima, Braden stressed his re-spect for Haya's "knowledge and vision."[59] Haya, for his part, described himself as very impressed with Braden and especially with his "pro-labor sympathies."[60] He was also enthusiastic about George Butler, the deputy director of the Office of American Republic Affairs during much of Bra-den's tenure as assistant secretary. Butler had been ambassador to Lima during much of the Second World War, and Haya considered him "the friendliest and most understanding diplomat that we have had in Peru."[61]

Like Eduard Bernstein in Germany a generation earlier, Haya had come to the position that progressive movements should seek to become the heirs of capitalism rather than its assassins: that they should devote themselves to the struggle for political democracy and practical measures of reform.[62] The fact that Haya's focus was on what he considered the semifeudal and semicolonial countries of Indoamerica should not obscure the underlying affinity. This is particularly worth stressing because Haya was given to claiming that all European ideologies were intrinsically foreign to Latin America. Europe, he maintained, was not only at a different stage of historical development; developments in Europe would inevitably be different because they were European. Indigenous solutions tailored to meet the problems of Latin America's particular time and place were what was needed.[63]

Aside from successful Aprista movements, capable of carrying out social democratic reforms and welcoming and regulating foreign capital, the indigenous mechanism through which Haya hoped to foster economic development in Latin America was a series of national economic congresses. Each congress would unite representatives of labor and capital—including foreign capital—in a given country in a consultative body that could advise the state as to the best economic policy to pursue. Then an inter-American congress would meet and offer advice to all of the states in the hemisphere. This congress would address the need for an inter-American customs union, an inter-American development bank, better and less expensive methods of communication and transportation, improved safety standards for workers, and so on.[64]

Addressing the foundations of Apra's economic policy in a public lecture in October 1945, Haya reminded his audience that fascism and communism had each presented totalitarian planning as the answer to capitalism's failures. The United States, in contrast, had shown how democratic planning could simultaneously preserve political liberty and promote social justice. This was the great historic significance of the New Deal. American experience could not simply be transplanted to Latin America, but it was clear on the basis of this experience that the prophecies of capitalism's imminent demise had been mistaken. Marx and Engels had made a good effort at diagnosis for the time and place in which they had been writing, but they had been unable to perceive the dynamism and capacity for evolution that capitalism would manifest in the United States. They had been unable to foresee how a democratic state could itself become a productive factor in the economy.[65]

This was the basic economic message that Haya and the Apristas would propagate in Latin America during the early Truman years. In the interest of Latin American emancipation, they made a more deliberate appeal to American reformist traditions than had been seen in the region since the days of Alberdi and Sarmiento. This was combined with a direct and sustained attack on various alternative sources of inspiration:

> We do not consider democracy as a stage, as a preliminary step on the road to socialism or communism; for us, democracy is an end in itself. We do not want bread without liberty, as in Russia, or liberty without bread as in other places, we want both. The Four Freedoms which President Roosevelt proclaimed are more revolutionary than any socialist doctrine because they apply not merely to one class but to every class. We do not wish to take the wealth of the rich away in order to give it to the poor. We seek instead to create new wealth for those who do not have any.[66]

In April and May of 1946, Haya brought his message to Chile and to a congress of socialist and popular parties in Latin America that had been organized by the Chilean Socialist Party. In September and October of that year he traveled to Venezuela, Colombia, Panama, Costa Rica, and Guatemala. The highlights of these visits, and the reactions they drew from American officials, are worth review. Commenting on Haya's continual emphasis on the need for unity among the twenty Indoamerican republics, one official suggested that this was a threat to the American interest in the maintenance of friendly inter-American relations. "I still have to be convinced," Braden's special assistant wrote in reply, "that Haya's objectives and our own best interests necessarily clash."[67]

The American ambassador to Chile, Claude Bowers, was greatly impressed with Haya. He described him as not merely stealing the show at the Socialists' conference, but as doing extraordinarily well with every political faction in Chile except the Communists. Communism was foreign to the Americas, Haya told the conference, and should be met with the united opposition of all other parties. It was as though he was successfully reviving the wartime national unity position, Bowers suggested, only with the communists excluded. His first words on arriving in Chile were to explain why Aprismo was a philosophy with appeal beyond the confines of socialist parties:

> We Apristas are not Socialists in the Chilean sense. Marxism itself, within our philosophical and social concepts, is a valuable antecedent in the doctrinary field but is in no way our aim or our guide. We look sympathetically on any party which publicly announces reforms

which favor the progress of nations and the welfare of the working-man. This is the bond which unites us to the Chilean Socialist Party. That is a long way from the acceptance of a Socialist International. The only International which the APRA accepts is that of the conglomerate of Indo-American nations, for you will remember the well-known APRA definition, "Indo-America is a nation of twenty states."[68]

Emphasizing the participation in the conference of the Cuban Auténticos and the Venezuelan Adecos, as well as the Chilean Socialists, one Aprista leader boasted that Aprismo had transcended national limits and become an effective Indoamerican instrument for building social peace and progress.[69] The conference's resolutions could hardly have been more to Haya's liking. They called for the establishment of a common Latin American citizenship, democratic planning so that the state could take an active role in economic development, national economic congresses, programs of agrarian reform, improving relations with the United States on the basis of greater good neighborliness. "The unity of the Latin American peoples," the statement of principles declared, "does not imply a hostility toward Saxon America."[70]

Haya's speeches during his visit, and the adoption of Aprista positions by the conference, may have been a source of irritation to some of the Chilean Socialists. Salvador Allende would recall this conference with bitterness years later as helping to persuade him that Apra, Acción Democrática, and other similar movements had forsaken a genuine commitment to anti-imperialism and thrown their lot with the enemy.[71] But if he held such views at the time, they had no immediate impact.

Haya did draw substantial criticism during his visit from the Chilean Communists. They were outraged by his public comments that he did not see any danger in Yankee imperialism and his observation that Apra did not subscribe to the romantic idea of the abolition of capitalism.[72] Haya traveled widely in the country and organized a forum that included leading industrialists, members of the Catholic Church, including the vice rector of the Catholic University, and all of the major candidates for the upcoming Chilean presidential elections. It made no sense, he told those participating in this forum, for Peru to be producing wine when the best wine in the New World was available in Chile, or for the United States to produce synthetic nitrate when Chile had nitrate in abundance. Similarly, it did not make sense for Chile to produce its own sugar when better and cheaper sugar was available in Cuba and Peru. What was necessary was an inter-American economic congress that could eliminate customs barriers and stimulate economic development. Since Latin America and the United States were obliged by geography to be neighbors, it was important to establish good relations between them. Here the greatest obstacle to be overcome was Latin America's inferiority complex and its failure to develop a technique of united resistance within a spirit of harmony: a form of cooperation that would seek to build on the fact that Latin America and the United States needed each other. The realization of a democratic inter-Americanism without imperialism would also be aided by the development of an informed public opinion within the United States that would enforce its decisions on the State Department. This kind of public opinion already existed with regard to Europe, but not with regard to Latin America.[73]

Both Eduardo Cruz Coke, the leading Conservative candidate for president, and Gabriel González Videla, the Radical Party candidate, were in agreement with the substance of Haya's remarks, Bowers reported to the State Department. Bowers also summarized the comments of former Chilean president Arturo Alessandri, whose son was another candidate in the upcoming election, before offering his own conclusion on Haya's visit:

> Ex-President Alessandri, while not commenting on the above points, agreed in general with Haya de la Torre and stated that America cannot be too grateful to him for what he is doing, and that never before had such a group as that attending the forum been brought together in Chile. He observed that always, when the Fatherland is at stake, all Chileans unite, and that he was especially impressed by the kinship existing among those present at the forum. It would appear that Haya de la Torre has done an amazing job of salesmanship for his country as well as of his person, first in dealing separately with all Chileans except the Communists, and then in bringing them together at the forum meetings.[74]

In Venezuela, Allan Dawson, the counselor of the American embassy, reported that Haya had been an excellent campaign speaker for the Adecos during the fall of 1946.[75] In public lectures, not merely in Caracas but in numerous cities throughout the country as well, he had given junta president Betancourt and other Acción Democrática leaders "an opportunity to appear before the Venezuelan people in the company of a man of continental stature, whose fame is secure in liberal, intellectual Venezuelan circles."

Asked at one point by a Catholic daily newspaper representative about the threat of communism, Haya replied that the communists were serving the interests of a foreign power as Stalin's slaves. However, he added, he was opposed to the suppression of free speech and was convinced that democratic parties presenting genuinely progressive programs would provide the most effective opposition to communism. Asked about Yankee imperialism, he pointed out that the United States was strong because it was united and observed that of the two currents in its politics (the Republicans and the Democrats), the latter was the dominant current, democratic and anti-imperialist. Such liberty and independence as the Indoamerican states enjoyed, he said, was due to the fact that the United States was not wholly imperialistic.[76]

Dawson met with Haya on a number of occasions during his visit to Venezuela, both alone and together with Betancourt, and got to be quite friendly with him. He was particularly impressed "with Haya's apparent intellectual domination over Betancourt despite the fact that Betancourt was a Chief of State in his own country." Commenting favorably on Haya's visit in a letter to Braden, he noted that Haya had asked him to convey a message:

> The gist of Haya's message for you was that there were, in his opinion, two great menaces which democracy must face in the New World, Fascism and Communism. Of these, he thought Communism was the more dangerous since it was the instrument of an extra-continental imperialism, used ruthlessly by the latter, whereas Fascism, in Argentina and elsewhere, had no point of importance outside of the Continent toward which to look for support.[77]

In Colombia, the American embassy reported that Haya was received with great honors and welcomed by all political elements except the communists. The sector of organized labor that was close to the Colombian Liberal Party was "especially interested in Haya as a bulwark against Communism."[78] In Guatemala, Haya gave a long lecture at the Guatemalan National Palace that was attended by the president, the cabinet, members of the National Congress, Army officials, and members of the diplomatic corps. In spite of the fact that he had been invited to the country by President Juan José Arévalo, however, the Guatemalan labor federation adopted a resolution to boycott his meetings.[79] A public lecture in Costa Rica was "greeted by enthusiastic applause," according to the embassy report, but Haya was also accused by the weekly *Trabajo* of having repudiated the opposition to Yankee imperialism that he had propounded on his previous visit in 1928.[80]

In Panama, Haya stressed the fact that his movement had always supported the internationalization of the Panama Canal and then added that the canal's defense against foreign attack—like the Venezuelan oil fields he had just visited—was a matter of common interest to every country in the Western Hemisphere. "Why all this fuss?" he asked the representatives of a student federation protesting over the continued presence of American bases on Panamanian soil. "What do you expect to get by agitating when you could accomplish so much more through cordial negotiations?" Unfortunately, the American embassy noted ruefully, there were no reporters present at this interview. While in the Canal Zone, Haya toured the various defense installations and the locks and was the luncheon guest of the zone's commanding general, Willis D. Crittenberger.[81]

At least during 1945, American officials within Peru were much less taken with Haya. This was partly in response to actions he took and partly because of their own prejudices. Responding to the Braden memorandum in June of that year, Ambassador John White disparaged its call for unilateral American action on behalf of democracy. Perhaps the states of the region could do something on a multilateral basis to encourage respect for human rights. A start in this direction had been made with the demand for the freedom of external news messages. If those who held power did not have to fear reprisals upon leaving office, they might be more willing to leave. This would facilitate the development of democracy. But there were severe limits on what the United States could hope to accomplish, at least in the short term:

> From time to time the Embassy has been urged to make some move in favor of the elements which consider themselves democratic. Such, however, is the complication of racial and other factors here and the generally low level of political experience and practice, that it is a question in my mind whether the so-called democratic elements would, if they were in power, behave any better than the oligarchs— at least for a considerable time. Therefore, my judgement of the situation is that unless we are prepared to come and police the country, which of course we are not, we had better let the Peruvians take care of their own domestic problems; placing the main emphasis on protecting American interests and on friendly relations.[82]

Although the American embassy did nothing deliberately to help the Apristas, its pursuit of American interests and friendly relations was not a significant obstacle in the way of Apra's legalization. The fact that Apra sympathizers attended embassy functions may even have indirectly contributed to the party's legal recognition by conveying the impression that the United States was in sympathy with their cause. Peruvian president Manuel Prado Ugarteche's police sent him continuous reports on all guests to the embassy and the homes of ranking embassy officers.[83] Fundamentally, however, Apra's legalization came about because of its organizational strength and lasting popular support, the widespread discredit into which undemocratic governments had fallen in Latin America with the end of the Second World War, and a rivalry within the traditional elite in Peru over who was to be the official candidate in the elections scheduled for 1945.

In 1936, Peruvian president Óscar R. Benavides had canceled the results of an election—when it was clear that the candidate backed by the underground Apristas had won—and persuaded the Peruvian Congress to dissolve itself after extending his term by three years.[84] His successor, Manuel Prado, was not in a position to follow this lead and ignore the constitutional prohibition against succeeding himself at the expiration of his six-year term. Initially, Prado and Benavides sought to find an acceptable civilian candidate. When José Luis Bustamante y Rivero insisted that Prado agree to free and fair elections as a condition of becoming the official candidate, Prado refused to consider him. An American embassy report would later note that Prado had claimed he would not go the way of Batista in Cuba. Without an acceptable civilian candidate, Prado turned to General Eloy Ureta. This provoked a break with Benavides; the American embassy reported that this break was mirrored in the army with the added possibility of some young "Sánchez Cerro" in the wings waiting to take advantage of the situation and a faction opposed to any form of military government.[85]

With Benavides's support, and with the support of Apra, José Luis Bustamante y Rivero became the candidate of a newly created opposition movement, the Frente Democrático Nacional (FDN). Under public pressure not only from Apra but also from Bustamante and from important conservative elements within the FDN, Prado agreed to Apra's legalization under the name of the People's Party on 16 May 1945. Four days later, for the first time since the early 1930s, Haya de la Torre addressed a public gathering in Peru. This gathering was, in the words of the American ambassador, a "monster demonstration."[86] The American assistant military

attaché placed the crowd at a hundred thousand and marveled at the organizational strength and discipline displayed and the skill with which party
monitors directed the peaceful demonstration. There was little doubt, he
reported, that victory for Bustamante would spell government in Peru by
Apra.[87]

The tone of Haya's address on 20 May 1945 was both conciliatory and
aggressively self-confident. The ideals for which their movement had
struggled for fifteen years were triumphing in the world, he told the
crowd, and so, despite the many years of suffering, "We return to legal life
with an outstretched hand and with neither reproaches nor resentment."
Every genuine martyr knew how to forget the pain and forgive those who
had known not what they did. Democracy was a moral equilibrium of
rights and obligations. Having fought against a tyranny that deformed and
exaggerated obligations, it was essential to uphold the responsibilities that
were part of the civic dignity Apra had always stood for and sought to
establish in Peru. "Let no one talk or speak to us of emancipatory dictatorships. Here, we have suffered from them sufficiently." Social renovation
required both liberty and social justice. There was no place in Peruvian
politics for either the Red or the Black Internationals. Reaffirming Apra's
1931 program of economic and social reform, Haya rebuked those who had
criticized it without even bothering to read it. Just as democratic elections
were necessary, it was necessary to insure that this democracy had an economic and social content and did not ignore the fundamental problems of
the country. We must know how to make ourselves worthy of freedom, he
told the crowd in his conclusion. "Do not forget that you must be exemplary citizens of an exemplary party."[88]

In the elections of 10 June 1945, Bustamante received 144,433 votes and
General Ureta only 64,600.[89] The American chargé noted that while Prado
administration officials had spoken superficially of a completely free election, they had actually succeeded in holding down the FDN vote in a variety of ways. "APRA spokesmen have insisted that if they had been allowed
a little more time they could have greatly bettered their showing in the
congressional struggle, and their view seems well founded."[90] As it was,
Apra could normally count on at least 64 of the 138 votes in the Chamber
of Deputies and 21 of 46 votes in the Senate. After the June 1946 by-elections, the party's assured strength increased to 74 out of 147 votes in the
lower house and 24 of 49 votes in the upper, which gave it effective majority control of Congress.[91]

One of the most striking features of Peruvian politics in the immediate aftermath of the elections was Haya's emergence as a respectable member of high society. Several of the leading blue bloods of Lima organized dinners in his honor, and *El Comercio* and *La Prensa*—staunchly reactionary papers that had enthusiastically backed General Ureta's candidacy—consented to publish Apra advertisements. Only a few weeks before, *El Comercio* had been comparing Haya to Hitler and Apra to the Nazi Party.[92] Since the elections, the American chargé reported, there had been rumors that the family behind this paper was planning to abandon Peru. The appearance of an Apra advertisement in its pages, after ten years in which Apra had been portrayed as the archenemy, "has been considered here as equivalent to a white flag on the part of the powerful Miró Quesada family."[93]

This sense of respect for, or acquiescence in, the outcome of the elections—and the widespread willingness to maintain civil relations among the different factions in Peruvian politics—did not last long. By the end of 1945, severe signs of strain were already showing. On the political right, there was fear of Apra's size and strength and its program of economic and social reform. No other political faction in Peru had anything like its mass base, and many years of unremitting hostility on the part of influential papers such as *El Comercio* and *La Prensa* had helped to color views of what Apra might do with executive authority with more than a tint of paranoia. Even among the non-Aprista elements of the FDN, there seems to have been great concern over what it would mean for Apra to "take control." These fears and concerns were exacerbated by the sense of purpose and party discipline that Apra representatives showed in the Congress and by their obvious loyalty to a man who held no official title or position in the government. Growing labor strife—produced both by economic conditions and by a struggle between the Apristas and the communists for control of the labor movement—was an additional source of nervousness. So was the proliferation of organizations, at once social and political, which Apra sought to establish. Bustamante, in particular, seems to have been put off by Aprista efforts to organize young women and involve them in political life.[94] These anxieties, so much a part of the political atmosphere among the traditional elites of Peruvian politics, were initially shared to a considerable extent by the American embassy.

Barely three months after the elections, in late September 1945, the new American ambassador was already commenting favorably on an anti-Apra editorial in *La Prensa*. "There is everywhere a manifest suspicion of the motives and policies of the APRA and of its essentially totalitarian structure," William Pawley reported to the State Department. If he could be authorized to say that the United States would very much regret a situation in which a particular political party or faction would place its own selfish interest ahead of the nation's welfare, this would help to prevent a premature rise to power by Apra and would strengthen Bustamante's hand.[95] "As long as Haya de la Torre runs the APRA Party as a one-man show, depriving individual party members of any initiative or the right of expressing their own independent judgement," he insisted a few weeks later, "I cannot regard it as a democratic organization."[96] Rejecting Pawley's request for permission to intervene against Apra, George Butler noted that much of the criticism directed against the party came from privileged interests who would be opposed to any popular movement, that Apra represented a very substantial portion of the Peruvian electorate, and that the appropriate standards for judging its democratic credentials were not such things as party discipline but "whether or not it is opposed to representative government, civil liberties, freedom of the press, subjection of the individual to the State, aggressiveness and so forth."[97]

For their part, the Apristas felt that a series of elections had already been stolen from them, that they had been unfairly excluded from open political life for more than a decade, and that, because they enjoyed substantial popular support, they should have substantial influence in a democratic government. Having greatly helped Bustamante to win his victory, they expected to enjoy a role of comparable importance in his government and were angered and disappointed when the only cabinet posts he offered them were Agriculture and Treasury. They felt that the need for social and economic reform was urgent, that there was a serious danger that communism would triumph in Peru if a democratic government failed to improve living standards for the mass of the population, and that Bustamante was backing away from the commitment to reform that he had made as a candidate.[98]

In his memoirs, Bustamante captured an important part of the underlying conflict in postwar Peruvian politics in an unintentionally revealing sentence: "Although the government over which I presided was national rather than partisan, the circumstance of Apra being the only organized group among those that supported my candidacy made it feel from the first moment like the official party."[99] The idea that a "national" government could function without significant organized support—either in the country at large or in the Congress—was Bustamante's first serious contribution to the breakdown of Peru's democratic opening. His continued unwillingness, from his assumption of office until his overthrow, to form a cabinet led by Apristas was evident, even though Apra was unquestionably the dominant political party in the country and especially in the coalition that elected him. The fact that Apra had provided the overwhelming majority of his votes mattered far less to him than the fact that he was the one who had been elected: he could represent the nation; they, as far as he was concerned, could not.

The first serious contribution the Apristas made to the breakdown of Peru's democratic opening was in trying to exercise, through their dominant position in the Congress, the substantial influence in government to which they thought they were entitled. During the very brief period between Apra's legalization and the elections, Haya had rejected suggestions that he renounce his support of Bustamante and run for the presidency himself, on the grounds that Apra was bound by "commitments of honor" to support the FDN ticket. A party that has waited fifteen years, he told his supporters, can wait five more.[100] Had the Apristas managed to stick to the strategy that comment implied, the course of events might have been significantly different.

On being offered nothing more than Treasury and Agriculture in Bustamante's first cabinet, the Apristas chose not to participate in it at all and instead sought to transform the Congress into a real branch of parliamentary government. This was perhaps compatible with Peruvian constitutional theory, but it had never before been put into practice, and the effort contributed greatly to the nervousness not only of overwrought reactionaries but also of more moderate non-Aprista elements in the FDN. Beyond this, the Apristas sought to further reduce the power of the Executive through the restoration of the locally elected municipal authorities that had been abolished under the Leguía dictatorship.[101] Investigations were opened into the conduct of the previous regime, and funds for the secret police were eliminated as were the restrictive emergency laws under which Apra had been repressed. By the fall of 1945, a bill had been proposed for the creation of a national economic congress, and Apra was offering strong support to Finance Minister Montero Bernales's effort to reach an agreement with the United States for repaying the large debt that Peru had acquired under Leguía almost twenty years earlier.[102]

Having abolished previous mechanisms for press censorship, Apra was criticized for a proposed press law that was held to be a new means of control. Street fighting broke out between communist and Aprista strong-arm elements at a protest meeting against the proposal, adding further to political tension. Although a modified version of the press law was passed unanimously by the Congress in December 1945, Bustamante went out of his way to say that he would have vetoed the bill if it had not been amended. This, the American chargé reported, provoked the president of Bustamante's cabinet to threaten to resign because he considered it an un-justifiable, and presumably impolitic, attack on Apra; all the worse for hav-ing been made gratuitously and without his prior knowledge. To avert this resignation, Bustamante issued a statement declaring unity between the government and the FDN and referring to the good relations between the Congress and the Executive. As if to make a mockery of this statement, Apristas in the Congress repealed the 1939 plebiscite from which Bustamante derived his authority to veto legislation. When he vetoed this measure, they overrode his veto and in the assessment of the somewhat excitable American chargé, "paved the way for a dictatorship by the Con-gress."[103]

The resulting crisis in the Peruvian government was partially resolved with the formation of a new cabinet with Aprista ministers in charge of Agriculture, Treasury, and Development. If the Apristas had provoked the crisis for the purpose of securing substantial cabinet representation, they failed to get significantly more than they could have had at the outset with no difficulty. If they were not trying to win executive authority through congressional pressure, there was even less justification for setting a bad precedent by severely tampering with the "rules of the game." Luis Alberto Sánchez has claimed that Apra was only trying to restore the legal situation under the 1933 constitution—which contained no presidential veto—but the Apristas could hardly have been unaware that this action would be perceived by other elements in Peruvian politics as a "dictatorial" grab for power.[104]

From the perspective of the American embassy, the entry of Apra into the cabinet in early February 1946 marked a turning point.[105] While there would be occasional disagreements with Aprista tactics after this, embassy perceptions were increasingly favorable and sympathetic.[106] This was par-ticularly true after Prentice Cooper replaced Pawley as the American am-bassador on the eve of the June 1946 by-elections. Reading anti-Apra cam-paign editorials in *La Prensa*, Cooper observed that many of them—and others in the Communist, Socialist and Unión Revolucionaria (UR) pa-pers—were "defamatory in the extreme." The UR's scandal sheet, he reported, had concluded a recent editorial with the words: "Anti-Aprismo means Peronism in Argentina; the greed of ex-Ambassador Pawley means the imperialism of Braden. In Argentina General Perón defeated Braden; in Peru anti-Aprismo will defeat Pawley." During the course of the campaign an assassination attempt was made on the life of Fernando León de Vivero, a popular Aprista leader and the president of the Chamber of Deputies. But while reactionary groups like the UR had attempted to turn the election into an anti-Apra referendum, Apristas won eleven of the fourteen contested seats for the Chamber of Deputies. Even winning two additional seats in the Senate, however, they were still short of an absolute majority in that body.[107]

Relations between Haya and Bustamante remained tense during 1946, but by the latter half of the year they managed to establish a working relationship through a series of long personal conferences. As part of this arrangement, Bustamante's veto power was restored through new legislation. As a further result of these conferences, Cooper reported, "The President has assured Haya de la Torre that his Administration will support early settlement of the foreign debt, approval of the Sechura contract, the petroleum code, and the Economic Congress, and combat Communism."[108] The new petroleum code to which Cooper referred was intended to encourage exploration by removing features of the 1922 and 1937 laws that the major private oil companies had found objectionable. The International Petroleum Company (IPC) had signed a contract for the exploration of the coastal Sechura Desert area, but this had yet to be ratified by Congress.[109] Measures like the Sechura contract, the new petroleum code, and especially the debt settlement generated strong reactionary and communist opposition and even with Apra's backing would have required the support of Bustamante's faction of the FDN to pass in the Congress.

The cordial relations that the Aprista minister of development, César Elías González, established with the IPC would prove of unexpectedly immediate benefit to Peru. During the Second World War, Prado's government had been unable to purchase any equipment for road construction and repair. With the end of the war, the U.S. government was selling such equipment at a discount, but Peru was short of cash and its credit was adversely affected by its outstanding debt. Elías approached the IPC and persuaded it to extend to the Peruvian government a five-million-dollar interest-free loan for the purchase of the equipment. Acceptance of this loan was then authorized by the Peruvian Congress.[110]

The Breakdown of Peruvian Democracy

While there were some reasons for optimism in 1946, these were soon dispelled. On 7 January 1947, *La Prensa*'s Francisco Graña Garland was murdered. It was widely rumored that the crime had been a political assassination, and various Apristas were named as suspects. Although no one was ever convicted, and Aprista authors have argued persuasively that there was no rational motive for an Aprista to kill Graña, his murder was a great windfall for Apra's opponents.[111] Bustamante immediately asked for the party's withdrawal from the cabinet so that there would be no doubt as to the impartiality of the investigation.[112] As his new minister of government he chose General Manuel Odría, the man who would overthrow his government less than two years later. Apra, attempting to fall back on its position in Congress, was confronted by a boycott of twenty-two reactionary senators, which deprived that body of a quorum and prevented the Congress as a whole from functioning. This left Bustamante in a position to rule by decree.[113] An Apra protest strike against this situation in August 1947 was met by Bustamante with a suspension of constitutional guarantees and a postponement of the by-elections scheduled for September.[114] As early as the previous November, the American embassy had noted Aprista complaints that Bustamante's minister of labor was actively favoring communist unions.[115] Such support was stepped up in 1947, and by September the embassy was reporting that the government had recognized a communist union in the oil fields in place of the previously established Aprista union.[116] In the long run, Cooper observed, it was probable that American interests in Peru would be adversely affected "by present trend of the Bustamante Government away from democratic principles."[117]

In January 1948, Bustamante attempted to prevent Apra from hosting an inter-American labor conference in Lima. About a week before it was scheduled to open, he appealed to the State Department to intervene with its sponsors to have the conference moved to another country. The conference would be exploited by the Apristas for domestic political purposes, the Peruvian chargé in Washington asserted, and this would hamper the president in his effort to steer the country down a middle course. He insisted that the State Department had only to ask its own embassy in Lima to ascertain that this was true.[118] On being asked, however, Cooper urged the State Department to encourage the holding of the conference as scheduled. Bustamante, he maintained, could not afford to call it off by decree, and it would aid in the fight against communism in Latin America and have wholesome political repercussions within Peru. Cooper's analysis of the conference's domestic impact is worth quoting as a window onto the deteriorating state of Peru's democratic opening:

> Bustamante administration now strongly anti-Aprista and controlled by Aprista-hating Odría and his backers. Labor convention would be dominated by Aprista party as far as Peru is concerned. Odría fears exposure of his secret dealings with Peruvian Communist groups and that Apristas will use the occasion to air out current Odría alliance with Communist labor group. The Communist labor group known as the "Frente de Unidad y Independencia Sindical" is controlled by an employee of General Odría's ministry. Anticipated political repercussions are that convention will tend to strengthen Aprista party in Peru and build up party morale and in equal measure weaken and discourage Communist labor groups in Peru. There will be a further tendency toward discouraging Peruvian Government further aligning itself with Communist labor groups. Further effect of convention will be to uphold constitutional and democratic government as opposed to arbitrary strong-arm methods currently sponsored mainly by General Odría.[119]

Faced with Odría's growing power and with Bustamante's increasingly autocratic practices, the Apra leadership had only two real choices: appeasement or aggressive self-defense. A variant of the first option was pursued without success, and a variant of the second was soon to have been attempted when Apra's capacity for action was overtaken by events. The most obvious course of appeasement would have involved coming to terms with the Unión Parlementaria (UP), the reactionary group that was boycotting the Peruvian Senate and preventing the functioning of the Peruvian Congress. This would probably have involved Apra support for UP control of the leadership of both houses of Congress. Luis Alberto Sánchez, who had personal friendships with some of the UP leaders, had twice been involved in negotiations "to get the Congress going by means of our partial or complete surrender."[120] The Apra leadership might also have adopted a course of waiting and campaigning for the 1950 presidential elections. This would have meant hoping that Bustamante and Odría would not attempt to prevent these elections from taking place, would count the vote fairly, and would respect the outcome.

Aggressive self-defense on Apra's part could have entailed a move to take control of the government by force, utilizing the party's support among trade unionists, students, local officials, the police, and the military. This had been seriously considered by some of the leading Apristas and some of their supporters in the military as early as February 1948, but it was rejected on the grounds that public opinion was unready for such a move and that organizational preparations were insufficient.[121] When senior figures in the military suggested an "institutional coup," which would install an interim government and pave the way for new elections and an end to rule by decree, the senior Apra leadership welcomed their proposal. The date set for this coup was 8 October 1948.[122] Five days before this, on the morning of 3 October, a revolt among junior officers broke out in Callao. Dissident Aprista elements were involved in this revolt, but they had not informed the Apra leadership of their plans, and they appear to have harbored some resentment against senior party leaders such as Sánchez and Manuel Seoane for their opposition to such an effort.[123] Who would be so stupid, Haya de la Torre reportedly asked on the afternoon of 3 October, as to attempt a popular revolution on a Sunday when the mass of the population could not be mobilized.[124] Bustamante and Odría took full advantage of the situation.[125] They quickly crushed the revolt and the following day outlawed Apra. As the hoped-for "institutional coup" failed to materialize, leading Apristas went underground or fled into exile. Less than a month later, on 27 October, Odría put an end to what remained of Peruvian democracy and replaced Bustamante.

The CIA's assessment of developments in Peru in October 1948 was brief and to the point: "The new regime cannot be expected to achieve more than a short-term stability; and the chances for the re-establishment of a more broadly based, democratic government—the prerequisite for long-term stabilization—have been reduced by the outlawing of APRA, the most popularly based party in the country."[126] The possibility of attempting to influence Peruvian politics in a more favorable direction does not seem to have occurred to American officials in the weeks following the coup. On the other hand, one cannot easily imagine how they might have exercised a positive influence with any hope of success.

Haya took refuge in the Colombian embassy in Lima, where he would remain a virtual prisoner for the next five years. It was there that he would hear that Odría's dictatorship had been granted diplomatic recognition by the United States in late November 1948 and, a few days later, that democracy in Venezuela had been overthrown in a military coup. In the spring of 1949, he smuggled out a memorandum to the State Department criticizing

American policy and warning of the effectiveness among the oppressed Latin American masses of a communist propaganda effort based on envy and hate. This propaganda presented the United States as a privileged nation responsible for Latin America's political and economic sufferings, serving as the armory of Latin America's military tyrannies and profiting from the world's miseries.

> The democratic parties and those of the left (but anti-Communist) such as APRA, the Democratic Action party of Venezuela, the Argentine Radical party and others, promised the people that democracy would be defended by the conquerors of totalitarianism. And the motto of those parties was clear: "Communism is not necessary for the realization of social justice, liberty and human dignity; the new democracy based on the Four Freedoms renders Communism needless." However, Communist propaganda replies: "Now you have your democracy under the military dictators gained by Fascist armies armed by the United States, while the latter stands by immobile and watches the fall of constitutional government and the destruction of political and labor democracy—while the United States recognizes and aids these dictatorial governments—and gives more arms to Perón and closes its eyes at the tremendous abuses of the totalitarian military tyrannies." In the face of this factual argument, what can the persecuted democratic parties reply? What reply can be made by the non-Communist labor unions destroyed by the dictators, armed with the most modern equipment?[127]

American officials were willing to provide Haya with some limited practical assistance. In particular, they sought a peaceful solution to the conflict between Colombia and Peru over his continued presence in the Colombian embassy, a solution that would keep him out of the hands of the Peruvian government. Rightly or wrongly, Deputy Assistant Secretary of State Thomas Mann observed, "Haya de la Torre personalizes for many people in the US and in Latin America the struggle in Latin America for *orderly* democratic growth and social justice and it would be lamentable if he were treated roughly."[128] When charges that American officials had accused Haya of drug trafficking began to appear in the Lima press, Assistant Secretary of State Edward Miller went so far as to deny them.[129] Unwilling to go beyond such limited assistance, most American officials sharply denied Haya's assertion that they had any responsibility, or practical ability, to do more.

"The Haya memorandum seems mostly silly to me," Miller commented in a marginal note.[130] As far as he and his supporters were concerned, the United States had done nothing to contribute to the military
revolts of which Haya complained, and no amount of American financial
assistance could have prevented them.[131] Meeting with one of the exiled
Aprista trade union leaders, he argued that the United States was concerned with the long-term welfare of the *people* of Peru and that to engage
in either active or passive sanctions against Peru—"merely because we
might not approve of its type of Government"—could bring about economic depression and "possibly even more repressive measures on the
part of the Government."[132]

From Alienation to Reconciliation

Notwithstanding his frustrations with the Truman administration, Haya
was dismayed by Dwight Eisenhower's election and by the rise of
McCarthyism. In May 1953 he described the United States as suffering
from hysteria.[133] The following year—having finally been allowed to go
into exile—he described Uruguay as much more democratic than the
United States. "In Uruguay, the political persecution of a party or a citizen
would be inconceivable; the appearance of a McCarthy a monstrosity, and
discrimination against a Negro something beneath contempt."[134]

One of the central defining moments of the Eisenhower administration's policy toward Latin America, as far as Haya and many others were
concerned, was the overthrow of the government of Jacobo Arbenz in Guatemala. Apra, and other parties of the democratic left such as Venezuela's
Acción Democrática, had not been on good terms with the Arbenz government. Their exiles, after having found refuge under Arévalo, had been accused by Arbenz of being agents of Yankee imperialism.[135] Writing to
Serafino Romualdi, Haya described the remarks he had made on the coup
in Guatemala during a recent visit to Uruguay:

> [I] explained that Arbenz and Castillo Armas, the one an agent of
> Moscow and the other of Washington, were nothing but miserable
> military mercenaries, like all of the military dictators in our coun-
> tries. I attacked the cowardice of Arbenz, who should have fought and
> died like a soldier struggling against the North American interven-
> tion; but I said that he would never have done so because he, Arbenz,
> was nothing but an agent of the other intervention. I conveyed what
> I am trying now to say: that both sides use the same methods (ty-

rants, gauleiters, satellites) in order to oppress the peoples. And that the *free world* is as false in its freedom as the communist world is false in its justice. Against communism there is only one response: that of European social democracy. The North American policy of persecuting supposed "communists" (we are all such) and supporting such tyrants as Tito, Franco, Castillo Armas, Odría and company, is a suicidal policy.[136]

Writing to Frances Grant, Haya claimed that Eisenhower's policy was more disastrous than any since Calvin Coolidge. The assistance the United States had provided to Costa Rica in its recent struggle with Nicaragua was perhaps "a sort of small candy for the bitter mouths of Latin Americans after Guatemala. But, although we must make [ourselves] smiling players of optimism, I think that military dictators are the ideal Latin pro-counsels for the White House. I admire your fight for Democracy and Freedom, and as far as I can, I shall do my best to offer you my humble cooperation, with the same confidence that Don Quixote felt every time he gently fought for justice and freedom."[137]

Haya would spend the next few years in northern Europe, writing admiringly of Sweden, Norway, and Denmark and critically of American policy.[138] He was greatly encouraged by the wave of democratization that began to sweep over Latin America in the late 1950s. First Juan Perón was overthrown in Argentina in 1955. Then an *apertura* began in Peru, and Odría stepped down in 1956. The following year, Julio Lozano Díaz in Honduras and Gustavo Rojas Pinilla in Colombia were both overthrown, and by 1958 the Marcos Pérez Jiménez dictatorship in Venezuela had been toppled as well.[139] That the dictatorship of Fulgencio Batista was replaced by that of Fidel Castro was no cause for rejoicing as far as Haya was concerned. In January 1962, he suggested in broad terms what he thought it meant for Latin America.

We have had an epoch of dollar diplomacy. But now another epoch is beginning in Cuba, the diplomacy of the ruble. The diplomacy of the dollar, like the diplomacy of the ruble, is the payment of those that give. The term surplus value, which agitates so many, is very well known in theory. Surplus value is made with the hard labor of the peoples in order to pay those who lend the capital to develop under-developed countries. So, we ask ourselves: is it better to develop our peoples with freedom or without it? We, while receiving North American financial aid, have the possibility and the ability to say:

"Down with imperialism!" and no one will tell us anything. We have the ability to organize ourselves, to create our own trade unions, to exercise our legal rights, to protest, and to strike. In other words, with the diplomacy of the dollar, certain restrictive and coercive stages have been overcome that correspond to the first exercise of the diplomacy of the ruble.[140]

Haya was welcomed by the Cold War liberals of the Kennedy administration, such as Arthur Schlesinger Jr. and Richard Goodwin, as a symbol of the kind of politics they wished to support in Latin America.[141] Touring Latin America in early 1961, Schlesinger stopped in Peru and met with Haya. Together with Jack Neal, of the embassy in Lima, he marveled at Haya's "remarkable freedom from bitterness" and his "buoyant confidence" in the future. "The APRA party, which Haya de la Torre founded thirty-five years ago," Schlesinger wrote in a memorandum of his tour, "has been the prototype of the disciplined, mass, non-Communist, leftish South American political party. It has undergone a considerable evolution in doctrine since 1924. Beginning as a socialist and anti-US party, it is now explicitly pro-US, pro-foreign investment, pro-mixed economy and strongly anti-Communist."[142]

Since the beginning of Peru's democratic opening in 1956, Haya and Apra had given Peruvian president Manuel Prado support and loyal opposition. They had concentrated their efforts on contributing to the institutionalization of democracy in Peru and on preparing for the elections scheduled for June 1962. Faced with widespread rumors that the Peruvian military might not accept an Apra victory, the State Department decided that "it was not in the United States interest to have a military takeover in Peru if APRA won." The American ambassador, James Loeb, was informed of President John Kennedy's decision that he should use his discretion in applying pressure to deter such a coup but that if he thought it would not be counterproductive, he could go so far as to indicate that the United States would find it "impossible" to recognize or aid a government installed by the military.[143]

While Haya won a plurality among the three major contenders in the 1962 elections in Peru, he did not win the third of the vote required to take office. After it became known that he had made a deal with one of the other candidates—the former dictator Odría—the military pulled off a coup. The United States delayed recognition until the military promised to hold free elections, but when the promised elections were held in 1963, they were won not by Haya but by Fernando Belaúnde Terry.[144] Five years later, when it looked as though Haya would win the elections scheduled for 1969, the military again pulled off a coup.[145]

Before Haya's death in July 1979, another wave of democratic openings had begun in Latin America and Apra was again the largest party in Peru. At age 83, Haya had finally been elected to public office—the president of Peru's constituent assembly. One of his last acts was to sign the constitution that this assembly drafted.[146] While he continued to address political issues until his death, the clearest statement of his view of Yankee imperialism in his last years was written in 1977 as part of the introduction to his collected works. In this introduction he again championed his vision of Latin American unity, claiming that there was a historical law of growing interdependence among the countries of the region and looking forward to "a sovereign continental community, just, peaceful, and free."[147] He also referred at length to the Marxist antecedents of Aprismo. He drew a striking analogy between Marx's views of the impact of English imperialism on India and his own views of the impact of Yankee imperialism on Latin America.[148]

England [he quoted Marx as writing] has to fulfill a double mission in India: one destructive, the other regenerating—the annihilation of old Asiatic society, and the laying of the material foundations of Western society in Asia. Arabs, Turks, Tartars, Moguls, who had successively overrun India, soon became Hindooized, the barbarian conquerors being, by an eternal law of history, conquered themselves by the superior civilization of their subjects. The British were the first conquerors superior, and therefore, inaccessible to Hindoo civilization. They destroyed it by breaking up the native communities, by uprooting the native industry, and by leveling all that was great and elevated in the native society.[149] . . . England, it is true, in causing a social revolution in Hindoostan, was actuated only by the vilest interests, and was stupid in her manner of enforcing them. But that is not the question. The question is, can mankind fulfill its destiny without a fundamental revolution in the social state of Asia? If not, whatever may have been the crime of England she was the unconscious tool of history in bringing about that revolution.[150]

Here, Haya insisted, were concepts that bore a close relation to Aprismo's descriptions of the revolutionary role of imperialism in initiating the first stage of capitalism among underdeveloped peoples—even if these peoples were dogmatically referred to by Marx as of "inferior civilization." Here, Haya suggested—in Marx's description of the needless stupidity of Britain's pursuit of its interests and the havoc its imperialism wrought on the native economy and society—was sufficient reason for organizing an anti-imperialist movement uniting workers and peasants with the middle classes to guide the inevitable economic, political, and social transformation.[151]

Haya's view of Yankee imperialism, and the appeal of this view among Latin American democrats, was undoubtedly influenced by the New Deal, the Good Neighbor policy, and the Alliance for Progress. But careful examination reveals a continuity of vision that transcends and antedates such influences—an ideological perspective Haya had already fully developed by the late 1920s. Haya's conception of imperialism as the first stage of capitalism did not lead him, as some of his critics would have it, to "sell out" to Yankee imperialism. Throughout his long career he showed himself capable of bitterly criticizing the United States and American policy whenever he thought such criticism was warranted. His closest American allies were always to be found among those intellectuals and trade unionists who were willing to criticize their government's support of dictatorial regimes. But his faith in the existence of historical laws, and above all in the dialectic of historical progress, probably did make him into the first anti-imperialist in Latin American history who believed that Yankee imperialism—if met with sufficient Latin American resistance and cooperation—was ultimately destined to do more good than harm.

A Venezuelan Visionary

In the 1930s and 1940s Rómulo Betancourt and his allies began looking for a close relationship with the American government just as the State Department and, later, the CIA were coming to view reformist movements such as Betancourt's Acción Democrática as the best possible bulwark against communism in Latin America.[1] The resulting international relationship during the three years of democratic government in Venezuela known as the *trienio* was cordial and potentially durable. Its success is indicative of the wisdom of an Aprista approach to inter-American relations. Its failure is indicative of both the importance of local political leadership in the maintenance of democratic openings and the strength of nationalist notions of political legitimacy in American policy.

As was the case in Peru, neither the Cold War nor American policy was a significant factor in the overthrow of Venezuelan democracy in 1948. American officials saw Marcos Pérez Jiménez as less friendly to American interests than the Acción Democrática government that he overthrew. Had it not been for a lack of imagination on the part of the American ambassador, and above all his excessive faith in nonintervention as a means of harmonizing American and Latin American interests, American policy might well have helped the Adecos to maintain their hold on power. Even without American assistance, it seems probable that a better strategy on the part of the Adeco leadership when the moment of crisis came in November 1948 would have given Venezuela's first democratic opening another chance.

In the spring of 1945, the Braden memorandum had argued that liberal and democratic forces were the natural allies of the United States in Latin America, particularly for combating the danger of communism in the postwar period. During the next few years this was the dominant perspective among American officials. The Acción Democrática government in Venezuela, in particular, came to be seen as exemplary, and it maintained that status after Braden left the State Department. From the beginning of Betancourt's term in office in October 1945, he had publicly and repeatedly indicated that he was sympathetic to the United States and especially to the reformist tradition in American politics. General Douglas MacArthur, he observed in a nationwide radio address in mid-December 1945, was insisting on the abolition of the Japanese *latifundia*. If an American general who could hardly be characterized as an extremist was advocating agrarian reform in Japan, surely this urgent necessity could be addressed in Venezuela, particularly where the vast properties of the former dictator, Juan Vicente Gómez, were concerned.[2] A few weeks later, he publicly praised Braden for his liberal attitude and welcomed the American endorsement of a Uruguayan proposal calling for collective intervention on behalf of democracy and human rights. "If intervention is collective," he declared, "there is no danger whatever in it."[3] Antidemocratic regimes, he told an audience in Panama a few months later, were a threat that required a response:

> As long as there is a single government in America that does not guarantee the free competition of political parties; that does not guarantee freedom of the press and the free spoken and written expression of all ideological currents; as long as there is a government that does not guarantee the Four Freedoms of Franklin Roosevelt, the freedom of the entire continent will be threatened.[4]

As early as 5 February 1946, in a remarkable conversation with Allan Dawson, the counselor of the American embassy in Caracas, Betancourt made it clear that his government considered its values and interests to be largely compatible with those of the United States and that he expected a strong measure of democratic solidarity from American officials. He began the conversation by saying that Juan Perón would undoubtedly win the upcoming elections in Argentina. In any fair elections he would be defeated, despite the weakness of the democratic candidate, but there was no chance of the elections being fair. "Sr. Betancourt expounded for some time on Perón and his machine. He characterized Perón as a Latin Huey Long in his rabble-rousing abilities and fascistic tendencies without the latter's saving grace of really having some interest in the common man."[5]

Through his comments on a wide range of issues, over the course of this conversation, Betancourt appears as an eloquent vindication of the Braden memorandum's emphasis on the role of Latin American liberals in the fight against both fascism and communism in the hemisphere.

Turning to the situation in Chile, Sr. Betancourt said that only a miracle and the decisiveness of the Socialist Party there had prevented "Peronista" Army elements from taking over the country. The great difficulty in the recent past had been that the Socialist Party had played into the hands of the Communists, on the one hand, and the Fascists, on the other, by its policies. Bernardo Ibáñez was a very able man but he had made a fetish of the unity of the working classes which got him too tied to the Communists and enabled the reactionary forces to wave the red flag. Fortunately, on his recent visit to Venezuela, Ibáñez had seen that Acción Democrática had grown stronger, not weaker, by adopting a vigorous anti-Communist line and wresting control of labor unions from the Communists instead of letting them infiltrate into its own organization. Ibáñez had written him (Betancourt) several letters commenting upon his intention to follow Betancourt's policies in this particular; the entrance of the Socialist Party into the Chilean Cabinet and Ibáñez's break with the Communists on the subject of the general strike indicated that he really had changed his tactics.[6]

Having focused on Argentina, Betancourt suggested, the United States had left itself vulnerable to an Argentine propaganda that accused it of not being concerned with the other dictatorships of the hemisphere. This propaganda claimed that what the United States was really perturbed about was Argentine rivalry as an exporting nation.

The Argentines cleverly pointed to the fact that we had taken no similar steps against dictatorships in the Caribbean region, those of Chapita (Trujillo), Tacho (Somoza) and Tiburcio (Carías), as proof that the form of government or the extent of civil liberties did not really interest us if we had control over the economic factors. He (Betancourt) and other liberals in Latin America, who knew something of history and the honesty and stability of our policies, realized the complete fallacy of the Argentine arguments but they had an insidious and very serious effect on many people who should know better and, above all, on the Latin American masses. . . . While we and he (Betancourt) understood the difference between fascistic dictatorships and the old personalistic ones which were traditional in parts of the Americas, the average Latin American did not, never having had any close experience with fascism. In any event, when one had no civil rights, it made little difference whether the oppression came from a dictator who was just intent on filling his pockets and those of his friends or one who had an ideology better developed than that of the robber baron.[7]

The best answer to Argentine propaganda, Betancourt argued, would be to move more forcefully against the Caribbean dictatorships. To Dawson's claim that the United States already showed its support of democracy in its entire foreign policy, Betancourt replied that "he thought we were trying to do so but that our international commitments prevented us from taking a clear line in much of the world; that, however, these considerations did not hold in the Americas where we had an open field unless we lost our moral leadership through lack of courage." The Caribbean dictatorships were more vulnerable than Argentina to U.S. pressure, Betancourt maintained. "If northern America were all democratic, the American republics save Argentina and its satellites could turn their attention to the peril of fascism in this hemisphere with clean hands and single purpose."[8]

Betancourt's view of the United States—and of American–Latin American relations—had evolved along a path similar to Haya de la Torre's, but with a significant detour.[9] From its founding in 1931 until he left exile to return to Venezuela in 1936, Betancourt was active in the Costa Rican Communist Party, took a leading role in putting out its journal, *Trabajo*, and frequently attended meetings of its central executive committee.[10] While he never publicly glorified totalitarian social control as Trotsky did and never showed anything like Lenin's tremendous private contempt for human life, he did for a time agree with their fantastic vision of themselves as the leaders of a Soviet Union in the vanguard of a progressive and historically necessary global transformation.[11] During this period, he became an articulate member of the antidemocratic left—someone who clearly expressed the view that democracy itself would ultimately be an obstacle to the kind of social revolution that was desperately needed. At most, democracy and amelioristic reforms could be supported as a tactical maneuver in the broader struggle for the establishment of the dictatorship of the proletariat. This is clearly evident in his letter of 2 August 1935 to close friend and comrade Raúl Leoni:

> Remember what I told you in an earlier letter: to launch a program to conquer the masses without bourgeois-democratic slogans, in a despoticized country like Venezuela, would be like jumping into the river to swim with one's arms tied behind one's back. It is not necessary to speak of the conception we have of putrid bourgeois democ-

racy. It is not necessary to say that we, communists, see in it nothing but a more-or-less cunning veil for the dictatorship of a handful of imperialists and millionaires. The backward masses of a country where the prevailing regime has not allowed the proletariat to educate itself politically do not reason thusly. They have constitutional illusions, faith in democracy. And even more than the proletariat, the petty bourgeoisie, which—in conformity with Lenin's already classic schema—weighs most heavily in the bourgeois-democratic stage of the revolution. Our attitude in this situation cannot be to say: bourgeois democracy is a swindle; we struggle not for bourgeois democracy but for soviet power. That is, to my way of thinking, a mechanical, and not a dialectical, means of posing the question.[12]

A better approach, Betancourt continued, would be to put forward a minimum program calling for a "civil" and "alternative" government and elementary economic reform such as an eight-hour day, while connecting this program to a maximum program for the education of the masses and the conquest of power. This was the approach that had worked for the Bolsheviks in Russia, Betancourt insisted, and he and Leoni and their comrades should make use of this rich experience in Venezuela.[13]

Betancourt did voice some criticisms of Stalin during his years on the antidemocratic left, and many criticisms of the Comintern, but these had more to do with tactics than strategy.[14] He was far more fundamentally critical of the United States. His changing conception of the problem of Yankee imperialism and the means by which it might be overcome defined the trajectory of his political outlook as he moved from a communist to a social democratic perspective. A close examination of this ideological journey sheds light on both worldviews and on the radically different meanings that "anti-imperialism" could have for each one. It also suggests that despite the fundamental ideological dichotomy, there was a common desire for a social transformation that would benefit the mass of humanity; a common desire that facilitated Betancourt's movement from one position to the other.

The social democratic position in Latin American politics in the early 1930s was articulated most forcefully by Haya de la Torre and Apra. Campaigning for the presidency of Peru in August 1931, Haya declared that while capitalism was sick, the remedy the communists offered would be worse than the illness.[15] "We must not forget," he warned a crowd of his supporters, "that communism and fascism are extremes that meet in a deformed, totalitarian and tyrannical vision of the state. Our mission, the mission of America and of Peru, is to save our peoples from the disgrace of despotism as much as from misery and backwardness."[16]

As far as the Apristas were concerned, there were two great competing interpretations of Marxism in the world: social democratic and communist. To charges that Apra was "communist," Haya would respond that anyone with the remotest familiarity with international politics knew that there were fundamental differences among Marxists:

> There are two great Marxist schools and two great Marxist Internacionales: the Second International of Amsterdam and the Third International of Moscow. One is reformist, evolutionary, autonomist. The other is revolutionary and Bolshevik. The socialist parties of France, Germany, Belgium, Austria, and Argentina and the Independent Labor Party in England all belong to the Second International. They are neither revolutionary nor communist. Blum, Kautsky, Bebel, Vandervelde, Justo, and Maxton are all Marxists. Kautsky was a personal friend and disciple of Marx and Engels and is the executor of their papers. None of them are communists. Those who have read Lenin's and Trotsky's attacks on the socialists or the social democrats know this well.[17]

Initially, Betancourt appears to have been drawn to social democracy. In 1928, he helped lead student demonstrations against the twenty-year-old dictatorship of Juan Vicente Gómez and participated in an attempted coup against the regime.[18] In exile in Costa Rica the following year, he became active in the Costa Rican section of Apra.[19] He remained close to the Apristas until 1932 and later in life would maintain an essentially Aprista position. From 1932 until sometime after 1935, however, he accepted a communist rather than Aprista view of Yankee imperialism.

For the Apristas, anything that contributed to the unity of Latin America and to the triumph of genuine national sovereignty and economic and social progress within the individual countries of Latin America was anti-imperialist.[20] Yankee imperialism came about because Latin America was weak, fragmented, and semifeudal, while the United States was strong, cohesive, and economically advanced. If the traditional obstacles to Latin America's progress were overcome, the threat of Yankee imperialism would be overcome with them. If they were not, Yankee imperialism would be able to absorb Latin America and make of it what it would. With an Aprista party in power, foreign investment and trade could help to over-

come imperialism—dialectically—by contributing to the abolition of feudalism within a social context in which a popular and nationalist party was
carrying out social reforms. Greater progress was not possible as long as
capitalism remained dominant in the metropolitan countries. From a communist perspective, in contrast, Latin America's backwardness and semicolonial position was caused by capitalism. Only the defeat of capitalism
could overcome imperialism. Only actions that contributed to that goal
could be called anti-imperialist. There could always be tactical compro-
mises, but, since capitalism was by nature parasitic, there could never be
mutually beneficial relations with it. Those who were genuinely opposed
to Yankee imperialism had to ally themselves with the global movement
that would bring about its overthrow—the global movement constituted
by the Communist International. By 1932, Haya de la Torre represented
one perspective and Betancourt had come to articulate the other.

The reasons for Betancourt's oscillation between an Aprista and a communist position remain somewhat obscure. The social democratic character of Haya's ideology was just beginning to be clearly articulated when
Betancourt joined the Costa Rican section of Apra. That section dissolved
soon after his arrival in the country, in any case, and most of the membership joined the newly formed Communist Party. There was, as Alejandro
Gómez has observed, no other leftist political group in Costa Rica with
which Betancourt could have been active.[21] But local conditions were only
a part of the picture. Betancourt wanted very much to maintain political
solidarity with a group of Venezuelan friends in exile in Colombia, a group
that included Raúl Leoni, Ricardo Montilla, and Valmore Rodríguez.[22] He
feared that they might become a mere collection of intellectuals without a
political party. Together, he hoped, they would constitute an anti-Stalinist
revolutionary group at the margin of the Third International that could
take over the Venezuelan CP.[23] His involvement in the Costa Rican CP was
in effect a model for this endeavor.

Betancourt combined an unusually strong faith that radical change was
necessary with an equally strong conviction that politics was a practical
vocation. In the early 1930s, the Costa Rican CP could seem congenial to
such a temperament. It maintained a fair degree of autonomy from the
Comintern, both tactically and doctrinally, and was willing to allow a Venezuelan exile like Betancourt a leading role.[24] Ultimately, however, the
dogmatism and impracticality of communist politics was bound to alienate
someone with Betancourt's pragmatic bent. From the beginning, he was
frustrated with the Comintern:

The Caribbean Bureau of the International is the most perfect example which one could give of stupidity and vain verbosity. To date,
after almost a year of contact with the group here, it has not been able
to reach an agreement. This is because what they call "accepting the
line of the International" amounts to accepting, without the benefit
of an inventory, all of the abstract clichés—a hundred miles and more
removed from reality—that are cranked out on copy sheets in New
York. Without any resolution of the essential points, they continue,
undaunted, to send the same directives with every mailing: on such
and such a day, great(!) mass demonstrations of workers against the
danger of imperialist war on the Soviet Union; on such and such a
day, a meeting of protest in front of the American Legation over the
murder of the Scottsboro Negroes. All of this leaves the impression of
a suffocating bureaucratism: of a disdain for fundamental questions
in favor of a preoccupation with what is mechanical and formalistic—
with the politics of mimeographed circulars.[25]

Writing for *Repertorio Americano* in March 1930, Betancourt showed
nothing but admiration for Haya de la Torre as a leader whose name was
"tied to every effort in these times for Latin American emancipation."[26]
Haya and José Carlos Mariátegui "embodied the thought of a new generation," he wrote in another article later that year.[27] In a letter to two Peruvian friends in May 1931, he promised to keep writing on behalf of their
cause both because it was just and because Apra was the only Peruvian
party that would, on reaching power, help the Venezuelans to make their
own revolution.[28] In the summer of 1931, a month after the founding of
the Costa Rican CP, Betancourt called a comrade's attention to the profound lack of militant figures in Latin America capable of realizing a program for change once they had political power:

> Of the few that there are, the most capable is Haya de la Torre, the
> current candidate of the Peruvian left for the presidency of the repub-
> lic; and precisely because he is so valuable, there has descended over
> his person, his work, and his ideology—very similar to ours, I might
> add—all of the virulent phobias of the embarrassed reds. They call
> him a "sissy" because he does not frequent cabarets; Gustavo
> Machado, in contrast, the maximum leader of Venezuelan commu-
> nism, confuses revolution with the tango. . . . We have gained nothing
> by calling ourselves "comrades" and believing ourselves united in a

single ideological front if this makes fundamental methods of appraisal and tactical determination more difficult.[29]

Yet by May 1932, Betancourt could write to his closest Venezuelan comrades in Colombia that his illusions about Aprismo had been completely dispelled. What he had taken to be a tactic of the moment, something adopted prior to adoption of a frankly revolutionary position, he was now convinced was a firmly established reformist strategy.[30] In spite of this judgement, his attitude toward Apra remained ambiguous for several months, and there is some evidence that he felt forced to trim his sails in his criticisms of the movement. Members of the Venezuelan CP had been denouncing him and his comrades in Colombia, and the Comintern had written the Costa Rican CP "sending a kind of questionnaire about my activities, my position within the party, about the attitude I have adopted toward the Venezuelan revolution and the CP."[31] He may, accordingly, have felt under some pressure to criticize an organization that was anathema to the Comintern. But it was precisely his comrades in Colombia who were most influential in getting him to denounce Aprismo. In a letter of October 1932 to one of his less-radical colleagues, he bemoaned the fact that Peruvian friends such as Magda Portal and Luis Alberto Sánchez no longer replied to his letters. He would have given them indications of his sympathy for Aprismo, he wrote, but his position was compromised.

> I could not tell them why, but you I can tell. It has to do with the group of *compañeros* in Colombia—Leoni, Montilla, etc.—they sent me a serious reprimand for the enthusiasm I had "casually" demonstrated for a party that was following, as they saw it, a policy that was too equilibristic; a line too sinuous and of little consequence. . . . To be sure, *compañero*, I am incapable of believing such idiocies as "Aprismo: an instrument of English imperialism," etc.; but I could not deny that the observations of the *compañeros* in Colombia reinforced a conception I was already forming: that Aprismo, with its policy of a liberally interpreted united front, had allowed social sectors within its ranks that would inhibit an effectively revolutionary policy. What do you think on this point? Tell me with complete frankness how it looks to you.[32]

Despite Betancourt's ambivalence and the complexities of his political situation—both within the Costa Rican CP and among the Venezuelan exiles—there is no reason to doubt that by May of 1932, and for several years thereafter, his views were sincerely irreconcilable with Aprismo. A Peruvian Aprista's description of their goal as a "functional democracy" with a "mutual control of classes," particularly irked him.[33] By this time, he believed that there was ultimately only one class that should rule. It was this belief in the proletariat's exclusive claim to legitimate authority in society (in practice the exclusive claim of the vanguard party) that was at the center of the antidemocratic left's ideology for most of the twentieth century. Leszek Kolakowski has suggested that this belief rested, in turn, on a deep-seated tendency within Marxism to define human progress in terms of the establishment of a unity of civil and political society and that logically the aspiration for such unity must be rejected by any democrat.[34] Certainly, a desire for the exclusive rule of the proletariat was at the heart of Betancourt's pamphlet "Whom We Are With and Whom We Are Against," the most extensive expression of his views while a leader of the Costa Rican CP.[35]

Presenting his perspective in a broad historical context, Betancourt described the period of the War of Independence in Venezuela—and by extension in Latin America—as a French revolution that failed: a revolution that failed to establish an autonomous industrialism, on a national capitalist base, capable of sustaining a powerful liberal bourgeoisie and a stable institutional order. The bourgeoisie of the period made a grave tactical error. Rather than rule as a class for itself, it allied with the old feudal elements in an effort to rule through the military. The resultant *caudillaje* led to backwardness and barbarism. Extortion and monopolies, rather than free trade and free industry, introduced capitalism. The presidency of the republic became the culmination of a successful military career and the formation of the political consciousness of the masses was impeded. Into this backward economy with its correlative political superstructure came colonizing capital: imperialism. It further deformed the economy with its typical tendency toward monoculture and tied it to a single industry: petroleum.[36]

In the early 1930s, Haya de la Torre, hoping to persuade the U.S. government to accept and cooperate with a reformist government that he would lead, was willing to sit down and talk with the American ambassador to Peru. Betancourt had not the slightest desire to do anything similar: "The Yankee government is not 'democratic' nor is it 'great.' It is an oligarchy of Quakers and adventurous and unscrupulous Jews that has committed, is currently committing, and is disposed to commit at every moment, the worst acts of banditry against our disorganized Latin American peoples."[37] The contrast between Haya's and Betancourt's positions was not rooted in different interpretations of the Good Neighbor policy, the New Deal, or the threat posed by nazism. All of these were still in the future. It was rooted in their conception of Yankee imperialism and the means by which it might be overcome. Haya saw the possibility of utilizing the positive aspects of Yankee imperialism in a dialectical effort to overcome it. Under such a scenario, social democratic movements in Latin America would become the heirs of capitalism, rather than its assassins. He was confident that the political triumph of a social democratic party would be a great victory for anti-imperialism. While Betancourt adopted a similar approach a little more than a dozen years later, in 1932 he considered such reformism—by definition—as a profound betrayal of anti-imperialism. "Independently of the capacity for sacrifice and the ingenuous good faith of some of its honored leaders," he wrote in early 1933, "Apra is a reformist and opportunistic party that, by failing to situate itself in the camp of the proletariat and its ideology, has objectively fallen into the opposing camp of capitalism."[38]

To agree with Haya that it was possible to establish mutually beneficial relations with the United States was to agree that it was possible to have mutually beneficial relations with capitalism. This was the exact opposite of what Betancourt then considered to be political wisdom:

At base, all of our social problems are aspects of the universal conflict between the forces that create wealth—the workers—and those that exploit wealth and its creators for the benefit of parasitic minorities—the capitalists. From this perspective, we see that Gómez and his regime and its passionate defenders within the country are all part of a vast international system of organized exploitation. We derive as a first consequence of this theoretical conception—which is neither an a priori nor a sentimental conception, but one extracted dialectically from our reality—an active position of struggle not only against the transitory political regime denominated "Gómez" but also against the fundamental economic constants, the permanent determinants, of governments of his type. For that reason, beyond the destruction by revolutionary means of the despotism, we seek the destruction of its social base—the capitalist-*caudillista* alliance. Our irreconcilable enemies, in consequence, are (a) the international imperialist bourgeoisie, indirect ruler of our economy, and its native allies: the national class of large landowners together with the great figures of commerce and industry; and (b) the military *caudillaje*.[39]

Both communists and Apristas called themselves anti-imperialists, but the term's meaning had relatively little common import within their antagonistic ideologies. The Apristas were committed to a vision of political democracy in which multiple classes and multiple parties had rights and interests that had to be at least partially reconciled. They believed that Apra should be a multiclass party and that on reaching power it should seek to establish mutually beneficial relations with the United States. They held that it was simply impossible for Latin Americans to destroy a capitalist economic system whose roots were in other continents. "We must be ready to confront the inevitable crisis of the system," Haya urged his supporters, "but also to utilize its technological and progressive contributions, to control its excesses and impede its abuses, and to organize the economies of our peoples from the perspective that the crisis of capitalism will be a long one." There was nothing to be gained by looking to the Russian Revolution; it was not going to supplant capitalism, sick as it was, and in any case offered a remedy that would be "worse than the sickness and far from a constructive and salvationary economic and social order for the world."[40]

For communists like Betancourt, in contrast, it was the global communist movement that would bring an end to imperialism. It was the exclusive rule of the proletariat that would bring genuine human emancipation:

> It will be the working classes, revolutionarily oriented, rigorously disciplined, dignified by the awareness of their destiny and by the unshakable conviction that the logic of history designates them as the successors of the bourgeoisie in the government of peoples, who, on coming to power, will realize our national possibilities, forging a new type of state, socialist and anti-imperialist—an instrument of the people for the achievement of social justice.[41]

Throughout his time on the antidemocratic left, Betancourt generally sought to publicly downplay the antagonism between communism and social democracy in the interest of furthering his movement's chances of acquiring political power (and perhaps also of winning social democrats over to a communist position), but his ability to pursue such a course before the Comintern changed tactics and adopted the popular front was severely circumscribed. Welcoming the opening to Aprismo when the party line changed, Betancourt wound up being persuaded by events—and perhaps by those Apristas he had sought to persuade—that he and not they had been mistaken.[42]

With the death of Juan Vicente Gómez in 1935, a period of political opening and social reform began in Venezuela under General Eleázar López Contreras.[43] Betancourt soon emerged as a major figure among those pressing for greater democratization. Here his interest in practical politics brought him into conflict with others whom he would later describe as following a policy "that did not agitate consciences toward justice, but rather passions toward demagoguery."[44] When the new regime cracked down somewhat in 1937, Betancourt went underground until he was finally caught at the end of 1939 and briefly exiled. He returned to Venezuela in February 1941 when López Contreras's successor, General Isaías Medina Angarita, was beginning his electoral campaign. During his time underground, Betancourt severed his remaining relations with the Venezuelan CP and wrote more than six hundred columns for the newspaper *Ahora*.[45] Although he was in hiding and his "Economy and Finances" column was technically anonymous, it contributed substantially to his growing reputation—particularly as the police did not seem to be able to catch him. In these columns, with a tone fairly free of hortatory exaggerations, Betancourt increasingly articulated an Aprista position, both economically and politically.

International commercial relations had to be based on strict reciprocity, Betancourt argued in March 1937, if they were to be stable and mutually beneficial.[46] Free trade was doubtless a just and reasonable policy, but since all of the great economies of the world had forsaken it, there was nothing for a small country to do but follow the established path. This meant that it was neither logical nor just to purchase so much in Japan when that country purchased so little in Venezuela, or to purchase textiles, machinery, and tools in England when that country would buy neither Venezuelan coffee nor cocoa. It was more natural to buy in Germany, France, or the United States—countries with a strong demand for Venezuelan products—or in Denmark, Finland, and Norway, where a favorable balance of trade offered a field for the development of Venezuelan production.[47] Trade with the United States was to be particularly encouraged:

> We buy most of the machinery and manufactured goods that we consume from the United States and this is natural by proximity and because the United States receives, without limitations, the greater part of our products. Everything suggests that commercial relations between the two countries will grow in importance, and we believe

that our government should persistently encourage that growth with
every means available to it while always maintaining our freedom of
action and our choice of markets.[48]

On numerous occasions during this underground period, Betancourt
indicated that he remained concerned about the dangers posed by colonizing capital. Roosevelt's "good neighborliness" was too evident to be denied, he wrote in October 1939, but the attitude of those on Wall Street
was different: "They are dedicated to exploiting us with the same enthusiasm, and with the same avid rapacity, as they demonstrated in the days
when a Coolidge or a Hoover was in the White House."[49] The countries of
Latin America, he suggested, should take advantage of the fact that
Roosevelt was in the White House to free themselves—to the extent that
such economically backward countries could free themselves—from the
tutelage of foreign capital.[50] Companies like United Fruit had attempted to
constitute a state within a state in the countries in which they operated,
and there was, therefore, good reason to establish the Venezuelan banana
industry without foreign capital.[51] As far as Venezuelan oil was concerned,
the foreign companies were interested in exploiting it as rapidly as possible. Venezuela, in contrast, should be interested in using its oil wealth
over time to develop other industries and agriculture as well. This could
hardly be done with the low taxes and salaries that prevailed in the oil
industry. If the minimum paid to an oil worker in the United States was
$4.00 a day, Betancourt argued, surely the Venezuelan oil workers were
not being unreasonable in asking for $3.33.[52]

"We recognize the need, because of our backwardness, for the foreign
capital and the advanced technology of the highly industrialized countries," Betancourt wrote in the spring of 1939. "But we insist on regulating
this imported capital so that it respects the dignity of the national workers
it employs."[53] Nationalization of the Venezuelan oil industry was simply
not yet a viable option.[54] Moreover, even where oil had been nationalized,
as in Mexico, there was still a need for foreign capital. Foreign investors,
Betancourt predicted, would continue to make a profit in Mexico, and the
oil industry there would continue to benefit from their expertise, but it
would be on the basis of a negotiated arrangement with a social democratic
and anti-imperialist state.[55]

Betancourt commented favorably on Roosevelt's observation that the
abuses of capital, if unchecked, could bring capitalism itself to an end.
Where he had previously welcomed the prospect of such a demise, he now
saw hope instead in the fact that there were people of vision who, without

renouncing their adhesion to the established social order, sought to modernize and humanize it.[56] Roosevelt, he wrote, had recognized that the old economics had failed and sought to move beyond it. That supply and demand ought to regulate prices, that the state is a bad administrator, that only private initiative is progressive, all of these dogmas had disappeared internationally.[57] There was no longer any question as to whether the state would intervene in the economy. The question was whether the state that intervened would be democratic and progressive or fascist and reactionary.[58]

Fascism, as far as Betancourt was concerned, was a new and threatening form of economic despotism in which the state intervened on behalf of reactionary interests. As an example, he described the many ways in which fascist powers in Europe—while claiming to uphold private property— were in fact dispossessing the Jews in those countries of their belongings.[59] British policy, which had taken a harder line against the nationalization of Mexican oil than against fascist aggression in Czechoslovakia, disgusted him.[60] He was sympathetic to Roosevelt's argument, in his Quarantine Address, that aggressor states should be cut off from the rest of the world. The fact that the Soviet Union was unwilling to go along with such a policy he considered irrelevant:

> The attitude the Soviet Union adopts means nothing to those who have never looked to Moscow for signs to inform their judgement. For this reason Venezuelan democracy—which in its most dense sector is not communist—will continue to staunchly defend the thesis that aggressor states should be surrounded and immobilized by the most rigorous economic boycott.[61]

If war were to break out, Betancourt observed in late August 1939, the United States might well follow the same course it had followed during the First World War and not enter the conflict immediately. Latin America would then be faced with a situation in which the United States would constitute practically the only market for its products and the only source of the manufactured goods that it imported. With sufficient economic coordination, it would be possible to establish a tolerable autarchy in the New World. In working for such an arrangement, Latin American economic interests would be served by the formation of a bloc in which to negotiate. Given the danger of fascist aggression, however, it would be necessary for this bloc to conclude not only an economic agreement with the United States but a defensive alliance as well.

This alliance would exclude the presence of Yankee or British marines on our territories on the pretext of defending North American
and English investments. It would also meet the danger of a situation
of colonial dependency—once the United States and Great Britain
had emerged, fortified, from a triumph over the Axis Powers—by a
defensive force that could quickly deploy 100 million men ready and
willing to defend the sovereignty of each and every one of our
twenty-one nationalities, fragments of the great and single Boli-
varian fatherland.[62]

A few months after writing this, Betancourt was again in exile, this time
in Chile, where he forged close ties to the Chilean Socialist Party. The
Hitler-Stalin Pact had led the communist parties of Latin America to claim
that the Second World War was just another imperialist conflict, like the
First World War, and that the countries of the New World ought to stay out
of it. This, in turn, had led to a bitter dispute between the Chilean Socialist
and Communist Parties and to considerable controversy on the Latin
American left in general. Partly in response to this controversy—and with
the help of the Peruvian Aprista leader, Magda Portal, the Argentine socialist leader, Leonilda Barrancos, and a number of Chilean socialists—
Betancourt organized a congress of democratic and popular Latin American parties. Held in Santiago from 3 to 8 October 1940, it adopted
resolutions arguing that there was a fundamental difference between democracy and fascism and urging the establishment of a defensive entente
between the two Americas. Denouncing Betancourt for this position in
April 1941, the Venezuelan communist newspaper, *El Martillo*, described
him as a traitor: "In the face of the palpitating problem of the imperialist
war, to cite only one case, he does not vacillate in putting himself behind
the interests of the Yankee bankers, and with unhidden preoccupation he
calls for support of the democratic policy of the Roosevelts and Rocke-
fellers." Having returned to Venezuela in February 1941, Betancourt had
already indicated where he stood in an interview with *Ahora:* "I reject the
Communist Party, with all the force of my Venezuelan intransigence, because its dependence on Moscow converts it into a simple bureaucratic
appendage of the Soviet state."[63]

Even before the somewhat byzantine Venezuelan elections of 1941—
whose result was a foregone conclusion—Isaías Medina had promised that
he would legalize opposition political parties. In deciding to run the well-
known novelist Rómulo Gallegos against Medina, Betancourt and his allies undoubtedly thought that the opportunity to organize was worth

whatever legitimacy their participation might confer upon the elections. The political party they established, Acción Democrática, was very much in Apra's mold: a multiclass party committed to a program of social democratic reform and the pursuit of mutually beneficial relations with the United States. Once legalized, it steadily gathered strength over the next few years as it established its own newspaper, *El País*, and wrested control of most of the growing Venezuelan labor movement from the communists.[64]

The American Reaction to Betancourt

The key figures in the American embassy in Venezuela initially ran hot and cold in their attitudes toward Betancourt after the coup that brought him to power on 18 October 1945. For much of 1946, they were uncertain if they had been correct in their judgement that he was genuinely committed to political democracy and to a cooperative relationship with the United States. They were, however, predisposed to like him. Both the ambassador and the counselor of embassy were old friends of Braden's and they shared with him a belief that all of America's basic interests in Latin America would be advanced by the triumph of reformist and democratic forces in the region and a conviction that American policy could be of direct assistance. As early as October 1943, the embassy had described Acción Democrática as just such a force; as a party that "demands the establishment of the basic requirements of democracy such as free and direct elections and education for the masses, economic and agrarian reform to the end that the farmer may own his land and thereby achieve for the country an improvement in agricultural production, and economic nationalism to the end that the nation may secure a more effective control over her natural resources."[65] In January 1944, the embassy offered an assessment of Betancourt that was remarkable for its accuracy:

> He is the real political power in the leftist opposition political party "Acción Democrática" and could be called "National Chairman" of the Party. While his views are inclined to the left, he is not a Communist, although he is frequently accused of being one and it is understood that at one time he was a member of the Communist Party in Costa Rica. Due to his strong agitation for political and economic reform under the regime of López Contreras, he was branded as a Communist and expelled from Venezuela. However, he fights the Communists at every opportunity and, in addition, is bitterly anti–

López Contreras. He is well-informed, aggressive, and a good speaker. He was one of the leaders of the fight to bring about revision of Venezuelan oil legislation and often speaks out concerning United States oil interests in Venezuela. Although violently critical of United States influence as it manifests itself in Venezuela, he is believed to be more nationalistic than anti-United States. He now writes a daily column for the "Acción Democrática"–inspired "El País." He is a stubborn individualist and is a political force to be reckoned with.[66]

Frank Corrigan, the American ambassador to Caracas, had already been in the country for half a dozen years when Betancourt came to power, and he was intimately familiar with Venezuelan politics. A political appointee, he had an unusual background, having worked as a surgeon in a hospital in Chile from 1917 to 1919 and for many years in Cleveland, before becoming minister to El Salvador in 1934.[67] It was during his time in Chile that he and Braden became friends.[68] As minister to El Salvador, he had urged a policy similar to the one Braden would advance in 1945 and seek to implement as ambassador to Argentina and as assistant secretary. Writing to the State Department on 21 January 1936, Corrigan suggested that dictatorially inclined leaders in the region were threatening to treat American self-restraint as an excuse to do what they wished while claiming Washington's blessing. Given the bad feeling against the United States on account of its previous interventions, it had been natural to emphasize the purely negative aspects of the Good Neighbor policy—the commitment to self-restraint and nonintervention—but there had to be positive aspects to that policy as well:

> Failure of a Mission to use its influence constructively may become a sin of omission with consequences fully as grievous as the former sins of commission. It would be useful to know the Department's point of view as to possible preventive steps which might be taken in advance of the rapidly developing situation alluded to in the earlier part of this despatch. Liberal elements, some of which have been formerly active critics of the United States and bitter opponents of intervention have indicated to me that the co-operation (by diplomatic means) of the United States is more than welcome when it seeks to retain progress and prevent bloodshed and the establishment of autocratic régimes and actual setting up of dictatorships such as the Machado régime in Cuba and the Gómez dictatorship in Venezuela. They feel that a Liberal Government like that of the United States

with its immense power and moral influence should lend its aid and cooperation in every peaceful way to retain progress and ideals and to aid the evolution of these countries toward real democratic republican government such as at present exists in Costa Rica.[69]

Corrigan's position won some initial support from Assistant Secretary of State Sumner Welles before Laurence Duggan, the chief of the Division of Latin American Affairs, talked him out of it.[70] Such politically uncertain situations were often so delicate and complex, Duggan argued, that deliberate inaction would be better than action the precise consequences of which could not be foreseen. "On more than one occasion inept handling of these situations by our own representatives has not only served to make these situations worse but has resulted in embarrassment for and intense criticism of the United States."[71] Defeated within the State Department in 1936, Corrigan would maintain his outlook and act upon it in Venezuela.

Although an advocate of democratic solidarity, Corrigan was not a wild enthusiast for the promotion of democracy abroad. In the summer of 1945, he lent a copy of a cautionary article on the subject to his more optimistic counselor of embassy, Allan Dawson. Dawson had been Braden's assistant in the negotiations to end the Chaco War and was a staunch supporter of Braden's policy.[72] The cautionary article was by A. G. Keller, professor emeritus of sociology at Yale.[73] Keller maintained that those who urged a program of world democratization were following a faith near enough to religion to allow of comparison. It was not a program likely to succeed, at least not any time soon. The transplantation of democracy would require the right kind of cultural soil, and this was simply not likely to be found in many countries. The effort to establish a republic in Germany, for example, appeared to have been almost as incomprehensible to the national Weltanschauung as a comparable effort in Japan. Political systems were a "natural growth" requiring the right nutritive deposits accumulated in folkways over historic periods. No hothouse efforts could adjust for unfavorable soil. By all means, Keller concluded, let us have all the democracy possible and attempt to encourage it wherever it has a chance to grow. "But let us consider the several kinds of ground mentioned in the Parable of the Sower, and not bank heavily upon the thin and stony soil, even if out of it certain showy sprouts spring up forthwith; for, later on, their withering away or their grotesque parody of genuine blossoming may have to be embarrassingly explained."[74]

After reading the piece, Dawson told Corrigan that he had found it interesting and that he considered Keller a worthy successor to William Gra-

ham Sumner, but that he himself was a convinced democrat, not a sociolo-
gist.

> In other words, I am under the handicap, in this particular, of being a
> fellow who has a religion instead of looking at matters from the ob-
> jective point of view of one who dissects religion. I agree thoroughly
> that democracy cannot be imposed but has to be a growth from
> within. However, elements of democracy exist in practically every
> community and culture. It seems to me that the cue of those of us
> who believe that democracy is the ideal way of life which evolution
> will eventually bring to all, even if it may be long-delayed, is to do
> what we can to nurture these feeble sprouts by example and encour-
> agement. Certainly, the totalitarian ideologies, both right and left,
> use proselytizing and conquest as weapons. While I do not advocate
> following their methods, we should at least defend what we believe to
> the extent of giving it a chance to develop naturally, and not leaving
> the field to democracy's ruthless opponents.[75]

Whether there was any great difference between Dawson's and Corrigan's outlook is doubtful. In the diplomatic record they appear to be largely
in agreement. Contemporary opinion, however, did detect a difference. The
Venezuelan military, in particular, as Dawson told Corrigan in October
1946, "consider me a buddy of the Acción Democrátistas while you are
supposed by them to be more conservative."[76] This was not without some
foundation. Three days before the coup, finding out that Betancourt was
broke, Dawson had even lent him twenty *bolívares* or about six dollars.[77]

While the American embassy had excellent contacts and had even heard
a few rumors that something was up, the events of 18 October 1945 still
came as a surprise.[78] Explaining the underlying reason for the coup in a
letter to his son, Corrigan indicated that it had turned on the question of
who would succeed Isaías Medina as the governing party's candidate for
the upcoming elections.

> Politically the thing began with the nervous breakdown of Escalante
> who probably would have won with the Government's backing. His
> departure for a sanatorium on an Army plane left the Government
> without a candidate. Then Medina's P.D.V. party held a convention
> which was pure rubber stamp and put up a non-entity, Biaggini,
> whom everybody recognized as a puppet of Medina. Foreseeing the
> renewal of a Gómez type dictatorship with Medina playing the part
> of Gómez, set up a wave of revolution throughout the country.[79]

While this account ignored certain issues, it was basically correct. Angel Biaggini, the minister of agriculture, had virtually no constituency of his own whereas Diógenes Escalante, the Venezuelan ambassador to Washington, had been widely acceptable, even to the Adecos. Beyond this, there had been a concern among both the Adecos and elements in the military that López Contreras might attempt a return to power, and there was also considerable resentment among the junior officers over issues of pay and promotions. Even at the price of cooperating with such officers—who might have taken action without them—the Adecos were undoubtedly drawn by the opportunity to begin to put their ideals into practice and to move Venezuela toward social reform and genuine elections with widespread suffrage.[80]

The American reaction to the coup was generally sympathetic. Meeting with the Colombian ambassador to Washington on 25 October 1945, Braden quickly ascertained that they were in agreement as to the previous week's developments in Venezuela: that "the Junta was in control of the country; that the revolution had been free from any foreign influence; that the Junta had expressed its intention to comply with all international agreements previously entered into by the Venezuelan Government; and that it appeared to be democratic in its orientation."[81] Later in the day, Braden spoke with the Cuban, Brazilian, and Bolivian ambassadors and the Argentine chargé. He indicated that the United States was favorably impressed and disposed to accord recognition after consultation with the other American republics.[82]

The honeymoon between the Venezuelan junta and the American embassy was relatively brief. On 31 December 1945, the junta issued Decree 112 placing a retroactive tax on income over 800,000 *bolívares* that had been earned during the year. More than 98 percent of this tax—which gave the junta an additional $26.5 million (Bs. 89 million)—was paid by the oil companies.[83] As this affected taxes paid to Washington, it also took about $3 million out of the United States Treasury.[84] The sums of money involved were not so great as to alienate either the larger oil companies or the embassy. In the face of wartime and postwar petroleum shortages oil prices were rising rapidly, and even after it paid an extra $18 million under the decree, Creole Petroleum still earned over $90 million in Venezuela in 1945.[85] On the other hand, the suggestion that this decree was not considered a serious problem because it merely reflected an attempt to insure a fifty-fifty profit split agreed to in 1943 is clearly mistaken on many levels.[86] The unilateral character of the decree and the prospect that future relations would follow a similar pattern contributed to genuine concern within the American embassy. Dawson went so far as to describe it as part of a "demagogic and radical" path that Betancourt had chosen to adopt.[87]

Corrigan saw himself and his embassy, with some reason, as a progressive force on the oil question, promoting Venezuelan as well as American interests. Within a month of arriving in Caracas in 1939, he was arguing that the oil companies were obliged by their position in Venezuelan society to contribute to the amelioration of social conditions in the country and to help the Venezuelan government in reformist projects such as the construction of homes, schools, hospitals, and roads.[88] For the next few years, against the background of expropriations in Mexico and Bolivia and the wartime need for Venezuelan oil, he was involved in efforts to reach an understanding between the oil companies and the government of Venezuela that would be more favorable to the Venezuelans than those reached under Gómez. Such an understanding would be seen as more legitimate in Venezuela and therefore would be more durable. This process of negotiations culminated in the revision of Venezuela's oil legislation in 1943. "I can honestly say," Corrigan boasted in a contemporary memo, "that but for our unpublicised efforts the happy result would not have been attained."[89]

Under the 1943 legislation, as Bryce Wood has observed, existing concessions were reaffirmed with the following changes: "(1) an increase in royalties to the government from rates varying between 7½ and 11 percent to a uniform rate of 16⅔ percent; (2) the establishment of a new base on which the royalties were calculated that was more favorable to the government than the one used previously; (3) a reduction in the customs exemptions formerly enjoyed by the companies."[90] William F. Buckley, the general agent for Pantepec, one of the smaller oil companies, would later go so far as to claim that the Venezuelan government had been willing to settle for a one-eighth royalty and that it was the State Department's representative in the negotiations who had proposed that the royalty be made one-sixth.[91] In any case, Corrigan assumed that the U.S. government, the Venezuelan government, and the oil companies had all come to a mutual understanding that would advance their common interests and that negotiation was the proper mechanism for reaching such understandings. Decree 112 suggested that the Venezuelan junta might have other ideas about its interests and the means by which they could be advanced.

Betancourt's New Year's Day address raised further questions for the American embassy, which described it as disappointingly vague, primarily because of its failure to set a date for the promised elections but also in its economic proposals.[92] Betancourt spoke of the need to rescue the majority of Venezuelans from backwardness and misery and promised that the economic program of the junta would free Venezuela from foreign tutelage in many respects. The Institute for the Increase of Production, which was to be financed by Decree 112, would provide long-term credit, machinery, and technical assistance to both industry and agriculture in an effort to reconstruct the Venezuelan economy. Public housing would be built in urban areas, and agrarian reform would provide land to landless agriculturists by utilizing the properties acquired from those found guilty of corruption by the Tribunal of Civic and Administrative Responsibility as well as the lands that had belonged to Gómez. Venezuelan commerce would be imported and exported in a national merchant marine.[93]

Commenting on Betancourt's speech, Dawson suggested that it bore the marks of having been drafted by a committee and not carefully thought out:

> While the objectives announced are excellent, hardly a start can be made on them during the next few months. Offhand, it would appear to an independent observer that they would more properly be the object of a long-term program to be put into effect by a permanent, constitutional administration after thorough study and that there are many short-term measures, neglected in the program, which might better lead to meeting the unquestioned need for improved living conditions and lowering the cost of living in Venezuela. . . . That the program was not prepared as soundly as would have been advisable is shown by the stress laid on the development of a national merchant marine as one of the basic objectives. Actually, the high freight rates on imported merchandise are but a relatively small factor in the inordinately high cost of imported goods, much more important being the heavy Venezuelan import duties and the tremendous profit taken by middlemen. The junta has as yet taken no effective measures on either score.[94]

Another issue contributing to increasing tension between the junta and the embassy had to do with the contracts of an American-owned firm, Constructing Engineers, CA. In early February 1946, Dawson told Corrigan that a government official, Luis Lander, had summarily informed this company that all of its contracts were canceled on account of a "lack of confidence."

> Parsons, Brinkerhoff, etc., the Constructing Engineers' parent com-
> pany, is one of the top two or three engineering firms in the States, it
> employs a larger percentage of Venezuelans in responsible jobs than
> any other foreign company in the country and without any differen-
> tial in salaries, and it has charged a substantially smaller percentage
> on its work than is customary in its field. This all adds up to the fact
> that Lander is trying to make political capital by an anti-gringo blow
> before taking up his job as Secretary General of A.D. It is a stinking
> mess.[95]

At least as troubling to the embassy as the economic issues, even given the security implications attached to Venezuelan oil, were the antidemo- cratic tendencies the junta appeared to demonstrate in its first months in power. To the continuing delay in announcing a definite date for elections, and the similar delay in announcing the restoration of constitutional guar- antees—suspended by the Medina regime as one of its last acts—the junta added a series of arrests of political opponents including, most notably, Antonio A. Pulido Villafañe, the chief justice of the Supreme Court.[96] Al- though the junta claimed to be acting in self-defense, after having uncov- ered a counterrevolutionary plot, Dawson saw it as taking action against a man who might become the focus of opposition although he had done nothing subversive. "The Pulido 'plot' was pure eyewash, as Morales has admitted to me," he told Corrigan.[97]

When the draft of the electoral statute came out on 5 February 1946, Dawson did acknowledge that the Adeco in charge of the project, Andrés Eloy Blanco, had done a good job.[98] The favorable impact it might have had on public opinion he thought had been largely counteracted by a speech on the same day by Interior Minister Valmore Rodríguez. Aside from allow- ing indoor political meetings in theaters and the like, this speech essen- tially reaffirmed the suspension of constitutional guarantees and the junta's promise "not to permit defense of the overthrown regimes." Since practically any criticism of the junta had been considered as falling into this category in the past, Dawson noted, this meant that there would be no lessening of the informal but effective controls on the press. In his report to the State Department, he quoted Valmore Rodríguez's reply to a jour- nalist when asked if the Partido Democrático Venezolano—the party of the

Medina regime—would enjoy the same political liberties as those granted to other political organizations: "Is there any PDV? I have heard that that party retired from the public stage together with its leader and its principal supporters. In any event, could that party do anything else, if it has not perished, than work for the resurrection of the old Medina regime?"[99]

In March 1946, Corrigan commented that Betancourt "now seems a very different person from the modest, straight-thinking man who came into office last October." Betancourt might say that it would be his greatest pride to turn over power to whomever the people elected, friend or foe, but if opposition leaders were deported or imprisoned and the organization and functioning of opposition parties was made difficult, what were the chances of a foe being elected?

> Certainly, many persons have been arrested in Venezuela under the Junta regime with no charges against them ever made public and many of those detained for alleged "conspiracy" seem actually to have been merely persons who were too vigorous in their oral opposition to the Junta and might become dangerous. However bad the Medina regime was, and the graft, corruption, and rigging of elections under it did reach to inexcusable extremes, it held not a single political prisoner when it was overthrown, a record which the Junta cannot begin to rival. That Sr. Betancourt has difficulty in taking a soundly democratic position to opposition is indicated by his stricture concerning the campaign against the Jury of Civil and Administrative Responsibility which "has now dared to raise its head in the pages of the daily press." His statement that "perhaps this Tribunal has made some mistakes; but the Revolutionary Government will see to it that the decisions of the Tribunal are complied with" also has a strangely undemocratic ring.[100]

Although he does not appear to have raised the idea with the State Department, Corrigan had decided as early as 14 February 1946 that the embassy would have to use its influence at some point in an effort to improve the situation. He suggested that Dawson consider meeting with Betancourt and the other key members of the junta and explaining to them the desire of the United States for a genuinely cooperative relationship with Venezuela, its interests in the country, and its concern that those interests had been adversely affected in recent months. The justification for such a course of action Corrigan thought was clear enough:

In the first place, we were their friends when they needed a friend very badly. We have tried to be in every way a good neighbor to Venezuela. We have spent some millions of dollars as a contribution to their health and welfare. We have furnished them any kind of expert they wanted, upon demand. Certainly what we have done has resulted in their having received an excellent press, early recognition of the present government, and an inspiration of confidence in it. The net results of their government so far, not speaking of the blood that was spilt in the revolution, is that conditions are certainly no better for the people of Venezuela, and much worse for our own interests: our interests both in democracy and its progress, and our material interests as represented by American investments and activities in Venezuela. . . . Now, they want a lot of things, and they are going to need a lot of things, and without our friendship and good will their future, to say the least, is dubious. So, there has to be a showdown. Are they our friends, and do they want to play ball with us and have the kind of sincere friendship and cooperation that we are ready to give them, or are they not?[101]

In a follow-up letter the next day, Corrigan softened his tone somewhat before continuing in the same vein. Noting that he had once sought to encourage an utterly downcast Andrés Eloy Blanco about Acción Demo-crática's prospects, Corrigan suggested that he be included in the meeting. In the discussion, Dawson might remind the Adecos of the utter failure of the British Labour Party the first time it took power: "There is a lesson in that for them if they will heed it." That a huge howl had not yet gone up from the hundreds of thousands of stockholders that companies like Cre-ole had in the United States was a near miracle for which the embassy could take some credit. If such a howl was to start, they would be in real trouble because Venezuela's oil position was already extremely vulnerable internationally. "What they are doing is stupid and criminal in the light of the real interests of their country. Ignorance and stupidity can cause losses that will make the amounts taken in graft and peculation look like small change in comparison."[102]

When the showdown finally came, on 30 April 1946, it would be be-tween Corrigan and Betancourt during a three-hour private dinner at the Miraflores Palace followed by coffee, liqueur, and Havana cigars.[103] In ad-dition to his offer of American friendship in general, Corrigan brought to the table the authority to release surplus military airplanes for delivery to

Venezuela that he knew the Venezuelan military wanted. The Venezuelan air attaché in Washington had already informed Betancourt, on the basis of his contacts in the War Department, that delivery was being blocked by the State Department. Betancourt, in turn, had already indicated to Dawson that he knew that this was the case.[104]

After expressing his appreciation for American assistance to Venezuela's health and sanitation program, Betancourt turned to the question of supplies in general—under what remained of Washington's wartime regulations—and suggested that Venezuela had not been treated favorably. Corrigan, having anticipated the complaint, presented him with a detailed memorandum suggesting that Venezuela had in fact received preferential treatment, relative both to American and European consumers, in various categories of foodstuffs, agricultural machinery, and automotive vehicles. Betancourt next turned to the issue of the military mission and the planes that the Venezuelan military desired. Assuming that Betancourt's prestige with the military would depend to a considerable extent on a favorable answer, Corrigan wanted to get certain assurances before providing it:

> I, therefore, said to him, "I would like to discuss with you the basic issues in which we are interested. They are two in number: (1) The orientation of your government and the opinions of its members with regard to our own devotion and commitments towards the ideals of democracy and the preservation and development of democratic processes, and (2) The protection of our material interests which are in large part important not only economically but also strategically for ourselves and from the standpoint of continental security." He gave me categorical assurances on both points using the word "categoricamente" in assuring me each time.[105]

Betancourt stressed the democratic character of his administration, noting that López Contreras's recent denunciation of it as a dictatorship had been published in all the Caracas papers. He said that he had been deeply moved by a recent newsreel showing commemorative ceremonies on the first anniversary of Roosevelt's death. He had lived all his life as a poor man and expected to die as such, and it was his only ambition to be mourned as Roosevelt was mourned. His administration was now buying desks and benches so that schoolchildren would have a place to sit in the buildings built by his predecessors. A greatly increased number of school lunches were now being served across the nation. Conceding that Betancourt made a good case for the social good intentions of his administration,

Corrigan turned to the issue of political prisoners and asked how many remained in Venezuelan jails. He was surprised to learn that there were only five left, that Pulido was now in Cuba, and that his family and the families of all of the exiled generals were receiving an allowance from the government or their regular pensions. Defending the delay in the elections, Betancourt noted that his party could easily have taken advantage of its organizational strength to win early elections but wanted to insure a fair contest by giving opposition parties an opportunity to organize. The Adecos' ability to have won an early election Corrigan acknowledged.[106]

Conceding the sincerity of Betancourt's devotion to democracy, Corrigan turned to the question of material interests. "In his answer to this," Corrigan later told the president of Creole Petroleum, "he mentioned your name and told me that Mr. Proudfit, with whom he had recently discussed the subject at length, was thoroughly familiar with his feelings and knew that he considered that the Venezuelan Government and the oil companies were partners (socios) and that their interests in economic exploitation of the country's petroleum under conditions which would enable Venezuela to compete in world markets were identical."[107] Beyond this, Betancourt indicated that he had no desire to see the oil workers establish themselves as a "labor aristocracy" and that his government would protect the oil companies from unreasonable labor demands. Having been satisfied as to both material and ideal interests, Corrigan informed Betancourt that he could take credit with the military members of the junta for obtaining the military planes.[108]

While there would be future occasions for complaint, American attitudes toward Betancourt and Acción Democrática improved steadily as it became increasingly apparent that Betancourt was in fact not only sincere in his convictions but was also capable of pursuing his aims skillfully and with popular support. The first hard evidence for this came in the fall of 1946 with the election of a constituent assembly to write a new constitution. Several political parties had emerged by this time: the Partido Social Cristiano (Copei), an essentially Christian democratic party whose leading figure was Rafael Caldera; the Unión Republicana Democrática (URD), a leftist and more personalist party centered on Jóvito Villalba; the Partido Comunista de Venezuela (PCV), led by Juan Bautista Fuenmayor; and the Partido Revolucionario Proletario (PRP), a communist splinter faction that ran a joint ticket with the PCV but was much more vocally hostile to the junta.[109]

On 27 October 1946, in contrast with the 5 percent of the population who had voted in previous elections, more than a third of the Venezuelan people went to the polls. The URD and the Communists each garnered around 50,000 votes, and each gained 2 members for their parties in the assembly. Copei elected 19 assembly members with a little less than 190,000 votes. AD, with well over a million votes, elected 137 members of the assembly.[110] While the opposition parties accused the Adecos of employing unfair tactics during the campaign, none of them raised charges of electoral fraud.[111] The ballot was secret, Corrigan informed the State Department, and the election was carried out with relative liberty and correctness on the part of the supervising electoral boards.[112] In a private letter to Braden, Dawson commented on the election's political impact:

> The election results here surprised all of us by the overwhelming majority Acción Democrática received although it was quite clear in advance that it would get a majority, not just a plurality. The poor showing of URD and the Communists just goes to show that, as Haya de la Torre said, a well-organized left-wing party with popular bases in this section of South America leaves little for the international Marxists or other left-of-center groups to work on. COPEI will furnish at least a vocal opposition on the Conservative side and the country is in no danger from reactionary elements as long as reasonable young Caldera is the conservative leader. So far as I can see, Acción Democrática's tremendous majority ensures peace and quiet in Venezuela for some time.[113]

None of us realized a year ago how much executive ability Betancourt had in him, Corrigan reported to the State Department after the elections. Yet his overall assessment was much less sanguine than Dawson's. In large part, this was because he concentrated on the impact of the elections on the Venezuelan military. Most of the military leadership, he noted, came from the Andean state of Táchira, where the victory went to Copei. They were astonished at the way the vote had gone nationally and were afraid that they had created a Frankenstein. For a year they had believed that they had put Rómulo in and could throw him out. Now, with AD's overwhelming victory at the polls, they were not at all confident that even all of the army would follow them in an attempt to override the expressed will of the people. They feared and resented their loss of influence and this, combined with AD's mistakes, created tension and instability.[114]

Betancourt, Corrigan maintained, "might have become a great national leader." Instead, having given in to petty demagoguery and a needless vindictiveness best exemplified in his treatment of López Contreras, he had become the leader of a sector rather than the nation.[115] Over the course of November 1946, as the embassy heard rumors of coups being plotted, Corrigan became increasingly worried. He invited Betancourt to an informal luncheon to discuss the danger. Betancourt told him that the government was aware of everything that was going on and assured him that there was no reason for concern. The government would have no difficulty in maintaining control, and he was in fact going to the country to work on his message to the constitutional convention. His assessment proved to be correct; all that materialized was a local revolt on 11 December 1946 that was quickly put down. Still, Corrigan told the State Department, the judgements of the Tribunal of Civil and Administrative Responsibility had left such strong resentments behind that they constituted a fertile field for the growth of a counterrevolutionary movement.[116] Were López Contreras to lead such a movement—in response to the attempt to smear his name and impoverish him—he would have a solid block of Andean support. This was the last serious obstacle remaining to the success of the October revolution. It would have to be dealt with, either by diplomatic means or civil war, before the Venezuelan political situation could be called stable.[117]

By March 1947, Corrigan could write the State Department that the past fifteen months had been a period of great development for Betancourt whose courage and initiative "have caused me to marvel." Like Assistant Secretary of State Braden, Corrigan commented, Betancourt was convinced that communism could not be successfully combated by reactionaries and that "it must be the task of the liberal-thinking people of the world to defeat Communism." In the event of any trouble with Russia, Betancourt had assured him, the Venezuelan government would be with the United States 100 percent. Its first action in such a case would be to imprison all the active communists in the country as the fifth columnists they were.[118] In a newspaper interview, Betancourt stressed his agreement with Truman's argument—in the speech enunciating the Truman Doctrine—that hunger, misery, and unemployment were the ingredients that gave rise to extremist ideologies. The communists in Venezuela were weak, he suggested, because the Venezuelan people were strongly nationalistic and because the present government had shown a disposition to address the problems of the masses, to satisfy their needs and raise their living standards.[119]

Corrigan agreed that communism was weak in Venezuela and declining in strength. The reds had taken a big tumble during the past year, he declared in a Miami newspaper interview in May 1947, and had "reached the stage where they are just noisy."[120] That the Adecos were in a particularly strong position to do battle with the communists was driven home to many observers later that summer. Interpreting a strike by two communist-dominated transport unions (one for electric car operators and one for autobus operators) as part of a broader effort to gain control of the labor movement, the American embassy was worried over its prospects for success. Rejecting communist demands to join the strike, the AD-dominated union kept the buses running while the police provided protection against communist attacks. Noting that the real question for the future would be whether the AD unions could convince the majority of the workers, including those in communist unions, that they could get more from the employers with less effort than the communists could, the embassy's second secretary, William Krieg, was nevertheless clearly impressed:

> To my mind, all this adds up to the fact that a popularly-supported government with strong roots in the working class is the best instrument for combating Communism. I doubt whether a conservative group in this country would have had the courage to take as strong action against the strikers as AD has. If conservatives did take strong action, they would very probably be faced with a general strike of all labor which not even the use of the Army would be able to beat down.[121]

Arthur Proudfit, the head of Creole Petroleum, told the American embassy that he had found the attitude of the minister of labor, Raúl Leoni, to be very reasonable. This feeling was doubtless mutual as the wages of Venezuela's oil workers had risen between 35 and 50 percent in 1946. Combining salaries and benefits, the oil workers were making between $4,000 and $5,000 a year, which was roughly what their counterparts in the United States were making. Asked by the embassy if he thought there would be any requests for wage increases in 1948 when the oil industry's collective labor contract came up, Proudfit replied in the affirmative. He added that some increase would be justified in view of increasing living costs and increased earnings at least on the part of his company.[122]

Having drafted a new constitution and having seen it enter into effect, the constituent assembly retired and the stage was set for general elections. Corrigan had indicated that he would be interested in a transfer once the transition to constitutional government had been made, and in early November 1947 he became part of the American mission to the United Nations.[123] His replacement, Walter Donnelly, was regarded by Secretary of State George Marshall and others in the State Department "as probably the finest FSO we have."[124] He arrived in Caracas in time to witness the later part of the electoral campaign and Acción Democrática's second landslide.

On 14 December 1947 elections were held in Venezuela for the presidency of the republic, for Congress, and for the state legislatures. Given its poor showing at the last elections, the URD had decided not to run a candidate for president. This probably helped Copei. Its candidate, Rafael Caldera, came in second with around 262,000 votes. AD's candidate, Rómulo Gallegos, won easily with a little more than 871,000 votes. The Communist candidate, Gustavo Machado, received 36,514 votes, or roughly 3 percent.[125] Commenting on the elections in a report to the State Department, Donnelly stressed that they were genuinely free and fair. "There was liberty of the press, radio and speech. While both the Government and the various opposition parties charged that partisan groups disrupted some meetings, the right of assembly was exercised frequently, usually without untoward incidents, in all parts of the Republic; and Acción Democrática was the only Party to officially demand of its members respect for the rights of the opposition." The Venezuelan people had an ample opportunity to hear and decide for themselves, and they had done so with a secret ballot in an atmosphere completely lacking in coercion.[126]

The respect that officials in the State Department had come to have for Acción Democrática was shared by analysts in the Central Intelligence Agency. Since CIA perspectives on Latin America are only beginning to be clarified with the aid of declassified documents, the CIA's report on the Venezuelan elections is worth quoting at length:

> The social and economic progressivism of the revolutionary Junta (to a continuation of which the newly elected Government is firmly committed) has been clearly demonstrated. Acción Democrática's leaders, out of an avowed determination to make AD a "popular" party, have deliberately sought, and won, support from all segments of the population. AD is not, therefore, a strictly working-class party, but rather a coalition of those groups that are seeking to promote the

industrialization of the country, extensive land reforms, better standards of living, health measures and cultural opportunities for the people; and the establishment of a tradition of democratic processes. The Junta's accomplishments in education, housing, in extension of the trade-union movement, in improving working conditions in the country's industrial concerns, in basing taxation on ability to pay, in agrarian reform, and in the promotion of agricultural and pastoral production, attest to the progressive trend in Venezuelan public policy.... Acción Democrática's policies, and its avowed political philosophy as well, look to a rapid advance in Venezuela toward political, economic, and social equality; and its enemies, especially among the elements that governed the country in the past, miss no opportunity to identify it as a "radical" party and as a threat to the status quo. Some go still further, and describe it as a disguised Communist party; but all the evidence available points to the conclusion that (a) it is not only non-Communist but anti-Communist, (b) it is so regarded by the Communists themselves, and (c) it has gone out of its way to alienate any Communist support.... The Acción Democrática does not deserve the Communist label its enemies have sought to fix on it. In fact, the great popular support won by the party in the December elections is another indication that, in the special conditions of Latin American politics, an active non-Communist progressive party constitutes one of the best guarantees against a strong Communist movement. In foreign policy the AD is pro-US and anti-USSR.[127]

Hearing that Betancourt might have a legal problem visiting the United States after he left office—because of his membership in the Costa Rican Communist Party more than a dozen years earlier—Donnelly was outraged. "Evidence that Betancourt is anti-Communist," he telegraphed the State Department, "is overwhelming. He has clearly demonstrated that he not only believes in but practices democracy and that he is friendly to US and American interests in Venezuela."[128] The visa was provided without difficulties, but the issue of Betancourt's communist background would reappear to cause trouble in later years.[129]

On leaving office, Betancourt complied with one of the anticorruption laws his government had established, filing a sworn statement estimating his net assets at 1,143.60 *bolívares* (roughly $380). This represented a considerable drop from the meager 7,500 *bolívares* he had listed on entering office. The American embassy in Caracas noted that he had lived in a modest house on a modest scale during his presidency and had used the presidential palace only for entertaining. There was no hint that he had hidden assets. Considering the temptations he had withstood, one State Department official commented, his conduct had been remarkable. "He may reasonably depend on being supported in his old age by the government, provided that all goes well."[130]

The Overthrow of Venezuelan Democracy

Even more than Betancourt's junta, Gallegos's government was looked upon with favor by American officials. It had been freely and overwhelmingly elected and—according to a CIA estimate of May 1948—had shown increasing concern over the potentialities of the Soviet threat and had moved more and more into the American orbit. Communist control of organized labor was decreasing, the estimate noted, and Acción Democrática appeared "determined to remove the Communists from the labor field in general and from the petroleum industry in particular."[131]

In July 1948, Gallegos spent two weeks in the United States as Truman's guest. Celebrating American independence on the fourth of July and Venezuelan independence on the fifth, Truman and Gallegos traveled by train together to Bolivar, Missouri, where they dedicated a statue of Simón Bolívar. "We are especially honored that this statue is presented by the distinguished leader of the Venezuelan people," Truman declared. "I am proud to be associated with the great statesman who today directs the destinies of Venezuela with the same lofty ideals that motivated the father of his country."[132] The visit was an outstanding success, Ambassador Walter Donnelly reported. Gallegos had been greatly impressed with American social, economic, and political accomplishments. "In brief, his visit to the United States confirmed his faith in democratic principles and his determination to strengthen them in Venezuela. It is apparent that he is now convinced that the progress of Venezuela must rest upon free enterprise, free initiative, improved educational facilities and work."[133]

The State Department was well aware that Venezuela's democracy had significant internal opponents, but it seriously underestimated their strength and their prospects. A State Department memo sent to the White House before Gallegos's visit noted that rightist civilian elements were seeking to overthrow his government. They had received moral and perhaps material assistance from Trujillo and might be expected to collaborate with a military revolt should one be attempted. "Since these elements commanded only about one fifth of the popular vote in the elections of

1946 and 1947 and since most of the population supports the present Government with more devotion than is usual in Latin American countries, a serious revolutionary outbreak—should it occur—would be expected to fail eventually, but only after considerable bloodshed."[134] This analysis took insufficient account of anti-Adeco sentiment within the Venezuelan army and compounded its error by assuming that the Venezuelan minister of defense, Carlos Delgado Chalbaud, would put his loyalty to Gallegos ahead of his loyalty to the army.

Growing resentment within the Venezuelan military at its diminishing political influence under a freely elected administration was apparent within a few months of Gallegos's inauguration in February 1948.[135] It added substantially to existing resentment over various Acción Democrática policies such as the sanctions applied to members of previous governments found guilty of corruption and the encouragement of union organization.[136] This animosity was skillfully cultivated by Army Chief of Staff Marcos Pérez Jiménez and by Assistant Chief of Staff Luis Felipe Llovera Páez,[137] both of whom, it should be stressed, were seen by the American embassy as unfriendly to the United States.[138] The subversive movement also benefited greatly from the strident anti-Adeco rhetoric of Copei and the URD and from Manuel Odría's success in seizing power in Peru in late October. At the height of the crisis, on 20 November, the American military attaché had an interview with Delgado Chalbaud, who specifically "blamed the tension on the desire of the younger officers to have a larger role in the Government and who were encouraged in their desire by the recent coup in Peru and by the constant criticism of the Government by the opposition."[139]

In late December 1948 the third secretary of the American embassy, John Thompson, prepared a well-informed summary of the overthrow of Venezuelan democracy the month before. The crisis, he suggested, had begun on 16 November when Pérez Jiménez met with Delgado Chalbaud and informed him that the armed forces would no longer support a government under the control of Acción Democrática and that they would no longer support him as minister of defense if he continued to support the Gallegos government as it was constituted. At that point, the demands of the military subversives who sided with Pérez Jiménez appear to have included exiling Rómulo Betancourt and forming a coalition government in which the Adecos could retain four posts with the rest filled by "independents" and army men. On learning of their demands from Delgado Chalbaud, Gallegos requested a meeting with these officers. At noon on 17

November they presented him with a list of the specific changes in the cabinet and the state governorships upon which they would insist. By this point, they were reportedly willing to tolerate only one Adeco at the cabinet level: Juan Pablo Pérez Alfonso, the minister of development. Gallegos replied that while he recognized certain defects in the government, he was the freely elected head of the government and the commander in chief, and he would not tolerate their interference in his administration. To this the commander of the La Guaira garrison replied that the army wanted no more words, but action. The meeting adjourned with both sides apparently feeling that they had made their positions clear.[140]

On 18 November 1948, senior Adeco party leaders met with the commander of the Maracay garrison, Jesus Manuel Gámez Arellano. Gámez told them that he was loyal to Gallegos. Later in the day he informed them that the chief of services of the armed forces, José Leon Rangel, had sought to persuade him to change sides, but that if necessary he would march on Caracas to the rescue of the government. This appears to have been the first information the Adecos had that Rangel, a potential rival of Pérez Jiménez, had become disloyal. Throughout the day, Delgado Chalbaud argued that a solution should be sought through negotiations rather than bloodshed. Pérez Jiménez and others pressed for more immediate action. They agreed to give Gallegos some time in which to act; otherwise, they would seize control. This message was conveyed to Gallegos on the evening of 18 November. The following morning, a pro-Adeco paper, *Ultimas Noticias*, carried a warning that the support of 300,000 organized industrial and farm workers was necessary to govern Venezuela. At a meeting between Gallegos and most of the senior military leadership, Gallegos indicated that he would accept suggestions for improvements in his administration, but not under the threat or use of force. The military leaders agreed to try to calm down the more hotheaded officers, and Pérez Jiménez, finding himself in the minority, agreed to this retreat from previous demands.[141]

On 20 November 1948, Gallegos met with his cabinet and discussed the army's "petitions." No changes were made in the cabinet, and the only announcement made was a decree suspending constitutional guarantees because of an undefined "state of alarm." For junior officers who had been expecting a victory for their position by means of violence, and for those senior officers who had been hoping for some sort of compromise, this was a source of frustration. Over the course of the next two days, military frustration grew as changes in the government were not forthcoming. Before noon on 23 November the secretary of the presidency, Gonzalo Barrios, announced that the cabinet had resigned. No names for a new cabinet were provided, however, and although it was frequently announced that Gallegos would speak to the nation, he failed to do so. That afternoon, in an effort to strengthen the government's position, Lieutenant Colonel Mario Vargas returned to Venezuela from the United States where he had been undergoing treatment for tuberculosis. He was unable to significantly alter army opinion, which was turning against a negotiated settlement.[142]

Early on the morning of 24 November, Valmore Rodríguez, Ricardo Montilla, Luis Lander, and other Adeco leaders went to Maracay to set up a provisional government in the event of a coup. Rumors had circulated for some time that Acción Democrática was stockpiling weapons and that a general strike would soon take place. These rumors would later be presented by apologists for the military as threats indicating that Gallegos had lost control to party militants and thus forced them to take action. By early afternoon, troops had moved to seize control of the Miraflores Palace, the various ministries, and the radio stations. Finding his Maracay garrison unwilling to support him in a defense of the government, Lieutenant Colonel Gámez resigned. By nightfall, aside from some minor armed skirmishes, a few student and union protests, and some clandestine radio broadcasts, Venezuelan democracy had been crushed. A military junta consisting of Delgado Chalbaud, Pérez Jiménez, and Llovera Páez was established and the Constitution of 1936 was declared the law of the land.[143] In succeeding months, members of both major opposition parties joined in the new government.[144] The Venezuelan Communist Party also remained legal and continued to function.[145]

Coming so soon after the Peruvian coup—and within three days of the American recognition of the Odría dictatorship—the Venezuelan coup generated considerable disappointment with American policy in liberal and democratic circles in Latin America.[146] Disappointment threatened to turn into hostility when Gallegos charged, on his arrival in Havana, that the American military attaché, Edward Adams, had acted as a "counselor or cooperator" for the coup plotters and suggested that American oil companies had also been involved.[147] Gallegos's charges greatly worried Donnelly for their potential influence on Latin American public opinion and on Acción Democrática, which he thought would probably regain power at some point in the future.[148] At his suggestion, a special delegate was dispatched by Truman to meet with Gallegos and explain that Adams's presence among Venezuelan army officers on the day of the coup was accidental, that Adams had not intervened but only sought information, that no evidence had been found indicating intervention by American officials or American interests, and that the United States had always been friendly toward his administration.[149] Gallegos accepted these explanations publicly in a statement to the press and also in a personal letter to Truman.[150]

Gallegos was apparently unaware of the activities of another American, Robert Brinsmade, and no attempt was made to inform him of Brinsmade's conduct.[151] A private American lawyer in Caracas, Brinsmade boasted to Donnelly of having provided the coup plotters with advice and assistance on the day of the coup.[152] He was reprimanded for damaging America's reputation for neutrality in internal Venezuelan politics and informed that the State Department could not undertake to protect him in the event that a subsequent Venezuelan government brought charges against him for his activities.[153] Donnelly thought that Gallegos might consider Brinsmade to be an agent of the oil industry. He was convinced that this was not the case and that the oil companies had remained neutral.[154] He was certainly correct that the larger oil companies like Creole had established a good working relationship with the Adecos and recognized that their long-term interests would be threatened by forsaking political neutrality.[155] Gallegos had, in fact, no information indicating oil company involvement. He had merely suspected that some of the companies were hostile to Acción Democrática and might have acted on that hostility.[156] At least as far as one of the smaller companies was concerned, he was undoubtedly correct in his assumption as to their attitude. In a letter to George Marshall of 5 December 1948, the chairman of the stockholder committee of Pantepec Oil, William F. Buckley, Sr., left no doubt of the hatred that he and his colleagues had for the Adecos.

> The Betancourt-Gallegos regime received an estimated $378,000,000 for oil royalties alone for the period January 31, 1946 to the present time. Revenue from oil taxes, other than royalties, and other taxes, undoubtedly amounted to three times this figure. Only a small part of this income has been accounted for, and it is generally believed in Venezuela that the difference has been used to subsidize scurrilously anti-American newspapers (notably El Nacional of Caracas, official party organ of the Accion Democratica Party), pro-Moscow propaganda in the balance of Latin America and, in direct violation of the Pan-American Pact, in armed attempts to unseat the governments of Nicaragua and Santo Domingo, and to strengthen irresponsible Red-dominated labor unions. In short, Betancourt, a professed ex-Com-

munist, and his puppet, Gallegos, have used the vast dollar resources of the country which they controlled to further Russian communistic interests in the Western Hemisphere, and they have forced American capital to provide the money for this anti-American campaign. . . . The new government, in my opinion, has the backing of those Venezuelans who believe in free enterprise and in the old doctrine of working for a living.[157]

A brief digression is in order at this point with regard to the American military attachés in Latin America. Some of them held views of the world that bore roughly the same relation to reality as Buckley's. Although it is not unreasonable to suspect those with such a warped perspective of engaging in antidemocratic activities, it must be stressed that no evidence has yet come to light to justify such suspicions. In general, the military attachés appear to have recognized their subordination to civilian authority and followed the orders of the ambassador and the State Department. They were often poorly trained, however, lacking fluency in the local language, and prone to accept the opinions of their local sources of information.[158] Nowhere were their weaknesses more painfully apparent during the Truman years than in Venezuela. Within a few weeks of the October coup that brought Betancourt's junta to power in 1945, the assistant military attaché in Caracas was developing a lengthy argument from "authoritative" sources that this change of government was merely part of a larger conspiracy in which Betancourt and the others were planning to turn power over to López Contreras. "This masterpiece of untrammeled imagination," Ambassador Frank Corrigan commented to the State Department, "does not even have the merit of as much logic as is to be found in current paper-backed detective stories."[159] Within a few months, Corrigan and Allan Dawson, the counselor of the embassy, would be nostalgic for such relatively mild errors. By January 1946, Dawson was referring to the reporting of the military attaché as "typical of his hysteria, lack of judgement and failure to consult Embassy in time of stress," and urging the State Department to ignore it.[160] By early February, he was suggesting to Corrigan that it was time to get the military attaché office cleaned out. The military attaché and his assistant had just put out a thirteen-page report devoted to "proving" that Betancourt and his colleagues were really communists, that their unfriendliness to the Communist Party was just a ruse, and that they were embarked on a deep plot to communize the country. Plans should be made, the MA had advised, in case counterrevolutionary activity failed to resolve the matter without American action.[161]

While the personnel of the military mission were replaced, the problem of poor military intelligence persisted as the military air attaché adopted a similar line.[162] He, too, was replaced. Edward Adams, ironically enough, was an improvement over some of his predecessors. Nor was the problem of poor intelligence restricted to the military mission in Caracas. In Washington, army intelligence dissented from the CIA's enthusiastic assessment of Acción Democrática and the Venezuelan elections of 1947. It suggested that the Adecos might cooperate with the communists in the future if it seemed expedient, that the junta had not been democratic in its orientation, that it had accomplished little in the way of social and economic reform except on paper, that AD's nationalism might pose a threat to American interests, and that its pro-U.S. policy represented expediency.[163] It was not until May 1948 that army intelligence was willing to join with the rest of the intelligence community in a strongly favorable assessment of AD and its intentions.[164]

Even before becoming assistant secretary of state in September 1945, Spruille Braden had sought to deal decisively with the problem of poor military intelligence. He suggested to Nelson Rockefeller that reporting by military and naval attachés "be limited to the technical subjects on which they are competent and they should *not* report on political, economic, social and other problems extraneous to their training, experience and usually their abilities."[165] While Braden did not succeed in that endeavor, he did generally succeed in making it clear who was in charge.[166] This is evident in a report Dawson sent Corrigan after attending a conference of military attachés and other intelligence officers for Latin America. Predicting that the MAs would be more cooperative than in the past, Dawson observed that "it has been made clear to them innumerable times by their own people that the Ambassador or Charge d'Affaires ad interim is the chief representative of the United States in the country in which stationed, the coordinator of *all* activities and, thus, the boss."[167]

In a series of memos to the State Department on this conference, Dawson praised its work and suggested ways of building upon it. While the final report was not authoritative, he observed, a copy might be sent to the ambassadors in the region, where it could prove useful "in dealing with their Military Attachés if the latter tend to get off the reservation ideologically."[168] The newer MAs seemed to him much more professional than the older ones. They were delighted to restrict their political reporting and follow the embassy's lead.[169] As an indication of this progress, Dawson noted that most of the MAs appeared to largely reflect the views of their ambassadors.[170] In the conference's final report, he was particularly pleased with the explicit recognition that there had been no widespread move to reduce military forces in Latin America with the end of the war. He expected that this would be useful in future discussions with army representatives on the need for armaments limitation. He was also pleased with the political section, where, "contrary to some military thought, a clear distinction is made between communism and the native socialistic parties which are friendly to the United States, with it being stated clearly that the latter have grown more than the former."[171]

While evidence has yet to come to light suggesting that American military or business interests played a significant role in overthrowing the Gallegos government—or any other government in Latin America during the Truman years—the fact remains that American policy did nothing to help preserve Venezuelan democracy. Although Donnelly appears to have genuinely sympathized with the democratic side in the struggle, he prided himself on having maintained political neutrality with regard to an internal Venezuelan dispute. He was oblivious, as Bethany Aram has observed, to any role he might have played in preventing a coup.[172] He did not engage in any calculation as to how seriously American interests would be adversely affected by a military seizure of power, he simply took it for granted that he should not look for ways to tip the scales in the struggle in an effort to avoid such an outcome. As a result, he overlooked a number of opportunities in which a mild American intervention might have helped to do just that.

A few weeks after the coup, Donnelly met with Rómulo Betancourt in the Colombian embassy in Caracas. Betancourt stated emphatically that he and Acción Democrática were satisfied that the American oil companies and the United States government had maintained a neutral position throughout the crisis. Gallegos, he suggested, had not believed that the military would dare to overthrow him and had been taken by surprise.[173] In hindsight, it certainly seems as though Gallegos could have preserved Venezuelan democracy either by timely concessions to strengthen the hand of the more moderate elements in the Venezuelan military or by mobilizing AD's strength for a showdown that would have established his authority over the military and enabled him to exile the more important military subversives. The latter course would have risked civil war and the former would have risked inciting those one was attempting to appease, but in both cases the danger of such eventualities seems fairly small. Had Donnelly met with Gallegos at any point during the crisis and expressed his concern over the seriousness of the situation—as Frank Corrigan had done with Betancourt in December 1946—that action alone might have helped to awaken Gallegos to the need to act. With a little more spunk, Donnelly could have offered to make any public or private statements of support for Venezuelan democracy that Gallegos would have considered useful. A clear public statement hailing Venezuela's democratic progress and praising peaceful political change—along the lines of Adolf Berle's speech in Brazil in September 1945—might have contributed significantly to the survival of Venezuela's democratic opening.[174]

In September 1948, more than two months before the crisis broke, American embassy officials were already aware that Pérez Jiménez appeared to have subversive intentions and that Gallegos had seriously considered replacing him with Jesus Manuel Gámez, the commander of the Maracay garrison. Delgado Chalbaud's reluctance to move against Pérez Jiménez had been reported as the reason why Gallegos had not done so.[175] On the basis of the American interest in the program of arms standardization for the hemisphere—to which Pérez Jiménez was opposed—American officials might have urged Delgado Chalbaud to consider the potential benefit to American-Venezuelan relations of a different army chief of staff.[176] This was not done for the same reason that an effort was not made on behalf of Venezuelan democracy during the crisis: a belief in the wisdom of avoiding intervention where it was possible to do so.

"It is apparent that some changes are in the offing," Donnelly reported at the outset of the crisis on 17 November 1948, "and I fear the tendency is to move away from democracy in the direction of restrictions on the liberties of the people. I hope this does not transpire because Venezuela is trying to make democracy work for the first time in its history."[177] Donnelly clearly sympathized with the cause of Venezuelan democracy, but he considered himself powerless to act on its behalf. The peoples of Latin America themselves, he argued in early 1949, were struggling for freedom and would ultimately obtain it. "Their efforts in this direction must be free of outside assistance; the people must settle their own domestic affairs in their own way."[178]

Embracing a nationalist definition of self-determination, Donnelly could convince himself that the Venezuelan people as a whole had somehow chosen to go along as a subversive group of soldiers became dominant in the army and then used that power base of a few hundred armed men to overturn the freely expressed judgement of more than two-thirds of the Venezuelan electorate. This was not the only definition of self-determination an American ambassador could have adopted. In choosing to adopt it, Donnelly does not appear to have considered alternatives or made any calculation as to what the consequences of different political outcomes in Venezuela would be for American interests. He simply took it for granted that he was pursuing a course that would, in the long run, best serve the interests of everyone involved. Nor was there any reason for him to doubt that the United States could probably come to a tolerable arrangement with almost any Venezuelan political faction that might come to power.

Under a more optimistic scenario—in which American officials successfully intervened on behalf of Venezuelan democracy—basic weaknesses in Venezuela's democratic opening would still have remained. Some sort of accommodation between AD and the other major civilian political parties would have to have been reached for the situation to stabilize. If a showdown with the subversive elements in the Venezuelan military had been postponed, sooner or later it probably would have been necessary. That these were not insurmountable obstacles is shown by the history of Venezuela after 1958. A persuasive argument can be made that a decade of dictatorial misrule made it easier for the civilian political parties and the more professional elements within the military to agree on the value of compromise, civility, and democratic "rules of the game."[179] But aside from this basic shift, there is little reason why Venezuelan democracy could not have been consolidated in the late 1940s instead of the early 1960s. Neither the Cold War, anticommunism, capitalism, American hegemony, American ideology, nor Venezuelan economic dependency were significant obstacles to such a consolidation. All of these factors were as important in 1958 as they were in 1948. As far as democratic political development in Venezuela was concerned, they were simply not very important. The factors of decisive importance were Venezuelan and largely those of political leadership. By helping to tip the scales to the Adecos' side during the crisis in November 1948, a different American policy might—at most—have helped to give Venezuela's democrats another chance.

Victory in Costa Rica

The officials who formulated American policy toward Ecuador in 1947 and Costa Rica in 1948, were less optimistic than those who had formulated American policy toward Cuba in 1944 and Brazil in 1945. But they continued to believe that American and Latin American interests could be harmonized and that an American policy that combined nonintervention and democratic solidarity would help to achieve this result. They continued to consider this more important than the short-term maximization of exclusively American interests. This is particularly apparent in the case of Ecuador, where a would-be dictator was denied diplomatic recognition in spite of the fact that he was seen as much more pro-American than the government he had overthrown and, at least initially, appeared in firm control of the machinery of government. It is also evident in the case of Costa Rica, where the American embassy was unwilling to actively encourage a victory by force of arms in the civil war—even one that promised to eliminate communist influence from the Costa Rican government. Instead, throughout the crisis, the American ambassador championed a negotiated settlement among all of the contending parties designed to preserve constitutional institutions and avoid bloodshed.

In both Ecuador and Costa Rica, American policy contributed significantly to the success of the democratic cause. In Ecuador, an American and inter-American denial of diplomatic recognition of the new government helped encourage constitutionalist forces to launch a successful counterattack. In Costa Rica, American and inter-American diplomatic pressure helped to prevent Anastasio Somoza from intervening on the government's side. By refusing to allow either side to purchase weapons in the United States, and by encouraging other states to adopt this position, American policy also helped to weaken the Costa Rican government's position and contribute to the victory of an insurgency determined to restore Costa Rican democracy.

Tipping the Balance in Ecuador

Ecuador's dramatic military defeat by Peru in 1941, and the country's loss of most of its Amazonian provinces in the peace settlement that followed, greatly discredited the administration of President Carlos Arroyo del Río. In May 1944 he was overthrown. A political coalition that included Communists, Conservatives, Socialists, dissident members of the Liberal Party, and the dominant sector of the military then brought José María Velasco Ibarra to the presidency. A constituent assembly was elected in July 1944 to draft a new constitution, and it, in turn, chose Velasco as constitutional president. But tension between Velasco and the dominant liberal and leftist sectors of the assembly soon developed. In May 1946, he repudiated the Constitution of 1945 and reestablished the Constitution of 1906. He then called for elections to a new constituent assembly. These elections were boycotted by the Liberals and the Left. As a result, the Conservatives won a national election for the first time in more than half a century. In the opinion of the American embassy, only military hostility to the idea of a Conservative presidency, and direct military pressure on the assembly, were responsible for the assembly's decision to allow Velasco to serve out the rest of his term. It was against this background that Velasco agreed to hold elections for a regular national congress in June 1947.[1]

Three major parties contended in the congressional elections of June 1947: the Conservatives, the Liberal-Radicals, and the National Civil Democratic Movement, a new party organized by moderate liberals and socialists and led by the former Ecuadoran ambassador to Washington, Galo Plaza Lasso.[2] The predominance of the latter two parties in the new Congress appears to have led Velasco to seek to bolster his support within the military by placing Colonel Carlos Macheno in charge of the Ministry of Defense. Whatever Velasco's intention, this was a mistake. On the evening of 23 August 1947, Macheno promoted himself to the presidency by means of a coup d'état. Velasco resigned and was put on a plane to Colombia. Denying any personal ambition, Macheno stated that he would call a meeting of all the political parties to designate a new cabinet.[3]

In some ways, Macheno at first appeared impressive to the American embassy. His coup had won solid military support and been conducted quickly and efficiently. Government employees were continuing at their posts, and the new regime appeared to thoroughly control the machinery of government. There was no active opposition to be seen and the public attitude appeared one of general acceptance. Macheno had promised to uphold all of Ecuador's international agreements and was reported as saying that the Communists would have no part in his government. He was "believed to be very well disposed toward the US considerably more so than was Velasco Ibarra."[4]

There were rumors in Ecuador that the United States would offer Macheno early recognition. If it had done so, his position would probably have been securely established, at least for the short term. Macheno's opponents would have been discouraged by such recognition, and Ecuador's representatives would not have been turned away by the Rio Conference. But American policy was not designed to pursue a short-term maximization of exclusively American interests. Nor was John Simmons, the American ambassador to Ecuador, inclined to such a course. Simmons had been a strong supporter of the Braden memorandum, and he urged the State Department to consider the weaknesses as well as the strengths in Macheno's case:

> As to the point, which he is now stressing, that after all Velasco did resign and did hand the presidential power over to him, my observation is (1) that he only resigned under strong compulsion and (2) that the decision as to who should succeed him was not his to make but rather should be a constitutional question. He unquestionably has by his action disavowed the Congress recently elected by free expression of opinion of the people. Summing up, I believe that recognition of the Macheno regime, if based upon the three criteria now usually observed under international law and under the policy of the U.S. would have considerable justification but that, if the manner of his coming into power should be an important consideration, his case would obviously be greatly weakened.[5]

On 26 August 1947, Simmons noted the publication in the Ecuadoran press of a decree from Mariano Suarez Veintimilla, the constitutional vice president. In this decree, Suarez claimed presidential authority under Article 103 of the Constitution and ordered all government employees to remain in their positions. His effort to challenge Macheno appeared to Simmons to be "foredoomed to failure."[6] Suarez was a member of the Conservative Party and had been elected by a constituent assembly boycotted by the other major parties. His claim to represent the Constitution

of 1946 did not carry the sanction of tradition or much solid backing beyond his own party. Nevertheless, he quickly won strong and public support in his endeavor from Galo Plaza. In addition to representing moderate
liberals and socialists, Plaza was a former minister of defense who had retained good contacts within the armed forces. In an interview in *El
Comercio,* he suggested that Suarez's partisan affiliation was hardly relevant in the face of the danger of a military dictatorship. Everyone, including the army, had to realize that a return to constitutionality was essential.
Enemies of militarism constituted a majority within the armed forces,
Plaza continued, and were aware of their sacred mission. They were also
aware of the danger to the army's prestige that past experience had shown
was inherent in any effort to "save the country." What was necessary was
the immediate transfer of supreme power to the vice president and the
restoration of constitutional procedure. "This step should be taken before
the termination of the Rio Conference, not only in order to save our international prestige as a civilized and democratic country, but also in order
that the solution of problems vital for Ecuador may be discussed."[7]

The disqualification of Ecuador's delegation to the Rio Conference, and
the conference's refusal to allow the Ecuadoran foreign minister to sign
the final document, was a major blow to Macheno's regime.[8] By 30 August
1947, Simmons could note that while the country was superficially calm,
latent animosity toward Macheno was widespread. There was strong resentment that in the eyes of the hemisphere Ecuador had been placed in
the same category as Nicaragua.[9] Over the next few days military forces
in Riobamba, Guayaquil, and other cities launched a constitutionalist
counterrevolt. Turning down a last-minute offer of communist support,
Mancheno decided that additional resistance was futile and on 3 September accepted asylum at the Venezuelan embassy.[10] On the same day, Suarez
Veintimilla established his government at Riobamba, called for a special
session of the newly elected Congress to be held on 15 September, and
promised to resign at this session in favor of a candidate chosen by the
Congress. Constitutionalism had assumed a new importance in Ecuador,
Simmons reported to Washington. "It has given them something to grasp,
something which redeems their national shame at the circumstances and
timing of the abortive Macheno coup d'etat."[11]

By a vote of 103 to 3, Carlos Julio Arosemena, a compromise candidate
from Guayaquil, was chosen by Ecuador's Congress to serve as president
until succeeded by the victor of the elections scheduled for June 1948.[12]
Although beginning with goodwill among the major civilian political par-

ties, Arosemena faced opposition within the military. The day after his election, Simmons reported that a large group of army officers was still loyal to Macheno.[13] Wishing to aid the new government, the State Department determined that "the most friendly and helpful action it could take" would be notifying the other American republics that it was resuming normal diplomatic relations with Quito. This it did on 18 September 1947.[14]

The victor in the Ecuadoran presidential elections of 1948 was Galo Plaza, a man who defined himself politically "as a leftist, as far as that is synonymous with progress, justice and liberty." He stressed that his administration would seek to solve problems within a spirit of "harmonious conciliation."[15] Liberals and socialists were predominant in his cabinet, and he actively sought to encourage the growth of a new export industry, bananas. He was the first Ecuadoran president in many decades to both enter and leave office as the result of a competitive electoral process.[16]

The Crisis of Costa Rican Democracy

The first half of 1948 was a high-water mark for the democratic left. The newly inaugurated Venezuelan government of Rómulo Gallegos was preparing an agrarian-reform law. The Peruvian Confederation of Labor was sponsoring a continental labor congress from which the region's principal labor federation was to emerge. In Cuba, the former minister of labor, Carlos Prío Socarrás, was elected president. Guatemalan president Juan José Arévalo was strongly sympathetic to the cause of the democratic left internationally and was popular even if his supporters were not organized into a movement analogous to the Cuban Auténticos, the Peruvian Apristas, or the Venezuelan Adecos. Much the same could be said of Ecuador's Galo Plaza. In Uruguay, President Luis Batlle Berres had his political base in the Colorado Party, one of the oldest parties of the democratic left. Chilean president Gabriel González Videla had recently repudiated an alliance with the Chilean Communist Party and even pushed legislation through the Chilean Parliament outlawing it. He was increasingly supportive of the democratic left and before the end of his term would oversee legislation extending suffrage to women. Puerto Ricans, recently granted the right to elect their own governor, were anticipating a victory for Luis Muñoz Marín and the Partido Popular Democrático.[17]

Against this background, the breakdown of democracy in Costa Rica was particularly striking. Yet the timing of the institutional crisis worked to the advantage of Costa Rica's democrats in three key ways: (1) the democratic left and its allies were in a position to provide decisive assistance; (2) a de facto government in Nicaragua, seeking to gain recognition, was more susceptible to pressure not to interfere than it would otherwise have been; and (3) the coincidence of the crisis and the Bogotá Conference provided additional means for discouraging Nicaraguan intervention.

American policy toward Costa Rica during the crisis—at least the policy of the State Department—was shaped by internally contradictory desires to avoid intervention, to help preserve Costa Rican democratic institutions, to discourage a regional escalation of the conflict, and to encourage the elimination of communist influence in the Costa Rican government.[18] At first glance, the American ambassador to San José at the time would not appear well suited to such a task. Nathaniel "Pen" Davis had no background in Latin America and would rather have been assigned to Panama, which he considered "preferable to Costa Rica in every way except climatically."[19] On numerous occasions, however, he was willing to risk his life crossing enemy lines in pursuit of a negotiated settlement that he hoped would avoid bloodshed and preserve the Costa Rican Constitution. He was not an unbiased mediator, but his biases were not incompatible with successful mediation given the local correlation of forces. He was convinced that an extraconstitutional solution to the extreme polarization of Costa Rican politics, even one that eliminated communist influence in the government, might do more harm than good.

> [A] negotiated settlement, genuinely acceptable to opposition and Republicano Nacional leaders and deputies, offers the nearest approach to serving the best interests of the United States; it being assumed that to be acceptable to both parties such a settlement would have to include some restraint on private political armies—specifically the Vanguardia shock brigades. Whether or not such a settlement is currently possible cannot be stated with any assurance. But as of the moment, this much seems clear: A settlement imposed by force of arms through victory of either side will be an unstable one boding no good for Costa Rica or, consequently, in the long run for us.[20]

In the end, an extraconstitutional solution proved enormously beneficial to Costa Rica and advantageous to the United States as well. But while Davis was mistaken in his assessment, and while events did not follow the course he preferred, the civility of his position was genuine and his efforts did help the cause of Costa Rican democracy. They helped to bring about a negotiated surrender that averted prolonged fighting over San José and

facilitated the transfer of power to a group of reformers who were determined to restore Costa Rican democracy and more securely establish its
foundations. Had this victory been imposed after bloody street fighting in
the capital city, the restoration of Costa Rican democracy might well have
been more difficult.

The polarization of traditionally civil Costa Rican politics can be traced
back to the administration of Rafael Ángel Calderón Guardia. Chosen by
President León Cortés Castro to be his successor, Calderón soon demonstrated his independence and his willingness to break with old patterns.
From 1940 to 1944 he introduced important labor and social legislation to
Costa Rica with the support of Archbishop Victor Sanabria Martínez,
brought the Costa Rican Communist Party into alliance with his National
Republican Party, and engaged in considerable corruption and electoral
fraud.[21]

Calderón chose to ally himself with the Communist Party, which had
been under the leadership of Manuel Mora Valverde since its foundation
in the early 1930s. The party had changed its name several times before
finally coming to be known as the Popular Vanguard Party (PVP), but
there is no indication that its basic ideology was much different from what
it had been when Rómulo Betancourt was a member of its inner circle.[22] To
the alliance of Mora's and Calderón's parties, the Victory Bloc, the PVP
brought solid and well-organized support, particularly among Costa Rican
trade unionists. During the fighting in 1948, its forces would come to constitute, according to one estimate, "some 70 percent of the police and
army."[23] But Mora also provided the extremely heterogeneous opposition
with a convenient target upon which they could all agree. This opposition
included elements of the traditional elite opposed to social reform and social reform advocates such as Father Benjamin Núñez, the head of the Rerum Novarum labor federation. It included the young activists of the Center for the Study of National Problems, who were introducing the country
to Aprista ideas, and many others, such as Otilio Ulate Blanco, a prominent
editor and publisher, who were principally concerned with a restoration of
electoral honesty.[24] After 8 July 1942, it also included José Figueres Ferrer.

Figueres was a progressive farmer who had lived and studied in the
United States and married an American. On 4 July 1942 he was horrified
by six hours of rioting and looting in downtown San José. Two days earlier
a Nazi U-boat had sunk the *San Pablo*, a Costa Rican ship, and the polit-
buro of the PVP had adopted as its slogan "An eye for an eye and a tooth
for a tooth." "The country is full of traitors," it declared. "The fifth column

moves with cunning and energy. These traitors ought to be smashed by the people without pity or delay." At a demonstration organized for 4 July, twenty thousand protesters were given an opportunity to do their part by sacking the businesses of Costa Ricans of Italian and German ancestry and their presumed collaborators. Mora and Calderón both addressed the crowd and made no effort to calm it. In all, 76 persons were injured and 123 buildings were damaged.[25]

Purchasing airtime to make his views known, Figueres addressed the country in a live radio broadcast on 8 July 1942. He bitterly condemned the government for failing to maintain public order. The worst form of sabotage, he argued, was incompetence. The president had spoken at the demonstration in good faith, but he had shown an absolute lack of practical foresight. All property in a period of wartime emergency was public property, and this was especially true of any enemy property. The rioters had destroyed more public property than the U-boat that sank the *San Pablo*. It was said that the government had been obliged to embrace the Communist Party because it had been abandoned by the ruling classes and other groups. Perhaps it had been abandoned. That was no excuse for playing politics instead of governing. If the government was in the hands of the Communist Party, and if that party thought it had to satisfy roguish and thoughtless rabbles, "we arrive at the sad conclusion that this administration has handed the country over to the mob that sacked the capital on the night of July fourth." Prevented from finishing his address by the police who had arrived to arrest him, Figueres had just enough time to offer a closing line: "What the government should do is, get out!" Overnight this speech, and his subsequent exile, made Figueres a national figure in Costa Rican politics.[26]

In exile Figueres authored an essay, "Palabras gastadas," to further clarify where he stood. The version of democratic socialism that he championed in this essay particularly endeared him to the young activists of the Center for the Study of National Problems. What was needed, he suggested, was something better than a capitalism that did not provide milk for all and a class struggle that would simply kill the cow. He offered no practical alternatives—beyond insisting that it would require a democratic political context—but he made it clear in subsequent articles that he favored taking advantage of the world market while simultaneously using the government to promote the general welfare. If Costa Ricans could produce greater wealth from coffee than from wheat, he argued in one of these articles, then they should produce coffee and import wheat. To clear land for a small plot of corn, or *milpa*, would destroy more wealth than a *milpa* could possibly produce. Instead, money should be invested in the most profitable sectors of the economy and the proceeds used to pay for needed goods and services.[27]

Since Calderón was prohibited by the Constitution from succeeding himself, he chose Teodoro Picado Michalski to be his successor and helped to insure his election. During the campaign the PVP's shock brigades attacked opposition newspapers and radio stations and broke up opposition rallies. On the day of the election—the "darkest day in the history of Costa Rica," according to Figueres—the government went so far as to stuff and steal ballot boxes.[28] Picado acknowledged to the American ambassador to San José, Hallett Johnson, that he had been the beneficiary of electoral fraud, but he also expressed considerable remorse and a desire to make amends. He told Johnson that while he "came in by the window," he wished to "go out by the door."[29]

The 1946 congressional elections generated additional charges of electoral fraud and helped the diverse opposition to unify around Otilio Ulate as a candidate for the 1948 elections. A twelve-day general strike in the summer of 1947 won an agreement from Picado to a "Pact of Honor" to insure the integrity of these elections. Signed by Picado, Calderón, and Ulate, it authorized the National Electoral Tribunal to investigate electoral irregularities and, if necessary, to remove culpable public officials. Each of the parties agreed to accept as definitive and beyond appeal the decision of the electoral tribunal as to who had won the elections. While these developments were encouraging to many in the opposition, Figueres was convinced that they would not be enough to prevent Calderón from trying to steal his way back into the presidency. He thought that an armed uprising would be necessary and was determined to be ready to lead it.[30]

Figueres needed an arsenal. The failure of the Cayo Confites expedition against Trujillo in the summer of 1947 had left a considerable arsenal in the hands of the Cuban government.[31] Where this extraordinary arsenal came from is an interesting question. While it is obvious that the Cuban government provided support, and reasonably clear that the Guatemalan and Venezuelan governments did so as well, it is conceivable that there was covert American involvement. Perhaps the arsenal that Colonel King and John Cabot had suggested could be put together for use against Perón in Argentina was actually assembled, was transferred to Cuba for use in the Cayo Confites expedition against Trujillo, and finally was used successfully in Costa Rica.[32] The leadership of the Cayo Confites expedition gave the impression that most of their rifles and machine guns had been acquired in Argentina by Guatemalan envoys who persuaded Perón that they were to aid a country menaced by North American imperialism and who even persuaded him to donate $350,000 to this unspecified cause. This, at any rate, was what Rolando Masferrer, a member of the Dominican Central Revolutionary Committee, wrote in the 12 October 1947 issue of the Cuban weekly *Bohemia*. Charles Ameringer takes this account at face value and may be correct to do so.[33] On the other hand, it should be remembered that Guatemala had hardly endeared itself to Perón with its strong support of the Larreta doctrine and that Perón was not known for giving large sums of money to unspecified causes.

Whatever its origin, obtaining this arsenal became one of Figueres's principal concerns.

> Various friends of mine, Nicaraguans and Hondurans, were also looking for arms for liberation and asked Dr. Arévalo to write to the president of Cuba, Dr. Grau San Martín, requesting the arms of the frustrated expedition of Cayo Confites. Grau acceded to this request and sent the military equipment to Guatemala. They told me that beneath his meek exterior this doctor and Cuban university professor who had become president was a man of intrigue. Then began our struggle to obtain these arms in order to begin the work of liberation in Costa Rica. Time was drawing short. I tried to convince my exiled friends that the first step in the crusade against tyranny in the Caribbean would have to be taken in Costa Rica. It was important that the first blow should triumph. The Caribbean and Central American satraps counted on powerful military forces. In Costa Rica the national sentiment was ripe and any act tending to impede the consolidation of a dictatorship would therefore receive the support of the people. Besides, the armed forces, aggressive and arrogant when oppressing unarmed citizens, would not know how to face a group of determined men with arms in their hands.[34]

With these arguments Figueres apparently persuaded his Dominican and Nicaraguan exile allies. On 16 December 1947, in Guatemala, they signed a pact of alliance to overthrow the dictatorships of the Caribbean, the resources of each liberated country being pledged "to the extent humanly possible" to aid the fight against the other dictatorships.[35] By means of this pact Figueres obtained not only arms and equipment but also a considerable number of highly skilled volunteers for his army.

Meanwhile, within Costa Rica, events were moving more or less along the course that Figueres had anticipated. With only forty districts still to be accounted for in the election of 8 February 1948, the electoral tribunal released figures showing Ulate with a commanding lead—54,000 votes to Calderón's 44,201. The Calderónistas, however, claimed that tens of thousands of their supporters had been prevented from voting by an electoral registrar who was sympathetic to the opposition and had dropped their names from the list. To this charge the opposition responded that they had suffered from delays and mistakes in the preparation of the voter lists and identification cards as much as anyone else. A fire in the women's college where the ballots were being stored added to the tension by preventing the electoral tribunal from completing a ballot-by-ballot count. Presented with a petition to annul the elections, the tribunal waffled and declared itself incompetent to rule on the question. While two of its three members maintained that the outcome of the elections was clear and had been duly recorded and certified, the third suggested that all of the relevant documents should be turned over to the Costa Rican Congress, which alone had the constitutional authority to proclaim the president. Since the Calderónistas had a majority in the old Congress—which they retained in the elections—this was effectively an invitation for them to reject the tribunal's certification of Ulate's victory. On 1 March they did so. They simultaneously annulled Ulate's election to the presidency and affirmed the legitimacy of the outcome of the congressional races. The fact that the same voter lists and identification cards had been used for the presidential and congressional contests did not appear to trouble them.[36]

After the Calderónistas broke the Pact of Honor, there were rumors that the opposition would launch an armed rebellion. About fifty troops, some in police uniforms and others in khaki, surrounded the house of Dr. Carlos Luis Valverde, where Otilio Ulate was staying. Machine guns were deployed and a short while later open conflict broke out between armed Ulate supporters within the house and the government forces. The house was put under siege and Valverde was fatally wounded. It was only after the intervention of Archbishop Sanabria that General René Picado, the minister of public security and the president's brother, agreed to accept personal responsibility for Ulate's safety. On the evening of 2 March 1948, Ulate was taken into custody by General Picado as Archbishop Sanabria, Ambassador Davis, and the British and Colombian ministers watched to make sure that nothing untoward happened. He was released under court order a short while later.[37]

News of the situation in Costa Rica was sent to Victor Raúl Haya de la Torre by Luis Alberto Monge, the second in command of the Rerum Novarum labor federation. Haya was then on a tour in the United States. Speaking at Yale University on 3 March 1948, he warned that Costa Rica might become "the Czechoslovakia of the Western Hemisphere." It was a phrase designed to grab attention, and it succeeded. Gonzalo Facio, a close ally of Figueres who was then trying to marshal support in the United States for the coming insurrection, later recalled that it completely changed the atmosphere: "It produced an intense interest to know what was going on in our little country." Before the end of the month, it would be quoted with approval by a State Department official in an internal memorandum.[38]

Within Costa Rica, Ambassador Davis was urging a negotiated settlement on everyone who came to see him. The only alternative to bloodshed, he suggested, was compromise: a compromise candidate for president, a bipartisan committee to remedy defects in the electoral law, and an agreement on the part of the Congress to reimburse the parties for their campaign expenditures.[39] Negotiations did take place at Archbishop Sanabria's residence between Ulate, Calderón, and Mora, but despite Davis's hopes and efforts these negotiations went nowhere.[40] On 10 March 1948, a message reached Figueres that Ulate had given the Calderónistas his final offer. The following day, he was advised that Calderón had rejected it.[41] Negotiations would in fact resume within a matter of days but in a context altered by the outbreak of fighting and in the end decisively shaped by the course of the war.

Launching what would come to be known as the War of National Liberation on 11 March 1948, Figueres's forces seized the airfield at San Isidro and immediately sent planes to Guatemala to pick up arms. They also brought back volunteers from the failed Dominican exile invasion of the year before who would serve as officers in the Army of National Liberation and help to train the recruits. Having carried off this operation without a hitch, the revolutionary forces established a defensive line about twenty miles south of San José at Empalme where they could block off the Inter-American Highway and look down on approaching forces from a high ridge. Driven out of his farm by government troops after a brief skirmish, Figueres joined them there. Perhaps not taking seriously the military threat posed by Figueres, these troops contented themselves with sacking and burning his property. Figueres, who had been counting on the natural defenses provided by the mountains of Tarrazú, mourned the loss

of his farm but welcomed the delay in fighting as an opportunity to pre-
pare for the next stage of the war.[42]

By 15 March 1948, Somoza in neighboring Nicaragua had already become worried about Figueres's revolt. He told the American chargé in
Managua, Maurice Bernbaum, that the Costa Rican government would be
forced into the hands of the communists if outside assistance was not
forthcoming and that he intended to airlift one thousand Nicaraguan National Guard officers to San José. Reporting to Washington, Bernbaum
suggested that Somoza was fearful that such intervention would jeopar-
dize his own prospects for recognition and was looking for a "go-ahead
signal" from the United States or at least acquiescence.[43] Presented instead
with strong protests, Somoza "confirmed cancellation [of] his projected intervention in deference to Department."[44]

The Costa Rican ambassador to Washington had earlier defended his
government's right to receive military assistance from Nicaragua. He had
maintained that under the Havana Convention of 1928 there was a fundamental difference between helping an insurrectionary movement (as he
charged Guatemala was doing) and helping an internationally recognized
government at its own request (as he acknowledged Nicaragua sought to
do).[45] But when confronted with the claim that the sending of so many
Nicaraguan troops would constitute an unwarranted intervention, he
proved unable to formulate an effective response and "apparently somewhat reluctantly agreed."[46]

Acting without substantial Nicaraguan support, Costa Rican government forces attacked Empalme and San Isidro simultaneously on 20 March
1948 and for a few days managed to regain part of San Isidro before being
routed on the twenty-third. While the fighting was going on, Picado gave
a Canadian citizen, Alex Murray, a safe-conduct pass to Figueres's lines to
see if he would accept Manuel Francisco Jiménez as a compromise candidate for the presidency. On his return, Murray stopped by to see Davis and
told him that Figueres's answer had been a resounding no. He added that
Figueres was clearly intent upon military victory. He had risked everything he had for the success of the movement in which he believed and had
prepared for it thoroughly. He had carefully determined the best terrain
from which to launch an armed revolt, and his military position was excellent.

> His program is to declare Ulate President, suppress militant commu-
> nism, and unseat all the deputies who voted to annul the elections. He
> is sure he will win, that the mass of the people support him, that he is

fighting world communism and not just a local affair, and thinks the US should intervene on his side in some way or other, not necessarily militarily, as part of our world wide struggle with communism. He wants us to break relations with the Picado government and embargo supplies to the government.[47]

Murray's favorable assessment of Figueres's military position was shared by Lieutenant Colonel James K. Hughes, the American military attaché. Hughes had toured behind Figueres's lines, and he viewed Figueres's defensive position as nearly impregnable in relation to any force that might be sent against it and his capacity for offensive action as almost equally impressive. Davis had his doubts. Without dramatic military victories on Figueres's part, he thought that the Costa Rican public would soon yearn for peace. Davis was still hoping for a compromise settlement, and he thought that such an arrangement would leave Figueres "in the unhappy position of a rebel, not only against the constitutional government, but also against the will of the people as expressed by its leaders." His doubts about Figueres's prospects would be dispelled only by the course of events.[48]

On 11 April 1948, Puerto Limón fell to a force airlifted in from San Isidro. The crucial role of Horacio Ornes and other exiles in this operation perhaps encouraged Figueres to designate the military group responsible as "La Legión Caribe." In any case, the name soon caught on and acquired a life of its own.[49] While Limón was falling to this Caribbean Legion, Figueres led a six-hundred-man force against Cartago. Government efforts to retake the city on 13 April led to the bloodiest fighting of the war, and the defeat of the government forces left no doubt as to where military supremacy lay. With two thousand men already killed in the fighting, the only remaining question seemed to be whether San José would also have to be taken by force.[50]

Even before their defeat at Cartago, the forces of the ancien régime were becoming desperate. On 11 April 1948, the Costa Rican foreign minister asked Davis for help in reaching a settlement, saying "the government would accept anything I could arrange with Figueres." The following morning, representatives of the Calderónistas came to Davis's house to plead with him. "They would have agreed to make me dictator if I had asked it," he wrote in his diary. Later that afternoon, the foreign minister told him that he was going to ask the diplomatic corps to place San José under its protection. The corps, in turn, selected the U.S., Mexican, Dominican, and Panamanian ambassadors, the papal nuncio, and the Chilean chargé to meet with Figueres and see if some means of sparing San José could be found.[51]

Meeting with Figueres, the representatives of the diplomatic corps soon discovered that he had no interest in any compromise with the government or in a constitutional succession. He explained to them that the constitutional order in Costa Rica had not existed since the fraudulent elections of 1944.

> We commented that whatever might be his political philosophy on that point, the fact is that the present government is recognized by all countries as the constitutional one and that any forceful overthrow would raise a question of recognition. Therefore, whatever he may think of the previous elections or the government which resulted from them, it is important for him to remember that in the eyes of the world his overthrowing it would be considered as a revolution against the constitutional government.[52]

Rather than argue the fine points of diplomatic recognition under international law, Figueres simply suggested that if they wanted a constitutional transition they could arrange for the resignation of the president and the vice president and his election by Congress along with that of two of his principal aides. He offered guarantees as to life and property and promised an amnesty. When this was presented to Picado, he balked at the demand for a complete surrender and attempted to suggest previously mentioned presidential compromise candidates to the members of the diplomatic corps. He was told that this would not do, in terms strong enough that he would later describe the corps as "heavily exerting pressure upon me to give the Presidency to Mr. Figueres." Finally, he suggested that it would be desirable to discuss matters with someone representing Figueres.[53]

On the morning of 14 April 1948, under gunfire from a nearby hill, Davis and the other representatives of the diplomatic corps picked up Father Benjamin Núñez at Figueres's lines and brought him back to San José. This procedure of escorting Núñez across enemy lines would be repeated many times in the days ahead, usually with Davis taking Núñez in his car.[54] It soon became apparent that the crux of the negotiations was between Núñez and Mora. When the Mexican ambassador suggested at one point that Calderón should join in their discussions, "Mora said with a smile that the Costa Ricans present probably understood the finer points of Costa Rican politics better than the diplomats and he felt quite certain that in the present circumstances it was better that only he and Núñez consult. Calderón said nothing but nodded a very sour assent."[55]

As of 16 April 1948, it looked as though the conversations between Mora and Núñez would bear fruit. Mora had expressed his relief at a promise from Figueres to maintain existing social legislation and indicated his willingness to support a compromise slate in which his party would have no representatives. On the way back to Figueres's lines, however, Núñez explained to Davis that this had largely been for show and "told me of the real state of affairs and the imminence of a general Central American war." Calderón and Somoza had made arrangements for a Nicaraguan invasion of Costa Rica in defense of the Calderónistas, and Mora had offered to join forces with Figueres to fight them. Figueres, however, would probably reject Mora's offer. He had been prepared to fight a Somoza-Calderón alliance that included Mora's forces—counting on a Guatemalan promise to invade Nicaragua if Nicaragua invaded Costa Rica—and would probably stick to that resolution.[56]

By the afternoon of 17 April 1948, Somoza had airlifted several hundred troops to Chiles, La Cruz, and Villa Quesada (the last city being deep within Costa Rican territory) and had several thousand more in place along the border. To Maurice Bernbaum in Managua, Somoza explained that these forces had been sent at the request of the Costa Rican government and that their purpose was to prevent an invasion of Nicaragua. He added that he had explained this in a telegram to the Nicaraguan delegation to the Bogotá Conference and gave a copy to Bernbaum. On hearing this news, Acting Secretary of State Robert Lovett sent a message to Bogotá urging the American delegation there to try to marshal multilateral pressure against the Nicaraguan action. The effectiveness of unilateral American representations, he noted, had been cast in doubt.[57]

On 18 April 1948, the usual participants in the Costa Rican peace negotiations gathered at the Mexican embassy: Picado, Calderón, Mora, Núñez, several other Costa Rican officials, and the members of the group representing the diplomatic corps. Davis asked the Mexican ambassador to read to this group part of the text of Somoza's telegram to the Nicaraguan delegation in Bogotá. As soon as he had finished, Davis suggested that while they had been trying to find a basis to restore peace in Costa Rica, they now had to be concerned with the preservation of peace in Central America. Without even consulting their governments, Davis continued, they knew that none of them would allow such a breach of the peace and would punish those responsible. It was therefore necessary to know

whether Somoza's statement was true. Picado replied that this appeared to
be a misunderstanding, that there was a long-standing agreement allowing
Costa Rican and Nicaraguan border patrols to pass into each other's territory, and that since he had not been in touch with the frontier area he could
not say if any Nicaraguan forces had entered the country. This provoked
the Mexican ambassador to interrupt and say that the matter was too serious for subterfuges. Furious, Picado said that he would have to consult and
left the room. He returned with a statement categorically denying that he
had ever authorized the entry of Nicaraguan troops into Costa Rica and
one to his minister in Managua instructing him to immediately demand
the withdrawal of all Nicaraguan forces from the country. Within the
week, Davis would claim in his diary that he had acquired documentary
proof that Picado had given Calderón the authority to do as he saw fit in
securing Nicaraguan assistance. Picado had never authorized the entry of
Nicaraguan troops into Costa Rica, he had allowed Calderón to do so for
him.[58]

Deprived of Nicaraguan assistance, Picado was in a very poor bargaining position. It was a position that American policy had made worse in
several ways. The first and most important of these was helping to block
Nicaraguan assistance. The second was refusing to sell arms to either side
in the conflict and encouraging other states to adopt a similar position. At
one point, a shipment of weapons from Mexico was blocked just as it was
about to leave for Costa Rica. Mexican officials had been unaware of the
purchase, and when it was brought to their attention by the American
ambassador, they decided to cancel it. Although these actions were taken
by American officials in the belief that they were compatible with a policy
that sought to avoid intervention and any escalation of the conflict, they
were seen in a very different light by the Costa Rican government. They
helped to demoralize Picado and give him the feeling, as he wrote to
Calderón and Mora, "that insuperable forces are absolutely determined to
have us lose this contest."[59]

There is no indication that Ambassador Davis ever hoped to have the
Calderónistas lose or that he ever wanted the Costa Rican Communist
Party to be defeated by force of arms. On the contrary, he appears to have
consistently hoped and worked for a compromise settlement that would
preserve constitutional government and avoid further bloodshed. At many
points during the course of the crisis, he would have eagerly embraced a
compromise that left the strength of the Calderónista forces intact. Fortunately, it was not his decision to make. Ultimately, the course of the nego-

tiations was decided by the relative strength of the contending military forces and by the skill of the negotiators directly involved. After the defeat of the government's counterattack on Cartago on 13 April 1948, these considerations clearly favored Figueres's forces, and the only obstacle remaining to securing a negotiated settlement was persuading the other parties to the conflict of just how true this was in the absence of outside intervention.

When the representatives of the diplomatic corps visited Figueres on the evening of 18 April 1948, they appear to have hoped that the Mora-Núñez compromise agreement would be acceptable to him. Figueres treated them to dinner before disabusing them of that aspiration:

> After dinner, Figueres made a speech telling us that in view of all the circumstances he was unwilling to agree to the formula worked out by Núñez and Mora. In effect, it amounted to delivering the government into communist hands and joining forces with the commies and Calderóns. As to Vanguardia, he had no quarrel with its sociological aspects; he was opposed to it politically because it had joined forces with the corrupt Calderón machine; he was opposed to it internationally because his policy was based on firm friendship with the United States and the other American countries for geographical, ideological and sentimental reasons and for family ties. He wanted no part of any leanings toward Russia or any other European country.[60]

The negotiated settlement that finally emerged on 19 April 1948, the "Pact of the Mexican Embassy," included Picado's resignation, an interim presidency to last until 8 May, guarantees as to life and property, a provision for the retirement of the government's forces, and a measure for the departure from the country of certain persons (Mora, Calderón, Picado, and others). It also included a reference to a letter from Figueres's Army of National Liberation to the head of the PVP that stated, among other things, that "existing social guarantees will not only be respected, but also applied in effective form in all the areas in which they still have not been."[61]

On 8 May 1948 Figueres and his allies established the founding Junta of the Second Republic to enact various social, economic, and political reforms and hold elections for a constituent assembly, before turning power over to Otilio Ulate. During their eighteen months in office, the junta saw the fracturing of the opposition coalition and harassed their defeated foes; they also faced numerous obstacles, including considerable resentment over their inexperience, a fiscal crisis, and an invasion by exiles supported by Somoza. Nevertheless, they left office chastened yet having firmly established themselves as a progressive force in Costa Rican politics and with a determination to fight electorally for what they believed in. In 1953, their social democratic Partido de Liberación Nacional won the elections, and Figueres was returned to the presidency with a 65 percent electoral majority.[62] Since then, the country has enjoyed an unbroken succession of democratically elected leaders.[63]

Cold War Conservatism in Latin America

The establishment of military governments in Peru and Venezuela in late 1948 was a turning point in Latin American politics. It marked the end of the optimism of the immediate postwar period. Accepting the State Department's assurances that American officials and American interests had not been involved in the overthrow of his government, Rómulo Gallegos suggested to Truman that diplomatic recognition of the new Venezuelan regime would be the standard by which American policy toward Latin America would be judged. Previous American administrations had not known how to win the goodwill of the Latin American peoples, he observed, or else had not wished to do so. This had changed with the Good Neighbor policy.

> But now it happens—and I must put this matter with absolute sincerity—that if Your Excellency's legitimate government, in the exercise of its sovereign will, which I respect fully, were to recognize the spurious régime in my country or were to continue to maintain friendly relations with it, all the noble work of the Good Neighbor policy would be fruitless and we would have to witness the definitive failure of our highest aspirations to cordial understanding: in peace, in common efforts to create collective welfare and happiness, as well as in the face of threats of war endangering the material and spiritual unity of our continent. Because in this instance we Venezuelans could not consider anyone a Good Neighbor, worthy of our friendship, if, for motives of a material nature, he were to acquiesce in violations of right by force.[1]

In his response, Truman indicated that the overthrow of Gallegos's government had come as a great shock, that he was sincerely moved by Gallegos's letter, and that he considered the use of force to effect political change to be deplorable. The United States, he indicated, had initiated a consultation among the American republics to see what steps could be taken to encourage democratic and constitutional procedures in the region. Nonrecognition, however, was not a step the United States would readily take. It was seldom if ever effective, and it precluded the influence in favor of democratic procedures that could be exercised through normal diplomatic channels.

> The possibility of withholding recognition was very carefully considered from all points of view, and it was my opinion and that of my advisers that it was not the course best adapted to achieve the ends which you and I both heartily desire. Since the administration of President Jefferson it has been the general policy of this Government, with certain exceptions, to maintain diplomatic relations with whatever Government held control of the administrative machinery of any state, provided it was both able and willing to carry out its international obligations and gave reasonable evidence of stability. It has not been and is not now the intention of this Government to pass judgement upon the internal arrangements of other Governments.[2]

Precisely how the United States was to encourage democracy without passing judgement on the internal affairs of other states, Truman left unsaid. Nor did the consultation to which he referred provide many constructive suggestions. As early as 10 December 1948, the director of the State Department's policy planning staff, George Kennan, had asserted that the use of force as a means to political change in Peru and Venezuela was deplorable. "It should be stressed that we cannot remain indifferent to this sort of thing, and that if there is an increased resort to this sort of procedure in other American countries, this will create a serious issue which will have to engage the attention of the American community as a whole."[3] But when it came to suggesting practical measures of response, the best the State Department could offer was the idea of adding the text of Article 5(d) of the OAS Charter to the diplomatic notes indicating a resumption of relations with Venezuela.[4] The reaction to even this extremely mild proposal was not encouraging. The Chilean government indicated a willingness to go along, but the Mexican government thought it could be seen as a form of intervention in Venezuela's internal affairs.[5] The Peruvian ambassador to Washington spent nearly an hour "discussing the conditions in his country, attacking the APRA party and explaining . . . that his country was not yet ready for either British or American types of democracy."[6]

There is no reason to doubt that senior American officials were sincere in their concern over the increasing strength of dictatorial forces in the hemisphere and in their desire to use American influence on behalf of the democratic cause. This is evident in both private and classified correspondence in which they had little or no reason to dissemble. The problem was a widespread lack of imagination as to what might be done without violating the American commitment to nonintervention and an even more widespread unwillingness to reconsider the value and legitimate extent of that commitment.

In a letter to Claude Bowers of 28 January 1949, Truman did indicate that he thought the prohibition on unilateral political and economic sanctions in the OAS Charter was unfortunate. He told Bowers that he was very much worried about the program of Latin America's dictators and that the United States would have to be exceedingly careful not to find itself in the position of supporting them. He noted that he was having the State Department make a survey of the problem and that he hoped "we can find a solution for such conditions as those existing in Peru, Venezuela, Santo Domingo, Nicaragua and Costa Rica."[7]

In April 1949, apparently in response to Truman's request, a draft statement of principles to guide American policy in Latin America was sent by the State Department to all of the American ambassadors in the region for their comments. The ambassadors were asked to respond as soon as possible to paragraph 16.[8] That paragraph dealt with the promotion of democracy:

> Since dictatorial governments always have existed and still exist in some Latin American countries although democratic principles are the expressed basis for the Organization of American States—and since non-intervention is an accepted principle of the American republics, the US should continue to use present means and try to find new means to persuade the governing and privileged classes of the Latin American countries to accept their direct responsibility for more rapid progress toward representative, stable and honest government as an important factor affecting hemisphere security and welfare. The withholding of recognition of anti-democratic governments probably is not an effective or appropriate means to deter the establishment and maintenance of such governments. To publicly state US support of democratic institutions and principles is desirable, although there should be no insistence upon "model USA." The Latin American peoples themselves must solve their political problems.[9]

Several responses indicated that the State Department had been misguided in its thinking about diplomatic recognition. Ralph Ackerman argued that recognition should be withheld for as long as necessary to ascertain that the usurper government was firmly in control and able to maintain itself against the democratic forces it had replaced. "In spite of the recognized weakness of this instrument, it should not be wholly discounted, for at times it has encouraged democratic forces to make the effort necessary to dislodge dictators."[10] Nathaniel Davis stressed that much of the utility of nonrecognition would depend on whether "a substantial, intelligent and historically successful anti-dictatorship element exists within the country."[11] Claude Bowers stressed the importance of timing. Easy and speedy recognitions, he argued, were "a serious disillusionment and discouragement to the democratic and liberal elements in South America, and an encouragement and incentive to fascistic and dictatorial elements."[12] Were the United States to simply consult with the other American republics and abide by the views of the majority, he warned, it might well find itself in the position of having antidemocratic regimes dictate American policy. In contrast with this assessment of the prospects for collective action, a number of responses referred to the need for something like the Larreta doctrine.[13] One suggested that even if collective measures to promote democracy could not yet be agreed upon, open advocacy of such measures would still have a beneficial effect.[14]

Many of the respondents employed a form of class analysis and seemed to believe that overcoming social and economic problems was the key to overcoming political problems. The measures they suggested were often lacking in direct relevance to the ongoing political struggles in the region. What they did have in common was a tendency to throw cold water on the assumption that the "governing and privileged classes" of Latin America could easily be persuaded to become more democratic. While these classes were impressed with the accomplishments of the United States, Fletcher Warren suggested, they were not willing to admit that these were the consequence of American political and economic practices. "They believe that their present small ruling classes are capable to develop the political and economic life of their nations and they are unwilling to see those classes lose control of their political and economic systems."[15] Noting a tendency among upper-class civilian and military groups to deny the people the right to govern themselves, Walter Donnelly stressed their belief "that they are rendering society a favor by molding the destinies of the masses to their own thought and to their own class advantage."[16] Perhaps the bleakest picture of class-based hostility to democracy in Latin America came from Harold Tittman, the American ambassador in Peru:

> Unfortunately for the cause of democracy, the ruling class just described is at all times conscious of the threat to its existence of an aroused Indian population vastly more numerous although thus far unorganized. They have become convinced that there is no solution to the racial and social problem except violence and they desire to postpone the inevitable clash as long as possible. For this underlying reason, they have consistently opposed (in spite of protestations to the contrary) democratic tendencies in politics which they fear they might not be able to restrain and which might lead to unrest among the Indians.[17]

Tittman's proposed solution was a program in which large numbers of Peruvian adolescents could be trained in American schools during their formative years. The expenditure of half a million dollars a year on this project, he asserted, would create a political climate favorable to democracy in a fairly short time. Donnelly also urged student exchanges, but in addition he stressed the value of training Latin American army officers and particularly of providing younger officers with political indoctrination. He also advocated an exchange program for trade unionists to help strengthen the ties between labor organizations in the United States and noncommunist labor organizations in Latin America. Many American companies, he observed, were setting good examples, "but unfortunately a segment of American business labors under the mistaken impression that governments which maintain themselves in office by force are good for business. These companies' own selfish interests are not served by dictatorial governments which invite revolution and strengthen the hand of the extreme left."[18]

Ellis Briggs urged Washington to decide between treating all of the American republics alike and discriminating in favor of the democracies and against the dictatorships, but he did not offer any concrete suggestions as to how the latter course might be pursued. He simply reiterated his old advice against seeking unanimity among the American states as a substitute for genuine solidarity. The most striking feature of his response was his pessimism about political conditions in much of Latin America and the unusual proposal that this helped to generate. Fully half of the American republics, he suggested, might never amount to anything. Their populations might be condemned to suffer a submarginal existence and successive political upheavals in perpetuity. Perhaps the United States should encourage federations or amalgamations leading to a total of seven states in the region instead of continuing to support the fragmentation that had produced twenty. "Where would the United States be today," he asked, "if our western boundary had remained the Appalachian Mountains, the Mississippi River, or even the Continental Divide of the Rockies?"[19]

By August 1949, a revised statement of principles had been drawn up incorporating the responses that had come in from the field. It is instructive to contrast these principles of 1949 with the principles of 1945. In both, the triumph of political democracy and economic prosperity in Latin America was seen as the key to protecting American security interests in the region.[20]

> U.S. should act upon the justified assumption that governmental or private actions which ignore human rights and the need for higher standards of living will inevitably lead to the unrest and misery which contribute substantially to the spread of communism. The principle to guide U.S. policies should be that the sound growth of the inter-American system along the established lines of freedom and individual rights, in which the development of an effective free labor movement is of great importance, is the best means to eliminate communist influence.[21]

This was a statement with which Braden and the other Cold War liberals would have readily agreed. They had also stressed the importance of democratically oriented labor movements in the struggle against communism and had seen poverty and dictatorship as breeding grounds for extremist ideologies. Nor would they have had any difficulty in agreeing with the principle that while private enterprise was essential to the economic development of Latin America, the state could play an important role. "If they want to do it themselves and not have private enterprise, that is their affair, we have nothing to say about it," Braden told one group of State Department officials.[22] He would certainly have agreed that "we should be neither surprised at nor attempt to use our power to block new economic undertakings by Latin American governments simply because at another time and in other countries they would have seemed suitable only for private enterprises."[23]

The central difference between the principles of 1945 and the principles of 1949—the principles of the Cold War liberals and those of the Cold War conservatives—was that the former contained a practical set of rules for discriminating against dictatorial and disreputable governments. Beyond the advantages that such governments could derive from the maintenance of diplomatic and private economic relations with the United States, they were to be denied the kinds of economic, military, and rhetorical assistance that had been routinely provided during the Roosevelt years. It was the systematic nature of the effort to uphold this discriminatory position that gave American policy in the early Truman years its distinctive character. If Braden and his allies exaggerated the impact that such "aloof formality" could have on regime maintenance and regime change in the hemisphere, they were nevertheless engaged in a proactive policy. They were seeking to encourage democratic forces and discourage dictatorial ones through a consistent pattern of rhetoric and action that was visibly at odds with the recent past. They were also seeking to influence everyone in Latin America who was interested in politics, and not simply "the governing and privileged classes." Sincere as American officials in the later Truman years were in their preference for democracy, they formulated no analogous set of rules to guide their conduct. American economic and military assistance did continue to go overwhelmingly to the remaining democratic governments, or to Mexico.[24] But beyond this, and beyond the influence of their rhetoric, American officials were responding to political events as they occurred.

In January 1949, for reasons unrelated to Latin America, Dean Acheson was appointed secretary of state. Acheson had been one of Braden's strongest supporters at the beginning of the Truman administration but had overturned Braden's policy on arms sales to Argentina in 1947 on the grounds of its apparent impracticability. As assistant secretary of state for inter-American affairs, he brought in Edward Miller, who was fluent in Spanish and familiar with the region. The assistant secretary position had been vacant since Braden's departure, and the work of the office had been divided between the director of the Office of American Republic Affairs and the undersecretary of state for political affairs. Miller's appointment seemed to indicate a renewal of American concern with the region. In Acheson's first major address on Latin America, on 19 September 1949, he sought to emphasize the value of Latin America to the United States and to make common cause with Latin America's democrats. At the same time, he sought to explain why the American contribution to political progress in Latin America would inevitably be a limited one:

We would like to see a world in which each citizen participates freely in determining periodically the identity of the members of his government. This is an objective for which we will continue to work, subject always to our common policy of nonintervention. In the Americas we have had periods of high hope and periods of bitter disappointment as we have seen democratic institutions flourish in some countries, only to see them subverted in others. We always deplore the action of any group in substituting its judgement for that of the electorate. We especially deplore the overthrow by force of a freely elected government. In such situations we do not cease to hope that the people will regain the right to choose their leaders. We realize, however, that the attainment of the democratic ideal in any country depends fundamentally upon the desires and efforts of the people of that country, The nature of democracy is such that it can be achieved only from within.[25]

In both Venezuela and Peru, American officials did attempt to exercise some influence on behalf of a return to civilian rule and for the release of political prisoners. Defending the State Department's recognition policy in a letter to Claude Bowers, Miller went so far as to claim that nonrecognition would not only be completely futile but "completely negative in the sense that the withdrawal of our Ambassador would in effect constitute the withdrawal of what in countries such as Venezuela today constitutes the vanguard of democracy."[26] Miller's imaginative characterization did have a slight foundation in reality. Presented with a Uruguayan threat to raise the issue of Venezuelan political prisoners in the General Assembly of the United Nations, American officials were worried that this would present the Soviet Union with an opportunity to divert attention from its own abuses. They persuaded the Uruguayans to wait while Donnelly made it clear to the Venezuelan government that only through its own action in releasing prisoners could "an embarrassing situation be avoided."[27] This appears to have contributed to the release of a few Adecos.[28]

In his speech of 19 September 1949, Acheson indicated that if another freely elected government were overthrown, the United States might not automatically recognize the usurper regime but instead might initiate a process of inter-American consultations. Even if the United States were to eventually recognize the new regime, he insisted, this would not constitute approval. Nothing more would be involved than the recognition of a set of facts and the realization that American interests could best be served by maintaining a channel of communications. Recognition was not an endorsement and "need not necessarily be understood as the forerunner of a policy of intimate cooperation with the government concerned."[29] Two months later, he would have the opportunity to put this new policy to the test.

On 19 November 1949, the Panamanian national police commander, José Antonio Remón, and men the American ambassador described as his "gangster associates" demanded that the president of Panama resign before 2:00 A.M. on the following day.[30] When President Daniel Chanis made clear his intention to resist, the police prepared to attack. Ten chiefs of mission accredited to Panama then called on the police barracks asking for an extension of the deadline on humanitarian grounds. The American ambassador, Monnett Davis, "emphasized especially the importance which the United States has always attached to democratic processes and to constitutional methods."[31] As a result of this diplomatic interference an extension of the deadline was granted during which time Chanis decided to resign in order to avoid bloodshed.[32]

Vice President Roberto Chiari became president for a few days, but in a second coup on 25 November 1949, Remón decided to place the losing candidate of the 1948 elections, Arnulfo Arias, in the presidency. This was a shrewd move in that Arias had considerable popular support and had claimed to have been cheated out of an electoral victory.[33] Davis responded, however, by writing of "obviously dishonest legal fictions" and urging the State Department to adopt a determined policy of nonrecognition to counter any pressure that might arise with "all measures short of intervention."[34] At a press conference on 25 November, Miller stated that recent events in Panama were a serious blow to the progress of democratic principles and to the inter-American system in general. In view of these circumstances, he continued, diplomatic relations between the United States and the Arias regime in Panama did not exist.[35] This position was reiterated in a statement by Acheson that was released to the press on 30 November. In this statement Acheson referred to the "deplorable disruption during the past 10 days of constitutional and democratic processes of government in Panama," reaffirmed the absence of diplomatic relations, and added that there would be consultations among the American republics about various aspects of the situation.[36] The result of these consultations, however, was a general agreement that there had been no outside intervention; that Arias had been fraudulently deprived of victory in 1948; that no question of civil liberties seemed to be involved; and that the regime intended to live up to its international commitments.[37] On 14 December 1949, the American embassy was instructed to resume diplomatic relations with Panama.[38]

The Primacy of Pessimism

The ineffectual character of Acheson's and Miller's tentative antidictatorial effort in Panama was yet another source of pessimism about the prospects for democracy in Latin America and about the ability of American policy to improve those prospects. It was on such pessimism that the position of the Cold War conservatives rested. In a sense, Miller and Acheson both became Cold War conservatives in response to a long series of unfavorable political developments in the region. At the beginning of the Truman years, the Cold War liberals had expected that American and Latin American interests would both be advanced by the triumph of democratic movements such as the Auténticos in Cuba, the Adecos in Venezuela, and the Apristas in Peru. By the end of the Truman years both the political prospects of such movements, and their capacity for establishing lasting democratic regimes, were widely seen as uninspiring.

Convinced that the democratic left would not be back in power any time soon, Miller grew increasingly tired of its criticisms of American policy. In a letter to Claude Bowers of 29 January 1952, he suggested that those who engaged in such criticism were simply and predictably attempting to mask their own failures:

> I have felt it inevitable that both the APRA and the Acción Democrática in Venezuela would turn against the United States during their period of suppression. This is due in large part to the general tendency of virtually everybody in Latin America to blame their troubles on the U.S. and specifically on the Bureau of Inter-American Affairs of the Department of State. I have no doubt that in the atmosphere of plotting and conniving that goes on among the "democratic" exiles of Peru, Venezuela, Argentina and the Dominican Republic, the atmosphere is necessarily slanted against the existing order of things and particularly against the U.S.[39]

While the Cold War was not in any way responsible for the shift in Miller's outlook, it did provide a useful excuse with which to respond when asked why the United States was not doing more. This is particularly evident in a revealing memorandum of conversation of 12 June 1952 drawn up by Miller after a discussion with José Figueres. Figueres had come to visit the United States before embarking on his presidential campaign in Costa Rica. Meeting with Miller, he reminded him that Haya de la Torre was still trapped in the Colombian embassy. He mentioned the fact that Miller had once tried to intervene in the case and asked if he might not do so again.

> Mr. Figueres said that if we did this the United States would be doing one thing at least to help the democrats of Latin America. I told him that I thought this statement, which carried the implication that the United States generally acted in a way displeasing to democrats, appeared inconsistent with his earlier protestations of admiration of this country. I told him that it was our concern to keep our country and our institutions free at home while at the same time bearing the burden of the fight against Communism. I said that I thought that in itself was enough to put us in good standing with democrats in other countries. I also summarized to him what I had said at the luncheon in February of the Inter-American Council for Freedom and Democracy where I had said that the establishment of democratic conditions in other countries could only be brought about by the people in those countries and could not be imposed by us. I said that, as I had told Dr. Eduardo Santos at that time, I felt that even if Latin Americans would be willing (as I surely thought they would not be) to delegate to the United States responsibility for judging the governments of other countries, the only way we could take action about conditions in those countries was through military occupation. Mr. Figueres dropped the subject at this point.[40]

At the beginning of the Truman years, Spruille Braden had argued that opposition to dictatorships in Latin America was essential to the fight against communism in the region. By the end of the Truman years, Miller could portray the two struggles as unrelated—the United States would bear the burden of the fight against communism, and the heavily outgunned peoples of the dictatorial countries would bear the burden of their fight against dictatorships. That the primary responsibility in the struggle for democracy in Latin America rested with the peoples of Latin America was a proposition with which Braden certainly agreed. The idea that the only way the United States could take action to help them was by "military occupation" he would have found ludicrous. Conversely, the "aloof formality" toward dictatorial regimes with which Braden had hoped to make a difference was doubtless seen by Miller as completely ineffectual if not counterproductive.

In hindsight, Braden appears to have been excessively optimistic and Miller excessively pessimistic. Neither of them conceived of American influence as something that should generally be brought to bear in unsettled situations in such a way as to tip the scales toward one side or the other in a political struggle. Such a conception was at odds with the commitment to nonintervention which both men shared. Braden, however, was keenly aware that this commitment to nonintervention carried a risk of associating the United States with dictatorial and disreputable regimes. Miller was both less aware of this risk and less inclined to think that it was worthwhile or even possible to avoid some measure of complicity. Braden's hope for avoiding such complicity had rested on the conviction that there were democratic forces in most or all of the countries of Latin America with reasonable short-term prospects for coming to power and presiding over a consolidation of democratic institutions. All the United States had to do was look for ways to encourage an autonomous trend that was already well under way. By the later Truman years, there appeared much less reason in recent history to maintain such an optimistic view.

To some extent, the influence of the practical rules that Braden and his allies had established continued throughout the Truman years. As late as November 1951, on being asked by the White House about the advisability of inviting President Paul Magloire of Haiti for a state visit, the State Department could reply that since Magloire had come to power in a military coup, to invite him would run "counter to the custom which we have followed in recent years of selecting freely-elected presidents from countries in Latin America with 'democratic' forms of government."[41] Told by the American ambassador to Venezuela, in February 1952, that American companies might be contributing to the political campaign funds of the governing party's candidates, the State Department strongly criticized any such practice. Ambassador Fletcher Warren was reminded of the importance of having American companies observe a strict impartiality with regard to local politics:

> The suggestion that contributions can be considered as directed against the communists simply doesn't hold water for, unless conditions have changed greatly since I was there, communist strength is relatively small compared with that of the COPEI, URD and Accion Democratica supporters. If it should become known that contributions to the government party have been made, all three of these non-

communist groups would be antagonized and no one can be sure that one or all of them will not one day exercise political power in Venezuela. If contributions were made in order to obtain concessions, the concessions, if they were granted, would be tainted with fraud which, if established later, would probably be considered by most Venezuelans ground for their cancellation. Not only would the concessions obtained through fraud be in peril but the investments in them as well. The position of other concessions not tainted with fraud would likewise be weakened.[42]

Braden's stand on keeping American businesses out of active involvement in local politics was retained throughout the Truman years; it was his effort to maintain a posture of aloof formality toward dictatorial regimes that was rejected. As early as 23 February 1951, the American ambassador in Peru reported that Odría had personally assured him "that there was not the slightest vestige of hard feelings remaining after the Haya contretemps."[43] In October of that year, Miller suggested to the dictatorial regime in Venezuela that "one good way of getting a valuable ally in the Senate would be for some university in Venezuela to confer an honorary degree on Lyndon Johnson."[44] Commenting to the American ambassador in Nicaragua on the 1952 presidential campaign in the United States, Miller suggested that he "tell Tacho that which ever of the two wins, he will still have a good friend in the White House."[45] Such encouragement and support for dictatorial regimes was not considered by American officials as a violation of their commitment to nonintervention. Nor was it particularly important to the regimes in question. This support was continued and increased under the Eisenhower administration, and this did not prevent a host of such regimes from being overthrown in the late 1950s. Yet at least in hindsight, much of the complicity seems gratuitous. If its absence would not have dramatically helped the cause of Latin American democracy, it is hard to see how its presence significantly advanced American interests.

Early in 1950, Acheson suggested to Miller the preparation of an article on inter-American policy similar to Kennan's "X" article on policy toward the Soviet Union. Under the cloak of anonymity, this article could express official policy in a frank manner without concern for the susceptibilities of other governments. By August, Miller could inform him that such an article, an "excellent restatement of our Latin American policy," had been prepared by Louis Halle and published in the July issue of Foreign Affairs.[46]

The title of "Y"'s article was "On a Certain Impatience with Latin America." In it Halle argued the need for a broader historical perspective in assessing developments and formulating policy toward Latin America. "The reactionary coups that took place in 1948 and 1949 in Peru, Venezuela and Panama, and the degeneration of the political situation in Colombia," Halle noted, "gave rise to a wave of editorial alarm and pessimism in the United States (and throughout the hemisphere), where to some it seemed that all the gains of democracy were being wiped out by a landslide of reaction." But this was not the case, as even in this period constitutional government had been restored in Costa Rica and there had been movements toward democracy in Honduras and Bolivia. From the perspective of a century and a half, steady progress was visible. "In the alternation that so many countries experience between elective and arbitrary governments, the periods of the former appear to be growing longer, those of the latter shorter." Patience was necessary, for democracy was the product of a slow process of "maturation."[47]

The United States had gained its independence because it had come of age and was ready for it. Most of the societies of Latin America, Halle claimed, were not yet ready to assume the responsibility of self-government when the Spanish Empire fell apart under the impact of Napoleon. "The result was a sordid chaos out of which Latin America has still not finally emerged."[48] The existing American republics varied in their degree of development. They were shades of gray, and it was not possible to draw a clear line for purposes of policy, Halle asserted, between the sheep and the goats. Uruguay was among the few outstanding democracies of the world while Nicaragua and the Dominican Republic were truly stifling dictatorships, but in between there was a wide range. Although the United States had a special responsibility as the oldest and most "mature" as well as the most powerful of the twenty-one republics, this responsibility should not be exercised paternalistically. The United States had attempted paternalism earlier in the century, and there was no evidence that it had brought Haiti, the Dominican Republic, or Nicaragua nearer to maturity.[49]

The United States, Halle suggested, could promote democracy by focusing international opinion in general terms and by helping to remove economic and social obstacles to political progress. While he did not specifically describe all efforts to exercise a direct influence on behalf of democracy as paternalistic, the thrust of his argument was in that direction. By renouncing intervention in the 1930s, he claimed, the United States had formally accepted the other American republics as "adults." The achievement of "greater maturity" would depend on the experience of the Latin American states in exercising their responsibility as "adult nations." To further this process the United States should cultivate close working relations with Latin American statesmen in dealing with world affairs. "Nothing is so conducive to the achievement of adult stature as to be treated like an adult, nothing so stultifying to development as to be treated like a child."[50]

Halle's metaphors glossed over the question of who, precisely, was being treated cordially as an "adult." His approach enabled those who accepted it to believe that whatever occurred was somehow contributing to a process of "maturation." It enabled them to believe that History was on the side of progress and that they were on the side of History. All that was necessary was a continuation of the Good Neighbor policy. The advent of this policy and its consequences, Halle tried to present in especially glowing terms:

> It may in fact be said that at the Montevideo and Buenos Aires Conferences of 1933 and 1936 we joined with the Latin Americans in formally declaring them of age. The evolution that reached this conclusion was more in themselves than in us. They had arrived at the stage, with respect to us, that we had arrived at with respect to England in the 1770s. Unlike the England of George III, however, we had sense enough to join them in their declaration of independence, which we had resisted at Havana in 1928. More than that, having taken the new direction from them, we proceeded to place ourselves in the lead. It was an act of statesmanship such as has rarely been displayed by any world Power. The era of good feeling that followed was its reward.[51]

Halle's analysis systematically exaggerated the importance of American policy as a factor influencing public and elite opinion in Latin America in the 1930s and 1940s. Like many other American officials, he ignored or failed to take seriously the influence of such other factors as the Great Depression, the New Deal, the recovery of American capitalism, the threat posed by Nazi Germany and the common hemispheric response to that threat, the aspirations and solidarity of democratic and progressive movements in the region, and the opportunistic pro-Americanism of communist movements for several years before the Hitler-Stalin Pact and for several years after the Nazi invasion of the Soviet Union. Having convinced themselves that a policy of nonintervention had brought about Latin

American goodwill, these officials simply assumed that a continuation of this policy would suffice to maintain it.

There has often been a strong basis for pessimism about the prospects for democracy in Latin America and about the ability of American policy to improve those prospects. Even during the optimistic period of the mid-1940s, there were prodemocratic American officials who expressed considerable caution. In March 1945, Ambassador John Wiley in Bogotá urged the adoption of a policy that would have concentrated American attention and support on "those few countries in Latin America which do not treat democracy as they treat God—something one talks about constantly but never sees." With these few democracies he expected a spontaneous parallelism of political views and objectives that would outweigh any other advantages that could possibly be achieved. One of these rare countries was Colombia. For forty-four years it had not had a major revolution, an experience unique in all of Latin America. Its capital did not overshadow the rest of the nation. Indeed, the country approximated a league of city-states that made any sort of coup d'état much more difficult. Its cultural level was high and so was the quality of its statesmen. There was, moreover, real opportunity to help. Colombia was still as Humbolt had described it: "a rich country with a poor economy." Colombian cattle raising could be revolutionized, a thriving small industry of consumer goods could be substantially expanded, and a flourishing tourist trade could be established, particularly in the region of Cartagena. While there was a substantial foundation for Wiley's vision of a Colombia enjoying continuous progress under a democratic government inclined to cooperate closely with the United States, it was less solid than he imagined. As Colombian interparty antagonism degenerated into civil war in the late 1940s, it was a vision without any immediate prospect of realization.[52]

The unfavorable trend of events in Colombia and elsewhere in Latin America was captured succinctly in a CIA survey of 16 November 1949:

> The interest of the US in seeing Latin American countries maintain or develop stable representative forms of government has been adversely affected by several recent developments. In Colombia, violent clashes between Conservatives and Liberals have culminated in the declaration of a state of siege. In spite of President Ospina's statement to the contrary, holding elections during the state of siege and under present political conditions is virtually impossible. In Peru much the same situation exists as regards democratic procedures in a different local context of political power. There, announcement of the possibil-

ity of holding elections is merely evidence that the members of the present military *junta* are confident they can manipulate the electoral process to their satisfaction.[53]

What is noteworthy about American officials in the later Truman years is not just that they were pessimistic. There were obvious and serious reasons for pessimism. What is noteworthy is the way some of these officials elaborated their pessimism into a rigid moralistic or legalistic dogma: "Nothing we do in the way of direct interference in Latin America is going to alter this situation materially," George Kennan claimed, "particularly for the better."[54] These officials underestimated their own capacity to make a positive difference and greatly overestimated the importance of their own self-restraint for the maintenance of Latin American goodwill. Rather than attempt to assess the probable consequences of their actions for the outcome of particular political struggles, especially in unsettled circumstances in which their potential influence was at its greatest, they sought to guide their conduct by an abstract rule of deliberate abstention from the exercise of any direct influence on behalf of regime maintenance or regime change as long as American security was not directly threatened. The civility informing their self-restraint was genuine, and their faith that their conduct would be seen by others as following this rule is touching. On the other hand, there is a certain absurdity to the insistence on the part of some of these officials that they were acting exclusively on behalf of a "realistic" conception of American interests.

Flawed as some of Latin America's democratic regimes were, they would prove considerably more favorable to American interests than some of their replacements. This is particularly evident in the case of Cuba. Despite its weaknesses, Cuban democracy contained within itself established mechanisms for reform and for peaceful change of governments. The corruption and destruction of these mechanisms under Batista's dictatorship would directly pave the way for Castro's triumph. Even during the later Truman years, there was some appreciation of the actual and potential cost to American interests imposed by dictatorial regimes in Latin America. After the coups in Peru and Venezuela, the CIA made a point of stressing that it was "doubted that governments installed by military coups can provide long-term social and political stability."[55] Yet when presented with an opportunity to help save Cuban democracy in 1952, American officials chose to forsake tangible American interests in the situation and do nothing. As in Venezuela in 1948, they did not think of doing otherwise primarily because they took it for granted that they were obliged to avoid "intervention." In the Cuban case, however, they were even less likely to consider the possibility of a prodemocratic intervention because of a mistaken assessment that the overthrow of Cuban democracy was likely to prove beneficial to American interests.

The Breakdown of Cuban Democracy

In the Cuban elections of 1 June 1948, the Auténtico Party won its second national victory and Carlos Prío Socarrás replaced Ramón Grau San Martín as president. A few months later, an extensive CIA study of Cuba was completed. Although acute and perceptive in many of its descriptions, this study suggests that even at the beginning of Prío's term, some of the mistaken judgements about Cuban politics that were to influence American policy in 1952 were already in place. Chief among these was a remarkably generous assessment of Fulgencio Batista. No mention was made in this study of the corruption associated with Batista's rule and scant mention of the cordial relations he had established with the Cuban Communist Party. Instead, he was presented as one of the great figures of Cuban politics in the aftermath of the Machado dictatorship. He was portrayed as an authoritarian political leader who had held an honest election in 1944, gracefully accepted defeat at the polls, and then voluntarily left the country for a four-year exile.

> Batista has an intuitive understanding of Cuba and its people. His political astuteness is a product of this understanding in combination with great native intelligence. Upon his return to Cuba he will become a significant factor affecting the island's future. While he performed a great service in bringing Cuba from revolutionary chaos to republican stability, he appears to lack idealism or any integrated concepts for his country's future. His talent appears to lie in the conciliation of opposing forces in the interest of order, stability and the peaceful maintenance of the status quo. His political development has been in the direction of increasing conservatism, but realistic political opportunism remains stronger in him than devotion to a particular ideology.[56]

The contribution the Auténticos had made to the struggle for Cuban democracy was not mentioned by the CIA. The CIA also ignored the extent of their devotion to the democratic cause, and that of the other Cuban political parties. Nor was any thought given to the connection between

Cuba's form of government and its orientation in international politics. That the Cuban government would support the American position in any serious international situation, and would solidly align itself with the United States in the event of a major war, was recognized, but taken for granted. It was explicitly assumed to be a natural consequence of Cuba's basic economic interests, its location, and the convictions of the vast majority of the Cuban people. The CIA acknowledged that there was no chance that the communist minority could ever maneuver Cuban nationalists into supporting the Soviet Union against the United States. It also recognized that the Auténticos had greatly strengthened the position of anticommunist elements within the Cuban labor movement. But it failed to see the underlying connection between the nationalism of the Auténticos, their loyalty to democratic institutions, and their support for the American side in the Cold War. Instead, it viewed their nationalism with mistrust and expected them to seek "to exploit every opportunity at international and inter-American conferences to make patent Cuba's sovereignty and to try to win for Cuba enhanced international prestige by initiating independent, and sometimes anti-US moves."[57]

In terms of their political fortunes, the Auténticos were presented as having benefited from a strong global demand for sugar and the economic progress this was bringing to the island. Since 1941, there had been notable increases in Cuban wealth in nearly every category. A sustained balance-of-payments surplus had left Cuba with $831 million of gold reserves and short-term dollar assets. The national debt was less than the value of gold deposits to Cuba's account in the United States and considerably less than the government's annual income. Ninety percent of this debt was in Cuban hands. Under pressure from the Cuban labor movement, real wages for many types of workers had risen substantially. The average wage among sugar workers had more than doubled since 1944. On the other hand, many people believed that the Auténticos were guilty of "gross dishonesty and corruption." Gangsters who had fought against the police under Machado and Batista as "revolutionaries" had been brought into the national police itself under the Auténticos. They had extended protection to malefactors of all kinds, and rival gangs within the police had even engaged in open conflict.[58]

If an economic downturn or some other issue were to provoke sufficient stress, the military might again become a determining factor in Cuban politics. It was at this critical conceptual juncture that the CIA offered a particularly poor forecast:

At such a time, tendencies toward division within the army into pro-Batista and pro-Auténtico factions would not, it is estimated, be sufficient to neutralize the army as a political force. On the contrary, in a time of stress, one of the two factions would emerge ascendant and would, by open espousal of particular issues, win for itself sufficient support from the Cuban civilian population to enable it to take control of the government. Such a situation, it is estimated, could evolve from disputes over domestic rather than foreign issues. No matter which army faction came to power, it would probably not be anti-US but more favorable to the US point of view than the present majority of Cuban civilian politicians.[59]

This was only a forecast and not a policy prescription. Offered more than three years before the overthrow of Cuban democracy, it is highly unlikely that it played any role in the course of events. Yet the attitude it embodies was similar to that expressed in 1952 by Assistant Secretary of State Edward Miller. This attitude severely deprecated the value of Cuba's democratic institutions and politicians and grossly overestimated the political capacity of the Cuban military and Fulgencio Batista. It was an attitude that made it easier for these officials to embrace "nonintervention" as an appropriate response to Batista's coup. Adopting a specious assumption that any military faction that came to power would be more favorable to the American point of view than the majority of Cuban politicians, those who held this attitude failed to consider what would happen if this new military government were to prove incompetent and unpopular. This failure is particularly striking on the part of CIA analysts who were capable of writing astutely about the way Machado had become a hated symbol of Cuba's political and economic subservience to the United States.[60] That Batista might easily become another such symbol never entered their thinking.

Initially, it looked as though Batista would participate in the elections scheduled for 1 June 1952 and demonstrate again his capacity to lose a free election. The Ortodoxo candidate, Roberto Agramonte, was widely judged to be a more serious threat to Carlos Hevia, the Auténtico candidate, than was Batista.[61] But early in the morning of 10 March 1952, Batista preempted the electoral campaign and transferred the contest to a more advantageous field. Between 2:44 A.M. and 5:00 A.M. he and his fellow subversives entered Camp Columbia in Havana and arrested Cuba's top generals.[62] Having simultaneously moved against the radio stations, the newspapers, and the telephone company, they could be reasonably confident of having cut Havana off from the rest of the country and especially from the less powerful but still significant provincial military commands. The wife of one of the generals arrested, however, managed to get word to Prío.[63] Ascertaining that the military commander at Santiago was prepared to support the government, Prío drafted a statement calling on the military to remain loyal and asking workers, students, peasants, industrialists, and businessmen to join in resisting "this dastardly attack." He then left Havana. By 8:15 A.M. a copy of his statement was presented to the American embassy, but given Batista's control of the radio stations, the statement remained unheard by the Cuban populace. By 10:00 A.M. an aide to Carlos Hevia had met with the American ambassador, Willard Beaulac, to ask if the American embassy could issue a statement regarding respect for democracy. He was told that the embassy was keeping the State Department informed. "I said we were not intervening," Beaulac added.[64]

Having reached an Auténtico safe house in Matanzas at about noon on 10 March 1952, Prío discovered that the commander of the Maceo regiment at Santiago had been replaced. "Without troops," he would later claim, "it was impossible for me to resist."[65] He returned to Havana and together with his family entered the Mexican embassy where they were granted asylum. The leadership of the Cuban Confederation of Labor (CTC) had in the meantime called a general strike, and by midafternoon the port and the dockworkers were out on strike and some of the sugar mills had been shut down.[66] With Prío's surrender, however, and with no apparent organized opposition activities on the part of governmental, political, or military groups, the CTC's prospects for successful resistance looked poor.[67] Discouraged, and fleeing an order for his arrest, the secretary-general of the CTC, Eusebio Mujal, asked for asylum from the American embassy. In keeping with standard American practice, he was refused.[68] Hoping to prevent further resistance from labor, Batista sent word to the CTC leadership that he would be willing to respect their autonomy. By the evening of 11 March, he had met with Mujal and established a tentative rapprochement.[69]

In his public statements in defense of the coup, Batista sought to give the appearance of a proven and competent leader whose personal devotion to democracy was evident in his history and who was moved to act by the force of circumstances. Intolerable graft and gangsterism within the government, he charged, had insured that Prío's candidate would be defeated in the elections and led him to plan a coup d'état of his own for 15 April. It was the need to prevent this coup, Batista insisted, that had forced him to act. He repeatedly referred to the honest elections over which he had presided in 1944, and he promised to establish a regime based on order, progress, and justice that would remain in power only long enough to secure those objectives and hold elections.[70]

Seeking to avoid being seen as a dictator, Batista did not attempt to prevent the Cuban press from publishing, although its reactions to his coup could hardly have been gratifying. Summarizing the first week of editorial responses, the American embassy noted that they were "almost unanimous in repudiating the move for its methods of force, its destruction of the work of fifty years in building democratic institutions, and for forestalling the elections only two and a half months away."[71] If Batista could draw any comfort, it was from the intense criticism of the Prío administration that also appeared. One commentator described Prío as having fallen like a piece of rotten fruit from an office that he saw as nothing more than a means of rapid enrichment. What this commentator considered even more damning, however, was the silence of the six political parties that had endorsed Carlos Hevia. None of them had said or done anything. The Cuban people, he charged, appeared without a soul, without self-esteem. They did not become indignant, or rejoice, or react profoundly at anything.

> Even employees who had positions of confidence and who are in charge of defending constitutional precepts do not consider themselves involved and stay on at positions which they should have resigned as soon as constitutional guarantees were suspended. Nobody resigns. Everybody crouches and waits for the storm to pass, and the serious part of it is not the political quarrel in itself; the really serious part is the disregard of the fundamental question which is the integrity of the regime, respect for the essential powers of the State that are the support for the democratic structure. Or does the Congress not consider it of any importance or any violation of law that the faculties it has received from the sovereign popular will should go unrecognized?[72]

Outraged as many Cubans were by Batista's seizure of power, they were inclined to view him as a known quantity. This contributed greatly to the ease with which his coup succeeded. Noting that some of the younger officers involved might have made the attempt on their own, Beaulac observed that "their chances of success would have been greatly diminished if Batista had not assumed leadership of the movement."[73] The same can perhaps be said of the ease with which the new government won diplomatic recognition from the United States. The origins of Miller's favorable assessment of Batista are unclear, but that he viewed him with sympathy is undeniable.

Miller had spent the first week of February 1952 visiting his mother in Havana and so was in a position to have his own direct impressions of Cuban politics and of the Cuban presidential campaign.[74] On the morning of 11 March 1952, he told the secretary of state's staff meeting that the coup in Cuba had come as a "complete surprise." There was, however, not the slightest indication of regret on his part at the course of events. Prío's government was corrupt, Miller told the meeting, and had given in almost completely to labor demands. "Batista is basically friendly toward the U.S. and undoubtedly his government will be no worse than Prío's, probably better."[75] In a letter to Claude Bowers on 27 March, Miller was even more emphatic. "Actually in Cuba from the coldblooded standpoint of U.S. interests, we have nothing to worry about from Batista, who is a proven friend of ours and who might possibly be tougher on the commies than Prío was."[76]

Like the authors of the CIA assessment of December 1948, Miller appears to have viewed Batista strictly on the basis of his reputation in ill-informed media circles, without bothering to look through the State Department's archives or seriously consider the circumstances in which a new Batista government would try to function. Beaulac, to his credit, was more balanced and astute in his first serious assessment on the day after the coup. He was less confident that the new government could be viewed as a known quantity or that it could be expected to be an improvement. Like Miller, and almost all other observers, he believed that Prío's government had been vulnerable because of its corruption and toleration of gangsters. But Miller was also aware of the advance toward constitutional government that had been made in Cuba since 1940 and the progress made under Prío's administration in particular.

> [I]t was generally recognized that the Prío regime was better than the regime of Ramón Grau San Martín, which preceded it. Toward the end of the Prío regime there was evidently much less peculation than at the beginning, and much less than during the Grau regime. Prío sponsored some excellent basic legislation which should be helpful to Cuba's economy and position in the future. His Government, under two successive honest and capable Ministers of the Treasury, collected ample revenues and spent a large part of them in constructing nu-

merous and useful public works. While it was generally alleged that Government did this for political reasons, the utility of the work accomplished cannot honestly be denied. Furthermore, President Prío supported and obtained the nomination for the Presidency of Carlos Hevia, an honest and capable citizen who promised to bring still further improvement into the conduct of Cuba's Government, if elected.[77]

Yet this tangible progress simply did not seem to matter much to Beaulac. He was convinced that democracy could only function where the people accepted discipline and sacrifice as a necessary part of self-government. Where they thought of government as an institution that doled out favors and privileges, progress toward democracy would be more apparent than real and upsets like Batista's coup would be inevitable. Summing up his political wisdom in a single sentence, he reminded the State Department that "governments in Cuba are made up of Cubans." The moral tone of the new government therefore might not be an appreciable improvement on the old. The enthusiasm for the new government shown by members of the army, navy, and police, he observed, directly followed the announcement of substantial increases in their pay.[78]

There was some concern in Washington over the possible antidemocratic implications of developments in Cuba for other countries. On 11 March 1952, Acheson wrote to Truman of the State Department's concern that the coup would have "a bad effect on other countries which are planning elections this year in South America."[79] As a result of this concern, American recognition was delayed until after Batista's regime had first been recognized by Switzerland, France, Brazil, Italy, Great Britain, and the Vatican, among others.[80] The fact remains that the United States recognized the new regime in less than three weeks, on 27 March 1952. Nor was there any condemnation from Acheson, as there had been in response to José Remón's coup in Panama in November 1949, of the "deplorable disruption . . . of constitutional and democratic processes of government."[81] American policy toward Panama in November 1949 was admittedly a failure. So was American policy toward Somoza's coup in Nicaragua in May 1947. In that case, diplomatic recognition had been suspended for almost a year without any visible effect on Nicaraguan politics. Forgotten among the more glaring failures was the success of nonrecognition in Ecuador in August 1947. Although a policy of nonrecognition and prodemocratic rhetoric was not considered by American officials, it is worth asking what such a policy might plausibly have accomplished and upon what considerations it could have rested.

The most forceful advocate of a significant alternative policy in 1952 was Jay Lovestone, an official of the American Federation of Labor. Hearing of the CTC's arrangement with Batista, he sharply criticized the strategy involved. In a letter to Serafino Romualdi of 20 March 1952, he laid out the reasons why this strategy was mistaken and why it should not be followed by the AFL. While Lovestone was not commenting on what American policy should be, his assessment and evaluation clashes sharply with Miller's, and it is worth quoting at length:

> I still disagree with the estimate of the situation made by our Cuban friends. Though I am not seeking to give them any advice as to what they should do in their country, I want to say I can't see how we can keep quiet about a situation where force and violence were used in a military putsch to overthrow a legally constituted democratically elected government. We cannot keep quiet about such crimes in our own backyard when we show much alertness to denounce military usurpers and totalitarian subverters of democracy in other lands. The double standard of morality is not good for international labor policies. Besides, I think an ostrich has to be buried ten feet under so that he will not be able to see that a) constitutional liberties have been suspended for forty-five days; b) [although] the property of the unions has been restored to them. A situation may arise in which it can be taken away very easily by the dictatorship c) the unions which were recently associated with the overthrown government have touched danger by uncritical association with its putsch usurpers so that its hands will not be clean and strong if and when the situation arises where a break between the two will come; d) I don't think we should play dumb to the fact that the first one to recognize Batista was Trujillo and the second one Venezuela; nor do I think it is insignificant that anti-labor, big business interests were celebrating the return of Batista to power; e) last but not least, is the fact that Batista has as his foreign minister one of the first signers of the Stockholm Peace petition. This convinces me that this "poor colonel" has another iron in the fire for future use. I know it is hard to believe that which we do not want to believe. I understand the difficulties of our Cuban friends. It is for them to resolve the difficulties alone. It is for them to solicit our help if and when they need and want it. But we

owe it to ourselves to be outspoken in behalf of the position we have taken in a number of other cases where democracy was destroyed by totalitarian grave-diggers.[82]

By 20 March 1952, the American embassy in Havana reported that for the first time in months, if not years, Prío was being applauded by movie theater audiences when he appeared on screen.[83] Batista's appearances, in contrast, were received with silence or whistles. Before political radio broadcasts were prohibited on 17 March, crowds had begun to gather before the transmitting stations whenever an Ortodoxo speaker was on the air. On one occasion, the police fired into the air to disperse the crowd. Soldiers also fired over the heads of a group of sixteen congressmen attempting to enter the capitol building against Batista's orders.[84] On 23 March, the Council of the University of Havana issued what Beaulac referred to as a "serious and dignified" manifesto denouncing the coup, insisting on the restoration of the 1940 constitution and calling for a provisional presidency under Articles 148 and 149 of that constitution.[85] None of this directly threatened the regime, and American recognition later that week was doubtless discouraging to Cuba's democrats. On the other hand, recognition in no way improved Batista's popularity.

Batista had effective control of Cuba's population and territory. He did not have much more than that. By June 1952, he felt sufficiently threatened by his lack of popular support to dissolve the political parties and try to prevent them from holding public meetings.[86] There were even indications of discontent within the military over forced retirements and at such dramatic promotions as the transformation of a lieutenant into a commodore.[87] While Batista had established a working relationship with the CTC's Eusebio Mujal, the American embassy reported "indications that certain important leaders of the movement are not pleased with this development, and would be tempted to openly oppose the Administration if given the opportunity."[88] The CTC leadership was uneasy, one State Department official observed. They were worried that Batista might attempt to replace them with his personal followers. The statements and writings of those persons in the American labor movement close to the CTC were opposed to the Batista regime, but neither the American labor leaders nor the CTC leadership appeared able to decide "just what to do about it."[89]

On 11 June 1952, shortly after the elections were to have been held, the American embassy reported the results of a poll allegedly conducted by one of the ministers in Batista's government. The question asked was

"Whom would you prefer as president at the present time, Carlos Prío, Agramonte, or Batista?" The answers showed about 37 percent refusing to commit themselves, 26.8 percent for Prío, 34 and a fraction for Agramonte, and only 1.6 percent for Batista. "If the percentage for Batista appears low," the acting counselor of embassy commented, "it is probably not a great deal higher in reality. Whatever popularity Batista may enjoy, it appears to this Embassy to be on the wane."[90]

The basic question—given the hostility or indifference to Batista of the overwhelming majority of the Cuban public—is whether sufficient popular pressure could have been mobilized in such a way as to prevent his consolidation of power. On the day of the coup, it would have been easy for the American embassy to convey Prío's call to resist to interested American and Cuban reporters—in time for American radio broadcasts to have some influence before the situation had clearly begun to settle in Batista's favor. This was never considered. Nor was any consideration given to issuing the statement in defense of democracy requested of Beaulac by Carlos Hevia's assistant. No calculation as to whether such a statement would advance or harm American interests was made. Instead, a policy of nonintervention was adopted.

Had a calculation of American interests in the outcome of the situation been made, it is easy to see much potential value to the United States, and hard to see any real costs, to having Secretary of State Acheson repeat what he had already said publicly three years earlier: "We always deplore the action of any group in substituting its judgement for that of the electorate. We especially deplore the overthrow by force of a freely elected government. In such situations we do not cease to hope that the people will regain the right to choose their leaders."[91] For that matter, it is hard to see any real cost to urging publicly that elections take place as scheduled, with an interim government formed under Articles 148 and 149 of the Cuban Constitution of 1940.[92] Such statements, in conjunction with a denial of diplomatic recognition, might have been enough to tip the scales.[93] They would have stiffened the spine of those CTC and student elements inclined to resist and perhaps encouraged the initially apathetic political parties as well. If enough of the various pockets of resistance and potential resistance had come to feel that they were not isolated but were part of a broader movement that enjoyed international support, they might have been capable of bringing about a dramatically different outcome.

The most likely cost of failure would have been nothing more than the embarrassment of a Great Power at urging something on a small power in its sphere of influence and having its advice ignored and its intervention denounced. Less pleasant outcomes are also conceivable. American condemnation, and increased Cuban resistance, might have led Batista to fight for power with renewed vigor and to adopt harsh repressive measures. An assertively prodemocratic American policy would have held some danger of encouraging a division in the Cuban military that might have degenerated into civil war. There is no such thing as a policy free of risks. But there is also no reason to assume that the risks of action are necessarily greater than the risks of inaction.

As it turned out, the loss of a legitimate mechanism for peacefully changing governments in Cuba would cost the United States dearly within the decade. Just how dearly, there was no reason for American officials in 1952 to be expected to foresee. But they should have at least considered the possibility that Batista might come to be viewed in much the same way as Machado had been. Instead, their radical overestimate of the political capacity of Batista and the Cuban military, and their excessive contempt for Prío, helped blind them to the value of Cuba's democratic institutions. They failed to realize that these institutions were considered by a great many Cubans as "theirs." If these Cubans were not willing to risk their lives in a direct confrontation with the Cuban army, they were nevertheless quite ready to become critical of an American policy that recognized and supported the dictator responsible for destroying the democratic progress Cuba had made.

In the Cuba of 1952, as in the Venezuela of 1948, there were many well-organized groups and institutions that could have been mobilized in defense of democracy. These included trade unions and political parties, newspapers, and student associations. While it was beyond the power of the United States to mobilize such groups, it would have been relatively easy to offer them encouragement at a decisive moment in the political history of their countries. Such encouragement could have given the democratic openings in both countries a second chance. At a minimum, it would have made it more difficult to associate the United States with two particularly disreputable dictatorships. Such an assertively prodemocratic policy, although it would have required some diminution of the American commitment to nonintervention, would not have required any great changes in the way the basic material and ideal interests of the United States were conceived. It would not have required any change at all in the strategic priority American officials gave to the Cold War and anticommunism. Nor would it have required any change in American capitalism. If Cold War liberals like Jay Lovestone had been in charge of American policy, instead of Cold War conservatives like Edward Miller, that would have been enough.

Democratic Solidarity in Eclipse

Wherever dictatorial governments succeeded in maintaining themselves in power in Latin America in the later Truman years, democratic solidarity was eclipsed as an effective component of American policy. Wherever democratic governments remained, however, this sense of solidarity continued to function to their benefit. This was particularly true in Chile. The only partial exception to this rule was Guatemala, where American officials perceived a threat to American security in the close relationship between the government of Jacobo Arbenz and the Guatemalan CP.[94] On 10 July 1952, CIA deputy director Allen Dulles met with Miller and Deputy Assistant Secretary of State Thomas Mann in an effort to gain their approval before supplying weapons and money to various would-be Guatemalan revolutionaries in an operation named PBFORTUNE. While Miller and Mann indicated that they wanted a new government in Guatemala, imposed by force if necessary, they "avoided direct answers when Dulles asked if they wanted the CIA to take steps to bring about that outcome." Dulles was willing to take this "vagueness" as implying approval, but CIA director Walter Bedell Smith was not. Yet rather than see Miller and Mann and attempt to clarify matters, he went to see Undersecretary of State David Bruce instead. He then signed the order to proceed with PBFORTUNE on 9 September 1952.[95] There is no indication that Miller and Mann, or for that matter Acheson, were aware of Bruce's conversation with Smith or ever approved of PBFORTUNE.

On 3 October 1952, Mann sent a memo to Acheson indicating that officials from Nicaragua, the Dominican Republic, Colombia, and Venezuela planned to undertake "indirect" military action against Guatemala and "would like to have a 'green light' from the U.S. and tangible support in arms." He went on to stress that both "Colombia and Venezuela fear Betancourt (former Acción Democrática leader in Venezuela) who presently lives in exile in San José, Costa Rica, more than they do Guatemala" and that Somoza was also fearful of developments in Costa Rica where Figueres was the leading presidential candidate. In responding to the Nicaraguan ambassador's description of the military action these Latin American governments planned to undertake, Mann told Acheson that he and Miller had explained where the United States stood and why:

Messrs. Miller and Mann, on separate occasions, stated as clearly as possible to Ambassador Sevilla Sacasa that the United States could never condone military intervention on the part of an American State against one of its neighbors, pointing out that non-intervention was one of the very keystones of the Inter-American system and that there are treaty commitments against such action. The Ambassador was reminded that the United States is fighting with its UN allies in Korea for the non-aggression principle. The Ambassador was told, however, that the United States has been concerned with the communist influence in the Guatemalan government and that it might be more appropriate to approach that problem through ODECA (Organization of Central American States) or, if that were not possible, through the regularly established procedures of the OAS, if practicable.[96]

Once PBFORTUNE's cover was blown, Nicholas Cullather has concluded, "Miller wasted no time in terminating it."[97] As late as March 1953, Mann was still willing to argue that if the United States allowed events to take their course, "the pendulum in Guatemala would swing back," but this was a position that steadily lost support in the new administration of Dwight Eisenhower over the course of that year.[98]

In helping to overthrow Arbenz in 1954, American policy certainly closed off whatever prospects existed for a peaceful outcome that would have preserved the democratic gains Guatemala had made since 1944. This is one of the more direct and significant contributions American policy has made to the dictatorial side of the ledger in Latin American politics. Yet the assumption that democracy would have survived in Guatemala in the absence of American intervention is highly problematic. There were many forces pushing Guatemalan politics in antidemocratic directions.

In his study of Guatemalan politics and American policy, Piero Gleijeses has made the case that Arbenz and the Partido Guatemalteco de Trabajo (PGT) were strategic, not merely tactical, allies and that their alliance was what drove the United States to intervene. He nevertheless suggests that this alliance was not a sufficient justification for intervention and maintains that it was not a significant threat to Guatemalan democracy. The interviews he conducted with former PGT leaders apparently convinced him that Arbenz and the PGT would not have attempted to impose a dictatorship of the proletariat on Guatemala because they recognized that the country first had to pass through a period of bourgeois democracy.[99] At the time, however, PGT secretary-general José Manuel Fortuny sang this tune at a different tempo. In a report to the party congress in 1952 at which the Guatemalan CP changed its name to the PGT, he argued that there was no need for the leadership of the Guatemalan Revolution to remain with the bourgeoisie and explicitly denied that the necessary capitalist period would have to be a long one.[100]

Arbenz was constitutionally prohibited from seeking a second term in 1956, and Gleijeses has acknowledged the possibility that he might have tried to circumvent this prohibition and remain in office: "The president would have had few moral qualms about setting the bourgeois constitution aside, but this action, tantamount to a coup d'état, would have been possible only with the army's support. And why should the military cooperate? Loyalty to Arbenz was not unconditional even among *Arbencista* officers, and it was progressively weakened by the mounting evidence of the president's ties to the PGT."[101] The unspoken assumption here is that Arbenz and the PGT would not have misread the correlation of forces, overreached, and provoked a military coup. But those with few moral qualms about violating "bourgeois" morality have again and again demonstrated remarkably poor judgement in estimating the strength of their opponents, and such an outcome in the event the United States had not intervened is by no means improbable.[102] This hardly justifies the intervention the Eisenhower administration undertook in 1954, but it should provide pause to those inclined to saddle American policy with exclusive blame for the many years of suffering following Arbenz's overthrow. So should the concern of two acute contemporary observers of Latin American politics who thought that if Arbenz had remained in power, Guatemala might have had "a post-World War II type of 'popular democracy' within six months to a year later."[103]

In contrast with Guatemala, and with every dictatorial regime in Latin America, Chile enjoyed a particularly high level of American support during the later Truman years. This was for three basic and related reasons: (1) because it was a democracy, (2) because of the policies pursued by the Chilean government, and (3) because the American ambassador to Santiago was the liberal Cold Warrior and popular historian Claude Bowers.[104] Bowers's tenure in Chile lasted from June 1939 to September 1953. Before the Truman administration began, he was already widely known and liked in Chile. On completing ten years of service in the country, he was formally honored by the Chilean Parliament.[105] He maintained an extensive correspondence with Presidents Roosevelt and Truman and was highly regarded by both.[106] He was particularly appreciated for his gift for succinct and biting commentary. "McCarthy is the most effective instrumentality Stalin has in the States," Bowers wrote to Truman in August 1951.[107]

Bowers had long been admired in liberal circles in the United States and was increasingly well thought of by Latin American democrats.[108] In March 1943, Henry Wallace could recall the keynote speech Bowers gave to the 1928 Democratic Convention as "the most inspiring political address to which I have ever listened."[109] In February 1957, Betancourt would write of the honor he had felt at hearing the comments of Bowers while receiving an award from the Inter-American Association for Democracy and Freedom. "In Latin America you are esteemed for your intellect and admired for your loyalty to the best North American democratic traditions. We see in you one of the faithful followers of the liberal ideology fashioned by the founders of the Republic in the Constitution of Philadelphia."[110]

On several occasions, Bowers would request and receive Truman's personal support for measures to help Chile, ranging from dealings with the World Bank to negotiations over copper prices to the prompt delivery of American military assistance. In his letters to Washington he continually stressed Chile's value to the United States as a genuine democracy, and his position on this point was widely shared. "I sincerely hope that Chile will have an election that will stand up in the eyes of the world," Truman wrote Bowers in July 1946, "and I am sure that they will."[111] Beyond the mere fact of Chilean democracy, American officials welcomed a series of policies pursued by the Chilean government for most of the Truman years. Urging the provision of economic assistance to Chile in April 1950, CIA director Roscoe Hillenkoetter stressed that these policies included: "(1) granting full support to the US in the Cold War; (2) backing democratic forces throughout Latin America; and (3) promoting closer economic ties with the US."[112]

Suggesting that the Chilean government was not properly appreciative of what the United States had done for Chile, Miller offered Bowers a laundry list of reminders in January 1952. Despite the petulant tone of this list, it is worth quoting at length as it can leave no doubt that Chile enjoyed an extraordinarily favored position among the countries of Latin America as far as American officials in the later Truman years were concerned:

1. Export-Import Bank loan for amplification of steel mill.
2. Obtaining of priorities for steel mill at strong insistence of the Department of State with NPA to obtain steel badly needed in our defense program.

3. Obtaining of priorities for construction of petroleum refinery which was equally as difficult as the priorities for the steel mill. The result of the obtaining of these two priorities puts Chile in as favorable a position for steel allocations as any country in the world and took a very great deal of urging.

4. Straightening out of Chile's long difficulties with the International Bank which as the President will remember was personally attended to by me when I was in Chile last March. At the time he seemed to express due gratitude for this although it seems to have slipped his mind since.

5. The sale of two cruisers to Chile at bargain prices *both* of which have been delivered to Chile in perfect form ahead of those bought by Brazil and Argentina.

6. Offer to negotiate a grant military aid agreement with Chile entirely unconditional upon any demonstration of Chile's interest in Korea.

7. Negotiation of a copper agreement with Chile under which Chile obtains 3 cents a pound for copper more than our own producers, copper being the only commodity with regard to which our producers get less than foreign producers.

8. Substantial increase in our Point IV activities in Chile especially in agricultural fields as desired by the President.

9. United States support of Chile for the Security Council of the UN and for the election of Sra. Figueroa as President of the General Assembly's Committee on Human Rights.[113]

The unusually high level of support the United States provided to Chile's democratic government in the later Truman years, like the lesser levels of support it provided to dictatorial governments in Nicaragua and the Dominican Republic, does not appear to have had any consequences for regime change or regime maintenance.[114] Chilean democracy would have survived without this support, and the Somoza and Trujillo dictatorships would have survived without it as well. The extent of American support for Chile is indicative of the residual strength of democratic solidarity as a component of American policy. Unfortunately, such solidarity was most needed by Latin American democrats in the later Truman years in countries where democracy was not yet established and above all where, as in Venezuela in November 1948 and Cuba in March 1952, its hold on power was being challenged by politicized and unprofessional military forces.

The Civility of Yankee Imperialism

Civility, the virtue of concern for the common good, was particularly evident among those American officials who recognized that they had more in common with many Latin American leftists and nationalists than they did with "pro-American" despots like Somoza and Trujillo. It was also particularly evident among those Latin American democrats who recognized that they had more in common with many American imperialists than they did with the "anti-imperialists" of the antidemocratic left. One need only look at the positions of democratic leaders such as Víctor Raúl Haya de la Torre, José Figueres, Rómulo Betancourt, Galo Plaza, Ramón Grau San Martín, and many others—and at the positions of American liberals such as Adolf Berle, Claude Bowers, Spruille Braden, Ellis Briggs, Allan Dawson, and many others—to recognize that they not only shared a good many interests, and fairly compatible strategies for pursuing them, but felt some measure of common affinity for all the peoples of the New World. Somewhat like the Greek intellectuals Polybius and Posidonius long before them, these Latin American democrats can be seen as trying to hold a not-entirely-foreign empire to the higher standards of a common culture.[1]

The international traditions that place a high value on democratic solidarity and respect for national sovereignty are part of the common culture of the modern world. Americans and Latin Americans alike have helped to cultivate these traditions. By discouraging consideration of some courses of action and suggesting the desirability of others, these traditions have helped to determine the character of American policy. They have helped make American officials more responsive than they otherwise would have been to the influence of Latin American leaders, to the arguments of Latin American intellectuals and publicists, and above all to the trend of political developments within Latin America.

The civility of American officials such as Edward Miller, Louis Halle, and George Kennan is harder to see. An explicit appeal to self-interest, including exclusively American self-interest, plays a larger role in their more conservative tradition. Their civility is evident, however, in their commitment to pursue a policy of nonintervention as long as the security of the United States was not seriously threatened by internal developments in another country. This commitment was no more the consequence of a careful calculation of interests than the analogous commitment of the liberals to pursue a policy of democratic solidarity. In both cases, we are dealing with a willingness to limit the pursuit of American interests out of respect for the rights and interests of others, a concern for the common good, and a belief that in the long run American interests would be best served by such civility.

Among those who have taken a hostile view of American policy in Latin America, and particularly among those who have described the United States as operating an empire, there has been a strong tendency to emphasize the resistance with which Latin Americans have responded to America's imperial ascendancy and to ignore or downplay their cooperation. These critics of Yankee imperialism tend to overlook the junctures at which solidarity between American and Latin American democrats has contributed to political progress in the region. They leave the impression that Latin Americans have never looked to the United States for leadership when in fact some have done so from the beginning. "Where, Oh noble and grand Washington, are the lessons of your politics?" asked the Argentine liberal Mariano Moreno in 1810: "Where are the rules which guided you in the construction of your great work? Your principles and your system would be sufficient to guide us—lend us your genius so that we may accomplish the results which we have contemplated."[2]

Pursuing a strategy that combined cooperation and resistance, Haya de la Torre, Betancourt, Figueres, and many others were often harshly critical of American policy and yet continued to see the United States as a potential source of hope. Figueres went so far as to argue that America's prestige as a democratic power and as the leader of the democratic cause in the world was of fundamental importance. "I know that many North Americans do not understand this. But I am bound by sufficient ties, cultural and emotional, with the United States, to feel entitled to fight for their reputation with my fellow Latin Americans. Especially since on this reputation, the survival of democracy in the New World depends."[3]

Correctly perceiving an American desire and capacity to contribute to the extension and defense of democratic government in Latin America that waxed and waned over time, these Latin American democrats faulted the

United States not so much for being a wealthy and powerful empire as for failing to extend sufficient support to fellow democrats. Testifying before the United States Congress in 1958, after Vice President Richard Nixon had been met with stones and spitting during a visit to Lima and Caracas, Figueres tried again to persuade American officials to adopt a consistently prodemocratic policy. Why, he asked, did the United States speak for liberty and human dignity in Russia but hesitate to do so in the Dominican Republic?

> Spitting is a despicable practice, when it is physically performed. But what about moral spitting? When your government invited Pedro Estrada, the Himmler of the Western Hemisphere, to be honored in Washington, did you not spit on the faces of all Latin American democrats? He deserved to be honored, we were told, because, as chief of police of a police state, he managed to maintain peace in Caracas, while a conference on human rights was held there over the screams of the tortured. You could easily keep peace in the world, if you turned it all into a huge cemetery. My government refused to participate in such a gruesome event. We provoked the ire of some United States Government officials and the criticism of some well-meaning North American newspapers. This was 1954, 4 years ago. The families of these dead are still spitting.[4]

Criticizing particular American violations of national sovereignty, moderate nationalists like Figueres, Haya, and Betancourt did not view the existence of the American empire itself as an intolerable injustice, at least not in the short term. Sympathetic to the democratic and reformist traditions of the United States, they recognized that American officials were capable of sharing with them, although with less consistency and intensity, an appreciation of the validity of their own claims to legitimate authority. Confronting the failure of the United States to do as much for the democratic cause in Latin America as they hoped, they correctly identified a periodic American desire and capacity to remain neutral in the internal political disputes of other countries as an important culprit.[5]

The rivalry between liberal and conservative impulses in American policy has been ignored by political scientists convinced that idealism plays no significant role in policy. "While national interests are often cloaked in the uplifting idiom of moral purpose," Peter Smith insists, "it is the quest for geopolitical and economic advantage—not idealism—that provides the driving force behind foreign policy and international behavior."[6] "For nearly two centuries," Lars Schoultz agrees, "U.S. policy has invariably intended to serve the interests of the United States—interests variously related to our nation's security, to our domestic politics, or to our economic development." Underlying this self-serving approach has been a consistent belief in Latin American inferiority that, according to Schoultz, "determines the precise steps the United States takes to protect its interests in the region."[7] Although in tune with an easy cynicism, the inadequacy of such a perspective has been amply demonstrated by this book. The rivalry between liberals and conservatives that did so much to shape American policy and its influence on Latin American politics was defined by competing conceptions of how the common good should be pursued far more than by differences over what constituted American economic and political interests.

Beyond changes in the political geography of Latin America, and in the related issue of the relative strength of liberalism and conservatism among American officials, American policy was shaped by individuals. Subtle differences in the outlook of individuals had a large impact on American policy and sometimes even a significant impact on the politics of other countries. Had the ambassador to Cuba in 1944 been someone other than Spruille Braden, Fulgencio Batista might well have retained his hold on power. Many other ambassadors would not have sought to avoid such an outcome. Had Adolf Berle not been ambassador to Brazil in 1945, it is not hard to imagine a military coup that would have placed Gomes in power with a less-than-peaceful outcome. Had John Simmons not been ambassador to Ecuador in 1947, the United States might have helped a would-be dictator consolidate power. Had Frank Corrigan been ambassador to Venezuela in 1948, instead of Walter Donnelly, the United States might well have sought to help keep a democratic government in power. The same point applies to Cuba in 1952: a less conservative ambassador than Willard Beaulac might well have made an effort on behalf of Cuban democracy.

A generation or two ago, American officials could find considerable sympathy and support among academics for their vision of the United States as an international good neighbor who normally played by the rules and was willing to lend a hand. Even an orthodox "realist" like Robert Osgood recognized that idealism and a concern for American security were combined in the Marshall Plan. "Realists" like George Kennan and Hans Morgenthau were critical of what they saw as the unwillingness of the American people to act on the basis of cold and selfish calculations of the national interest. But Osgood insisted on the positive contribution that had been made by an informed public opinion concerned with both ideals and self-interest. Skeptics might disparage the power of reason to govern the actions of a democratic people, he observed in 1953, but "the history of the last decade has shown that when the American people are convinced that their vital interests are at stake, reason is a more persuasive guide to policy than either wish or impulse. There is a strong element of pragmatic common sense in the American people. It needs only to be informed to be effective."[8]

Even when disagreeing with American policy, authors such as Samuel Flagg Bemis, Dana Munro, Arthur Whitaker, and Bryce Wood were inclined to see American officials as acting on the basis of many of the same values and ideas they themselves held dear. The Latin American policy of the United States, Bemis suggested in 1943, "has reflected constantly the vital necessities of national security and the idealism of the American people."[9] Franklin Roosevelt's Good Neighbor policy, Wood concluded in 1961, was "a rare amalgam of moral elevation and political achievement."[10] Having personally helped fashion the policy that Roosevelt repudiated, Munro argued that it had been well-intended—seeking to promote both American interests and the democratic cause—but had alienated public and elite opinion in Latin America. The military interventions of the first third of the twentieth century might have been forgiven, he suggested, "had it not been for the belief that the policy was inspired by sinister and sordid motives, which might well reassert themselves at some future time."[11] Providing a more generous interpretation of American motives, and demonstrating that there was solid evidence for such an interpretation, was one of the major purposes of Munro's work.

Ironically, the conservative impulse that the Roosevelt administration gave to American policy helped associate the United States with the support of Latin American dictatorships. Somoza, for example, arriving in Washington in May 1939, was greeted at the train station by the president, the vice president, the chief justice of the Supreme Court, leading members of Congress, a twenty-one-gun salute, a military honor guard, a motorcade down Pennsylvania Avenue, a state dinner in his honor, and an overnight stay at the White House.[12] The support inherent in such gestures did not go uncriticized, and the debate over the purposes behind American policy was intensified by American military interventions and covert operations after the Second World War. Already associated with Somoza and Trujillo, the United States was soon linked with the overthrow of governments such as that of Jacobo Arbenz in Guatemala. American policy toward Latin America came to be considered by many as something shameful. Americans, Ernest May observed in 1963, were inclined to say of their own country's record in Latin America what Gladstone said of Austria's role in Europe: that one could point to no place on the map and say, There, the nation did good. May argued that the intentions behind American policy had been legitimate.[13] Many of those who have written since the early 1960s have been less inclined to credit American officials with decent intentions. They have tended to a debunking attitude toward the intense patriotism of an earlier generation of scholars, referring, for example, to Samuel Flagg Bemis as "Samuel 'Wave the Flag' Bemis."[14] They often have sought to uncover the darker aspects of American policy, to stress its selfishness and self-centeredness, and have offered an account that places greater emphasis on the negative than the positive effects of American policy on other peoples.

"The past is the history of how the class-ridden remains of the Spanish empire turned into the revolution-ridden parts of the North American system," Walter LaFeber has concluded, arguing that the United States has responded to revolutionary aspirations for a better life with force and violence and so made a difficult situation still more difficult and violent.[15] The high levels of political and social turmoil that have characterized recent Central American history, John Coatsworth concurs, "are the result, in large part, of excessively close and subordinate ties to the United States."[16] Although the episodes of military and covert intervention on which scholars like LaFeber and Coatsworth focus have received greater attention, it is by no means clear that such episodes have been as important for the evolution of political life in Latin America as the kinds of political struggles examined here. In these struggles, where they were in a good position to exercise a significant influence with relatively little effort, American officials either sought to support the democratic side or to remain neutral. In the course of similar struggles over the decades, American officials may well have provided Latin America's democrats with more important support than Latin America's dictators.

The possibility that American policy has done Latin America's democrats more good than harm does not excuse the harm that was done or remove the moral obligation of seeking to do better in the future. It does suggest the desirability of recognizing the strength and potential of liberal and conservative impulses in American policy and harnessing them to good effect. In their promises to do right by the rest of the world, it is understandable that Americans have preferred to speak of "leadership" rather than "imperialism." If there were no such thing as collective guilt, there would never be an effort to whitewash the past. Yet the task for the foreseeable future involves more than a choice between liberal and conservative leadership. It involves recognition and concern for an empire that was built by both. It involves coming to terms with what that empire has meant to other peoples as well as to the people of the United States and seeking to construct a genuine "Empire of Liberty" upon its foundation. The power of the American empire is too deeply rooted in our emerging global society to disappear. By action and inaction it will continue to exercise an influence on developments around the planet regardless of whether an effort is made to conceive of American policy in imperial terms or not. The potential advantage of such a conception is a greater appreciation of when and how such influence has been helpful in the past and might be constructive in the future.

Notes

Preface

1. Lane Kirkland, eulogy of George Meany, 15 January 1980, text in *Free Trade Union News* 35, no. 1 (January–February): p. 1.

2. "My obsession," Polish activist Adam Michnik would note in 1999, "has been that we should have a revolution that not resemble the French or Russian, but rather the American." Roger Cohen, "The Accommodations of Adam Michnik," *New York Times Magazine*, 7 November 1999, p. 72.

3. Technically, the name of the organization had already been changed to the Young Social Democrats, but those of us who knew its history preferred to call it the YPSL ("Yipsel").

4. Schwartzberg, "Peace and Ideology," *Reed College Quest*, 24 March 1982.

5. My assumption was that the United States could find democratic allies everywhere in the world. See Schwartzberg, "Human Rights in El Salvador," *Chicago Tribune*, 10 August 1981.

6. On the motives behind postwar policy toward Japan, see Schwartzberg, "The 'Soft Peace Boys,'" pp. 185–216.

7. My use of the concept of civility is an extension of an idea elaborated by Edward Shils, with whom I had the good fortune to take a course in the political sociology of Max Weber in the spring semester of 1982. See Shils, *The Virtue of Civility*. See also Kantorowicz, *Der Geist Englischen Politik*.

8. William Clinton, State of the Union address, 27 January 2000.

9. Franklin Roosevelt, inaugural address, 1933, *The Public Papers and Addresses of Franklin D. Roosevelt* (New York: Random House, 1938), 2:14.

10. Betancourt, *El 18 de octubre de 1945*, p. 302.

11. Harry S. Truman, address to the governing board of the Pan American Union, 15 April 1946, text in *Bulletin of the Pan American Union* 78, no. 6 (June 1946): pp. 309–10.

12. Haya, address at a luncheon of Pan American Women's Association, 7 February 1948, file "PAWA Minutes," box 34, Grant Papers.

13. Rock, ed., *Latin America in the 1940s*, p. 35.

Chapter 1. Cold War Liberalism in Latin America

1. Braden, "President Batista and Communist Infiltration in Cuba," 28 August 1943, p. 2, file "Bra-Bre," box 29, Berle Papers. Thanking Braden for his memo, which he described as the most valuable on the subject of communist infiltration that the State Department had yet received from Latin America, Assistant Secretary of State Adolf Berle added that it was clear "the dissolution of the Communist International did not in any sense mean the renunciation by Moscow of its previous policy of using Communist Parties throughout the world and affiliated groups for the furtherance of Soviet interests." Berle to Braden, 4 September 1943, file "Bra-Bre," box 29, Berle Papers.

2. Braden, "Conditions in Cuba and Their Effect on Our Relations," June 1943, p. 3, file "Bra-Bre," box 29, Berle Papers.

3. Gellman, *Roosevelt and Batista*, p. 211. On the estimate of a $2,000,000 loss to Batista, see Braden, "Memorandum for Policy Committee on Conditions in Cuba and Our Policies in Respect Thereto," 1 August 1944, file "Correspondence 1945–Cuba A," box 15, Braden Papers.

4. Braden to Berle, 22 November 1943, included with Berle to Secretary of State Hull, 25 November 1943, file "Bra-Bre," box 29, Berle Papers.

5. Wood, *The Making of the Good Neighbor Policy*, p. 88.

6. See Thomas, *Cuba: The Pursuit of Freedom*, pp. 691–736.

7. Roca, *El triunfo*, p. 2.

8. Berle, diary entry of 29 August 1944, in Berle and Jacobs, eds., *Navigating the Rapids*, pp. 458–59.

9. Braden, "Agenda for Washington," n.d., pp. 1–2, 837.00/1–2045, National Archives (hereafter NA).

10. Dawson to Byrnes, 7 September 1946, file "Diplomatic Correspondence, 1946–47: A–D," box 20, Braden Papers.

11. Braden, "Agenda for Washington," p. 8.

12. Ibid., pp. 1–10; Braden to John Muccio, 27 January 1945, file "Correspondence 1945–Cuba A," box 15, Braden Papers.

13. Braden, "Policy Respecting Dictatorships and Disreputable Governments," 5 April 1945, pp. 1–7, 711.00/4–545, NA.

14. Ibid., pp. 6–7.

15. Ibid., pp. 7–9.

16. See Joseph Grew to certain diplomatic missions, 711.00/5–2845, NA; and Division of American Republics Analysis and Liaison, "Ambassador Braden's Proposed Policy Respecting Dictatorships and Disreputable Governments in the Other American Republics," October 1945, file "Dictatorships and Disreputable Governments," in Records of the Deputy Assistant Secretaries of State for Inter-American Affairs, 1945–56, lot files 57 D 598, 57 D 634, 58 D 691, NA. Those favorable included Ambassadors Claude Bowers (Chile), Hallett Johnson (Costa Rica), J. F. McGurk (Dominican Republic), William Dawson (Uruguay), Edwin Kyle (Guatemala), George Messersmith (Mexico), Orme Wilson (Haiti), and John Simmons (El Salvador). Those opposed included Ambassadors John C. White (Peru), Willard Beaulac (Paraguay), Walter Thurston (Bolivia), and John Erwin (Honduras).

17. Bowers to Grew, 14 June 1945, pp. 5–6, 710.11/6–1445, NA.

18. Minutes of the meeting of 25 June 1945, Records of the Secretary of State's Staff Committee, microfilm, M-1054, roll 3, NA.

19. Briggs, *Proud Servant* (unpublished manuscript, 1975), p. 325, box 1, Briggs Papers.

20. See Berle, diary entry of 4 April 1940, in *Navigating the Rapids*, p. 301.

21. Quoted in Braden to Franklin Delano Roosevelt, 27 March 1939, Official File 3193, Roosevelt Library.

22. See chapter 3.

23. Grew to Braden, 28 September 1945, MSAm1687 v. 121(13), Grew Papers.

24. Acheson to Braden, 30 August 1945, Catalogued Correspondence, boxes 1–3, Braden Papers.

25. Braden to J. Edgar Hoover, 9 July 1946, 810.00B/7–846, NA.

26. Bowers to Braden, 19 November 1945, file "Nov.–Dec. 1945," box 6, mss. II, Bowers Papers.

27. Braden to Bowers, 3 December 1945, file "Nov.–Dec. 1945," box 6, mss. II, Bowers Papers.

28. Braden to Bowers, 29 December 1945, file "Nov.–Dec. 1945," box 6, mss. II, Bowers Papers.

29. Bowers, *My Mission to Spain*.

30. Bowers to Byrnes, 3 December 1945, file "Nov. 9–Dec. 1945," box 6, mss. II, Bowers Papers.

31. Betancourt, speech of 26 July 1946, in Arévalo and Betancourt, *Venezuela y Guatemala*, p. 16.

32. Central Intelligence Agency, "The Venezuelan Elections of 14 Dec. 1947," ORE 65, 5 January 1948, pp. 3–4, and "CIA Reports ORE 1948, 58–65," box 256, President's Secretary's File, Harry S. Truman Library.

33. Briggs, *Proud Servant*, p. 93. When Briggs completed this memoir shortly before his death in 1975, Costa Rica, Venezuela, and Colombia were the only Latin American democracies. While the "predictable future" as he saw it looked bleak, Latin America was in fact on the eve of the greatest wave of democratic openings in its history.

34. Braden to Thurston, 26 August 1946, file "Diplomatic Correspondence, 1946–47: Q–V," box 20, Braden Papers.

35. In his memoirs, Briggs noted that while he and Braden thought Latin America was important to the United States, they recognized that for the next generation it would "not be so important as the reconstruction of Europe, or the stabilization of relations with the Soviet Union, or the solution of the problems of Asia." Briggs, *Proud Servant*, p. 93.

36. See Chalmers to Berle Jr., 7 September 1945, and Berle Jr. to Chalmers, 12 September 1945, file "Philip O. Chalmers," box 75, Berle Papers. Chalmers was the head of the Division of Brazilian Affairs in the State Department at this time.

37. Louis Halle, "Draft: Policy Governing Economic Assistance to the Other American Republics," 27 August 1945, attached to an office memorandum by William G. MacLean of 29 August 1945, 810.50/8–2945, NA. A later draft is attached to the letter of 7 September from Chalmers to Berle mentioned above. Halle was at this

time the acting assistant chief of the Division of American Republics Analysis and Liaison.

38. Department of State, "Current U.S. Policy toward the Other American Republics," *The American Republics* (tentative draft), 16 December 1946, pp. 1–2, 711.20/12–1646, NA.

39. Dana G. Munro, "Some Notes on Latin American Policy," 28 September 1945, p. 10, 710.11/9–2845, NA. Munro was at this point a special assistant to the director of the Office of American Republic Affairs.

40. Ibid., p. 3.

41. John Wiley, memorandum, 8 November 1945, file "South America," box 188, President's Secretary's Files, Truman Library. In a letter to Dean Acheson of 17 January 1946 enclosing a copy of this memo, Wiley mentioned that he had given a copy to Braden. Acheson's response noted only that he had read the memo "with interest." See Wiley to Acheson, 17 January 1946, and Acheson to Wiley, 4 February 1946, 810.00/1–1746, NA.

42. See Ameringer, *Don Pepe*, pp. 163–226.

43. Thomas W. Braden, "I'm glad the CIA is 'immoral,'" *Saturday Evening Post*, 20 May 1967, p. 10.

44. See chapters 3, 6, and 7.

45. Hillenkoetter to Braden, 16 July 1947, file "Resignation," box 22, Braden Papers. At this time, Hillenkoetter was still head of the Central Intelligence Group (CIG), which would only become the CIA under section 102(f) of the National Security Act of 26 July 1947. See M. Warner, ed., *The CIA under Harry Truman*, p. 134 and passim.

46. Braden, "Subject: Combating Communism," 12 May 1947, pp. 2–3, FW 810.00B/5–847, NA.

47. "Braden reunido con Haya de la Torre," *El Nacional* (Caracas), 14 March 1947.

48. Policy Planning Staff, PPS-26, "To establish U.S. policy regarding anti-Communist measures which could be planned and carried out within the Inter-American System," 22 March 1948, *FRUS, 1948*, 9:197, 200.

49. George Marshall to Diplomatic Representatives in the American Republics, 21 June 1948, U.S. Department of State, *Foreign Relations of the United States: 1948* (hereafter FRUS), 9:193.

50. PPS-26, 22 March 1948, *FRUS, 1948*, 9:199.

Chapter 2. A New Dealer and Cold Warrior in Brazil

1. See Mark, "Charles E. Bohlen and Acceptable Limits," pp. 201–13. See also Mark, "American Policy toward Eastern Europe," pp. 313–36.

2. Quoted in G. Smith, *The Last Years*, p. 44.

3. Quoted in the *New York Times*, 19 November 1943.

4. G. Smith, *The Last Years*, p. 53.

5. Quoted in Weil, *A Pretty Good Club*, pp. 190–91.

6. A. Berle, A–B/1, "Principal Problems in Europe," 26 September 1944, file "Records Relating to Miscellaneous Policy Committees," box 137, Papers of Harley A. Notter, NA. The text is reproduced in A. Berle, *Navigating the Rapids*, pp. 460–68.

7. A. Berle and Means, *The Modern Corporation and Private Property*, p. 353.

8. A. Berle, address to the Academy of Political Science, 2 May 1939, pp. 5–7, file "Speeches," box 77, Berle Papers.

9. Berle to Corrigan, 8 May 1939, file "Adolf Berle," box 1, Corrigan Papers.

10. A. Berle, address on Inter-American affairs at George Washington University, 5 December 1939, p. 6, file "Speeches," box 77, Berle Papers.

11. Berle to Roosevelt, Hull, and Welles, n.d., pp. 2–15, file "Post War Plans, 1942," box 65, Berle Papers.

12. Ibid.

13. A. Berle, "The Bases of the Present War, the Mechanism of a Progressively Developing Victory and of a Peace Based Thereon," n.d., pp. 3–8, file "Post War Problems: Economic and Political, 1942–43," box 65, Berle Papers.

14. Ibid., pp. 10–12.

15. A. Berle, address to the Association of American Universities, 15 November 1940, p. 1, file "Speeches," box 77, Berle Papers.

16. A. Berle, "The Bases of the Present War," p. 7.

17. See Schwartzberg, "The 'Soft Peace Boys,'" pp. 185–216.

18. Post War Programs Committee, minutes of the 25th meeting, 27 April 1944, p. 5, in Iokibe, *The Occupation of Japan*, 2–D-4.

19. A. Berle, "American Situation in Face of the Possibilities of Defeat of Germany," 6 September 1943, pp. 1–3, file "Post War Problems: Economic and Political, 1942–43," box 65, Berle Papers.

20. Ibid., pp. 5–6.

21. Ibid., pp. 6–8.

22. Berle's diary entries in 1944 and 1945 were frequently more pessimistic than his statements in governmental committees or in memoranda. He appears to have tempered his pessimism in those contexts in an attempt to gain official support for his basic views.

23. A. Berle, diary entry of 29 August 1944, in *Navigating the Rapids*, p. 458.

24. A. Berle, diary entry of 23 September 1944, box 216, Berle Papers. By the time Soviet planes dropped supplies, on 16 September 1944, it was "much too little too late to do any good." De Santis, *The Diplomacy of Silence*, p. 120. Tadeusz Bor-Komorowski was the senior military figure in the uprising. W. Averell Harriman was the American ambassador in Moscow.

25. Troy, *Donovan and the CIA*, pp. 13–20, 132.

26. Schwarz, *Liberal*, p. 172.

27. Dulles to Berle, 13 February 1953, file "Personal Correspondence," box 82, Berle Papers.

28. A. Berle, A–B/1, "Principal Problems in Europe," 26 September 1944, p. 5. Membership in the two committees was largely overlapping, and Berle played an important role in both. See Notter, *Postwar Foreign Policy Preparation*, pp. 208–12.

29. Policy Committee, minutes of the 79th meeting, 13 October 1944, pp. 2–3, file "Records Relating to Miscellaneous Policy Committees," box 138, Papers of Harley A. Notter, NA. Minutes cited hereafter by meeting number and date.

30. A. Berle, "Principal Problems in Europe," *Navigating the Rapids*, p. 463.

31. Policy Committee, minutes of the 79th meeting, 13 October 1944, p. 4.

32. A. Berle, "Principal Problems in Europe," *Navigating the Rapids*, pp. 464–65.

33. Ibid., pp. 466–67.

34. Ibid., pp. 464–68.

35. Policy Committee, minutes of the 79th meeting, 13 October 1944, p. 4.

36. Ibid., pp. 3–4. The four area office directors on the subcommittee with Berle were James Dunn, Europe; Wallace Murray, Near East; Joseph Grew, Far East; and Norman Armour, Latin America.

37. "Report to the Policy Committee Regarding United States Interests and Policy in Eastern and Southeastern Europe and the Near East from the Subcommittee Composed of Mr. Berle and the Directors of the Four Area Offices" (hereafter "PC-8," including annexes A through L), 1 November 1944, file "Records Relating to Miscellaneous Policy Committees," box 137, Papers of Harley A. Notter, NA; Policy Committee, minutes of the 81st meeting, 25 October 1944.

38. PC-8, pp. 1–2. As a separate point, the general position that territorial settlements should be left until the end of the war was reaffirmed.

39. PC-8, p. 1.

40. The subcommittee had envisioned sending the text of PC-8, if Roosevelt approved it, to the British and Soviet governments. Policy Committee, minutes of the 85th meeting, 8 November 1944, p. 6. I have been unable to find any record of Roosevelt's response. It appears that the recommendations for particular countries were incorporated into the background preparation for the conferences at Malta and Yalta. See FRUS, p. 42.

41. Stettinius to Roosevelt, 8 November 1944, *FRUS, 1944*, 4:1025–26. For Berle's role in the International Conference on Civil Aviation, see Schwarz, *Liberal*, pp. 239–53.

42. Dean Acheson, in a letter to David Acheson of 27 December 1944, observed that Berle's resignation had come "at Ed's request." He offered no insight into the reasons for this request. Berle was at times difficult to get along with ("Berle rhymes with surly," in *Time* magazine's formulation) and could have been ousted for that alone. In later years, he himself would maintain that he was fired because he had advocated tougher policies toward the Soviet Union than those of a pro-Russian group led by Acheson. Not only has no documentary evidence come to light that would support this charge, available evidence suggests that Acheson's thinking was actually evolving along lines similar to Berle's. In a memorandum on Poland written at almost the same time as PC-8, Acheson argued that while the United States wished to maintain friendly relations with the Soviet Union, and recognized that Poland would necessarily be under strong Russian influence, "it is also to the interest of this country, as well as that of Poland, that Russian influence does not become so dominant as to affect international political stability or restrict the exercise of the legitimate rights of third countries. The United States can only hope to exert some influence in this part of the world if some degree of equality of opportunity in trade, investment and communication, including access to sources of information, is preserved for outside countries, and exclusive privileges for one power are avoided." Acheson, *Among Friends*, p. 48; *Time* magazine quoted in Schwartz, *Liberal*, p. 208; G. Smith, *Dean Acheson*, pp. 55–57; Acheson, "Memorandum for the President: Reconstruction of Poland," 27 October 1944, pp. 1–2, file ECA-9, box 137, "Records

Relating to Miscellaneous Policy Committees," Papers of Harley A. Notter, NA. Acheson's authorship of this memorandum is indicated in Policy Committee, minutes of the 82nd meeting, 27 October 1944, p. 4. See also A. Berle, *Navigating the Rapids*, pp. 570, 586–87, 591; and Berle to Jones, 28 December 1949, file "Personal Correspondence," box 83, Berle Papers.

43. Berle to Truman, 25 June 1945, Confidential File, White House Central Files, Truman Library.

44. A. Berle, diary entry of 4 May 1945, *Navigating the Rapids*, p. 533.

45. A. Berle, diary entry of 15 July 1945, *Navigating the Rapids*, p. 539. For a succinct survey of the reactions of other American officials to the developments in Eastern Europe between October 1944 and the summer of 1945, see De Santis, *The Diplomacy of Silence*, pp. 126–54. See also G. Smith, *American Diplomacy*, pp. 137–56.

46. Berle to Truman and Byrnes, 13 July 1945, text in *Navigating the Rapids*, pp. 539–42.

47. See McCann, *The Brazilian-American Alliance*; and Desch, *When the Third World Matters*, ch. 3.

48. A. Berle, diary entry of 30 January 1945, *Navigating the Rapids*, p. 520.

49. Berle to Stettinius, 9 May 1945, 832.00/5–945, NA.

50. Dulles, *Vargas of Brazil*, pp. 13–80; Skidmore, *Politics in Brazil*, pp. 3–6.

51. Dulles, *Vargas of Brazil*, pp. 119–37; McCann, *The Brazilian-American Alliance*, pp. 27–33.

52. Skidmore, *Politics in Brazil*, pp. 20–24; Dulles, *Vargas of Brazil*, pp. 144–55; Jordan Young, "Luís Carlos Prestes," in Alexander, ed., *Biographical Dictionary*, pp. 363–64. On the Comintern's erroneous assessment of Brazilian politics, see Dulles, *Brazilian Communism*, p. 60.

53. Dulles, *Vargas of Brazil*, pp. 155–97; Skidmore, *Politics in Brazil*, pp. 24–33; McCann, *The Brazilian-American Alliance*, pp. 33–105.

54. Leslie Bethell, "Brazil," in Bethell and Roxborough, eds., *Latin America*, esp. pp. 41–42; Collier and Collier, *Shaping the Political Arena*, pp. 185–89.

55. Quoted in McCann, *The Brazilian-American Alliance*, p. 279.

56. Berle to Truman, 4 September 1945, Confidential File, White House Central Files, Truman Library.

57. McCann, *The Brazilian-American Alliance*, p. 445.

58. Hilton, "The Overthrow of Getúlio Vargas," esp. pp. 14–15.

59. See Bethell, "Brazil," esp. pp. 48–49.

60. Report of military attaché of 7 July 1945, attached to Berle to Byrnes, 10 July 1945, file "Ambassador's Despatches, 1945," box 74, Berle Papers.

61. Berle to Byrnes, 18 September 1945, 832.00/9–1845, NA.

62. Lima Cavalcanti was the other. Skidmore, *Politics in Brazil*, p. 29.

63. A. Berle, memorandum of conversation with Magalhães, 15 February 1945, file "Ambassador's Despatches, 1945," box 74, Berle Papers.

64. A. Berle, diary entry of 17 April 1945, *Navigating the Rapids*, p. 529. Lacerda's politics appear to have been both more ideological and more complex than Berle realized. Although Lacerda had never formally been a member of the Brazilian

Communist Party, it had attacked him as a profascist Trotskyite and "expelled" him in 1939. See Dulles, *Carlos Lacerda*, pp. 52–56.

65. A. Berle, diary entry of 27 April 1945, *Navigating the Rapids*, p. 531.

66. See Hilton, "The Overthrow of Getúlio Vargas," esp. pp. 6–9.

67. A. Berle, address before the Instituto dos Advogados, 30 August 1945, file "Speeches," box 77, Berle Papers.

68. A. Berle, diary entry of 8 February 1945, *Navigating the Rapids*, p. 521.

69. Dulles, *Vargas of Brazil*, p. 171.

70. Skidmore, *Politics in Brazil*, p. 60.

71. Berle to Byrnes, 22 August 1945, 832.00/8–2245, NA.

72. Berle to Berle, 5 November 1945, file "Alice Berle," box 74, Berle Papers.

73. Berle to Byrnes, 18 September 1945, 832.00/9–1845, NA.

74. Berle to Stettinius, 9 May 1945, 832.00/5–945, NA.

75. Hilton, "The Overthrow of Getúlio Vargas," p. 5; Berle to Truman, 18 May 1945, file "Hold," box 75, Berle Papers. This letter does not appear to have been sent.

76. Berle to Truman and Byrnes, 13 July 1945, text in *Navigating the Rapids*, p. 541.

77. Bethell, "Brazil," pp. 48–50; A. Berle, diary entry of 6 October 1945, *Navigating the Rapids*, p. 551.

78. Berle to Byrnes, 18 September 1945, 832.00/9–1845, NA.

79. A. Berle, diary entry of 25 September 1945, box 217, Berle Papers.

80. Chalmers to Berle, 2 October 1945, file "Phil Chalmers," box 75, Berle Papers; Braden to Dawson, 26 February 1946, file "Diplomatic Correspondence, 1946–47, A–D," box 20, Braden Papers.

81. Quoted in Skidmore, *Politics in Brazil*, p. 349 n. 11.

82. A. Berle, memorandum of conversation with Getúlio Vargas, 1 October 1945, file "Memoranda of Conversation," box 76, Berle Papers.

83. A. Berle, diary entry of 30 October 1945, box 217, Berle Papers.

84. A. Berle, address before the Sindacato dos Jornalistas do Rio de Janeiro, 29 September 1945, file "Speeches," box 77, Berle Papers. This citation applies to the next two paragraphs as well.

85. A. Berle, diary entry of 6 October 1945, *Navigating the Rapids*, p. 553.

86. Berle to Berle, 6 November 1945, file "A. A. Berle, Sr.," box 74, Berle Papers. Berle's initial judgement was that the speech "did contribute materially to stabilizing the situation." Berle to Byrnes, 4 October 1945, 832.00/10–445, NA.

87. McCann, *The Brazilian-American Alliance*, p. 477.

88. Berle to Byrnes, 30 October 1945, filed with a complimentary letter from Truman to Berle of 9 November 1945, Confidential File, White House Central Files, Truman Library.

89. Wieland to Berle, 26 October 1945, file "Memos," box 76, Berle Papers.

90. Dulles, *Vargas of Brazil*, pp. 271–74; McCann, *The Brazilian-American Alliance*, pp. 480–84.

91. Berle to Berle, 5 November 1945, file "Alice Berle," box 74, Berle Papers.

92. Berle to Chalmers, 14 November 1945, file "Phil Chalmers," box 75, Berle Papers.

93. Berle to Byrnes, "Communist Party in Recent Brazilian Change of Government," 5 November 1945, file "Ambassador's Despatches, 1945," box 74, Berle Papers. Actually, it appears that it was Vargas who rejected an offer by Prestes to mobilize last-minute support. Dulles, *Vargas of Brazil*, p. 272.

94. Berle to Byrnes, 22 August 1945, 832.00/8–2245, NA.

95. A. Berle, diary entry of 30 October 1945, box 217, Berle Papers.

96. A. Berle, diary entry of 1 November 1945, box 217, Berle Papers.

97. Text in *Correio da Manhã*, 31 October 1945. In an attached memo, Berle's cultural relations attaché called Berle's attention to this passage, adding that he had heard the speech in person: "The man is a thorough liberal . . . an electric orator who can lift his audience to its feet like William Jennings Bryan used to." Nash, memorandum, 31 October 1945, file "Memos," box 76, Berle Papers.

98. Dulles, *Carlos Lacerda*, p. 75.

99. Bethell, "Brazil," p. 55.

100. Dulles, *Vargas of Brazil*, p. 281.

101. Berle to Chalmers, 5 December 1945, file "Phil Chalmers," box 75, Berle Papers.

102. Memorandum of conversation, Berle and Luiz Flavio de Faro, 13 December 1945, file "Memos of Conversation," box 76, Berle Papers.

103. Dulles, *Vargas of Brazil*, pp. 283–84; "Brazil: Pulling the Eagle's Tail," *Newsweek*, 23 January 1950, 40.

104. On the breakdown of Brazilian democracy, see Alfred Stepan, "Political Leadership and Regime Breakdown: Brazil," in Linz and Stepan, eds., *The Breakdown of Democratic Regimes*, pp. 110–37.

105. Berle to Truman, 26 November 1945, file "Truman," box 77, Berle Papers.

106. Truman to Berle, 20 February 1946, file "Truman," box 77, Berle Papers.

107. The quotations in this paragraph are taken from "Translated Abstracts of Press Comment on Ambassador Berle's Resignation," dated 10 February 1946, and "Press Comment on Ambassador Berle," dated 1 March 1946, file "State Department and Other Government Agencies, 1945–54," box 97, Berle Papers. See also B. Berle, *A Life in Two Worlds*.

108. A. Berle, address to the IADF, 5 June 1958, file "IADF," box 106, Berle Papers.

109. A. Berle, diary entry of 9 December 1958, *Navigating the Rapids*, pp. 690–91.

110. "Report to the President-Elect of the Task Force on Immediate Latin American Problems," n.d., pp. 2, 8–12, file "Latin American Task Force Undated," box 94, Berle Papers. In his diary, Berle listed the membership of the task force as Arthur Whittaker, Lincoln Gordon, Robert Alexander, Arturo Morales-Carrión, Ted Moscoso, and Richard Goodwin. A. Berle, diary entry of 7 December 1960, *Navigating the Rapids*, p. 720. Jerome Levinson and Juan de Onís suggest that even among the members of the task force, Berle's emphasis on direct support for democratic movements soon gave way to a more limited focus on promoting economic development and social reform in general. Levinson and Onis, *The Alliance That Lost Its Way*, p. 56.

Chapter 3. The Yankee Cowboy and Argentina

1. Dahl, *Polyarchy*, p. 137.

2. See Díaz-Alejandro, *Essays on the Economic History of Argentina*, pp. 1–66.

3. See Peter H. Smith, "The Breakdown of Democracy in Argentina, 1916–30," in Linz and Stepan, *Breakdown of Democratic Regimes*, pp. 14–17.

4. Robustiano Patrón Costas was the candidate. See Mark Falcoff and Ronald Dolkart, "Political Developments," in Falcoff and Dolkart, eds., *Prologue to Perón*, p. 41.

5. See David Rock, "Argentina, 1930–46," in Bethell, ed., *The Cambridge History of Latin America*, vol. 8, esp. pp. 55–60.

6. Cordell Hull, statement of 10 October 1944, quoted in Wood, *The Dismantling of the Good Neighbor Policy*, p. 73.

7. The first document circulated to the broader GOU membership condemned both the Masons and the Rotary Club as Jewish conspiracies. The Masons were a threat to the established order—political and spiritual—and in the past had been responsible for the French Revolution and the Spanish Civil War. The Rotary Clubs were "an international Jewish propaganda and espionage ring in the service of the United States." See Potash, ed., *Perón y el G.O.U.*, pp. 101–3.

8. Text in *La Prensa* (Buenos Aires), 11 June 1944.

9. For the American diplomacy preceding this offer, see Wood, *The Dismantling of the Good Neighbor Policy*, pp. 80–92.

10. The Argentine chargé to the director general of the Pan American Union, 28 March 1945, *FRUS, 1945*, 9:371–72.

11. Resolution 7 dealt at length with the "extirpation of the remaining focal points of the Axis' subversive influence in the hemisphere." Resolution 19 dealt with enemy property. For the full texts, see *Acta final de la conferencia interamericana*, 5–6, 13–14. See also Grew to the Diplomatic Representatives in the American Republics, 4 April 1945, *FRUS, 1945*, 9:374–75.

12. See Blasier, *The Hovering Giant*, pp. 27–29.

13. "Guatemala es ya verdadera democracia, expresó Braden," *El Imparcial* (Guatemala City), 20 March 1945.

14. Braden to Stettinius, 2 April 1945, file "Correspondence 1945–Cuba C–F," box 16, Braden Papers.

15. Quoted in Braden to Davidson, 30 May 1945, 835.00/6–1545, NA.

16. Quoted in *La Prensa* (Buenos Aires), 29 August 1945. See also McGann, "The Ambassador and the Dictator," p. 351.

17. Luna, *El 45*, p. 101.

18. Carlos Alfredo Torquinst quoted in ibid., p. 101.

19. Quoted in Braden to Byrnes, 20 July 1945, *FRUS, 1945*, 9:397.

20. Braden to Bowers, 7 August 1945, Catalogued Correspondence, boxes 1–3, Braden Papers.

21. See Brown, *James F. Byrnes*, pp. 303–5.

22. In *Time* magazine, "shrewd, jolly Spruille Braden" had yet to become "hulking, excitable Spruille Braden." See May, "The 'Bureaucratic Politics' Approach," p. 152.

23. Senate Committee on Foreign Relations, "Nomination of Spruille Braden," 3

October 1945, p. 65, in Congressional Information Service, *Unpublished Senate Committee Hearings*, microfiche, 79SFO-T.2.

24. Rockefeller to Braden, 9 August 1945, Catalogued Correspondence, boxes 1–3, Braden Papers.

25. Braden to Byrnes, 21 August 1945, 111.12 Braden, Spruille/8–2145, NA.

26. Ibid. See also Byrnes's announcement of Braden's promotion, Department of State, *Bulletin* (26 August 1945), p. 291.

27. Braden, address at the Museo Social, 14 September 1945, pp. 9–19, file "Speeches 1945," box 29, Braden Papers.

28. "What Is Our Inter-American Policy," radio broadcast transcript, Department of State, *Bulletin* (6 and 13 January 1946), p. 27.

29. Whitaker, *The United States and Argentina*, pp. 133–34.

30. David Kelly, dispatch from Buenos Aires, 1 October 1945, quoted in Wood, *The Dismantling of the Good Neighbor Policy*, pp. 99–100.

31. Luna, *El 45*, pp. 267–69.

32. Braden to Cabot, 5 October 1945, file "General Correspondence: John M. Cabot," box 22, Braden Papers.

33. Acheson, memo of 29 September 1945, *FRUS, 1945*, 9:159.

34. Braden to Corrigan, 17 October 1945, file "Spruille Braden," Corrigan Papers.

35. Luna, *El 45*, pp. 269–73.

36. Ibid., pp. 302–32.

37. Quoted in Luna, *El 45*, p. 368.

38. Braden, memo of 26 October 1945, 835.00/10–2345, NA.

39. Cabot to Byrnes, 19 October 1945, *FRUS, 1945*, 9:422.

40. "Nomination of Spruille Braden," 3 October 1945, pp. 10–11.

41. Braden to Corrigan, 4 October 1945, file "Spruille Braden," box 1, Corrigan Papers.

42. "Nomination of Spruille Braden," 3 October 1945, p. 41.

43. Ibid., p. 48. Resolution 27 of the Mexico City Conference, it should be noted, stressed the essential obligation of all of the American republics "to guarantee to their peoples free and impartial access to sources of information" and to eliminate wartime censorship. For the full text, see *Acta final de la conferencia interamericana*, pp. 18–19.

44. "Nomination of Spruille Braden," 3 October 1945, p. 60. Braden did note that the possibility of collective intervention had some support among the diplomatic corps in Buenos Aires.

45. Ibid., 3 October 1945, pp. 10, 19, 56.

46. Ibid., pp. 60–61.

47. "Nomination of Spruille Braden," 10 October 1945, pp. 125–26, in Congressional Information Service, *Unpublished Senate Committee Hearings*, microfiche, 79SFO-T.3.

48. Quoted in McGann, "The Ambassador and the Dictator," p. 353.

49. Quoted in Wood, *The Dismantling of the Good Neighbor Policy*, p. 236 n. 24.

50. White to Stettinius, 7 June 1945, 711.00/6–745, NA.

51. Cabot to Byrnes, 18 October 1945, 835.00/10–1845.

52. Cabot to Braden, 22 October 1945, file "General Correspondence: John M. Cabot," box 22, Braden Papers.

53. Before coming to work for the CIA, according to Richard Immerman, Colonel King had worked in Latin America for the FBI. The FBI was responsible for surveillance and counterintelligence activities in the region until 1947. Immerman, *The CIA in Guatemala*, p. 139.

54. Cabot to Braden, 22 October 1945, file "General Correspondence: John M. Cabot," box 22, Braden Papers.

55. Thurston to Stettinius, 21 June 1945, 711.00/6–2145, NA.

56. Cabot to Braden, 22 October 1945, file "General Correspondence: John M. Cabot," box 22, Braden Papers.

57. Braden to Cabot, 1 November 1945, file "General Correspondence: John M. Cabot," box 22, Braden Papers.

58. Luna, *El 45*, pp. 438–42.

59. Shortly after Perón's comeback, Cabot reported close to a 50 percent increase—since 9 October 1945—in Perón's support among the workers of fifteen companies with American interests he had surveyed. Cabot to Byrnes, 23 October 1945, 835.00/10–2345, NA.

60. Cabot to Briggs, 17 November 1945, *FRUS, 1945*, 9:426–34.

61. Braden to Cabot, 11 December 1945, file "General Correspondence: John M. Cabot," box 22, Braden Papers.

62. Braden to Dawson, 26 February 1946, file "Diplomatic Correspondence: 1946–47, A–D," box 20, Braden Papers.

63. Department of State, *Consultation among the American Republics*, hereafter the "Blue Book."

64. Transcript of talks by Braden and Carl Spaeth before a group of State Department officers, 24 September 1946, p. 15, file "Speeches—Departmental Group," box 25, Braden Papers.

65. Braden to Bowers, 29 December 1945, file "Nov.–Dec. 1945," box 6, mss. II, Bowers Papers.

66. Byrnes to Berle, 20 February 1946, *FRUS, 1946*, 11:5.

67. See Unión Panamericana, *Consulta del gobierno del Uruguay*. See also chapter 3 below.

68. João Neves da Fontoura, note of 1 April 1946, forwarded to Byrnes by the American chargé in Brazil, *FRUS, 1946*, 11:8. See also "Summary of Replies of Other American Republics to Blue Book," 17 April 1946, folder "Argentina 1946–52," box 1, Records of the Deputy Assistant Secretaries of State for Inter-American Affairs, 1945–56, NA.

69. Braden to Cabot, 26 January 1946, file "General Correspondence: John M. Cabot," box 22, Braden Papers.

70. Acheson to Diplomatic Representatives in the American Republics, 1 April 1946, *FRUS, 1946*, 11:10–12; Department of State, press release no. 232, 8 April 1946.

71. Thorpe to Paul, 8 April 1946, CAR D-2, "2B.2 Argentina Committee, 1946–47," box 9, Intradepartmental and Interdepartmental Committees, lot file 122, NA. At the end of the war, wartime economic controls on exports had been maintained on

a small number of group "E" countries including Spain, Argentina, Austria, Italy, Bulgaria, Rumania, and Hungary. In his letter, Thorpe requested that the necessary removal of Argentina from this category be given as little publicity as possible. In explaining the State Department's reasoning for the decision, he emphasized the impossibility of securing multilateral cooperation in a program of economic pressure against Argentina and the spread of famine conditions in Asia and Europe. Willard L. Thorpe was at this time deputy to the assistant secretary of state for economic affairs and Arthur Paul an assistant to the secretary of commerce. On the earlier policy, see *FRUS, 1945*, 9:526–59.

72. Cabot to Byrnes, 18 January 1946, *FRUS, 1946*, 11:187.
73. Cabot to Byrnes, 23 January 1946, *FRUS, 1946*, 11:190.
74. Cabot to Byrnes, 8 February 1946, *FRUS, 1946*, 11: 201–2.
75. Byrnes to Cabot, 9 February 1946, *FRUS, 1946*, 11:204.
76. Braden to Byrnes, 17 July 1945, 835.00/7–1745, NA.
77. Braden to Bowers, 29 December 1945, file "Nov.–Dec. 1945," box 6, mss. II, Bowers Papers.
78. Quoted in Luna, *El 45*, p. 534.
79. Memorandum of telephone conversation, 13 February 1946, *FRUS, 1946*, 11:209.
80. Cabot to Byrnes, 14 February 1946, *FRUS, 1946*, 11:212.
81. Cabot to Byrnes, 21 February 1946, *FRUS, 1946*, 11:219.
82. Quoted in Díaz Araujo, *La conspiración del '43*, p. 85.
83. Luna, *El 45*, p. 583.
84. Acheson, *Present at the Creation*, p. 187.
85. Bowers to Braden, 13 March 1946, file "Jan.–April 1946," box 6, mss. II, Bowers Papers.
86. For an overview of Perón's impact on Argentine political development, see Carlos H. Waisman, "Argentina: Autarkic Industrialization and Illegitimacy," in Diamond, Linz, and Lipset, eds., *Democracy*, pp. 59–104.
87. Responding to Pope Clement VIII's protest over France's continued recognition of the Dutch rebels in a letter of 23 July 1601, Cardinal Ossat formulated the core of what has become the classical positivist position: "When princes are dealing with a considerable Power, they have not been accustomed to examine whether the potentate who sends them an ambassador is legitimate or not. Without further enquiry into title, they concern themselves only with the power and the possession." Quoted in Wight, "International Legitimacy," p. 5. See also Kelsen, *Principles of International Law*, especially pp. 387–89, 412–14.
88. See Kedourie, *Nationalism*.
89. See Dahl, *Polyarchy*.
90. For an example of this, see Schwartzberg, "The Lion and the Phoenix," pp. 139–77, 287–311.
91. Haya, "Plan para la afirmación de la democracia en América" [1941], in "La defensa continental" [1943], *Obras completas*, 4:364.
92. See George H. Butler, "Inter-American Relations after World War II," Department of State, *Bulletin* 13, no. 316 (15 July 1945), pp. 88–99.
93. The State Department's message can be found in the text of an informal note

of 11 October 1945 from the American ambassador in Uruguay to the Uruguayan foreign minister, attached to Dawson to Byrnes, 20 October 1945, 835.00/10–2045, NA.

94. Eduardo Rodríguez Larreta, *Note Verbale*, 19 October 1945, text attached to Dawson to Byrnes, 20 October 1945, 835.00/10–2045, NA. William Dawson was the American ambassador to Uruguay at this time.

95. Byrnes to Dawson, 24 October 1945, *FRUS, 1945*, 9:187. Although drafted by Carl Spaeth with Braden's help, a marginal note indicates that this paragraph was revised by the secretary of state personally before being sent. See Byrnes to Dawson, 24 October 1945, 835.00/10–2045, NA.

96. Eduardo Rodríguez Larreta, "Nota del gobierno del Uruguay dirigida a los gobiernos de las otras republicas americanas," 21 November 1945, Unión Panamericana, *Consulta del gobierno del Uruguay*, pp. 1–5; English translation in *FRUS, 1945*, 9:191–92.

97. Larreta, "Nota del gobierno del Uruguay," 21 November 1945, Unión Panamericana, *Consulta del gobierno del Uruguay*, p. 4; *FRUS, 1945*, 9:194.

98. James Byrnes, statement of 27 November 1945, text in Department of State, *Bulletin* 13, no. 336 (2 December 1945), p. 892.

99. Larreta, "Nota del gobierno," p. 5; *FRUS, 1945*, 9:196.

100. Editorial, "La tesis uruguaya," *El Tiempo* (Bogotá), 25 November 1945.

101. Department of State, *Bulletin* 13, no. 336 (2 December 1945), p. 892.

102. Corrigan to Byrnes, 27 November 1945, 835.00/11–2745, NA.

103. Ibid.

104. Alfaro to Larreta, 30 November 1945, Unión Panamericana, *Consulta del gobierno del Uruguay*, p. 63.

105. Toriello to Larreta, 30 November 1945, Unión Panamericana, *Consulta del gobierno del Uruguay*, pp. 42–43.

106. Briggs to Austin, 7 December 1945, 710.11/12–745, NA.

107. Fernández to Larreta, 7 December 1945; Trujillo to Larreta, 10 December 1945; Serrano to Larreta, 13 December 1945; Lescot to Larreta, 14 December 1945; Nájera to Larreta, 10 December 1945; Peña Batlle to Larreta, 14 December 1945; Unión Panamericana, *Consulta del gobierno del Uruguay*, pp. 24–27, 28–31, 32–37, 44–45, 52–54, 71–74; Berle to Byrnes, 14 December 1945, *FRUS, 1945*, 9:209.

108. Memorandum of conversation, newspaper correspondents and Braden, 15 December 1945, 710.11/12–1545, NA.

109. Braden to Bowers, 29 December 1945, file "Nov.–Dec. 1945," box 6, mss. II, Bowers Papers.

110. *New York Times*, 29 November 1945.

111. Braden to Butler, 19 February 1947, *FRUS, 1947*, 8:630–31.

112. See Valenzuela, "Paraguay: The Coup That Didn't Happen," pp. 43–55.

113. Londoño to Larreta, 24 December 1945; Unión Panamericana, *Consulta del gobierno del Uruguay*, pp. 14–15.

114. Department of State, press release no. 232, 8 April 1946. Braden later described Byrnes's statement as a retreat, rather than a reversal, from previous policy and attributed it to pressure from various senators. Braden to Wright, 20 November 1946, file "Diplomatic Correspondence 1946–47, W–Z," box 20, Braden Papers. Jesse

Stiller has called attention to a meeting at Blair House on 7 April 1946 between Byrnes and Senators Tom Connally, Walter George, and Wallace White as being decisive in this regard. The shift in policy, however, had been fully articulated a week before the meeting at Blair House. See Acheson to diplomatic representatives in the American republics, 1 April 1946, *FRUS, 1946,* 11:10–12; Stiller, *George S. Messersmith,* p. 229.

115. Joint Chiefs of Staff, memorandum of 21 February 1945, p. 3, enclosed with Matthews to Byrnes, 29 March 1946, 711.00/3–2946, NA.

116. Braden, "Memorandum on the Argentine Situation," 12 July 1946, and Truman to Braden, 22 July 1946, both in file "Harry S. Truman," Catalogued Correspondence, Braden Papers.

117. Braden, "Memorandum on the Argentine Situation," pp. 1–4 of the summary of conclusions and pp. 8, 18–22, 29–34 of the memorandum proper. For a more detailed exposition of Braden's reasoning on the subject of the Argentine government's "good faith," see Braden to Messersmith, 22 July 1946, 710.11/7–2246, NA.

118. Braden, "Memorandum on the Argentine Situation," pp. 2–3.

119. Ibid., pp. 10–11.

120. Braden to Wright, 24 October 1946, file "Diplomatic Correspondence 1946–47, W–Z," box 20, Braden Papers.

121. Braden, "Memorandum on the Argentine Situation," pp. 12–14, 34–37.

122. Braden, "The Arming of Argentina," second draft, n.d., pp. 11, 24, in file "Harry S. Truman," Catalogued Correspondence, Braden Papers.

123. For a detailed description of the problem Argentina was expected to at least partially address—including the names of key individuals and companies—see the State Department to the Officer in Charge of the American Mission in Buenos Aires, 25 September 1946, 111.12 Braden, Spruille/10–2346, NA.

124. Messersmith to Byrnes, 16 August 1946, p. 10, 111.12 Braden, Spruille/8–1646, NA.

125. Messersmith to Byrnes, 15 July [August] 1946, pp. 9, 13, 111.12 Braden, Spruille/8–1646, NA. This was in direct response to his receipt of a copy of Braden's "Memorandum on the Argentine Situation" of 12 July 1946. "We are all in general agreement," Messersmith had written on behalf of the American embassy in Mexico the year before, "with the sound and considered statements which Mr. Braden has made in his despatch." Messersmith to Byrnes, 9 August 1945, 710.00/8–945, NA.

126. Messersmith to Sulzberger, 25 September 1946, pp. 6, 38, 111.12 Braden, Spruille/10–2346, NA.

127. Braden, file "Outline of Speech for a Group of Officers in the War Department—Intelligence Personnel," 11 January 1946, p. 5, "Speeches, 1945–46," box 29, Braden Papers. As David Green has observed, Braden was opposed to Perón "*not* merely because he thought of Perón as a fascist but because he thought Perón's policies might ultimately benefit the forces of communism in South America." David Green, "The Cold War Comes to Latin America," in Bernstein, ed., *Politics and Policies of the Truman Administration,* pp. 172–73.

128. For Messersmith's view of Perón's potential helpfulness in combating com-

munism in Latin America, see Messersmith to Sulzberger, 25 September 1946, pp. 23–26, 111.12 Braden, Spruille/10–2346, NA.

129. Cold war conservatives and their outlook are considered at length in chapter 7.

130. For developments in Argentina under Perón, see Luna, *Perón y su tiempo.*

131. Quoted in the *Washington Post,* 10 March 1947.

132. Braden to Messersmith, 22 July 1946, 710.11/7–2246, NA. See also Roland Hussey, "Instances in which Argentina has asked us to pay tribute under the threat of an alliance with Russia," 5 August 1946, Memos of the Division of American Republic Research and Liaison, box 16, Records of the Office of American Republic Affairs, NA. Braden appears to have been a good deal more troubled by the possibility of a covert arrangement in which the Argentine communists would offer their effective support to Perón and receive his in return.

133. Some of the persons receiving letters from Messersmith during this time are listed in Messersmith to Byrnes, 3 October 1946, 111.12 Braden, Spruille/10–346, NA, and copies of many of these letters are available in this file; others are mentioned in Braden to Wright, 24 October 1946, file "Diplomatic Correspondence 1946–47, W–Z," box 20, Braden Papers.

134. Acheson to Spaeth, 23 October 1946, Acheson Papers.

135. Braden to Wright, 12 November 1946, file "Diplomatic Correspondence 1946–47, W–Z," box 20, Braden Papers.

136. Messersmith to Byrnes, 23 October 1946, p. 2, 111.12 Braden, Spruille/10–2346, NA.

137. Byrnes to Messersmith, 29 October 1946, 111.12 Braden, Spruille/10–2346, NA.

138. Braden to Wright, 24 October 1946, file "Diplomatic Correspondence 1946–47, W–Z," box 20, Braden Papers.

139. See the excerpts in Hoyt to Mann, "Ambassador Messersmith's Reports," 17 January 1947, 835.00/1–1747, NA.

140. Cecil Lyon, "Visit to River Plate Country," 18 April 1947, file "Memos Relating to General Latin American Affairs," box 13, Records of the Office of American Republic Affairs, NA. Lyon was at this time the acting assistant chief of the Division of River Plate Affairs in the State Department.

141. In the contemporary judgement of the U.S. political adviser for Germany, the Argentine government "evidently played a captious and legalistic game with the lists of German agents demanded by the United States for deportation. By using these specific lists as a basis for bargaining over their 'international obligations' and by eventually surrendering a limited number of the 'wanted' individuals, the Argentines were able at the end to get what they wanted—participation in the Rio Conference—without being seriously challenged on the score of the potentially far more dangerous Nazi nucleus of former NSDAP leaders." Murphy to Marshall, 30 August 1947, *FRUS, 1947,* 8:211–12.

142. On 31 March 1947, Truman told the Argentine ambassador that all that remained was the deportation of some twenty to thirty dangerous Nazis who were still at large. The ambassador replied that there were no Nazis in Argentina and that it was a calumny to say there were. Messersmith, on hearing of this, explained that

the Argentine ambassador was not well informed, that special squads were already scouring the country for the fugitives, that they were hardly dangerous since they would be apprehended on sight, and that Perón was doing all that could reasonably be expected. Stiller, *George S. Messersmith*, p. 260. For details, see *FRUS, 1947*, 8:186–201.

143. Wood, *The Dismantling of the Good Neighbor Policy*, p. 120.

144. "The real break seems to have come when the Secretary sent a letter to the White House giving the Department's support for the arms bill which Spruille had opposed. The documentation in this regard was drafted in Hilldring's office and Braden learned about the decision from Acheson a few hours after the letter had gone to the White House and actually after news of it had leaked to the press." Dawson to Corrigan, 6 June 1947, "Dawson, Allan," box 3, Corrigan Papers. See also Braden, *Diplomats and Demagogues*, pp. 367–69.

145. Pach, "The Containment of U.S. Military Aid," p. 227. This section has benefited from Pach's succinct presentation of the issue.

146. Braden to Acheson, 4 April 1947, 810.20 Defense/4–447, NA. Quoted in Rawls, "Spruille Braden," p. 479.

147. Braden to Byrnes, 16 December 1946, *FRUS, 1946*, 11:108–10.

148. Acierto, "A Marshall Plan for Latin America," p. 5.

149. Braden to Clayton, 21 June 1946, file "Memos Relating to General Latin American Affairs," box 11, Records of the Office of American Republic Affairs, NA; Byrnes to Certain Diplomatic Representatives, 21 March 1946, *FRUS, 1946*, 11:96. Panama, which had only a police force, was also excluded, as was Cuba for failure to pay back any of what it owed on Lend-Lease. Haiti, which had experienced a coup in January 1946, was initially excluded as well.

150. Braden to Byrnes, 16 December 1946, *FRUS, 1946*, 11:108–10. See also John Dreier, "Visit of Representatives of the AF of L Delegation to Argentina," 12 March 1947, file Memos Relating to General Latin American Affairs, box 13, Records of the Office of American Republic Affairs, NA.

151. For Acheson's support of Braden's position, see Acheson to Patterson, 19 March 1947, *FRUS, 1947*, 8:105–6. For Acheson's opposition to Braden's position, see minutes of meeting of the secretaries of state, war, and navy, 1 May 1947, *FRUS, 1947*, 8:114.

152. *FRUS, 1947*, 8:115 n. 27.

153. "Arms and the Man," *Time*, 2 June 1947, p. 24.

154. Dreier to Braden, 8 June 1947, "Resignation 1947," box 22, Braden Papers.

155. Pach, "The Containment of U.S. Military Aid," pp. 225–43.

156. Central Intelligence Agency, "Conditions and Trends in Latin America Affecting US Security," NIE-70 (12 December 1952), p. 8, President's Secretary's Files, Truman Library.

157. See Office of Intelligence Research, "Factors Affecting the Negotiation of Bilateral Military Assistance Agreements with Selected Latin American Countries," OIR 5830, NA. The seven countries were Brazil, Chile, Colombia, Cuba, Ecuador, Peru, and Uruguay.

158. Patterson to Byrnes, 18 December 1946, 710 Conference (W&PW)/12–1846, NA.

159. Henry Dearborn, memorandum of conversation with General Crittenberger, 23 January 1946, Memos Relating to General Latin American Affairs, box 11, Records of the Office of American Republic Affairs, NA. Lt. Gen. Willis D. Crittenberger was the commanding general of the Caribbean Defense Command.

160. Quoted in Dreier to Braden, 5 February 1947, Memos Relating to General Latin American Affairs, box 12, Records of the Office of American Republic Affairs, NA.

161. Patterson to Byrnes, 18 December 1946, 710 Conference (W&PW)/12–1846, NA.

162. Quoted in Dreier to Braden, 5 February 1947, Memos Relating to General Latin American Affairs, box 12, Records of the Office of American Republic Affairs, NA.

163. Patterson to Acheson, 27 March 1947, FRUS, 1947, 8:106–9.

164. Braden to Acheson, 4 April 1947, 810.20 Defense/4–447, NA. Cited in Rawls, "Spruille Braden," p. 480.

165. See Braden to Byrnes, 16 December 1946, FRUS, 1946, 11:108–10. See also Ellis Briggs, memorandum, 20 May 1947, FRUS, 1947, 8:221–24.

166. Braden to Marshall, 4 February 1947, FRUS, 1947, 8:219.

167. Braden to Marshall, 2 May 1947, FRUS, 1947, 8:220.

168. Inverchapel to Marshall, 21 May 1947, FRUS, 1947, 8:225; Braden to Acheson, 20 May 1947, 835.34/5–2047, NA. Cited in Rawls, "Spruille Braden," p. 475.

169. Ellis Briggs, memorandum, 20 May 1947, FRUS, 1947, 8:221–24.

170. Acheson, marginal note on Braden to Acheson, 20 May 1947, 835.34/5–2047, NA. Quoted in Rawls, "Spruille Braden," p. 521 n. 102.

171. Marshall to Truman, 26 June 1947, FRUS, 1947, 8:226. Truman approved the sale.

172. FRUS, 1947, 8:117 n. 31.

173. Hilldring to Acheson, 4 August 1947, and attached memo, FRUS, 1947, 8:117–20. John Hilldring was the chairman of the Policy Committee on Arms and Armaments.

174. George Marshall to the embassy in Argentina, 9 September 1947, FRUS, 1947, 8:227. This was a shortened statement of the policy. For the longer version, see Lovett to Royall, 29 August 1947, FRUS, 1947, 8:120–21. Robert Lovett was the acting secretary of state and Kenneth Royall the secretary of war.

175. See Dreier, "Arms Policy for Other American Republics," 4 November 1947, FRUS, 1947, 8:125–27.

176. F. K. Roberts, memorandum of conversation between George Marshall and Ernest Bevin et al., 18 December 1947, FRUS, 1947, 8:234–35.

177. The text of the Rio Treaty and the OAS Charter are available as appendices in Thomas and Thomas, The Organization of American States, pp. 413–33.

178. See especially Articles 6, 8, 13, and 17 of the Rio Treaty in ibid., pp. 430–32.

179. Text in ibid., pp. 415–16.

180. Fenwick to Braden, 25 July 1946, 710.11/7–2546, NA.

181. Sanders to Fenwick, 19 August 1946, 710.11/7–2546, NA.

182. Briggs, Farewell to Foggy Bottom, p. 186.

183. In a handful of cases, the existence of the Rio Treaty and the OAS has helped both Latin American democrats and the cause of hemispheric peace and security. Costa Rican democrats, in particular, have been the beneficiary of these institutions. In late 1948 and early 1949, and again in 1955, Costa Rica was threatened by an exile invasion from Nicaragua supported by Anastasio Somoza. In both cases, pressure from the OAS played a key role in foiling the invasions. See Ameringer, *Don Pepe,* pp. 80–83, 121–25.

184. Braden, "The Arming of Argentina," p. 6.

185. Lyon, "Visit to River Plate Country," 18 April 1947, Memos Relating to General Latin American Affairs, box 13, Records of the Office of American Republic Affairs, NA.

186. On the distinction between an ethic of ultimate ends and an ethic of responsibility, see Max Weber, "Politics as a Vocation" [1919], *From Max Weber,* pp. 77–128.

187. Braden, "The Arming of Argentina," pp. 9–10. In attempting to advance his position, Braden exaggerated the extent to which various civilian regimes, particularly those in Ecuador and Peru, could be considered "traditionally democratic" and also the extent of recent democratic progress, especially in Bolivia and Paraguay.

188. Cold war conservatives and their outlook are considered at length in chapter 7.

189. Braden to Briggs, 28 August 1943, file "Diplomatic Correspondence 1943: Briggs," box 10, Braden Papers.

190. Braden, "The Arming of Argentina," pp. 9–10.

191. Mecham, "Democracy and Dictatorship in Latin America," p. 299.

192. "Guatemala to Decorate Braden," *New York Times,* 27 December 1947; and "Guatemala Decorates Braden," *New York Times,* 21 January 1948. Richard Immerman mistakenly asserts that this award was presented to Braden by the Guatemalan dictator, Jorge Ubico. Immerman, *The CIA in Guatemala,* p. 230 n. 94.

193. Grant to Braden, 6 June 1947, file "Resignation," box 22, Braden Papers.

Chapter 4. Coming to Terms with Yankee Imperialism

1. On the aspirations of the leaders of the Wars of Independence, see Robertson, *Rise of the Spanish-American Republics.* Particularly interesting in this regard are the comments of Francisco de Miranda on his extensive visit to the United States. See Miranda, *The Diary of Francisco de Miranda, 1783–1784* (New York: Hispanic Society of America, 1928). See also Whitaker, ed., *Latin America and the Enlightenment.* For an overview of more recent work on this period that attempts to move beyond elite perspectives, see John Lynch, "The Origins of Spanish American Independence," Timothy Anna, "The Independence of Mexico and Central America," and David Bushnell, "The Independence of Spanish South America," all in Bethell, *The Cambridge History of Latin America,* 3:3–156.

2. "I was in command for twenty years, and from them drew only a few certain conclusions: (1) for us, America is ungovernable; (2) he who serves a revolution plows the sea; (3) the only thing that one can do in America is emigrate; (4) this country will inevitably fall into the hands of a rampaging mob and later into the hands of almost imperceptibly small tyrants of all colors and races; (5) devoured by

crime and destroyed by barbarism, the Europeans will not deign to conquer us; (6) if it were possible for part of the world to return to primordial chaos, this would be the final epoch in the cycle of America." Fragment of a letter from Simón Bolívar to Juan José Flores, 9 November 1830, in Bolívar, *Simón Bolívar obras completas*, 2:959–60.

3. Alberdi, *Bases y puntos de partida*, p. 49.

4. Domingo Faustino Sarmiento, *Recuerdos de provincia* [1850] (Buenos Aires: Kapelusz Editora, 1993), p. 216.

5. This is not to suggest that the emulators had not encountered strong resistance earlier, but rather to note that by and large their opponents had acted without developing an elaborate rationale. For most of their tenure in office, dictators like Juan Rosas in Argentina had relatively little need of such rationales—"having the united support of the social establishment and no significant political opposition, they did not need a doctrine." Frank Safford, "Politics, Ideology, and Society in Post-Independence Spanish America," in Bethell, *The Cambridge History of Latin America*, 3:396.

6. Rodó, *Ariel*, p. 80.

7. Ibid., p. 99.

8. Mark Berger has suggested that works such as the present one, with their implicit or explicit emphasis on the "success" of the United States and the "failure" of Latin America, are themselves part of an intellectual tradition that has contributed to the strength and resilience of American hegemony. Both liberal and Marxist scholarship, he claims, have linked past events to the fulfillment of the Western idea of progress and the rise of the liberal democratic nation-state in a way that has contributed to U.S. efforts to control and manage events in the Americas. As against such "teleological" approaches, Berger champions a "genealogical" approach—"a more diffuse conception of power, allowing historians and social scientists to be seen as neither subordinate to Washington nor independent from Washington (this often includes radicals). They are positioned in a broad and complex web of institutions, organizations, and structures linked together by a set of discourses, which, even when they are oppositional, can still have a complementary relationship to the maintenance of US hegemony." The claim that there are oppositional "discourses" that do not have a complementary relationship to the maintenance of U.S. hegemony is problematic. Rather than attempt to make this claim directly, Berger notes that some "discourses," even when oppositional, "can still have" such a complementary relationship. The grounds for believing that there are any "discourses" that do not have such a relationship are not presented. Instead, there is an implicit reliance on an emancipationist entelechy; a future without hegemony to which the advocates of the "genealogical" approach apparently wish to contribute and on behalf of which they can be seen as trying to "enlist" the past. The grounds for believing that their approach is capable of helping them make such a contribution—or that they stand in any different position in this regard than any other school (liberal, Marxist, or whatever)—are not presented. See M. Berger, *Under Northern Eyes*, pp. xi, 8–9, 11, and passim.

9. On Haya and Apra's influence on Acción Democrática in Venezuela, see Schwartzberg, "Rómulo Betancourt," esp. pp. 620–32. On Haya and Apra's influence on the Partido de Liberacíon Nacional in Costa Rica, see Ameringer, *Don Pepe*, esp. p.

15; and Gonzalo Facio, "La vida del mas grande luchador democrático de América Latina se encuentra en peligro," *Diario de Costa Rica* (San José), 26 March 1950. On Haya and Apra's influence on the Partido Revolucionario Cubano Auténtico in Cuba, see the documents in Castro, ed., *Haya de la Torre*, vol. 2, esp. pp. 115–31. On Haya's and Apra's influence on the Partido Revolucionario Dominicano in the Dominican Republic, see Miolán, *El perredé*, esp. pp. 15, 98. On Haya's and Apra's influence on the Caribbean Legion, see Ameringer, *The Caribbean Legion*, esp. pp. 1–3.

10. Alexander, *Aprismo*, p. 3.

11. Eugenio Chang-Rodríguez, "Víctor Raúl Haya de la Torre," in Alexander, *Biographical Dictionary*, pp. 209–10.

12. Even among Haya's friends, Serafino Romualdi could criticize the authoritarianism of Apra structures and practices and Rómulo Betancourt could seriously question Haya's tactical judgement. See Romualdi, *Presidents and Peons*, pp. 293–94; Betancourt and Alexander, conversation of 2–3 June 1964, in Alexander, *Venezuela's Voice for Democracy*, p. 88. Pike, *The Politics of the Miraculous in Peru*, reviews the standard criticisms and adds some new ones.

13. "I left Russia feeling a great joy. There, everything is wonderful and, after having lived a *short* while in the midst of its grand activity, one can know where the world is moving." Haya to Lovestone, 25 November 1924, file "Haya de la Torre," box 372, Lovestone Papers.

14. See Haya, "El aprismo como credo civil de nuestra América" [1930], in "Teoría y táctica del aprismo" [1931], *Obras completas*, 1:198–99; Haya, "Pensamientos de crítica, polémica y acción" [n.d.], published with "Impresiones de la Inglaterra imperialista y la Rusia soviética" [1933], *Obras completas*, 2:474–75; Haya, "El antiimperialismo y el Apra" [written 1928, published 1936], in Haya, *Obras completas*, 4:136. See also Alexander, *Aprismo*, pp. 7–8.

15. For a description of Inman's background and the background of his circle generally, see Robert David Johnson, "The Transformation of Pan-Americanism," in Johnson, ed., *On Cultural Ground*, pp. 173–96.

16. Haya, "El antiimperialismo y el Apra," 4:148.

17. Haya to Sánchez, 21 May 1953, in Haya and Sánchez, *Correspondencia*, 2:66.

18. On some occasions, Haya would use the terms "good intervention" and "bad intervention." Popular sovereignty remained the standard by which such actions were judged. See Haya, "Interamericanismo democrático sin imperio" [December 1943], in Haya, "Y después de la guerra ¿Qué?" [1946], *Obras completas*, 6:95–101.

19. With Roosevelt and the Democratic Party, Haya later recalled, "there had finally arrived at the White House that policy of *anti-imperialism* that since the end of the previous century William Jennings Bryan had represented." Haya, "Trienta años de aprismo" [1955], *Obras completas*, 6:350.

20. Haya, "A Democratic Hemisphere," *Common Sense*, November 1941, pp. 338–39.

21. Luis Alberto Sánchez reports that Haya's book was written in response to an attack on Apra by the Cuban communist Julio Antonio Mella and that after Mella was assassinated—presumably by the Cuban dictator, Gerardo Machado—Haya was unwilling to see it published and was reluctant even when Sánchez and Carlos

Manuel Cox took charge of the project in 1935. Sánchez, *Sobre la herencia de Haya de la Torre*, p. 12.

22. Haya, "El antiimperialismo y el Apra," 4:120–21.

23. Ibid., 4:89, 150; Hobson, *Imperialism*; Lenin, "Imperialism, the Highest Stage of Capitalism" [1916], *Selected Works*, 5:3–119.

24. Haya, "El antiimperialismo y el Apra," 4:89.

25. Ibid., 4:157.

26. Ibid., 4:185.

27. Ibid., 4:116–18. In a footnote on page 169, Haya also praised at length the reforms and nationalizations associated with the administrations of José Batlle y Ordóñez in Uruguay (1903–7 and 1911–15).

28. Haya, "El antiimperialismo y el Apra," 4:185.

29. Ibid., 4:177{ff}.

30. Although Haya referred to the destruction of indigenous small business at the hands of monopoly capital, he was always vague about the economic disadvantages of imperialism that Apra was to correct and the ways in which it would correct them. "The masses of workers who will be transformed into the modern proletariat," he argued, "will not perceive the violence of imperialist exploitation until much later. The modern type of imperialism, especially North American imperialism—so advanced and refined in its methods—only offers advantages and progress in its initiation." Haya, "El antiimperialismo y el Apra," 4:101. Haya's dominant concern seems always to have been with the political disadvantages of imperialism. "Generally," he claimed in one early and striking essay, "when the *criollo* politicians, agents of Wall Street, make a deal with the purchasers of the sovereignty of our peoples, there circulates a propaganda that rapidly converts itself into a literature. It speaks of 'progress,' of 'sewage systems,' of 'industrialization,' etc. It sings the praises of the 'friendship of the United States,' the 'vigor of the Saxon race,' and the benefits of 'capital investment.' Later come the first paved streets, modern plumbing, straight roads and houses made of cement. Then the imperialist literature becomes delirious and poets emerge writing sonnets to the new hygienic services. But no one asks how much this costs the country that receives it and what it gives in exchange." Haya, "Literatura imperialista" [November 1924], in Haya, "Por la emancipación de América Latina" [1927], *Obras completas*, 1:50–51.

31. For Haya's impressions of the Soviet Union, see Haya, "Impresiones de la Inglaterra imperialista y la Rusia soviética," *Obras completas*, 2:415–46. See also the additional letters and essays reproduced in Haya, "Ex combatientes y desocupados" [1936], *Obras completas*, 3:15–72. For his description of his differences with the Soviet leadership, see Haya, "El antiimperialismo y el Apra," 4:84–85.

32. "For Communism, there cannot exist another party of the left that is not an instrument of the Third International of Moscow, of Stalinist orthodoxy. Any political organization that Moscow does not command must be execrated and fought. After the [World Anti-Imperialist] Congress of Brussels in 1927, this was the case with Apra." Haya, "El antiimperialismo y el Apra," 4:87.

33. It is perhaps worth noting that the family Haya stayed with in Berlin, from 1929 to 1931, was Jewish. Sánchez and Vallenas, *Sobre la herencia de Haya de la Torre*, p. 68. His stay in Germany was initiated against his will when American

officials in the Canal Zone refused to let him disembark from a ship whose next stop was Bremen, Germany. This Haya soon turned into useful anti-imperialist propaganda. See Salisbury, "The Middle America Exile of Víctor Raúl Haya de la Torre," pp. 13–15.

34. Haya, "¿Qué quieren los Nazis?" [May 1931], in "Ex combatientes y desocupados," *Obras completas*, 3:226–28.

35. Haya, speech of 20 August 1931, text in "Política aprista," *Obras completas*, 5:48.

36. Ibid., 5:43–44.

37. Haya, speech of 23 August 1931, text in "Política aprista," 5:55–57, 60–61.

38. Alfredo L. Palacios, who wrote a prologue to the 1946 edition of Alberdi's classic work, helped to found the Argentine Socialist Party at the turn of the century and continued to be active in the Argentine Left until his death in the early 1960s. According to Luis Alberto Sánchez, he exercised a great influence on Haya during a visit to Lima in 1919. Sánchez and Vallenas, *Sobre la herencia de Haya de la Torre*, p. 53.

39. Véliz, *The New World of the Gothic Fox*, pp. 7–8.

40. Dearing to Kellogg, 7 September 1931, 810.43 APRA/102. Quoted in Davies, *Indian Integration in Peru*, pp. 110–11. Davies interprets this memo, and similar ones from other interviews with Haya, as proof that "Haya de la Torre was not sincere in his espousal of radical causes." He presents no evidence, however, to suggest that as far as matters of substance were concerned Haya was saying anything different in private than he was in public. In a less cynical interpretation, Peter Klaren suggests that "Haya, pulled increasingly toward the center by the exigencies of pragmatic electoral politics, considerably moderated his earlier shrill calls for 'revolution' and the construction of a socialist society." Klaren, *Modernization, Dislocation, and Aprismo*, p. 133. While there is much to recommend this view, it tends to underemphasize the influence on Haya's thinking of his years in Germany. Haya's analogies between fascism and communism, and his identification with the "democratic left," appear to reflect this experience rather than the moderating influence of participation in electoral politics.

41. Haya, "¿Qué es el A.P.R.A.?" [1926], in "Por la emancipación de América Latina" [1927], *Obras completas*, 1:129.

42. Congresso Nacional Aprista, "Plan de acción inmediata o programa minimo" [August 1931], text in "Política aprista," 5:11–29.

43. See Robert Alexander's discussion of this point in his introduction to "The Anti-Imperialist State," and the selections from Haya's writings that follow, in Alexander, *Aprismo*, pp. 161–222.

44. Haya to Sánchez, 8 November 1952, in Haya and Sánchez, *Correspondencia*, 2:17.

45. Sánchez and Vallenas, *Sobre la herencia de Haya de la Torre*, p. 12. In his conclusion, especially on pages 237–38, Sánchez argues that "mature" Aprismo emerged around 1930 and that it was significantly modified after 1940 by an emphasis on the need for a "democratic inter-Americanism without imperialism" and by a radical critique not only of communism and nazism, but also of all forms of state capitalism.

46. Apra in Peru in 1931 appears in many ways similar to Acción Democrática in Venezuela in 1945. While both parties failed in their initial attempts, the Adecos gained invaluable experience in three years in power, which helped them greatly in their later successful efforts. Even Acción Democrática's serious mistakes became part of a "known quantity" that could be contrasted with the military dictatorship that followed. In Peru, Apra would not get the chance to make mistakes with executive authority until the 1980s. On Apra's mistakes in power, see Ricardo Lago, "The Illusion of Pursuing Redistribution through Macropolicy: Peru's Heterodox Experience, 1985–1990," and the subsequent commentary in Dornbusch and Edwards, eds., *The Macroeconomics of Populism in Latin America*, pp. 263–330. On Acción Democrática's contribution to the transformation of Venezuela from a coup- and dictatorship-ridden country in the nineteenth and early twentieth centuries to one of Latin America's oldest democracies, see Alexander, *Rómulo Betancourt*.

47. See Stein, *Populism in Peru*, p. 193. For a list of other references on this question, see Pike, *The Modern History of Peru*, p. 364 n. 10.

48. Sánchez, *Testimonio personal*, 2:24.

49. For a succinct presentation of the Trujillo revolt and its background, see Klaren, *Modernization, Dislocation, and Aprismo*, pp. 136–41.

50. Haya, "El 'buen vecino': ¿Garantia definitiva?" [mistakenly cited in Haya's collected works as from February 1938; it contains an internal reference to an article written in April 1938], in "La defensa continental" [1943], *Obras completas*, 4:261–62.

51. Haya, "¿Hay un imperialismo democrático?" [April 1941], in "La defensa continental," 4:288–91.

52. Haya, "Sobre el frente democrático interamericano" [April 1941], in "La defensa continental," 4:340–43.

53. Haya, "Plan para la afirmación de la democracia en América" [1941], in "La defensa continental," 4:362.

54. Haya, "An Inter-American Democratic Front," *Free World* 4, no. 2 (November 1942): p. 152.

55. Haya, "Interamericanismo democrático sin imperio" [December 1943], in Haya, "Y después de la guerra ¿Qué?" [1946], *Obras completas*, 6:101.

56. See Schwartzberg, "Civility of Yankee Imperialism," chapter 5 in this volume.

57. See chapter 5.

58. For an insightful comparative study of the SPD in Germany and the SAP in Sweden that casts new light on the character of both movements and on social democratic politics in the first third of the twentieth century in general, see Berman, *The Social Democratic Moment*.

59. Braden to Cooper, 27 December 1946, file "Peru," box 5, Records of the Deputy Assistant Secretaries of State for Inter-American Affairs, 1945–56, NA.

60. Henry Dearborn, memorandum on a report from the military attaché in Lima on Haya's recent visit to the United States, 8 May 1947, file "Memos Relating to General Latin American Affairs," box 13, Records of the Office of American Republic Affairs, NA.

61. Quoted in Dawson to Braden, 4 October 1946, file "Diplomatic Correspondence: 1946–47, A–D," box 20, Braden Papers.

62. See E. Bernstein, *Evolutionary Socialism*. See also Gay, *The Dilemma of Democratic Socialism*. The description of social democratic movements as seeking to become the "heirs of capitalism rather than its assassins," I owe to John P. Roche.

63. On Haya's conception of Latin America, the United States, Europe, and various other parts of the world as occupying distinct "historical space-times," see the selections from his work and the commentary presented in Alexander, ed., *Aprismo*, pp. 31–85.

64. The idea of a Peruvian national economic congress had been part of the aprista campaign in 1931. See Haya, speech of 23 August 1931, text in "Política aprista," 5:68–70. The idea of an inter-American economic congress was presented most articulately in Haya, "Plan para la afirmación de la democracia en América," in "La defensa continental," 4:366–67.

65. Haya, "El plan económico del aprismo," a public address of 9 October 1945, text in *Obras completas*, 5:356–93. Much the same attitude was expressed by Juan José Arévalo in Guatemala. According to Arévalo, Roosevelt was the great "transformer" of democracy: "He showed us that there is no necessity for doing away with the concept of liberty in the democratic system in order to simultaneously breathe into that system a socialist spirit. Because of him we know that the concept of liberty is perfectly compatible with the concept of collective organization." Arévalo, *Informe presidencial*, p. 30.

66. Quoted in *La Tribuna* (Lima), 9 May 1946.

67. Carlos Hall, memorandum, 11 October 1946, and marginal note by GS (Gerald Smith), 810.00/10–1146, NA. Hall was in the Division of North and West Coast Affairs in the State Department, and Smith was the special assistant to the assistant secretary of state.

68. Bowers to Byrnes, 8 May 1946, 810.00/5–846, NA. Quoted in Bowers to Byrnes, 16 May 1946, 810.00/5–1646, NA.

69. Magda Portal, "Aprismo, doctrina indoamericana," *La Tribuna* (Lima), 4 May 1946.

70. Bowers to Byrnes, 8 May 1946, 810.00/5–846, NA.

71. The following is an excerpt from an interview Allende held with Régis Debray soon after coming to power:

Debray: You belong to a generation, shall we say the generation of Betancourt, Haya de la Torre, Arévalo and their peers. This generation is politically dead today. They are now a part of Latin American pre-history, and yet you are a central figure in its contemporary history, and will influence its future. Why were they left by the wayside, whereas you have continued to make progress?

Allende: Look, what you say is rather hard, but true enough. The truth is as follows: when it had been in existence for two or three years, the Socialist Party called a Conference of the popular parties of Latin America here in Chile. On that occasion, there were representatives of APRA and other populist movements, but there was already a noticeable difference, because the Socialist Party was a Marxist party, and we were categorically anti-imperialist; at the time, APRA also claimed to be an anti-imperialist party. The truth is sad. What happened? When the popular parties, for instance 'Democratic

Action,' came to power in Venezuela, they lacked the positive approach required to make the necessary changes, there was no struggle to change the
regime, the system—on the contrary they threw their lot with imperialism.
APRA, for example, has not come to power, but in its attempt to do so, it has
modified, mitigated and changed its attitude to imperialism. As a result, these
parties have been overtaken by history and do not represent or interpret the
aspirations of the Latin American peoples. (Debray, *The Chilean Revolution*,
pp. 68–69)

72. Bowers to Byrnes, 8 May 1946, 810.00/5–846, NA.

73. Bowers to Byrnes, 16 May 1946, 810.00/5–1646, NA.

74. Ibid.

75. Dawson to Byrnes, 4 October 1946, 831.00/10–446, NA.

76. Dawson to Byrnes, 10 October 1946, 831.00/10–1046, NA.

77. Dawson to Braden, 4 October 1946, file "Diplomatic Correspondence, 1946–
47: A–D," box 20, Braden Papers. In the margin next to this Braden wrote "good
point."

78. Wiley to Byrnes, 23 September 1946, 823.00/9–2346, NA.

79. Donovan to Byrnes, 23 October 1946, 810.00/10–2346, NA.

80. Gibson to Byrnes, 11 October 1946, 810.00/10–1146, NA; Cohen to Byrnes,
31 October 1946, 810.00/10–3146, NA.

81. Collins to Byrnes, 8 October 1946, 810.00/10–846, NA.

82. White to Stettinius, 7 June 1945, 711.00/6–745, NA.

83. Jay Reist, summary of conversation with Manuel Prado Garland, 17 June
1945, attached to Trueblood to Stettinius, 21 June 1945, 823.00/1–3045, NA. Reist
was the assistant military attaché at the embassy, Prado was the son of the outgoing
Peruvian president, and Trueblood was the chargé d'affaires ad interim.

84. Eugenio Chang-Rodríguez, "Óscar R. Benavides," in Alexander, *Biographical
Dictionary*, p. 52.

85. Trueblood to Stettinius, 30 January 1945, 823.00/6–2145, NA; Dwyre to
White, 16 February 1945, attached to Trueblood to Wells, 27 February 1945, 823.00/
2–2745, NA; White to Stettinius, 19 April 1945, 823.00/4–1945, NA. Dwyre was the
American vice consul in Arequipa and an acute observer.

86. White to Stettinius, 21 May 1945, 823.00/5–2145, NA.

87. Jay Reist, report no. R-267–45, 22 May 1945, attached to White to Stettinius,
29 May 1945, 823.00/5–2945, NA.

88. Haya, "Discurso del reencuentro," 20 May 1945, *Obras completas*, 5:344, 347,
353.

89. Trueblood to Stettinius, 21 June 1945, 823.00/6–2145, NA.

90. Trueblood to Stettinius, 11 July 1945, 823.00/7–1145, NA.

91. Office of Intelligence Research (OIR), Division of Research for the American
Republics (DRA), Department of State, "Plans and Activities of APRA Leader Victor
Raul Haya de la Torre," 17 October 1947, p. 10, OIR (R&A) 4336, NA.

92. White to Stettinius, 9 June 1945, 823.00/6–945, NA.

93. Trueblood to Stettinius, 29 June 1945, 823.00/6–2945, NA.

94. In his memoirs, Bustamante claimed that Aprista demonstrations included
"little girls and young women whose ingenuous impetuosity was unscrupulously

utilized to reinforce the activity of the adepts. The pretext for this premature initiation into political life was the right of women's suffrage in municipal elections, a right recognized by the constitution, but limited by it solely to women of age and to the mother of the family." Bustamante, *Tres años de lucha*, p. 58.

95. Pawley to Byrnes, 28 September 1945, 823.00/9–2845, NA.

96. Pawley to Byrnes, 15 October 1945, 823.00/10–1545, NA.

97. Butler to Braden and Briggs, 18 October 1945, FW823.00/9–2845, NA. Both Braden and Briggs approved Butler's position in marginal notes.

98. On Bustamante's offer of the ministries of agriculture and treasury to Apra, and the reasons for the party's refusal and its growing disenchantment with Bustamante, see the memoirs of one of the key Aprista parliamentary leaders, León de Vivero, *El tirano quedó atrás*, pp. 49–69. See also Sánchez, *Testimonio personal*, 2:366–71. As early as July 1945, the American chargé had reported a conversation with Haya in which he "seemed to be obsessed with the view that democracy was on trial and that if it failed Communism would be the next step. He returned time and again to this point." Trueblood to Byrnes, 6 July 1945, 823.00/7–645, NA.

99. Bustamante, *Tres años de lucha*, pp. 52–53.

100. White to Stettinius, 9 June 1945, 823.00/6–945, NA. Haya's comments were taken from a speech he gave in Callao on 6 June 1945.

101. Reist to Pawley, 17 August 1945, attached to Pawley to Byrnes, 21 August 1945, 823.00/8–2145, NA.

102. OIR, "Plans and Activities of APRA Leader Victor Raul Haya de la Torre," 17 October 1947, p. 10, OIR (R&A) 4336, NA; Trueblood to Byrnes, 28 December 1945, 823.00/12–2845, NA.

103. Trueblood to Byrnes, 28 December 1945, 823.00/12–2845, NA. Trueblood enclosed a summary of a conversation he had with Aprista leader Manuel Seoane in which the latter boasted that after the street fighting a great many members of the armed forces had congratulated him on Apra's anticommunist stand. Trueblood's impression, however, was that a protest meeting had been broken up.

104. Sánchez, *Sobre la herencia de Haya de la Torre*, p. 185.

105. Haya had effectively accepted responsibility for the success of Bustamante's government, Pawley reported, "and I find that he is successfully enlisting the assistance of many of the conservatives who a few weeks ago were attacking the Aprista Party, Montero, and myself because of the Government's determination to settle its foreign debt." Pawley to Byrnes, 6 February 1946, 823.00/2–646, NA.

106. In late April 1946, Pawley would report Bustamante's complaints over the Apristas' use of patronage in the ministries they controlled, their success in winning support at the municipal level and within the police, and the danger that they would win majorities in both houses of Congress and "take over" complete control of Peru and the government, but he no longer endorsed such fears and instead also reported Haya's view that Bustamante was relying on anti-Apra advisers and noted that while the gap between the two was widening, Haya was reiterating his desire to reach an understanding. Pawley to Byrnes, 24 April 1946, 823.00/4–2446, NA; and William Pawley to James Byrnes, 26 April 1946, 823.00/4–2646, NA.

107. Cooper to Byrnes, 10 July 1946, 823.00/7–1046, NA.

108. Cooper to Byrnes, 25 November 1946, 823.00/11–2546, NA.

109. For a succinct review of oil issues as they concerned American interests, see Levangie to Marshall, 2 December 1948, attached to Tittman to Marshall, 10 December 1948, *FRUS, 1948*, 9:736–37. George Levangie was the petroleum attaché in the American embassy in Lima, Charles Marshall a staff member of the Foreign Affairs Committee of the House of Representatives, and Harold Tittman the American ambassador.

110. León de Vivero, *El tirano quedó atrás*, pp. 72 n. 1, 86.

111. See ibid., pp. 119{ff}; Sánchez, *Testimonio personal*, 3:71{ff}; Bustamante, *Tres años de lucha*, pp. 107{ff}.

112. Bustamante, *Tres años de lucha*, p. 109.

113. Sánchez, *Testimonio personal*, 3:79{ff}; Bustamante, *Tres años de lucha*, pp. 113{ff}.

114. OIR, "Plans and Activities of APRA Leader Victor Raul Haya de la Torre," 17 October 1947, p. 16, OIR (R&A) 4336, NA; Bustamante, *Tres años de lucha*, p. 124. Among their infringements on Peruvian constitutional rights, Bustamante and Odría banned the showing of the American film *Boomerang* on the grounds that it would exacerbate popular animosities. The plot of the film, León de Vivero suggests, was very similar to the Graña case: "A priest is murdered in order to blame the killing on a popular group." León de Vivero, *El tirano quedó atrás*, p. 187 n. 5.

115. Cooper to Byrnes, 25 November 1946, 823.00/11–2546, NA.

116. OIR, "Plans and Activities of APRA Leader Victor Raul Haya de la Torre," 17 October 1947, pp. 16–17, OIR (R&A) 4336, NA.

117. Quoted in Nigel Haworth, "Peru," in Bethell and Roxborough, *Latin America*, p. 187.

118. Sheldon Mills, memorandum of conversation between Paul Daniels and Sr. Fernández-Dávilla, 2 January 1948, 810.504/1–248, NA.

119. Cooper to Marshall, 4 January 1948, 810.5043/1–448, NA.

120. Sánchez, *Testimonio personal*, 3:85.

121. Ibid., 3:101.

122. Ibid., 3:109, 111.

123. Ibid., 3:101. Bustamante refers to a letter of 14 April 1948 from the Apra archives—which the Peruvian government seized—in which one of the Callao conspirators promises Haya that his forces are "ready at the first order." There does not, however, appear to be any evidence that Haya ever gave such an order. Bustamante, *Tres años de lucha*, p. 184.

124. Sánchez, *Testimonio personal*, 3:111.

125. Bustamante presents himself in his memoirs as convinced that the Apra leadership was behind the 3 October 1948 revolt and could not be trusted not to try similar attempts in the future. He also claims that materials in the party's archives prove that it had a "totalitarian" structure. Bustamante, *Tres años de lucha*, pp. 178–87.

126. Central Intelligence Agency, "Review of the World Situation," CIA 11–48, 17 November 1948, pp. 9–10, file NSC Meetings, "Meeting No. 27," box 204, President's Secretary's File, Truman Library.

127. Haya, "Draft of a Memorandum on the Present Political Situation Existing in Latin America in General and in Peru in Particular, with Reference to Commu-

nism and the Latin American Policy of the United States," 12 May 1949, translated by Allan Dawson and forwarded to the State Department by the American ambassador to Chile, Claude Bowers, 15 July 1949, 810.00/7–1549, NA.

128. Mann to Kreig, 24 November 1950, file "Peru," box 5, Records of the Deputy Assistant Secretaries of State for Inter-American Affairs, NA. Spruille Braden's position on the subject is also worth noting: "Reverting to our correspondence regarding our mutual friend, Haya de la Torre, I have written to and discussed the matter with my friends in the Department. I find that they are doing everything possible in the premises and that, therefore, it would not be helpful for me to address a communication to the President, at least at this time." Braden to Grant, 19 December 1950, "Peru: Political Personalities: Haya," box 12, Grant Papers.

129. Actually, Serafino Romualdi sent Miller a letter of 11 April 1950 attacking inaccuracies in the content of letters allegedly sent by American narcotics agents and asking if his interpretation of them was "substantially correct." To this question Miller replied in the affirmative in a brief note of 1 May 1950. Both letters were then published. See file 6, box 5, Romualdi Papers.

130. Miller, marginal note, on Owen to Miller, 27 July 1949, FW710.11/5–2649, NA.

131. Owen to Miller, 27 July 1949, FW710.11/5–2649, NA.

132. Miller to Bowers, 29 January 1952, file "Jan.–Feb. 1952," box 7, mss. II, Bowers Papers.

133. Haya to Sánchez, 21 May 1953, in Haya and Sánchez, *Correspondencia*, 2:65.

134. Haya, "¿Qué llamarían ustedes una democracia ideal?" [November 1954], in Haya, "Mensaje de Europa Nordica" [1956], *Obras completas*, 3:250.

135. "The Acción Democrática people in Guatemala are thinking of leaving, because their situation there has become virtually impossible. The Communists are carrying on a tremendous campaign against them, and even President Arbenz had accused them of being Yankee agents." Alexander and Betancourt, conversation of 15 July 1953, in Alexander, *Venezuela's Voice for Democracy*, p. 25. One Aprista exile has written in his memoirs that he left Guatemala after the political atmosphere became too unpleasant. See Andres Townsend Ezcurra, *Cinquenta años de aprismo: Memorias, ensayos y discursos de un militante* (Lima: n.p., 1989), pp. 88–89. See also Gleijeses, *Shattered Hope*, esp. pp. 134–48.

136. Haya to Romualdi, 11 January 1955, file 4, box 6, Romualdi Papers.

137. Haya to Grant, 10 March 1955, file "Haya de la Torre," box 12, Grant Papers. On American support for Costa Rica in this period, see Ameringer, *Don Pepe*, pp. 121–25.

138. See Haya, "Mensaje de Europa Nordica," 3:393–450.

139. The best overview of these developments remains Porter and Alexander, *The Struggle for Democracy in Latin America*, pp. 74–141.

140. Haya, "El APRA trienta años después," *Combate* 4, no. 21 (March and April 1962), p. 56. Along with Norman Thomas, Rómulo Betancourt, Eduardo Santos, and José Figueres, Haya served on the editorial board of *Combate*. Whether he knew that it was receiving a subsidy from the CIA is an open question. Figueres would later observe that he had approached the CIA, not the other way around, and would

suggest that the outcry resulting from the disclosure of such activities in *Ramparts* magazine in 1967 was "silly and adolescent." Quoted in Ameringer, *Don Pepe*, p. 164.

141. Goodwin would still wax lyrical about Haya in the late 1960s: "If it were possible to fix an instant when Latin America entered the modern age, it might be the afternoon about 60 years ago when the teen-aged Haya walked from the level, green fields of his home town toward the crumbling ruins of the imperial city of Chimu in the drab, jagged foothills of the Andes." Richard Goodwin, "Our Stake in the Awakening," *Life*, 14 April 1967, p. 76.

142. Schlesinger Jr. to Thomas Mann, 15 March 1961, p. 21, file "Visits to and from Latin America," box 3, Bureau of Inter-American Affairs, Subject Files of the Assistant Secretary, 1959–62, NA. Jack Neal had played an important role in the CIG, the CIA's predecessor, and may have been the CIA's station chief in Lima at this time. When the CIA used State Department telegraphic cables in the 1940s, the headline code phrase was "Please inform Neal for Joyce." The use of this phrase is explained in William Eddy to Robert Lovett, 1 August 1947, 839.00/8–147, NA.

143. Ball to Loeb, 24 March 1962, *FRUS, 1961–1963*, 12:858.

144. Pike, *The Politics of the Miraculous in Peru*, pp. 253–57.

145. Had it not been for the coup, in the judgement of his old opponent Fernando Belaúnde Terry, Haya would have won the 1969 elections. See Clinton, "APRA: An Appraisal," p. 280.

146. Pike, *The Politics of the Miraculous in Peru*, pp. 276–83.

147. Haya, "Preliminares" [January 1977], in Haya, *Obras completas*, 1:xli.

148. In Haya's presentation, the following quotes are interspersed with commentary. I have chosen to present them together for convenience and also to quote from the original English rather than translate back from the Spanish. Although Haya was fond of quoting Marx, he does not seem to have quoted from his writings on India before this. It is possible that he had only encountered them the year before in the magnificent polemic by Rangel, *Del buen salvaje al buen revolucionario.* Haya recommends Rangel's book in a speech on the fifty-second anniversary of the founding of Apra. Haya, speech of 7 May 1976, in Haya, *Obras completas*, 7:485.

149. Marx, "The Future Results of British Rule in India" [8 August 1853, *New York Daily Tribune*], text and translation in Avineri, ed., *Karl Marx on Colonialism*, pp. 125–26.

150. Haya ends his quote just before Marx's disturbing concluding assertion that "we have the right, in point of history to exclaim, with Goethe: 'Sollte diese Qual uns quälen / Da sie unsre Lust vermehrt / Hat nicht Myriaden Seele / Timurs Herrschaft aufgezehrt?'"—"Should this torture then torment us / Since it brings us greater pleasure / Were not through the rule of Timur / Souls devoured without measure?" Marx, "The British Rule in India" [25 June 1853, *New York Daily Tribune*], text and translation in Avineri, ed., *Karl Marx on Colonialism*, p. 89.

151. Haya, "Preliminares," *Obras completas*, 1:xxxix–xlii.

Chapter 5. A Venezuelan Visionary

1. Much of this chapter has appeared in Schwartzberg, "Rómulo Betancourt."

2. Betancourt, "Versión taquigráfica del discurso radiodifundido a toda la nación por los micrófonos de 'La Voz del Táchira' en San Cristóbal," 14 December 1945, in

Betancourt, *Trayectoria democrática*, 2:20. By the end of 1947, slightly more than 73,000 hectares had been distributed to some 6,000 peasants. During Betancourt's second term, a little more than a decade later, more than 1.5 million hectares would be distributed to more than 60,000 peasant families. Alexander, *Rómulo Betancourt*, pp. 271, 504. Technically, there was no *latifundia* in Japan. The land reform imposed by the American occupation transferred landownership from roughly 2,341,000 landlords to some 4,748,000 tenants. See Schwartzberg, "The 'Soft Peace Boys,'" pp. 185–216.

3. Quoted in Dawson to Byrnes, 30 January 1946, file 13, box 55, Dozer Papers. On the Uruguayan initiative and the responses it drew, see Unión Panamericana, *Consulta del gobierno del Uruguay.*

4. Betancourt, "Versión taquigráfica del discurso pronunciado en Panamá," 28 July 1946, *Trayectoria democrática*, 2:180.

5. Dawson to Byrnes, 8 February 1946, 835.00/2–846, NA.

6. Ibid. For the situation in Chile to which Betancourt refers, see Barnard, "Chilean Communists," pp. 359–60.

7. Dawson to Byrnes, 8 February 1946, 835.00/2–846, NA.

8. Ibid.

9. For the following interpretation of Betancourt's views I am indebted to Arturo Sosa A., "Estudio introductorio," in Betancourt, *La segunda independencia*, 1:3–341; Aníbal Romero, Elizabeth Tinoco, and María Teresa Romero, "Estudio preliminar," in Betancourt, *Antología política*, pp. 7–39; Alejandro Gómez, *Rómulo Betancourt;* and Alexander, *Rómulo Betancourt.*

10. See Alexander, *Rómulo Betancourt*, pp. 74–75; and Gómez, *Rómulo Betancourt y el Partido Comunista de Costa Rica*, pp. 11–15 and passim.

11. Trotsky's succinct defense of totalitarianism is unrivaled on the antidemocratic left: "The foundations of the militarization of labor are those forms of State compulsion without which the replacement of capitalist economy by the Socialist will forever remain an empty sound. Why do we speak of *militarization?* Of course, this is only an analogy—but an analogy very rich in content. No social organization except the army has ever considered itself justified in subordinating citizens to itself in such a measure, and to control them by its will on all sides to such a degree, as the State of the proletarian dictatorship considers itself justified in doing, and does. Only the army—just because in its way it used to decide questions of the life or death of nations, States, and ruling classes—was endowed with powers of demanding from each and all complete submission to its problems, aims, regulations and orders." Trotsky, *Terrorism and Communism*, p. 141. For Lenin's view of the value of human life, see the documents in Pipes, ed., *The Unknown Lenin*. On Betancourt's view of Lenin and Trotsky as bringing Russia into the vanguard of the struggle for world socialism, see Betancourt to García, 28 November 1932, in Betancourt, *Antología política*, p. 430.

12. Betancourt to Leoni, 12 October 1935, in Betancourt, *Antología política*, pp. 511–12.

13. Ibid., pp. 512–13.

14. Although Betancourt described his position as caught between two fronts, the right and the ultraleft, Wall Street and Moscow, he found the latter much less threat-

ening. He thought that the Bolshevik Revolution had entered a Thermidorian phase and that Stalin—having dedicated himself to the idiocy of "building socialism in one country"—was a Bonaparte without Bonaparte's expansionary ambitions. See Betancourt to Herrera Umérez, 13 August 1931, and Betancourt to García, 28 November 1932, in Betancourt, *Antología política,* pp. 308, 431.

15. Haya, speech of 11 August 1931, quoted in Haya, "Treinta años de aprismo," *Obras completas,* 6:424–25.

16. Haya, speech of 20 August 1931, text in Haya, *Obras completas,* 5:48.

17. Quoted in Seoane, *Las calumnias contra el aprismo,* p. 34.

18. Alexander, *Rómulo Betancourt,* pp. 35–47.

19. Gómez, *Rómulo Betancourt y el Partido Comunista de Costa Rica,* p. 30.

20. The Aprista views in this paragraph are a summary of arguments contained in Haya, "El antiimperialismo y el Apra," *Obras completas,* vol. 4, esp. pp. 89, 120–24, 150, 157, 177{ff}, 185.

21. Gómez, *Rómulo Betancourt y el Partido Comunista de Costa Rica,* pp. 30, 44.

22. Valmore Rodríguez would be the interior minister in the first AD government, and Raúl Leoni would be the minister of labor. In the 1960s, Leoni would succeed Betancourt as president of the republic.

23. Betancourt to Rodríguez, Montilla, and Leoni, 3 May 1932, in Betancourt, *Antología política,* pp. 354–55.

24. For an excellent discussion of the Costa Rican CP's heterodoxies, see Alexander, *Rómulo Betancourt,* pp. 67–86. The best discussion of Betancourt's role in the party is Gómez, *Rómulo Betancourt y el Partido Comunista de Costa Rica.*

25. Betancourt to Rodríguez, Montilla, and Leoni, 27 January 1932, in Betancourt, *Antología política,* p. 335. Although some of the Scottsboro defendants had been sentenced to death at the time Betancourt was writing, they were ultimately released after the Supreme Court reversed their convictions on procedural grounds and one of the alleged rape victims recanted her testimony.

26. Betancourt, "Panorama de los movimientos estudiantiles de Latinoamerica y sus proyecciones," 15 and 22 March 1930 [in *Repertorio Americano*], in Betancourt, *Antología política,* p. 143.

27. Betancourt, "La verdad sobre la situación del Peru," 19 November 1930 [in *La Prensa* of Bogotá], in Betancourt, *Antología política,* p. 221. Mariátegui was a founder of the Peruvian Communist Party.

28. Betancourt to Portal and del Mar, 23 May 1931, in Betancourt, *Antología política,* p. 267.

29. Betancourt to Herrera Umérez, 29 July 1931, in Betancourt, *Antología política,* p. 300.

30. Betancourt to Rodríguez, Montilla, and Leoni, 3 May 1932, in Betancourt, *Antología política,* p. 361.

31. Betancourt to Hermanitos (Rodríguez, Montilla, and Leoni), 19 May 1932, quoted in Alexander, *Rómulo Betancourt,* p. 72.

32. Betancourt to Picón Salas, 12 October 1932, in Betancourt, *Antología política,* p. 426. Since the original Apra platform had only specified action against Yankee imperialism, a standard communist claim was that Apra was covertly allied with the British.

33. Betancourt to Rodríguez, Montilla, and Leoni, 3 May 1932, in Betancourt, *Antología política*, p. 361. The work that most bothered Betancourt seems to have been Seoane's *Las calumnias contra el aprismo*. On the one side, as Seoane comments on page 34, were the Russian Bolsheviks, who favored the immediate dictatorship of the proletariat and violent transformation. On the other were "almost all of the European socialist parties, advocates of the democratic system and of evolutionary transformation."

34. See Leszek Kolakowski, "The Myth of Human Self-Identity: Unity of Civil and Political Society in Socialist Thought," in Kolakowski and Hampshire, eds., *The Socialist Idea*, esp. pp. 24–25.

35. Betancourt, "Con quién estamos y contra quién estamos," May 1932 [in *Venezuela Futura*], in Betancourt, *Antología política*, pp. 378–400. Alexander follows Betancourt's misleading recollection of this document as attacking both conservative and communist positions. While it did attack a "New York" communist position, it also put forward a Venezuelan one—Betancourt's. Alexander, *Rómulo Betancourt*, p. 60.

36. Betancourt, "Con quién estamos y contra quién estamos," pp. 379–81.

37. Ibid., p. 397. The use of "Quakers" and "Jews" as part of a derogatory stereotype was not common in Betancourt's writing. This is the only example with which I am familiar. It may have reflected nothing more than the kind of simplistic association of "race" with economic backwardness or success that was common at the time. On the other hand, such formulations were not unheard of on the antidemocratic left, and Marx had set a particularly nasty precedent in an early formulation of his desire for the unity of civil and political society: "Christianity is the sublime thought of Judaism; Judaism is the vulgar practical application of Christianity. But this practical application could only become universal after Christianity as the perfect religion had completed, in a theoretical manner, the self-alienation of man from himself and from nature. Only then could Judaism attain general domination and make externalized man and externalized nature into alienable, saleable objects, a prey to the slavery of egoistic need and the market.... As soon as society manages to abolish the empirical essence of Judaism, the market and its presuppositions, the Jew becomes impossible, for his mind no longer has an object, because the subjective basis of Judaism, practical need, has become humanized, and because the conflict of man's individual, material existence with his species-existence has been superseded. The social emancipation of the Jew implies the emancipation of society from Judaism." (Marx, "On the Jewish Question" [written in 1843], in *Karl Marx*, ed. McLellan, pp. 61–62.)

38. Betancourt, "Guerra civil en el Peru y posición del partido aprista," 19 March 1933 [in *Trabajo*], in Betancourt, *Antología política*, pp. 470–71.

39. Betancourt, "Con quién estamos y contra quién estamos," pp. 397–98.

40. Haya, speech of 11 August 1931, quoted in Haya, "Treinta años de aprismo," *Obras completas*, 6:424–25.

41. Betancourt, "Con quién estamos y contra quién estamos," p. 400.

42. For Betancourt's enthusiasm with the popular front, see Betancourt to Leoni, 12 October 1935, in Betancourt, *Antología política*, pp. 518–21. See also Alexander, *Rómulo Betancourt*, p. 64.

43. In *Venezuela: Política y petróleo,* as Arturo Sosa observes, Betancourt attempted to portray López Contreras's regime as little more than a prolongation of the Gómez dictatorship. A very different picture emerges from his contemporary newspaper columns. See Arturo Sosa, "Estudio introductorio," in Betancourt, *La segunda independencia,* pp. 327–28.

44. Betancourt, "Venezuela: Tierra de riqueza y pauperismo," 25 February 1939, in Betancourt, *La segunda independencia,* p. 88; Alexander, *Rómulo Betancourt,* pp. 88–114.

45. For a discussion of the break between Betancourt's group and the communists, and of the importance of his "Economy and Finances" column, see Alexander, *Rómulo Betancourt,* pp. 118–47.

46. Betancourt, "Venezuela y el Japón," 21 March 1937, in Betancourt, *La segunda independencia,* 1:359.

47. Betancourt, "Nuestro comercio exterior," 24 March 1937, in Betancourt, *La segunda independencia,* 1:361–62.

48. Betancourt, "Los tratados de reciprocidad," 27 March 1937, in Betancourt, *La segunda independencia,* 1:364.

49. Betancourt, "La proposición venezolana en la conferencia de Panamá," 4 October 1939, in Betancourt, *La segunda independencia,* 3:451.

50. Betancourt, "América Latina y la política emprestista de los Estados Unidos," 11 May 1939, in Betancourt, *La segunda independencia,* 3:216.

51. Betancourt, "Con capitales nacionales debe fomentarse la industria bananera," 14 October 1937, in Betancourt, *La segunda independencia,* 1:622–23.

52. Betancourt, "Nuestra producción de petroleo crudo," 26 September 1937, in Betancourt, *La segunda independencia,* 1:592–94.

53. Betancourt, "La empresa 'Gran Ferrocarril de Venezuela' y sus abusos intolerables," 3 March 1939, in Betancourt, *La segunda independencia,* 3:98.

54. Betancourt, "Hacia la explotación nacional de nuestro petróleo," 24 and 25 January 1939, in Betancourt, *La segunda independencia,* 3:38–40.

55. Betancourt, "La expropriación petrolera mexicana y las perspectivas de un arreglo con las Compañías yanquis," 20 March 1939, in Betancourt, *La segunda independencia,* 3:124–26.

56. Betancourt, "Una frase de Roosevelt," 7 January 1938, in Betancourt, *La segunda independencia,* 2:10–12.

57. Betancourt, "La nacionalización de los ferrocarriles franceses," 3 September 1937, in Betancourt, *La segunda independencia,* 1:555–56.

58. Betancourt, "Economía dirigida frente a economía liberal," 5 January 1938, in Betancourt, *La segunda independencia,* 2:7–8.

59. Betancourt, "El 'antisemitismo' fórmula del despojo económico," in Betancourt, *La segunda independencia,* 3:59–61.

60. Betancourt, "La expropriación petrolera mexicana y las perspectivas de un arreglo con las Compañías yanquis," 20 March 1939, in Betancourt, *La segunda independencia,* 3:125.

61. Betancourt, "La 'Standard Oil' en la picota de la opinión norteamericana," 16 September 1939, in Betancourt, *La segunda independencia,* 3:430–31.

62. Betancourt, "Entente económica y defensiva interamericana con Estados

Unidos," 31 August 1939, in Betancourt, *La segunda independencia*, 3:411–13. Although the context provides no evidence, one may assume that the twenty-first nationality was Puerto Rican.

63. Alexander, *Rómulo Betancourt*, pp. 162–63.

64. Ibid., pp. 163–92.

65. Report no. 26, Consulate, Caracas, 19 October 1943, quoted in Roland Hussey, "Background Material on Acción Democrática in Connection with the Venezuelan Revolution," 24 October 1945, Memos of the American Republics Division of Research and Liaison, box 16, Records of the Office of American Republic Affairs, NA.

66. Confidential Biographic Data, January 1944, quoted in Roland Hussey, ibid.

67. Rabe, *The Road to OPEC*, pp. 73–74.

68. Braden to Corrigan, 13 January 1939, file "Braden, Spruille," box 1, Corrigan Papers.

69. Corrigan to Hull, 21 January 1936, *FRUS, 1936*, 5:126–27.

70. Welles to Duggan, 17 March 1936; Duggan to Welles, 25 March 1936; Welles to Duggan, 26 March 1936; *FRUS, 1936*, 5:127–31.

71. Duggan to Welles, 25 March 1936, *FRUS, 1936*, 5:130.

72. "I want you to know just how pleased and satisfied I was at your appointment to direct and formulate our Latin American policy. I can think of nothing that has ever made me happier. This is not only because you are patently the best fitted citizen for the long overdue job of revamping that policy and getting it back on the track but because your integrity, vigor and sound belief in democracy are so needed in the Washington councils." Dawson to Braden, 1 September 1945, file "Diplomatic Correspondence: 1946–47, A–D," box 20, Braden Papers.

73. Keller, "The Transplantation of Democracy," pp. 165–76.

74. Ibid., p. 175.

75. Dawson to Corrigan, 4 September 1945, "Dawson, Allan," box 3, Corrigan Papers.

76. Dawson to Corrigan, 9 October 1946, "Dawson, Allan," box 3, Corrigan Papers.

77. While denying that there was any foundation to communist charges of American support for the coup, Corrigan did mention Dawson's loan in passing. Corrigan to Byrnes, 1 July 1946, 810.00B/7–146, NA.

78. Corrigan to Flack, 22 October 1945, "Flack, Joe," box 2, Corrigan Papers. Flack was the head of the North and West Coast Division of the State Department at this time.

79. Corrigan to Corrigan, 27 October 1945, "1945," box 12, Corrigan Papers.

80. Alexander, *Rómulo Betancourt*, pp. 195–220.

81. Bainbridge Davis, memorandum of conversation between Braden and Carlos Sanz de Santamaria, 25 October 1945, 831.01/10–2545, NA.

82. Braden, memorandum, 25 October 1945, 831.01/10–2545, NA.

83. Rabe, *The Road to OPEC*, p. 102; Alexander, *Rómulo Betancourt*, p. 259.

84. Corrigan to Dawson, 15 February 1946, "Dawson, Allan," box 3, Corrigan Papers.

85. Rabe, *The Road to OPEC*, p. 102.

86. Stephen Rabe has suggested that the larger oil companies protested only

mildly because they were prospering, and they recognized that the 1943 oil legislation was designed to divide profits equally between themselves and the Venezuelan government and that Decree 112 insured such a division for 1945. See Rabe, *The Road to OPEC*, pp. 102–3. In fact, as Bernard Mommer has shown, a fifty-fifty profit split was not adopted in 1943, but only an agreement that centered on royalties. The Adecos did express the hope that this agreement, together with other taxes, would result in a sixty-forty profit split between Venezuela and the oil companies. Venezuela had, however, no legal commitment from the companies to such an arrangement or even to a fifty-fifty split. There was merely an expectation on the part of the Adecos that the 1943 agreement would, over the years, result in a fifty-fifty split. This had no practical implication for the division of any given year's profits. See Mommer, *La cuestión petrolera*, esp. pp. 84–96. I am grateful to anonymous referees from the *Journal of Latin American Studies* for calling my attention to this fine work.

87. Dawson to Corrigan, 12 January 1946, "Dawson, Allan," box 3, Corrigan Papers.

88. Corrigan to Hull, 9 October 1939, 831.6363/1155, quoted in Rabe, *The Road to OPEC*, p. 73.

89. Frank Corrigan, memorandum, 11 May 1943, "State Department," box 19, Corrigan Papers.

90. Wood, *The Making of the Good Neighbor Policy*, p. 276.

91. Buckley to Byrnes, 29 October 1945, 831.01/10–2945, NA.

92. Dawson to Byrnes, 3 January 1946, 831.00/1–346, NA.

93. Betancourt, "Mensaje de Año Nuevo dirigido por radio a la nación," 1 January 1946, in Betancourt, *Trayectoria democrática*, 2:61–66.

94. Dawson to Byrnes, 3 January 1946, 831.00/1–346, NA.

95. Dawson to Corrigan, 5 February 1946, file "Dawson, Allan," box 3, Corrigan Papers.

96. Dawson to Byrnes, 15 January 1946, 831.00/1–1546, NA.

97. Dawson to Corrigan, 16 January 1946; see also Dawson to Corrigan, 19 January 1946, both in file "Dawson, Allan," box 3, Corrigan Papers. The admission probably came from Carlos Morales, the foreign minister.

98. Dawson to Corrigan, 5 February 1946, file "Dawson, Allan," box 3, Corrigan Papers.

99. Quoted in Dawson to Byrnes, 5 February 1946, 831.00/2–546, NA.

100. Corrigan to Byrnes, 12 March 1946, 831.00/3–1246, NA.

101. Corrigan to Dawson, 14 February 1946, file "Dawson, Allan," box 3, Corrigan Papers.

102. Corrigan to Dawson, 15 February 1946, file "Dawson, Allan," box 3, Corrigan Papers. In a letter in this file from 28 January 1946, Dawson suggested to Corrigan that members of the junta went off on an anti–foreign capital bent when they wanted to impress the public, but that he and other members of the embassy had been working diligently "to make them realize what harm lack of confidence up North might mean."

103. Corrigan to Proudfit, 1 May 1946, file "Proudfit, Arthur," box 8, Corrigan Papers.

104. Bainbridge Davis, memorandum, 12 April 1946, file "Diplomatic Correspondence: 1946–47, A–D," box 20, Braden Papers. Commenting in a marginal note on the War Department's leak, Braden wrote: "This is getting to be the standard practice."

105. Corrigan to Byrnes, 2 May 1946, 831.00/5–246, NA. See also the attached memorandum, "The Venezuelan Supply Situation."

106. Corrigan to Byrnes, 2 May 1946, 831.00/5–246, NA.

107. Corrigan to Proudfit, 1 May 1946, file "Proudfit, Arthur," box 8, Corrigan Papers.

108. Corrigan to Byrnes, 2 May 1946, 831.00/5–246, NA.

109. For background on these parties, see Alexander, *Rómulo Betancourt*, pp. 229–34.

110. Alexander, *Rómulo Betancourt*, p. 237.

111. Dawson to Byrnes, 6 November 1946, 831.00/11–646, NA. Some of the complaints against AD's tactics were undoubtedly justified, but it seems impossible to get at the truth of some of the more important ones. Before a Copei mass meeting on 18 June 1946, for example, handbills were distributed in Caracas threatening that AD would disrupt the meeting. According to Robert Alexander, who was basing his account on an interview with Rafael Caldera, "Neither Gonzalo Barrios as governor of the Federal District nor Mario Vargas as minister of the interior responded favorably to Copei requests for police protection for the meeting. The threatened attack did take place, and three people were killed during it." Alexander, *Rómulo Betancourt*, p. 250. On 20 October 1946, in contrast, Copei held a large mass meeting in Caracas without the slightest untoward event. Gonzalo Barrios, Dawson reported to the State Department, "informed me before the meeting that he was morally certain that there would be no incidents. He said he had suggested to the COPEI leaders that the meeting be held in the afternoon instead of at night in order to make protection easier, had made arrangements for half of the Caracas police force plus Army detachments to be on hand and had called the principal Communist leaders (the Communists were blamed, probably with reason, for the June 18 fracas) into his office on Oct. 19 to tell them that he would hold them personally responsible and jail them if there were any disorder." Dawson to Byrnes, 21 October 1946, 831.00/10–2146, NA.

112. Frank Corrigan, "Comments on Recent Revolution in Venezuela," 13 December 1946, FW831.00/11–1346, NA.

113. Dawson to Braden, 30 October 1946, file "Diplomatic Correspondence: 1946–47, A–D," box 20, Braden Papers.

114. Corrigan to Byrnes, 7 November 1946, 831.00/11–746, NA.

115. Corrigan to Byrnes, 7 November 1946, 831.00/11–746, NA. Both Dawson and Corrigan were favorably inclined toward López Contreras for what they considered as his role in leading Venezuela away from the Gómez dictatorship. In early 1946, Corrigan had met with him and ascertained that he had completely separated himself from the Medina crowd and was willing to help Betancourt carry out a program that he considered similar to his own. Corrigan suggested that Dawson pass this information along to Betancourt and received this reply: "I finally had a chance to talk to Rómulo about General L. C. He has become more bitter against the old man

with the passage of time and, from his remarks, it was clear that he would not consider letting him come back as long as he is in power. In an endeavor to find an excuse for continuing the present repressive police system and detentions without formal charges, he and Rodríguez and the Junta as a whole are getting themselves in deeper and deeper with verbal attacks on 'reactionary forces' and 'the deposed regimes' (always with an 's'). Having created this bugaboo, they cannot well go back on their line and they are a vindictive crowd. I think I wrote you some time ago that Valmore had told me with glee that the Sustanciadora had uncovered some hidden assets of L. C." Corrigan to Dawson, 2 January 1946; and Dawson to Corrigan, 5 February 1946, both in file "Dawson, Allan," box 3, Corrigan Papers.

116. "By taking away not only ill-gotten wealth from former office holders and their sycophants, but legitimately acquired property as well, such an amount of hatred has been engendered that some of those affected have been driven to plotting against the Government. And, to the number of people who still have appreciable influence despite the fact that much if not all of their wealth has been taken from them, there must be added a very large number of other people who were deprived of their liberty and even subjected to torture for reasons probably more closely related to political vindictiveness than to any sound evidence of connection with conspiracy." Corrigan to Marshall, 22 January 1947, 831.00/1–2247, NA.

117. Corrigan, "Comments on Recent Revolution in Venezuela," 13 December 1946, FW831.00/11–1346, NA.

118. Corrigan to Marshall, 17 March 1947, 831.00/3–1747, NA.

119. Corrigan to Marshall, 22 April 1947, 831.00/4–2247, NA.

120. William Baggs, "Venezuelan Reds Losing Ground, U.S. Envoy Says," 1 May 1947, *Miami Daily News,* typed copy attached to Baggs to Corrigan, 5 May 1947, "Baa–Baz," box 1, Corrigan Papers.

121. William Krieg, quoted in Richard N. Post, "Notes on Recent Transportation Strike in Caracas, with Particular Reference to the Communist Situation," 28 August 1947; and Richard Post, "Strike of Communist-Led Caracas Transport Workers Ends in Virtual Government Victory," 10 September 1947, both in file "Venezuela," box 63, Records of the Office of American Republic Affairs, NA. Post was head of the Division of North and West Coast Affairs in the State Department. The victory was "virtual" and not "complete" because the government settled with the communist unions once they gave up their demand for a wage increase.

122. Maleady to Marshall, 1 October 1947, 831.00/10–147, NA; Rabe, *The Road to OPEC,* p. 103. Thomas Maleady was chargé d'affaires ad interim in the embassy.

123. See Corrigan to Flatau, 21 April 1947, file "Fl–Fz," box 2, Corrigan Papers.

124. Quoted in Lyon to Bowers, 15 July 1948, file "March–July 1948," box 7, mss. II, Bowers Papers.

125. Alexander, *Rómulo Betancourt,* p. 251.

126. Donnelly to Marshall, 26 December 1947, 831.00/12–2647, NA.

127. Central Intelligence Agency, "The Venezuelan Elections of 14 Dec. 1947," ORE 65, 5 January 1948, pp. 3–4, file "CIA Reports ORE 1948, 58–65," box 256, President's Secretary's File, Truman Library.

128. Donnelly to Marshall, 18 December 1947, 831.001 Betancourt, Rómulo/12–1847, NA.

129. On 24 November 1952, Alex Cohen, an attaché at the American embassy in Costa Rica, referred the State Department to "irrefutable evidence that as late as Sept. 25, 1934 (that is only eighteen years ago) Betancourt publicly stated 'I am and I will be a communist.' He may quite well have changed since that time, but his [recent] statement that he has fought communism for twenty years is a deliberate misstatement of fact." Cohen appears to have convinced himself that Betancourt could be a covert leader of a "little cominform" for Latin America. Alex Cohen, memo of 24 November 1952, 718.00/11–2452, NA.

130. Richard Post, "Honest Rómulo of Venezuela," 26 February 1948, FW831.00/2–2048, NA.

131. Central Intelligence Agency, "Vulnerability to Sabotage of Petroleum Installations in Venezuela, Aruba, and Curacao," ORE 31–48, 14 May 1948, pp. 2–3, file "CIA Reports ORE 1948, 30–39," box 255, President's Secretary's File, Truman Library. In general, American embassy assessments shared this view of declining communist influence. A report of early August 1948 did accept the thesis of a *Chicago Tribune* reporter that communist activities during the past month had become "bolder" and that the Venezuelan government was not effectively curbing the movement. By late September, however, the embassy would be praising the forthright response of the government to a resolution from a group of communist oil workers and suggesting that the Voice of America contrast this resolution with one from the anticommunist oil workers federation, which had expelled them. Donnelly to Marshall, 5 August 1948, 831.00B/8–548, NA; and Donnelly to Marshall, 30 September 1948, 831.00B/9–3048, NA.

132. Harry Truman, address of 5 July 1948, *New York Times,* 6 July 1948.

133. Donnelly to Marshall, 20 July 1948, 831.001 Gallegos, Rómulo/7–2048, NA.

134. Post, "Possibility of Revolutionary Attempt in Venezuela," 1 July 1948, 831.00/7–148, NA.

135. "The general feeling among the Army officers, according to José Giacopini, is that . . . Acción Democrática has absorbed many of the functions of the Government by placing civilian members of Acción Democrática in high positions which had formerly been under the control of the Army." Controlled American Source, "Revolutionary Movement Against the Venezuelan Government," 21 May 1948, p. 4, 831.00/6–448, NA. José Giacopini Zarraga had been secretary general of the junta and had been appointed a governor of the territory of the Amazon by Gallegos.

136. John Thompson, "Resume of Recent Overthrow of Government in Venezuela," 30 December 1948, p. 1, 831.00/12–3048, NA. Thompson was the third secretary of the American embassy at this time.

137. Post, "Renewed Activities of the Rightist 'Opposition' in Venezuela," 4 June 1948, 831.00/6–448, NA.

138. "Lt. Colonel Marcos Pérez Jiménez, Chief of Staff of the Venezuelan Army and one of the leaders of the young officers in the Venezuelan Army who brought about the Revolution of 18 Oct. 1945, is very ambitious. He is known to be in opposition to the United States, particularly with respect to its military policies regarding Latin America." Controlled American Source, "Revolutionary Movement Against the Venezuelan Government," p. 2. "Llovera Páez is liaison officer with the recently named petroleum industry committee on Communist sabotage, on which Embassy

Caracas has a representative. He has shown himself to be unfriendly to the United States." Post, "Renewed Activities of the Rightist 'Opposition' in Venezuela."

139. Thompson, "Resume of Recent Overthrow," p. 5.

140. Ibid.

141. Ibid., pp. 2–4.

142. Ibid., pp. 5–7.

143. Ibid., pp. 1, 7–8.

144. Thompson, "Theory and Practices of COPEI," 17 March 1949, esp. pp. 3–4, 831.00/3–1749, NA; and Thompson, "Policies and Practices of URD," 31 March 1949, esp. pp. 1, 3, 831.00/3–3149, NA.

145. In late March 1949, the new Venezuelan foreign minister told John Carrigan, the American chargé d'affaires ad interim, that to "take action against Communist unions, simultaneously with that against the AD unions, was not opportune." Carrigan, for his part, said nothing in defense of the AD unions and instead suggested the establishment of "apolitical" labor federations. Carrigan to Acheson, 1 April 1949, 831.00/4–149, NA. By August 1949, the military junta had exiled a few communists along with a large number of Adecos. See William Krieg, "Deportation of Communists from Venezuela," 29 September 1949, 831.00/9–2949, NA.

146. Disappointment was evident even before the Venezuelan coup as can be seen by the following in a column by Eduardo Rodriguez Larreta: "A characteristic sign of what we are talking about is the attitude adopted toward the Peruvian military coup; a coup conducted by force, and without extenuating circumstances, against the rule of law. Not even the traditional consultations among foreign ministries have been initiated to consider whether that government should be recognized. Today we learn that the United States has, on its own account, decided on recognition; an example which will surely be followed by others in the hemisphere. Just as we attribute part of the responsibility for retrograde developments to the weakness and disunity of the democratic forces, it doesn't hurt to add that the indifference which the United States is displaying toward the organization and life of the countries of the good neighborhood, conspires terribly against the future of these republics. The simple moral support of that formidable nation constituted a great point of leverage for the democracies against totalitarian tendencies. ("Latino-América crucificada," *El País* [Montevideo], 23 November 1948.)

147. Quoted in a press release issued by the State Department on 10 December 1948, reproduced in a circular to American ambassadors in Latin America, 13 December 1948, 831.00/12–1348, NA.

148. Donnelly to Marshall, 9 December 1948, 831.00/12–948, NA.

149. Mallory to Marshall, 13 December 1948, 831.00/12–1348, NA. C. Allan Stewart appears to have been the delegate dispatched.

150. Gallegos to Truman, 15 December 1948, Confidential File, White House Central Files, Truman Library. See also Flack to Acheson, 19 January 1949, 831.00/1–1949, NA.

151. Mallory to Marshall, 13 December 1948, 831.00/12–1348, NA.

152. Donnelly, memorandum of conversation with Robert Brinsmade, 7 December 1948, attached to Donnelly to Marshall, 10 December 1948, 831.00/12–1048, NA.

153. Lovett to the embassy in Caracas, 10 December 1948, 831.00/12–848, NA.

154. Donnelly to Marshall, 9 December 1948, 831.00/12–948, NA.

155. If anything, Creole's Arthur Proudfit appears to have desired a continuation of the Gallegos administration. In May 1948, he told Richard Post of the State Department's Division of North and West Coast Affairs that he had been worried about a possible rightist coup attempt in the months before Gallegos's inauguration, and while he could not imagine such a coup succeeding, he thought that it might do great harm both materially and politically. Post, "Renewed Activities of the Rightist 'Opposition' in Venezuela," 4 June 1948, 831.00/6–448, NA.

156. Mallory to Marshall, 13 December 1948, 831.00/12–1348, NA.

157. Buckley to Marshall, 9 December 1948, FW731.02/12–548, NA.

158. After the event, Edward Adams acknowledged that he had "thoughtlessly contributed to anti-United States propaganda" and that his presence among military officers at the start of the coup had been improper although it "appeared at that time to be a logical way to obtain information." He also admitted that during lunch at the tank battalion's officers' club, "a civilian at the table talked excitedly to me but his Spanish was entirely too rapid for me to comprehend; besides, I was trying to question the officers concerning their military plans." Edward Adams, memoranda of 6 December 1948, enclosed with Walter Donnelly to George Marshall, 11 December 1948, 831.00/12–1148, NA. Adams does not seem to have recalled being warned twice before by the ambassador to avoid contact with Venezuelan officers during the crisis. See Donnelly to Irwin, 22 March 1949, 831.00/12–1148, NA. LeRoy Irwin was head of army intelligence; in this letter Donnelly spelled out his reasons for wanting Adams transferred. Donnelly did not question Adams's motives, but he did deplore his judgement.

159. Corrigan, "Inaccuracy of Reports from Military Attaché's Office," 20 November 1945, and enclosures, 121.5431/11–2045, NA.

160. Dawson to Byrnes, 19 January 1946, 831.00/1–1946, NA.

161. Dawson to Corrigan, 7 February 1946, file "Dawson, Allan," box 3, Corrigan Papers.

162. After leaving his position as military air attaché, Carl Gordon Wagner remained in Caracas working for a local airline and continued to send reports to the embassy and to various people in Washington claiming that the principal Adecos were really communists. Although the issue was too clear for debate, an embassy employee explained to Richard Post, the ambassador did not wish to offend Wagner but rather to receive and consider any information that his excellent contacts in antigovernment circles might provide. Mann to Post, 12 January 1948, 831.00B/1–1248, NA.

163. Dissent of the Intelligence Division of the Department of the Army, enclosure "A," attached to Central Intelligence Agency, "The Venezuelan Elections of 14 Dec. 1947," ORE 65, 5 January 1948, pp. 3–4, "CIA Reports ORE 1948, 58–65," box 256, President's Secretary's File, Truman Library.

164. Central Intelligence Agency, "Vulnerability to Sabotage of Petroleum Installations in Venezuela, Aruba, and Curacao," ORE 31–48, 14 May 1948, pp. 2–3, "CIA Reports ORE 1948, 30–39," box 255, President's Secretary's File, Truman Library.

165. Braden to Rockefeller, 22 January 1945, 121.54/1–2245, NA.

166. See Chamberlin to Braden, 17 June 1946, and the enclosed directive of the same date by Deputy Chief of Staff Thomas Handy, FW121.54/6–1746, NA. Handy's directive reiterated civilian authority over the MAs and MA reporting, but it dug in its heels over requiring the MAs to reveal the identity of all sources upon request. It told the MAs only that they "may" reveal sources.

167. Dawson to Corrigan, 15 January 1947, file "Dawson, Allan," box 3, Corrigan Papers.

168. Dawson to Briggs and Dreier, 20 February 1947, Memos Relating to General Latin American Affairs, box 12, Records of the Office of American Republic Affairs, NA.

169. Dawson to Briggs and Dreier, 20 March 1947, file Memos Relating to General Latin American Affairs, box 13, Records of the Office of American Republic Affairs, NA.

170. Dawson to Braden, Briggs, and Dreier, 2 April 1947, file Memos Relating to General Latin American Affairs, box 13, Records of the Office of American Republic Affairs, NA.

171. Dawson to Briggs and Dreier, 20 February 1947, file Memos Relating to General Latin American Affairs, box 12, Records of the Office of American Republic Affairs, NA. At a second conference held the following year, Donald Dozer of the State Department's intelligence organization found a number of the attachés to be reactionary in their outlook. At the same time, he saw "an almost eager willingness on the part of most attachés to follow the behests of Washington in so far as those behests are known to them." Dozer, "Report on the Second Latin American Intelligence Conference," 18 February 1948, box 48, file 4, Dozer Papers.

172. Aram, "Exporting Rhetoric, Importing Oil," p. 97.

173. Krieg, "Conversation of Ambassador Donnelly with Rómulo Betancourt," 28 December 1948, FW831.001 Betancourt, Rómulo/12–1648, NA.

174. On Berle's speech and its impact, see chapter 3.

175. Donnelly to Marshall, 14 September 1948, 831.00/9–1448, NA. For an early warning of Pérez Jiménez's potential support for an anti-Gallegos revolt, see Post, "Possibility of Revolutionary Attempt in Venezuela," 1 July 1948, 831.00/7–148, NA.

176. In March 1948, Pérez Jiménez was sent abroad on a tour of Latin American countries. Reports from various American embassies indicated that he was opposed to arms standardization and also to sending Latin American troops outside the hemisphere. See Sheldon Mills, circular telegram, 2 December 1948, 831.00/12–148, NA.

177. Donnelly to Marshall, 17 November 1948, 831.00/1–1748, quoted in Aram, "Exporting Rhetoric, Importing Oil," p. 97.

178. Donnelly to Acheson, 25 May 1949, p. 2, 710.11/5–2549, NA.

179. See Daniel H. Levine, "Venezuela: The Nature, Sources, and Future Prospects of Democracy," in Diamond, Linz, and Lipset, *Democracy,* pp. 257–59.

Chapter 6. Victory in Costa Rica

1. Williamson to Hull, 23 June 1944, 822.00/6–2344, NA; Shaw to Byrnes, 20 May 1946, 822.00/5–2046, NA; Shaw to Byrnes, 31 October 1946, 822.00/10–3146,

NA; Shaw to Marshall, 6 June 1947, 822.00/6–647, NA; Shaw to Marshall, 30 June 1947, 822.00/6–3047, NA.

2. Shaw to Marshall, 30 June 1947, 822.00/6–3047, NA.

3. Simmons to Marshall, 24 August 1947, 822.00/8–2447, NA.

4. Simmons to Marshall, 25 August 1947, 822.00/8–2547, NA.

5. Ibid. This telegram was repeated directly to the American delegation to the Rio Conference. See Robert Lovett to the American delegation in Petropolis, 26 August 1947, 822.01/8–2647, NA. "I believe that Mr. Braden's suggestion has considerable merit and that we might well consider the advisability of denying, or at least withholding for long periods, the granting of loans, invitations to visit Washington and military cooperation as a means of impressing upon the dictators the fact that we are not in sympathy with their methods and their form of government." Simmons to Byrnes, 9 July 1945, 711.00/7–945, NA.

6. Simmons to Marshall, 26 August 1947, 822.00/8–2647, NA.

7. Datelined 26 August 1947, this interview appeared in *El Comercio* on 28 August. A translation was attached to Simmons to Marshall, 8 September 1947, 822.00/9–847, NA. Simmons praised Plaza's courage for speaking out when he did and observed, "While this article did not in itself turn the tide against Macheno, it nevertheless did have a strong influence among the many readers of *El Comercio* and has already become one of the most widely discussed newspaper articles of this whole period."

8. State Department records are unclear as to when and why this decision was taken. On 28 August 1947, Acting Secretary of State Robert Lovett noted merely that he had "heard from Rio that conference there had decided not to allow [Ecuadoran Foreign Minister] Trujillo to sign treaty." In this same note, he indicated that the Chilean government was opposed to recognizing the new Ecuadoran regime because it had come to power by unconstitutional means. Lovett to the American delegation in Petropolis, 28 August 1947, 822.01/8–2847, NA.

9. Simmons to Marshall, 30 August 1947, 822.00/8–3047, NA. On the inter-American denial of recognition to the de facto government of Nicaragua, see Clark, *The United States and Somoza*.

10. Simmons to Marshall, 3 September 1947, 822.00/9–347, NA.

11. Simmons to Marshall, 8 September 1947, 822.00/9–847, NA.

12. Simmons to Marshall, 16 September 1947, 822.00/9–1647, NA. See also Simmons to Marshall, 18 September 1947, 822.00/9–1847, NA.

13. Simmons to Marshall, 16 September 1947, 822.00/9–1647, NA.

14. Lovett to Simmons, 18 September 1947, 822.01/9–1847, NA.

15. Translation of interview with Galo Plaza from *El Comercio* of 23 November 1947. Enclosed with Simmons to Marshall, 3 December 1947, 822.00/12–347, NA.

16. Alexander, "Plaza Lasso, Galo," in Alexander, *Biographical Dictionary*, p. 358. Galo Plaza's administration was seen by American officials as serving the interests of the United States as well as of Ecuador: "Should he fall, there would undoubtedly be a scramble for power which might place the control of Ecuador in the hands of military groups less friendly to the United States than he is." Simmons to Marshall, 5 October 1948, 822.001 Plaza, Galo/10–548, NA.

17. For additional information on the individuals referred to in this paragraph, see Alexander, *Biographical Dictionary.* On Muñoz Marín's prospects, see the *New York Times*, 25 March 1948. In fact, he not only won the election in November 1948, he was reelected three times before deciding to retire in 1964. During his time in office, Puerto Rico became an exemplar of progress and stability, as well as a safe haven for many of the democratic left's leaders in exile. See Aitken, *Poet in the Fortress.*

18. My thinking on American policy toward Costa Rica in 1948 has benefited from a conversation with Marcia Quirós and the opportunity to read her paper, "The United States and the Costa Rican Civil War of 1948: The Case Against Intervention," in manuscript. It is possible that a different course was pursued by the CIA with the approval of President Truman. That there was a CIA representative in San José (at the latest by the fall of 1948) is clear from the following report by the American ambassador: "The Department is aware of the cordial and close cooperation already existing between the Embassy and the representative in this city of the federal agency that would bear a large part of the responsibility for carrying out any arrangement of the sort under discussion. His knowledge is at the disposal of the Embassy and its files are open to him. He has established relations of mutual confidence with the Costa Rican official primarily responsible for watching communist activities and has access to the latter's files. He has not, however, felt that he could return the compliment. The flow of information traffic such as it is, follows a one way street, and we are in complete agreement that to alter that arrangement at the present time would endanger our own security measures with no corresponding advantage, to us or to the Costa Rican government." Davis to Marshall, 20 October 1948, 810.00B/10–2048, NA.

19. Davis to Ravndal, 21 August 1947, Davis Papers.

20. Davis to Marshall, 22 March 1948, 818.00/3–2248, NA. To seat the opposition's candidate by force of arms over the objection of the National Republicans, Davis observed, "would serve our interests to a point although the resort to extra-constitutional means could more than over balance the desirable effects— within Costa Rica and abroad—of such action."

21. For background on Calderón's administration, see Ameringer, *Don Pepe*, pp. 9–21.

22. Robert J. Alexander suggests that the Costa Rican CP became more Stalinist and less independent of Moscow after Betancourt's departure and notes that the party only became a full member of the Comintern in August 1935 and had earlier displayed important heterodox tendencies. On the other hand, Alejandro Gómez's work has demonstrated that the party had shown a strong attachment to the Comintern line for several years before this. See Alexander, *Rómulo Betancourt*, pp. 67–87; and Gómez, *Rómulo Betancourt y el Partido Comunista de Costa Rica.*

23. William Tapley Bennett Jr., memorandum of 26 March 1948, *FRUS, 1948,* 9:502.

24. On the Center for the Study of National Problems, see Ameringer, *Don Pepe*, especially p. 15. Centristas like Gonzalo Facio were among those who welcomed Haya de la Torre on his visit to the country in 1946. See Gonzalo Facio, "La vida del mas grande luchador democrático de América Latina se encuentra en peligro,"

Diario de Costa Rica, 26 March 1950. Enclosed with Alex Cohen, "Costa Rica and the Haya de la Torre Case," 3 April 1950, 621.23/4–350, NA.

25. See Ameringer, *Don Pepe*, p. 17.

26. Figueres, "La situación del momento," address of 8 July 1942, text in Figueres, *Escritos y discursos*, pp. 33–39.

27. See Ameringer, *Don Pepe*, pp. 23–29. See also Figueres, "Palabras gastadas" [1943], text in Figueres, *Escritos y discursos*, pp. 43–71.

28. See Ameringer, *Don Pepe*, p. 26. In spite of the fraud, Ameringer suggests that Picado's margin was such that he would have won in any event.

29. Johnson to Stettinius, 21 June 1945, 711.00/6–2145, NA. Johnson seems to have believed that Picado was sincere in his desire for reform. He was convinced that "Picado's election had been corrupt but that he was doing his utmost to give the country an administration free from graft and based on democratic principles." Hallett Johnson, Spruille Braden, and Robert Newbegin, memorandum of conversation, 31 October 1945, 711.18/103145, NA.

30. See Ameringer, *Don Pepe*, pp. 31–38.

31. For the history of this expedition, see Ameringer, *The Caribbean Legion*.

32. On King's and Cabot's suggestion, see chapter 3.

33. See Ameringer, *The Caribbean Legion*, p. 34. For a translation of this part of Masferrer's account, see Lester Mallory, "Frustrated Plot to Invade the Dominican Republic—Summer of 1947 (Continued)," 19 December 1947, p. 8, 839.00/12–1947, NA.

34. Figueres, *El Espiritu del 48*, p. 127.

35. Ibid., p. 129.

36. Ameringer, *Don Pepe*, pp. 43–47. William Tapley Bennett Jr., "Ambassador Gutiérrez' Memorandum on Costa Rican Election," 8 March 1948, file "CPA-General-1948–Costa Rica," box 1, Records of the Office of Middle American Affairs, 1947–56, NA. On page 43, Ameringer presents a final count of 54,931 to 44,438. This presumably reflects the inclusion of tallies prepared by the electoral boards or telegraphic returns in the tribunal's possession.

37. Davis, diary entries of 1 March, 2 March, and 3 March 1948, Davis Papers. See also Ameringer, *Don Pepe*, p. 47.

38. Gonzalo Facio, "La vida del mas grande luchador democrático de América Latina se encuentra en peligro," *Diario de Costa Rica*, 26 March 1950. Enclosed with Alex Cohen, "Costa Rica and the Haya de la Torre Case," 3 April 1950, 621.23/4–350, NA. It was with this quotation from Haya that William Tapley Bennett Jr. concluded a memorandum warning that communist forces now accounted for 70 percent of the military strength on the Calderónista side. Bennett Jr., 26 March 1948, *FRUS, 1948*, 9:502. See also Ameringer, *Don Pepe*, p. 56.

39. Davis, diary entries for early March 1948, esp. 5 March, Davis Papers.

40. The Costa Rican ambassador to Washington, Francisco Gutiérrez, also hoped for a compromise agreement and thought that these negotiations would yield one. Paul Daniels, Francisco Gutiérrez, and Robert Newbegin, memorandum of conversation, 5 March 1948, file "CPA-General-1948–Costa Rica," box 1, Records of the Office of Middle American Affairs, 1947–56, NA.

41. This is according to a report the American embassy received on 21 March

1948 from an emissary who had recently visited Figueres. This report is attached to Davis to Marshall, 22 March 1948, 818.00/3–2248, NA.

42. Ameringer, *Don Pepe*, pp. 50–52. The property destroyed at Figueres's farm was of considerable value. His 1948 coffee crop alone had been mortgaged for $250,000 by Otil McAllister Company of San Francisco. Davis, diary entry of 23 March 1948, Davis Papers.

43. Bernbaum to Marshall, 15 March 1948, 818.00/3–1548, NA. See also Marshall to American diplomatic representatives in the other American republics, 22 March 1948, 818.00/3–2248, NA. Marshall gave the details of Somoza's proposed intervention and instructed his ambassadors to tell the governments to which they were accredited that the United States had expressed to Somoza "our deep concern over intervention by any foreign govt in Costa Rican internal affairs and our feeling that such intervention is particularly regrettable on eve Bogotá Conference."

44. Telegrams 71 and 73 from Managua, 22 March 1948, 818.00/3–2248, NA. See also *FRUS, 1948*, 9:499–500. On 23 March Robert Newbegin, chief of the Division of Central America and Panama Affairs, wrote to Bernbaum that he had intended for the Somozas to audit their telephone conversation the previous day and that he thought the quick action they had got was "due in part, at least, to eavesdropping." Newbegin to Bernbaum, 23 March 1948, 818.00/3–2248, NA.

45. Memorandum of conversation, Francisco Gutiérrez, Paul C. Daniels, Robert Newbegin, 19 March 1948, file "CPA-General-1948–Costa Rica," box 1, Records of the Office of Middle American Affairs, 1947–56, NA. Although the United States asked Guatemala, as well as Nicaragua, not to intervene in Costa Rica, the State Department seems to have been satisfied with Gonzalo Facio's claim that the arms had not come directly from the Guatemalan government. Memorandum of conversation, Facio and Bennett, 29 March 1948, 818.00/3–2948, NA.

46. Gutiérrez and Newbegin, memorandum of conversation, 29 March 1948, file "CPA-General-1948–Costa Rica," box 1, Records of the Office of Middle American Affairs, 1947–56, NA.

47. Davis, diary entry of 21 March 1948, Davis Papers; Davis to Marshall, 22 March 1948, and attached report by an emissary [Alex Murray], 818.00/3–2248, NA; Ameringer, *Don Pepe*, p. 53.

48. Davis, diary entry of 21 March 1948, Davis Papers; Davis to Marshall, 22 March 1948, 818.00/3–2248, NA.

49. Ameringer, *The Caribbean Legion*, p. 73.

50. Ameringer, *Don Pepe*, pp. 56–58.

51. Davis, diary entries of 11 April and 12 April 1948, Davis Papers.

52. Davis, diary entry of 13 April 1948, Davis Papers.

53. Ibid.; translated letter from Picado to Mora, 19 April 1948, 818.00/5–1248, NA. This is one of a number of documents taken from Mora by American officials after he left Costa Rica. The general tone of the letter is to absolve Mora from any responsibility for Picado's decision "to terminate the civil war at a cost of even sacrificing my self pride."

54. Davis thought there was a certain amount of danger in this as Núñez was easily recognized and "there must be plenty of Communists who would like nothing

better than to take a pot shot at him." Davis, diary entry of 15 April 1948, Davis Papers.

55. Davis, diary entries of 14 April and 15 April 1948, Davis Papers. Seeking to facilitate a visit to Figueres on the part of Archbishop Sanabria, Davis had already discovered that Mora was the man to talk to for a safe-conduct: "Such is the pass this government has come to. There is no longer any responsible head, but Mora, chief of the communist party, is able and willing to guarantee the safety of the head of the Church on a mission seeking to bring the fighting to an end." Davis, diary entry of 3 April 1948, Davis Papers.

56. Davis, diary entry of 16 April 1948, and attached memorandum of conversation of the same date, Davis Papers.

57. Bernbaum and Newbegin, memorandum of long-distance telephone conversation, 19 April 1948, file "CPA-General-1948–Costa Rica," box 1, Records of the Office of Middle American Affairs, 1947–1956, NA; Davis to Marshall, 19 April 1948, 818.00/4–1948, NA; Lovett to the American embassy in Bogotá, 17 April 1948, 818.00/4–1746, NA.

58. Davis, diary entries for 18 April and 21 April 1948, Davis Papers.

59. Lovett, Gutiérrez, Newbegin, memorandum of conversation, 13 April, 1948, and Newbegin, "Costa Rican Government's Inability to Obtain Arms," 13 April 1948, both in file "CPA-General-1948–Costa Rica," box 1, Records of the Office of Middle American Affairs, 1947–1956, NA; Picado to Calderón Guardia and Mora, 18 April 1948, quoted in Ameringer, *Don Pepe*, p. 63.

60. Davis, diary entry for 18 April 1948, Davis Papers.

61. Figueres, *El Espiritu del 48*, p. 273. The letter mentioned, in particular, improvements in legislation concerning social security, workmen's compensation, the right to strike, the right to organize, and so forth.

62. See Ameringer, *Don Pepe*, pp. 67–109.

63. See John A. Booth, "Costa Rica: The Roots of Democratic Stability," Diamond, Linz, and Lipset, *Democracy*, pp. 387–422.

Chapter 7. Cold War Conservatism in Latin America

1. Official translation of Gallegos to Truman, 15 December 1948, Confidential File, White House Central Files, Truman Library.

2. Truman to Gallegos, 3 February 1949, Confidential File, White House Central Files, Truman Library.

3. Kennan to the Acting Secretary of State, 10 December 1948, *FRUS, 1948*, 9:141.

4. The Acting Secretary of State to Diplomatic Representatives in the American Republics (marginal penned initials: HST), 16 December 1948, *FRUS, 1948*, 9:147–48. Article 5(d) reads: "The solidarity of the American States and the high aims which are sought through it require the political organization of those States on the basis of the effective exercise of representative democracy."

5. The Acting Secretary of State to Diplomatic Representatives in the American Republics, 28 December 1948, *FRUS, 1948*, 9:150.

6. Sheldon Mills, memorandum of conversation, 23 December 1948, *FRUS, 1948*, 9:116.

7. Truman to Bowers, 28 January 1949, file "Jan.–April 1949," box 7, mss. II, Bowers Papers.

8. Acheson to American Diplomatic Officers in the Other American Republics, 22 April 1949, 710.11/4–2249, NA.

9. Rusk to American Diplomatic Officers in the Other American Republics, 19 April 1949, 710.11/4–1949, NA.

10. Ackerman to Acheson, 12 May 1949, 710.11/5–1249, NA.

11. Davis to Acheson, 4 May 1949, 710.11/5–449, NA.

12. Bowers to Acheson, 6 May 1949, 710.11/5–649, NA.

13. Williams to Acheson, 24 June 1949, p. 3, 710.11/6–2449, NA. Williams was chargé d'affaires ad interim in Nicaragua at this time.

14. Bernbaum to Acheson, 22 June 1949, p. 4, 710.11/6–2249, NA. Bernbaum was chargé d'affaires ad interim in Ecuador at this time.

15. Warren to Acheson, 15 July 1949, p. 3, 710.11/7–1549, NA.

16. Donnelly to Acheson, 25 May 1949, p. 1, 710.11/5–2549, NA.

17. Tittman to Acheson, 10 June 1949, p. 2, 710.11/6–1049, NA.

18. Donnelly to Acheson, 25 May 1949, p. 2, 710.11/5–2549, NA.

19. Briggs to Acheson, 25 May 1949, pp. 2–3, 710.11/5–249, NA.

20. For a brief discussion of American foreign economic policy and Latin American economic development during the Truman years, see Schwartzberg, "The Civility of Yankee Imperialism," chapter 1, in this volume.

21. "Problem: To state principles which should govern the formulation of U.S. policies concerned with inter-American affairs," 29 August 1949, p. 28, 810.00/8–2949, NA.

22. Transcript of talks by Spruille Braden and Carl Spaeth before a group of State Department officers, 24 September 1946, p. 36, folder "Speeches—Departmental Group," box 25, Braden Papers. This attitude was reflected in a lending policy in which the United States would "not necessarily oppose credits to countries merely on the ground that they are conducting state enterprises or pursuing nationalization programs." Department of State, "Current U.S. Policy toward the Other American Republics," *The American Republics* (tentative draft), 16 December 1946, p. 23, 711.20/12–1646, NA.

23. "Problem: To state principles which should govern the formulation of U.S. policies concerned with inter-American affairs," 29 August 1949, pp. 26–27, 810.00/8–2949, NA.

24. From the beginning of 1946 through 1948, although some countries were allowed to purchase arms from the United States, no new American military assistance was provided to Latin America. Of American direct economic assistance to the region, 43.4 percent went to Mexico; 20.3 percent went to Brazil; 7.6 percent went to Peru; and each of the other countries received less than 5 percent, with Argentina receiving nothing and the dictatorships of Nicaragua, Honduras, and the Dominican Republic sharing 5.7 percent of the total. Of all Eximbank loans in this period, 94.3 percent went to four countries of which three were democracies: Brazil (31.5%), Mexico (30.8%), Chile (24.5%), and Colombia (7.6%). The World Bank made one loan in Latin America in this period, to Chile. From 1949 through 1952, 83.3 percent of all American military assistance went to four democracies: Brazil (57.9%), Chile

(14.4%), Uruguay (6.0%), and Ecuador (5.0%). Among the dictatorships, only Colombia (7.5%) and Peru (8.0%) received significant assistance. Of direct economic assistance, 52.5 percent went to Mexico; 6.6 percent to Guatemala; 5.5 percent to Brazil; and lesser percentages to the other countries. Of all Eximbank loans in this period, 25.7 percent went to Mexico; 21.1 percent went to Brazil; and 12.6 percent went to Chile. The Argentine dictatorship did receive a significant 20.5 percent of the total. More than four-fifths of all World Bank loans went to three countries: Brazil (41.0%), Mexico (28.1%), and Uruguay (11.5%). Among the dictatorships, only Colombia (10.5%) received a notable share. Figures derived from Agency for International Development, *U.S. Overseas Loans and Grants*, pp. 35–65, 203–12.

25. Acheson, "Waging Peace in the Americas," 19 September 1949, in Department of State, *Bulletin* (26 September 1949), p. 463.

26. Miller to Bowers, 8 December 1949, "Oct.–Nov. 1949," box 7, mss. II, Bowers Papers.

27. Acheson to Donnelly, 29 April 1949, 831.00/4–2949, NA.

28. Donnelly, "Release of Political Prisoners," 2 June 1949, 831.00/6–249, NA.

29. Acheson, "Waging Peace in the Americas," pp. 463–64.

30. Davis to Acheson, 25 November 1949, nos. 751 and 550, *FRUS, 1949*, 2:723–25.

31. *FRUS, 1949*, 2:723.

32. *FRUS, 1949*, 2:724.

33. According to a memorandum of 28 November 1949 by Murray M. Wise, the acting officer in charge of the Division of Central America and Panama Affairs, "There can be no doubt that he [Arias] won the election last year and was cheated out of the Presidency by the fraudulent actions of the electoral jury." *FRUS, 1949*, 2:729.

34. Davis to Acheson, n.d., *FRUS, 1949*, 2:727.

35. Department of State, *Bulletin* (12 December 1949), p. 910.

36. Ibid., p. 911.

37. Miller to Acheson, 8 December 1949, *FRUS, 1949*, 2:740.

38. Acheson to the embassy in Panama, *FRUS, 1949*, 2:743.

39. Miller to Bowers, 29 January 1952, "Jan.–Feb. 1952," box 7, mss. II, Bowers Papers.

40. File "Costa Rica," Records of the Assistant Secretary of State (Edward G. Miller), NA.

41. Magloire's coup followed an attempt by the elected president, Dumarsais Estimé, to remain in office in defiance of the Constitution. See Percy Hintzen, "Magloire, Paul Eugène," in Alexander, *Biographical Dictionary*, pp. 277–79. The idea of inviting Magloire had been suggested to Truman by Walter White of the NAACP. The State Department's opposition, which was successful, was also based on the assumption that there might be time for only one state visit from a Latin American leader and that it would be much more useful to invite the recently elected president of Brazil, Getúlio Vargas. White to Truman, 25 August 1951, and Scott to Dawson, 23 November 1951, both in file "Correspondence," box 42, Confidential File, White House Central Files, Truman Library.

42. Mann to Warren, 6 February 1952, "Venezuela, 1952," box 7, Records of the

Deputy Assistant Secretaries of State for Inter-American Affairs, NA. Mann was the deputy assistant secretary at this time, and his letter indicated that he was writing on Miller's behalf.

43. Tittman to Mann, 23 February 1951, file "Peru," box 5, Records of the Deputy Assistant Secretaries of State for Inter-American Affairs, NA.

44. Miller to Armour, 29 October 1951, file "Correspondence, A," box 1, Miller Papers. In a subsequent letter to Armour of 7 November, Miller attributed Johnson's rejection of this idea to an "anti-foreign and anti-State Department" attitude on the senator's part.

45. Miller to Whelan, 28 July 1952, file "Correspondence, W," box 3, Miller Papers.

46. Miller to Acheson, 7 August 1950, FRUS, 1950, 2:624.

47. Louis Halle ["Y," pseud.], "On a Certain Impatience with Latin America," pp. 566–68.

48. Ibid., pp. 565–66.

49. Ibid., pp. 570, 578.

50. Ibid., pp. 571, 575, 578.

51. Ibid., p. 571.

52. Wiley, memorandum of March 1945, file "Latin America, 1945," box 12, Wiley Papers. On the breakdown of Colombian democracy, see Alexander W. Wilde, "Conversations among Gentlemen: Oligarchical Democracy in Colombia," in Linz and Stepan, The Breakdown of Democratic Regimes, pp. 28–81.

53. Central Intelligence Agency, "Review of the World Situation," CIA 11–49, 16 November 1949, p. 7, NSC Meetings, file "Meeting No. 36," box 205, President's Secretary's File, Truman Library.

54. Kennan to Acheson, 29 March 1950, FRUS, 1950, 2:615.

55. Central Intelligence Agency, "Review of the World Situation," CIA 12–48, 16 December 1948, p. 8, NSC Meetings, file "Meeting No. 30," box 205, President's Secretary's File, Truman Library.

56. Central Intelligence Agency, "Cuba," SR-29, 23 December 1948, pp. 41–42, file "CIA Reports SR nos. 29–31," box 261, President's Secretary's File, Truman Library.

57. Central Intelligence Agency, "Cuba," pp. 13, 25–26.

58. Ibid., pp. 7, 11, 17, 31.

59. Ibid., pp. 33–34.

60. Commenting on the way Machado's regime had been combined in the public mind with the severe economic distress associated with sharply rising American tariffs after the crash of 1929, the CIA observed: "There was thus generated among the Cuban people widespread and bitter hostility, not only to the regime itself, but also to the ties that, in their opinion, made Cuba so dependent on the US that a change in the latter's tariff policy could plunge Cuba into poverty and suffering. Thus to many Cubans the revolution against Machado in 1933 was not only designed to put an end to a tyrannical domestic regime, but also to terminate Cuba's economic and political subservience to the US of which Machado was regarded as the principal symbol." Central Intelligence Agency, "Cuba," p. 25.

61. According to the American ambassador, "while the Prío regime cannot be

said to have been popular, it is unlikely that Batista could have polled as many votes in honest elections as Carlos Hevia. The group the Government was afraid of from the electoral standpoint was the *Ortodoxos,* not the Batista group." Willard Beaulac, "Batista's March 10, 1952, *Coup d'État,*" 11 March 1952, 737.00/3–1152, NA.

62. This is taken from an account by Francis McCarthy, the United Press International representative in Havana, which appeared in the Cuban periodical *Bohemia.* In transmitting a translation of his account to Washington, the American embassy indicated that it considered it Batista's version of events. Earl Crain to Dean Acheson, 9 April 1952, 737.00/4–952, NA. Crain was the acting counselor of embassy at this time.

63. This is drawn from an interview with Prío that appeared in the 11 March 1952 issue of *El Mundo.* Beaulac to Acheson, 12 March 1952, 737.00/3–1252, NA.

64. Beaulac, "Batista's March 10, 1952, *Coup d'État,*" 11 March 1952, 737.00/3–1152, NA. Beaulac quotes the complete Spanish text of Prío's appeal.

65. Carlos Prío Socarrás, "Datos para la historia," *Alerta* (Havana), 12 March 1952, enclosed with Beaulac to Acheson, 13 March 1952, 737.00/3–1352, NA.

66. In a telephone conversation held at 2:15 P.M. on the day of the coup, Beaulac indicated that the port and dockworkers were on strike. A day later, he indicated that the sugar mills that had been idle were operating again. Beaulac and Henry Wellman, memorandum of telephone conversation, 10 March 1952, 737.00/3–1052, NA; and Beaulac and Wellman, memorandum of telephone conversation, 11 March 1952, 737.00/3–1152, NA.

67. John Fishburn, Serafino Romualdi, and Francisco Aguirre, memorandum of conversation, 17 March 1952, 737.00/3–1752, NA.

68. Wellman, "Batista Coup d'État in Cuba," 11 March 1952, 737.00/3–1152, NA.

69. Fishburn, Romualdi, and Aguirre, memorandum of conversation, 17 March 1952, 737.00/3–1752, NA.

70. This presentation of Batista's views is taken from a nationwide address he gave at 6:00 P.M. on the day of the coup. See Wellman and Beaulac, memorandum of telephone conversation, 10 March 1952, 737.00/3–1052, NA; and Beaulac to Acheson, 10 March 1952, no. 607, 737.00/3–1052, NA. Batista reiterated these themes for days. See especially Earl Crain, "Press Conference Held by Batista," 13 March 1952, 737.00/3–1352, NA.

71. Crain, "Habana Editorial Comment on the Batista *Coup* during the First Week," 25 March 1952, 737.00/3–2552, NA.

72. Ramón Vasconcelos, "Men without Stature," translated by the American embassy from the 12 March 1952 issue of *Alerta,* enclosed with Beaulac to Acheson, 12 March 1952, 737.003–1252, NA.

73. Beaulac, "Memorandum Summarizing Events of March 10 *Coup d'État,*" 10 April 1952, 737.00/4–1052, NA.

74. Miller to Belt, 12 February 1952, 737.01111/2–452, NA. Miller told a friend that he was going to Havana "for what I hope is a little badly needed rest and possibly some judicious ear-to-the-ground work about Batista, Hevia, etc." Miller to Hannifin, 28 January 1952, file "Hannifin, Jerry," Miller Papers.

75. *FRUS, 1952–1954,* 4:868.

76. Miller to Bowers, 27 March 1952, file "March–April 1952," box 7, mss. II, Bowers Papers.

77. Beaulac, "Batista's March 10, 1952, *Coup d'État*," 11 March 1952, 737.00/3–1152, NA.

78. Ibid.

79. Acheson to Truman, 11 March 1952, Memoranda of Conversations, March 1952, box 67, Acheson Papers.

80. Earl Crain, "Countries That Have Recognized the BATISTA Regime," 1 April 1952, 737.00/4–152, NA; and Miller to Bowers, 27 March 1952, file "March–April 1952," box 7, mss. II, Bowers Papers.

81. Department of State, *Bulletin* (12 December 1949), p. 911.

82. Lovestone to Romualdi, 20 March 1952, file 2, box 4, Romualdi Papers.

83. Beaulac to Acheson, 20 March 1952, 737.00/3–2052, NA.

84. Wellman to Miller, 18 March 1952, 737.00/3–1852, NA.

85. Beaulac to Acheson, 25 March 1952, 737.00/3–2552, NA. Articles 148 and 149 of the Constitution of 1940 provided that the vice president should succeed the president, the president of the Congress succeed the vice president, and the most senior magistrate of the Supreme Court succeed the president of the Congress.

86. Crain to Acheson, 5 June 1952, 737.00/6–552, NA.

87. J. L. Topping and Paul Ryan, memorandum of conversation, 2 April 1952, 737.00/4–252, NA. See also Beaulac to Acheson, 3 June 1952, 737.00/6–352, NA.

88. Topping to Wellman and Miller, 15 May 1952, 737.00/5–1552, NA.

89. Topping, "Opposition to the Batista Administration in Cuba," 7 April 1952, 737.004–752, NA.

90. Crain, "Survey of Popularity of Batista, Agramonte and Prío," 11 June 1952, 737.00/6–1152, NA. The survey was reportedly conducted by Miguel Suarez Fernandez, an opportunistic former Auténtico who had gone over to Batista and was looking to see which way to jump next.

91. Acheson, "Waging Peace in the Americas," 19 September 1949, in Department of State, *Bulletin* (26 September 1949), p. 463.

92. The kinds of interests taken into account by American officials seem almost unbelievably petty and the emphasis on their immediate pusuit through diplomatic recognition extraordinarily myopic: "We have important interests in Cuba including our army, air and navy missions whose members draw pay from Cuban Govt; nickel mining and processing plant at Nicaro and Kenaf program. We are helping Cuba with geodetic survey and with minerals survey. Our milit assistance agreement requires implementation. It is in our interest we see all these activities continued or resumed at earliest practicable date." Beaulac to Acheson, 17 March 1952, 737.003–1752, NA. What Miller meant when he indicated that Batista might somehow be "tougher on the commies than Prío" is a mystery. At one point in September 1952, Beaulac indicated to the Cuban minister of information that he was distressed with "the freedom with which Cuban Communists were allowed to travel abroad." Perhaps an end to this freedom is what Miller hoped for. Miller to Bowers, 27 March 1952, file "March–April 1952," box 7, mss. II, Bowers Papers; Beaulac to Acheson, 5 September 1952, 737.00/9–552, NA.

93. Meeting informally with American officials in Washington, three days after

the coup, the Cuban chargé d'affaires explained that he was familiar with the American policy of recognizing foreign governments once certain criteria had been met without this action constituting any judgement on the government or on how it came to power. "He pointed out, however, that, since the United States recognition is considered in Latin America as the validation of a new government, failure to recognize after an appropriate time had elapsed would be interpreted as disapproval of the new government and might have undesirable consequences." Wellman and Dr. Espinosa, memorandum of conversation, 13 March 1952, 737.00/3–1352, NA.

94. See Gleijeses, *Shattered Hope.*

95. Cullather, *Operation PBSUCCESS,* pp. 18–19.

96. Mann to Acheson, 3 October 1952, 714.00/10–352, NA.

97. Cullather, *Operation PBSUCCESS,* pp. 18–19. An alternative interpretation would be that once Miller found out about the operation himself, he put an end to it.

98. Quoted in Cullather, *Operation PBSUCCESS,* p. 20; see pages 21–25 on shifting attitudes over 1953.

99. Gleijeses, *Shattered Hope,* pp. 147–48.

100. Alexander, *Communism in Latin America,* pp. 359–60.

101. Gleijeses, *Shattered Hope,* pp. 205–6.

102. It is almost as though these advocates of a "proletarian" perspective really believed that the opposition they encountered was merely a reflection of social and economic structures serving elite interests and that it would simply disappear if those structures were transformed. To be fair, however, even as astute a politician as Getúlio Vargas did not anticipate the reaction to his appointment of his brother as chief of the federal police in October 1945. It is easy to blunder in such matters, and the consequences for Guatemalan politics of such a blunder would probably have been much the same as those brought about by American intervention in 1954.

103. Porter and Alexander, *The Struggle for Democracy,* p. 70.

104. The relative uniqueness of Chilean democracy might be added as a fourth reason. Had all or even most of the countries of Latin America been democratic, it seems doubtful that Chile would have received quite as much attention and assistance.

105. It was at this time that Salvador Allende praised Bowers for the high value of his historical works and for his "permanent democratic convictions." Allende to Bowers, 9 September 1949, "Sept. 1949," box 7, mss. II, Bowers Papers.

106. There are well over a hundred letters from Roosevelt in the Bowers Papers and close to forty from Truman.

107. Bowers to Truman, 20 August 1951, "July–Aug. 1951," box 7, mss. II, Bowers Papers.

108. To those who are only familiar with Bowers's work on Reconstruction, this may come as a surprise. Even with regard to race relations, however, his views were more progressive than his history of the post–Civil War period would suggest. He appears to have admired the way Josephus Daniels endangered his newspaper in Raleigh, and broke with his friend William Jennings Bryan, to support placing a specific denunciation of the Ku Klux Klan in the 1924 Democratic Party platform. See Bowers to Miller, 26 September 1952, file "Sept. 1952," box 7, mss. II, Bowers Papers. See also Bowers, *The Tragic Era.*

109. Wallace to Bowers, 4 March 1943, file "Bowers," box 8, Wallace Papers.

110. Betancourt to Bowers, 26 February 1957, box 8, mss. II, Bowers Papers.

111. Truman to Bowers, 10 July 1946, file "July–Aug. 1946," box 6, mss. II, Bowers Papers.

112. Hillenkoetter, "Economic Outlook in Chile," 11 April 1950, Confidential File, White House Central Files, Truman Library.

113. Miller to Bowers, 7 January 1952, file "Jan.–Feb. 1952," box 7, mss. II, Bowers Papers.

114. For more information on policy toward Nicaragua and the Dominican Republic, see Schwartzberg, "The Civility of Yankee Imperialism," chapter 8 in this volume.

Chapter 8. The Civility of Yankee Imperialism

1. See Momigliano, *Alien Wisdom,* pp. 22–49.

2. Mariano Moreno, "Plan of Operations Which the Provisional Government of the United Provinces of the Rio de la Plata Should Pursue to Consolidate the Great Work of Our Liberty and Independence," excerpts in Robertson, *Rise of the Spanish-American Republics,* pp. 154{ff}.

3. Figueres, "Mixed Feelings," 10 February 1955, file "José Figueres," box 8, Grant Papers.

4. Figueres, statement of 10 June 1958, *Hearings before the Subcommittee on Inter-American Affairs,* p. 77.

5. See Krieg, "Conversation of Ambassador Donnelly with Rómulo Betancourt," 28 December 1948, FW831.001 Betancourt, Rómulo/12–1648, NA. This was part of the reason for Haya's insistence that "no pretext, no twisted interpretation of 'nonintervention in the internal affairs of another state,' can explain away the complicit tolerance of democratic governments with regard to cynical and cruel dictatorships." Haya, "La declaración democrática de Caracas," *Combate* 1, no. 5 (March and April 1959), p. 30.

6. Smith, *Talons of the Eagle,* pp. 7–8.

7. Schoultz, *Beneath the United States,* p. xv.

8. Osgood, *Ideals and Self-Interest,* p. 441.

9. Bemis, *The Latin American Policy of the United States,* p. 384.

10. Wood, *The Making of the Good Neighbor Policy,* p. 360.

11. Munro, *Intervention and Dollar Diplomacy,* p. 530.

12. *New York Times,* 6 May 1939. See also Clark, *The United States and Somoza,* pp. 63{ff}.

13. May, "The Alliance for Progress."

14. Mark Gilderhus, "Founding Father: Samuel Flagg Bemis and the Study of U.S.–Latin American Relations," *Diplomatic History* 21, no. 1 (winter 1997), pp. 1–13.

15. LaFeber, *Inevitable Revolutions,* p. 368 and passim.

16. Coatsworth, *Central America and the United States,* p. 216 and passim.

Bibliography

Archive Depositories

Franklin D. Roosevelt Library, Hyde Park, N.Y.
Harry S. Truman Library, Independence, Mo.
National Archives (NA), Washington, D.C. Record Group 43, Record Group 59.
   President's Secretary's Files.
   White House Central Files.
   White House Official Files.

Personal Papers

Acheson, Dean. Papers. Harry S. Truman Library, Independence, Mo.
Berle, Adolf A., Jr. Papers. Franklin D. Roosevelt Library, Hyde Park, N.Y.
Bowers, Claude G. Papers. Lilly Library, Indiana University, Bloomington, Ind.
Braden, Spruille. Papers. Rare Book and Manuscript Collection, Butler Library, Columbia University, New York, N.Y.
Briggs, Ellis Ormsbee. Papers. Hoover Institution on War, Revolution, and Peace, Stanford University, Stanford, Calif.
Corrigan, Francis P. Papers. Franklin D. Roosevelt Library, Hyde Park, N.Y.
Davis, Nathaniel P. Papers. Harry S. Truman Library, Independence, Mo.
Dozer, Donald Marquand. Papers. Hoover Institution on War, Revolution, and Peace, Stanford University, Stanford, Calif.
Grant, Frances R. Papers. Special Collections and Archives, Rutgers University Libraries, New Brunswick, N.J.
Grew, Joseph C. Papers. Houghton Library, Harvard University, Cambridge, Mass.
Kaiser, Philip M. Papers. Harry S. Truman Library, Independence, Mo.
Lovestone, Jay. Papers. Hoover Institution on War, Revolution, and Peace, Stanford University, Stanford, Calif.
Miller, Edward G., Jr. Papers. Harry S. Truman Library, Independence, Mo.
Romualdi, Serafino. Papers. Labor-Management Documentation Center, M. P. Catherwood Library, Cornell University, Ithaca, N.Y.
Wallace, Henry A. Papers. Franklin D. Roosevelt Library, Hyde Park, N.Y.
Wiley, John C. Papers. Franklin D. Roosevelt Library, Hyde Park, N.Y.

Books, Articles, and Published Documents

Acheson, Dean. *Present at the Creation: My Years in the State Department.* New York: W. W. Norton, 1969.

——. *Among Friends: Personal Letters of Dean Acheson.* Edited by David S. McClellan and David C. Acheson. New York: Dodd, Mead, 1980.

Acierto. "A Marshall Plan for Latin America." *Inter-American Economic Affairs* 1, no. 2 (September 1947): 3–20.

Acta final de la conferencia interamericana sobre problemas de la guerra y de la paz. Bogotá: Ministerio de Relaciones Exteriores, 1945.

Adams, John Quincy. *Memoirs of John Quincy Adams.* Edited by Charles Francis Adams. 12 vols. Philadelphia: J. B. Lippincott, 1874–77.

——. *Writings of John Quincy Adams.* Edited by Worthington Chauncey Ford. 7 vols. New York: Macmillan, 1913–17.

Aitken, Thomas, Jr. *Poet in the Fortress: The Story of Luis Muñoz Marín.* New York: New American Library, 1964.

Alberdi, Juan Bautista. *Bases y puntos de partida para la organización política de la república Argentina* [1852] with a prologue by Alfredo L. Palacios. Buenos Aires: W. M. Jackson, 1946.

Alexander, Robert J. *Communism in Latin America.* New Brunswick, N.J.: Rutgers University Press, 1957.

——. *The Bolivian National Revolution.* New Brunswick, N.J.: Rutgers University Press, 1958.

——. *Prophets of the Revolution: Profiles of Latin American Leaders.* New York: Macmillan, 1962.

——. *Organized Labor in Latin America.* New York: Free Press, 1965.

——. *Latin American Political Parties.* New York: Praeger, 1973.

——. *Aprismo: The Ideas and Doctrines of Víctor Raúl Haya de la Torre.* Kent, Ohio: Kent State University Press, 1973.

——. *The Right Opposition: The Lovestoneites and the International Communist Opposition of the 1930s.* Westport, Conn.: Greenwood Press, 1981.

——. *Rómulo Betancourt and the Transformation of Venezuela.* New Brunswick, N.J.: Transaction Books, 1982.

——. *Venezuela's Voice for Democracy: Conversations and Correspondence with Rómulo Betancourt.* New York: Praeger, 1990.

——, ed. *Biographical Dictionary of Latin American and Caribbean Political Leaders.* New York: Greenwood Press, 1988.

Alexander, Robert J., and Charles O. Porter. *The Struggle for Democracy in Latin America.* New York: Macmillan, 1961.

Ameringer, Charles D. *The Democratic Left in Exile: The Antidictatorial Struggle in the Caribbean, 1945–1959.* Coral Gables, Fla.: University of Miami Press, 1974.

——. *Don Pepe: A Political Biography of José Figueres of Costa Rica.* Albuquerque: University of New Mexico Press, 1978.

——. *U.S. Foreign Intelligence: The Secret Side of American History.* Lexington, Mass.: Lexington Books, 1990.

———. *The Caribbean Legion: Patriots, Politicians, Soldiers of Fortune, 1946–1950.* University Park: Pennsylvania State University Press, 1996.

Aram, Bethany. "Exporting Rhetoric, Importing Oil: United States Relations with Venezuela, 1945–1948." *World Affairs* 154, no. 3 (winter 1992): 94–106.

Arévalo, Juan José. *Informe presidencial sobre la situación política del país.* Guatemala: n.p., 1947.

Arévalo, Juan José, and Rómulo Betancourt. *Venezuela y Guatemala: Discursos con motivo de la visita del Presidente Betancourt a Guatemala.* Guatemala: Tipografía Nacional de Guatemala, 1946.

Atkins, G. Pope, and Larman C. Wilson. *The United States and the Trujillo Regime.* New Brunswick, N.J.: Rutgers University Press, 1972.

Barnard, Andrew. "Chilean Communists, Radical Presidents, and Chilean Relations with the United States, 1940–1947." *Journal of Latin American Studies* 13, no. 2 (1981): 347–74.

Barnet, Richard J. *Intervention and Revolution: The United States in the Third World.* New York: New American Library, 1968.

Beloff, Max. *An Historian in the Twentieth Century.* New Haven, Conn.: Yale University Press, 1992.

Bemis, Samuel Flagg. *The Latin American Policy of the United States.* New York: W. W. Norton, 1967.

Berger, Henry W. "Union Diplomacy: American Labor's Foreign Policy in Latin America, 1932–1955." Ph.D. diss., University of Wisconsin, 1966.

Berger, Mark T. *Under Northern Eyes: Latin American Studies and U.S. Hegemony in the Americas, 1898–1990.* Bloomington: Indiana University Press, 1995.

Berle, Adolf A., Jr. *Navigating the Rapids, 1918–1971.* Edited by Beatrice Berle and Travis Jacobs. New York: Harcourt Brace Jovanovich, 1973.

Berle, Adolf A., Jr., and Gardiner C. Means. *The Modern Corporation and Private Property.* New York: Commerce Clearing House, 1932.

Berle, Beatrice. *A Life in Two Worlds: The Autobiography of Beatrice Bishop Berle.* New York: Walker, 1983.

Berman, Sheri. *The Social Democratic Moment: Ideas and Politics in the Making of Interwar Europe.* Cambridge, Mass.: Harvard University Press, 1998.

Bernstein, Barton J., ed. *Politics and Policies of the Truman Administration.* Chicago: Quadrangle Books, 1970.

Bernstein, Eduard. *Evolutionary Socialism* [1899]. Translated by Edith Harvey with an introduction by Sidney Hook. New York: Schocken, 1961.

Betancourt, Rómulo. *Trayectoria democrática de una revolución.* 2 vols. Caracas: Imprenta Nacional, 1948.

———. *Venezuela: Política y petróleo.* Mexico City: Fondo de Cultura Económica, 1955.

———. "Mensaje para Venezuela y América." *Combate* 1, no. 4 (January and February 1959): 3–12.

———. *El 18 de octobre de 1945.* Barcelona: Sele Barral, 1979.

———. *Antología política, 1928–1935.* Caracas: Fundación Rómulo Betancourt, 1990.

———. *La segunda independencia de Venezuela: Compilación de la columna "Economía y Finanzas" del diario "Ahora," 1937–1939.* 3 vols. Caracas: Fundación Rómulo Betancourt, 1992.

Bethell, Leslie, ed. *The Cambridge History of Latin America*. Volume 3, *From Independence to c. 1870*. Cambridge, England: Cambridge University Press, 1985.

Bethell, Leslie, and Ian Roxborough, eds. *Latin America between the Second World War and the Cold War, 1944–1948*. Cambridge, England: Cambridge University Press, 1992.

Blasier, Cole. *The Hovering Giant: U.S. Responses to Revolutionary Change in Latin America, 1910–1985*. Revised edition. Pittsburgh: University of Pittsburgh Press, 1985.

Boeker, Paul H. *Lost Illusions: Latin America's Struggle for Democracy as Recounted by Its Leaders*. New York: Markus Wiener, 1990.

Bolívar, Simón. *Simón Bolívar obras completas*. Edited by Vicente Lecuna et al. 2 vols. Havana: Editorial Lex, 1947.

———. *Cartas del Libertador*. 8 vols. 2d ed., edited by Vicente Lecuna et al. Caracas: Italgráfica, C. A., 1964–70.

Bonilla, Heraclio, and Paul W. Drake, eds. *El Apra de la ideología a la praxis*. Lima: Editorial y Productora Gráfica "Nuevo Mundo" EIRL, 1989.

Bowers, Claude. *The Tragic Era: The Revolution after Lincoln*. Cambridge, Mass.: Houghton Mifflin, 1929.

———. *My Mission to Spain: Watching the Rehearsal for World War II*. New York: Simon and Schuster, 1954.

Braden, Spruille. "Foreign Trade Reconstruction—The Americas." *International Conciliation*, no. 419 (March 1946): 168–72.

———. *Diplomats and Demagogues*. New Rochelle, N.Y.: Arlington House, 1971.

Braden, Thomas W. "I'm glad the CIA is 'immoral.'" *The Saturday Evening Post*, 20 May 1967.

Briggs, Ellis. *Farewell to Foggy Bottom: The Recollections of a Career Diplomat*. New York: David McKay, 1964.

Brogan, Denis W. *American Aspects*. New York: Harper and Row, 1964.

Brown, Walter J. *James F. Byrnes of South Carolina: A Remembrance*. Macon, Ga.: Mercer University Press, 1992.

Bustamante y Rivero, José Luis. *Tres años de lucha por la democracia en el Perú*. Buenos Aires: Bartolomé U. Chiesino, 1949.

Caballero, Manuel. *Latin America and the Comintern, 1919–1943*. Cambridge, England: Cambridge University Press, 1986.

Cabot, John Moors. *First Line of Defense: Forty Years' Experiences of a Career Diplomat*. Washington, D.C.: School of Foreign Service, Georgetown University, 1979.

Carothers, Thomas. *In the Name of Democracy: U.S. Policy toward Latin America in the Reagan Years*. Berkeley: University of California Press, 1991.

Carter, Jimmy. Address at Commencement Exercises at the University of Notre Dame, 22 May 1977. *Weekly Compilation of Presidential Documents* 13, no. 22 (30 May 1977): 773–79.

Castro, Luis Alva. *Haya de la Torre: Peregrino de la unidad continental*. 2 vols. Lima: Fondo Editorial "V. R. Haya de la Torre," 1990.

Chomsky, Noam. *Deterring Democracy*. London: Verso, 1991.

Clark, Paul Coe, Jr. *The United States and Somoza, 1933–1956: A Revisionist Look.* Westport, Conn.: Praeger, 1992.

Clay, Henry. Speech of 25 March 1818. *Annals of the Congress of the United States.* 15th Congress, first session. Washington, D.C.: Gales and Seaton, 1854.

Clinton, Richard Lee. "APRA: An Appraisal." *Journal of Inter-American Studies and World Affairs* 12, no. 2 (April 1970): 280–97.

Coatsworth, John. *Central America and the United States: The Clients and the Colossus.* New York: Twayne, 1994.

Cobbs, Elizabeth A. *The Rich Neighbor Policy: Rockefeller and Kaiser in Brazil.* New Haven, Conn.: Yale University Press, 1992.

Coleman, Peter. *The Liberal Conspiracy: The Congress for Cultural Freedom and the Struggle for the Mind of Postwar Europe.* New York: Free Press, 1989.

Collier, Ruth Berins, and David Collier. *Shaping the Political Arena.* Princeton, N.J.: Princeton University Press, 1991.

Collings, Harry T. "The Congress of Bolívar." *Hispanic American Historical Review* 6, no. 4 (November 1926): 194–98.

Cullather, Nicholas. *Operation PBSUCCESS: The United States and Guatemala, 1952–1954.* Washington, D.C.: Central Intelligence Agency, 1994.

Dahl, Robert. *Polyarchy: Participation and Opposition.* New Haven, Conn.: Yale University Press, 1971.

Davies, Thomas M., Jr. *Indian Integration in Peru: A Half Century of Experience, 1900–1948.* Lincoln: University of Nebraska Press, 1974.

Debray, Régis. *The Chilean Revolution: Conversations with Allende.* New York: Random House: 1971.

De Santis, Hugh. *The Diplomacy of Silence: The American Foreign Service, the Soviet Union, and the Cold War, 1933–1947.* Chicago: University of Chicago Press, 1980.

Desch, Michael C. *When the Third World Matters: Latin America and United States Grand Strategy.* Baltimore: Johns Hopkins University Press, 1993.

Diamond, Larry, Juan L. Linz, and Seymour Martin Lipset, eds. *Democracy in Developing Countries: Latin America.* Boulder, Colo.: Lynne Rienner, 1989.

Díaz Araujo, Enrique. *La conspiración del '43.* Buenos Aires: Ediciones La Bastilla: 1971.

Díaz-Alejandro, Carlos F. *Essays on the Economic History of Argentina.* New Haven, Conn.: Yale University Press, 1970.

Dietz, James L., and Dilmus D. James, eds. *Progress toward Development in Latin America.* Boulder, Colo.: Lynne Rienner, 1990.

Dornbusch, Rudiger, and Sebastian Edwards, eds. *The Macroeconomics of Populism in Latin America.* Chicago: University of Chicago Press, 1991.

Dozer, Donald M. *Are We Good Neighbors? Three Decades of Inter-American Relations, 1930–60.* Gainesville: University Press of Florida, 1959.

Dulles, John W. F. *Vargas of Brazil: A Political Biography.* Austin: University of Texas Press, 1967.

———. *Brazilian Communism, 1935–1945.* Austin: University of Texas Press, 1983.

———. *Carlos Lacerda, Brazilian Crusader.* Volume 1, *The Years 1914–1960.* Austin: University of Texas Press, 1991.

Dumont, Louis. *German Ideology: From France to Germany and Back.* Chicago: University of Chicago Press, 1994.

Escudé, Carlos. *Gran Bretaña, Estados Unidos, y la declinación Argentina, 1942–1949.* Buenos Aires: Editorial de Belgrano, 1983.

Esquivel, Arturo Castro. *José Figueres Ferrar: El hombre y su obra.* San José: Imprenta Tormo, 1955.

Falcoff, Mark. *Modern Chile, 1970–1989: A Critical History.* New Brunswick, N.J.: Transaction Books, 1989.

Falcoff, Mark, and Ronald Dolkart. *Prologue to Perón: Argentina in Depression and War, 1930–1943.* Berkeley: University of California Press, 1975.

Federal Reserve System, Board of Governors. "United States Postwar Investment in Latin America." *Federal Reserve Bulletin* 39, no. 5 (May 1953): 445–46.

Figueres, José. Statement of 10 June 1958. *Hearings before the Subcommittee on Inter-American Affairs of the Committee on Foreign Affairs, House of Representatives.* 85th Cong., 2d sess. Washington, D.C.: Government Printing Office, 1958.

———. *El espiritu del 48.* San José: Editorial Costa Rica, 1987.

———. *Escritos y discursos, 1942–1962.* San José: Editorial Costa Rica, 1990.

Fitch, John Samuel. *The Military Coup d'Etat as a Political Process: Ecuador, 1948–1966.* Baltimore: Johns Hopkins University Press, 1977.

Freedom in the World: Political Rights and Civil Liberties. New York: Freedom House, 1978–1995.

Furet, François. "Democracy and Utopia." *Journal of Democracy* 9, no. 1 (January 1998): 65–79.

Galenson, Walter. *The CIO Challenge to the AFL: A History of the American Labor Movement, 1935–1941.* Cambridge, Mass.: Harvard University Press, 1960.

Gay, Peter. *The Dilemma of Democratic Socialism: Eduard Bernstein's Challenge to Marx.* New York: Columbia University Press, 1952.

Gellman, Irwin F. *Roosevelt and Batista: Good Neighbor Diplomacy in Cuba, 1933–1945.* Albuquerque: University of New Mexico Press, 1973.

———. *Good Neighbor Diplomacy: United States Policies in Latin America, 1933–1945.* Baltimore: Johns Hopkins University Press, 1979.

Gleijeses, Piero. *The Dominican Crisis: The 1965 Constitutionalist Revolt and American Intervention.* Translated by Lawrence Lipson. Baltimore: Johns Hopkins University Press, 1978.

———. *Shattered Hope: The Guatemalan Revolution and the United States, 1944–1954.* Princeton, N.J.: Princeton University Press, 1991.

Goldwert, Marvin. *The Constabulary in the Dominican Republic and Nicaragua: Progeny and Legacy of United States Intervention.* Gainesville: University Press of Florida, 1962.

Gómez, Alejandro. *Rómulo Betancourt y el Partido Comunista de Costa Rica, 1931–1935.* Caracas: Fondo Editorial de Humanidades y Educación de la Universidad Central de Venezuela, 1985.

Gompers, Samuel. *Labor and the Common Welfare* [1919]. Compiled by Hayes Robbins. Freeport: Books for Libraries Press, 1969.

———. *Seventy Years of Life and Labor* [1925]. Edited and with an introduction by Nick Salvatore. Ithaca, N.Y.: ILR Press, 1984.

Gompers, Samuel, and William English Walling. *Out of Their Own Mouths: A Revelation and an Indictment of Sovietism.* New York: E. P. Dutton, 1921.

Grant, Frances R. "Some Artistic Tendencies in South America." *Bulletin of the Pan American Union* 63, no. 10 (October 1929): 972–83.

———. "The Roerich Museum." *World Unity* 6, no. 1 (April 1930): 27–30.

———. "Brazilian Art." *Bulletin of the Pan American Union* 65, no. 1 (January 1931): 40–53.

———. "Nicholas Roerich's Plan of World Peace." *World Unity* 9, no. 5 (February 1932): 307–13.

———. *Oriental Philosophy: The Story of the Teachers of the East.* New York: Dial Press, 1936.

Grant, Frances R., and Mary Siegrist, et al. *Roerich–Himalaya.* 24 color plates and 78 halftone reproductions of works by Nicholas Roerich. New York: Brentanos, 1926.

Hanson, Simon G. "The Curtain That Shields the 'Diplomats.'" *Inter-American Economic Affairs* 4, no. 4 (spring 1951): 37–47.

Halle, Louis ["Y," pseud.]. "On a Certain Impatience with Latin America." *Foreign Affairs* 28, no. 4 (July 1950): 565–79.

Haya de la Torre, Víctor Raúl. "A Democratic Hemisphere." *Common Sense* (November 1941): 338–39.

———. "An Inter-American Democratic Front." *Free World* 4, no. 2 (November 1942): 150–52.

———. "La declaración democrática de Caracas." *Combate* 1, no. 5 (March and April 1959): 29–32.

———. *Obras completas.* 7 vols. Lima: Editorial Juan Mejia Baca, 1976.

Haya de la Torre, Víctor Raúl, and Luis Alberto Sánchez. *Correspondencia.* 2 vols. Lima: Mosca Azul Editores, 1982.

Hilton, Stanley E. "The Overthrow of Getúlio Vargas in 1945: Diplomatic Intervention, Defense of Democracy, or Political Retribution?" *Hispanic American Historical Review* 67, no. 1 (1987): 1–38.

Hobson, John Atkinson. *Imperialism: A Study.* London: J. Nisbet, 1902.

Hong, Wontack. *Factor Supply and Factor Intensity of Trade in Korea.* Seoul: Korean Development Institute, 1976.

Hunt, Michael H. *Ideology and U.S. Foreign Policy.* New Haven, Conn.: Yale University Press, 1987.

Huntington, Samuel P. *The Third Wave: Democratization in the Late Twentieth Century.* Norman: University of Oklahoma Press, 1991.

Hussey, Roland. *The Caracas Company, 1728–1784.* Cambridge, Mass.: Harvard University Press, 1934.

[IADF] Asociación Interamericana pro Democracia y Libertad. *Conferencia Interamericana pro Democracia y Libertad: Resoluciones y otros documentos.* Havana: ALFA, 1950.

ICFTU-ORIT. *The Permanent Struggle of the Free Trade Union Movement against Latin American Dictatorships.* Mexico City: ORIT Press and Publications, 1960.

Immerman, Richard H. *The CIA in Guatemala: The Foreign Policy of Intervention.* Austin: University of Texas Press, 1982.

Inter-American Association for Democracy and Freedom. *Report of the Havana Conference, Havana, Cuba, May 12–15, 1950.* Havana: Inter-American Association for Democracy and Freedom, 1950.

Iokibe, Makoto, ed. The Occupational Japan (microfilm), Washington, D.C.: Library of Congress.

Iriye, Akira. *Cultural Internationalism and World Order.* Baltimore: Johns Hopkins University Press, 1997.

Jefferson, Thomas. *The Writings of Thomas Jefferson.* 20 vols. Edited by Andrew Lipscomb and Albert Bergh. Washington, D.C.: Thomas Jefferson Memorial Association, 1903.

Johnson, Robert David, ed. *On Cultural Ground: Essays in International History.* Chicago: Imprint Publications, 1994.

Kampelman, Max M. *The Communist Party vs. the C.I.O.* [1957]. New York: Arno and New York Times, 1971.

Kantorowicz, Hermann. *Der Geist Englischen Politik und das Gespenst der Einkreisung Deutschlands.* Berlin: E. Rowohlt, 1929. Published in English as *The Spirit of British Policy and the Myth of the Encirclement of Germany.* London: George Allen and Unwin, 1931.

Kaufman, Stuart Bruce. *Samuel Gompers and the Origins of the American Federation of Labor, 1848–1896.* Westport, Conn.: Greenwood Press, 1973.

Kedourie, Elie. *Nationalism.* 4th ed. Cambridge, Mass.: Blackwell, 1993.

Keller, A. G. "The Transplantation of Democracy." *Scientific Monthly* 31, no. 3 (March 1945): 165–76.

Kelly, Janet. "Democracy Redux: How Real Is Democracy in Latin America?" *Latin American Research Review* 33, no. 1 (1998): 212–25.

Kelsen, Hans. *Principles of International Law.* 2d ed., edited by Robert W. Tucker. New York: Holt, Rinehart, and Winston, 1966.

Kennan, George F. *Memoirs, 1925–1950.* Boston: Little, Brown, 1967.

Klaren, Peter F. *Modernization, Dislocation, and Aprismo: Origins of the Peruvian Aprista Party, 1870–1932.* Austin: University of Texas Press, 1973.

Kofas, Jon. *The Struggle for Legitimacy: Latin American Labor and the United States, 1930–1960.* Tempe: Arizona State University, 1992.

Kolakowski, Leszek, and Stuart Hampshire, eds. *The Socialist Idea: A Reappraisal.* New York: Basic Books, 1974.

Kolko, Gabriel. *Confronting the Third World: United States Foreign Policy, 1945–1980.* New York: Pantheon, 1988.

Konvitz, Milton R., and Clinton Rossiter, eds. *Aspects of Liberty: Essays Presented to Robert E. Cushman.* Ithaca, N.Y.: Cornell University Press, 1958.

Krauze, Enrique. "Old Paradigms and New Openings." *Journal of Democracy* 3, no. 1 (January 1992): 15–24.

Krueger, Anne, and Jagdish Bhagwati, eds. *Foreign Trade Regimes and Economic Development.* 11 vols. Cambridge, Mass.: Ballinger Press, 1974–78.

Kunz, Diane B. "When Money Counts and Doesn't: Economic Power and Diplomatic Objectives." *Diplomatic History* 18, no. 4 (fall 1994): 451–62.

LaFeber, Walter. *Inevitable Revolutions: The United States in Central America*. 2d ed. New York: W. W. Norton, 1993.

Legrand, Catherine C. "Informal Resistance on a Dominican Sugar Plantation during the Trujillo Dictatorship." *Hispanic American Historical Review* 75, no. 4 (November 1995): 555–96.

Lenin, Vladimir Ilich. *Selected Works*. 12 vols. New York: International Publishers, 1938.

León de Vivero, Fernando. *El tirano quedó atrás*. Mexico City: Editorial Cultura, 1951.

Levenstein, Harvey A. *Labor Organizations in the United States and Mexico: A History of Their Relations*. Westport, Conn.: Greenwood, 1971.

Levine, Daniel H. "Venezuela: The Nature, Sources, and Future Prospects of Democracy." In *Democracy in Developing Countries: Latin America*, edited by Larry Diamond, Juan L. Linz, and Seymour Martin Lipset. Boulder, Colo.: Lynne Rienner, 1989.

Levinson, Jerome, and Juan de Onis, eds. *The Alliance That Lost Its Way: A Critical Report on the Alliance for Progress*. Chicago: Quadrangle Books, 1970.

Linz, Juan J., and Alfred Stepan, eds. *The Breakdown of Democratic Regimes: Latin America*. Baltimore: Johns Hopkins University Press, 1978.

Lombardo Toledano, Vicente. *Posición de la C.T.A.L. frente al imperialismo nazi-fascismo y las huelgas*. Montevideo: Ediciones Unidad, 1944.

———. *La C.T.A.L. ante la guerra y ante la postguerra*. Mexico City: Universidad Obrera de Mexico, 1945.

———. Lorwin, Lewis L. *The International Labor Movement*. New York: Harper and Brothers, 1953

———. *Obras completas*. 25 vols. Mexico City: Rosette y Asociados Artes Gráficas, 1991.

Lowenthal, Abraham F., ed. *Exporting Democracy: The United States and Latin America*. 2 vols. Baltimore: Johns Hopkins University Press, 1991.

Luna, Félix. *El 45: Crónica de un año decisivo*. Buenos Aires: Editorial Jorge Alvarez, 1969.

———. *Perón y su tiempo*. 3 vols. Buenos Aires: Editorial Sudamericana, 1984.

Lundestad, Geir. *The American Non-Policy towards Eastern Europe, 1943–1947*. Tromsö, Norway: Universitetsforlaget, 1978.

———. "Moralism, Presentism, Exceptionalism, Provincialism, and Other Extravagances in American Writings on the Early Cold War Years." *Diplomatic History* 13, no. 4 (fall 1989): 527–45.

Maier, Charles S. "The Politics of Productivity: Foundations of American International Economic Policy after World War II." *International Organization* 31, no. 4 (autumn 1977): 607–33.

Marcus, George. "The Uses of Complicity in the Changing Mise-en-Scène of Anthropological Fieldwork." *Representations* 59 (summer 1997): 85–108.

Mark, Eduard. "Charles E. Bohlen and the Acceptable Limits of Soviet Hegemony in Eastern Europe: A Memorandum of 18 October 1945." *Diplomatic History* 3, no. 2 (spring 1979): 201–13.

———. "American Policy toward Eastern Europe and the Origins of the Cold War,

1941–1946: An Alternative Interpretation." *The Journal of American History* 68, no. 2 (September 1981): 313–36.

———. "The War Scare of 1946." *Diplomatic History* 21 (summer 1997): 383–415.

Marx, Karl. "Bolívar y Ponte, Simón." In *The New American Cyclopeædia*, edited by George Ripley and Charles Dana. 16 vols. New York: D. Appleton, 1858.

———. *Karl Marx on Colonialism and Modernization*. Edited by Shlomo Avineri. Garden City, N.Y.: Doubleday, 1968.

———. *Karl Marx: Selected Writings*. Edited by David McLellan. Oxford: Oxford University Press, 1977.

May, Ernest R. "The Alliance for Progress in Historical Perspective." *Foreign Affairs* 41, no. 4 (July 1963): 757–70.

———. "The 'Bureaucratic Politics' Approach: U.S.-Argentine Relations, 1942–1947." In *Latin America and the United States: The Changing Political Realities*, edited by Julio Cotler and Richard R. Fagen. Stanford, Calif.: Stanford University Press, 1974.

———. "National Security in American History." In *Rethinking America's Security*, edited by Inin Graham Allison and Gregory F. Treverton, 94–114. New York: W. W. Norton, 1992.

McCann, Frank D., Jr. *The Brazilian-American Alliance, 1937–1945*. Princeton, N.J.: Princeton University Press, 1973.

McGann, Thomas F. "The Ambassador and the Dictator: The Braden Mission to Argentina and Its Significance for United States Relations with Latin America." *The Centennial Review* 6, no. 3 (summer 1962): 343–57.

Mecham, J. Lloyd. "Democracy and Dictatorship in Latin America." *Southwestern Social Science Quarterly* 41, no. 3 (December 1960): 294–303.

Millon, Robert Paul. *Mexican Marxist: Vicente Lombardo Toledano*. Chapel Hill: University of North Carolina Press, 1966.

Miolán, Angel. *El perredé, desde mi ángulo*. Santo Domingo: n.p., 1984.

Miranda, Francisco de. *The Diary of Francisco de Miranda, 1783–1784*. Edited by William Spence Robertson. New York: Hispanic Society of America, 1928.

Momigliano, Arnaldo. *Alien Wisdom: The Limits of Hellenization*. Cambridge, England: Cambridge University Press, 1975.

Mommer, Bernard. *La cuestión petrolera*. Caracas: Asociación de Professores UCV-TROPYKOS, 1988.

Moynihan, Daniel Patrick. "The United States and the International Labor Organization, 1889–1934." Ph.D. diss., Fletcher School of Law and Diplomacy, 1961.

Munro, Dana G. *Intervention and Dollar Diplomacy in the Caribbean, 1900–1921*. Princeton, N.J.: Princeton University Press, 1964.

———. *The United States and the Caribbean Republics, 1921–1933*. Princeton, N.J.: Princeton University Press, 1974.

Ninkovich, Frank. *Modernity and Power: A History of the Domino Theory in the Twentieth Century*. Chicago: University of Chicago Press, 1994.

North, Douglass C. *Institutions, Institutional Change, and Economic Performance*. Cambridge, England: Cambridge University Press, 1990.

Notter, Harley A. *Postwar Foreign Policy Preparation, 1939–1945*. Department of State Publication 3580. Washington, D.C., 1949.

Osgood, Robert Endicott. *Ideals and Self Interest in America's Foreign Relations: The Great Transformation of the Twentieth Century*. Chicago: University of Chicago Press, 1953.

Pach, Chester J., Jr. "The Containment of U.S. Military Aid to Latin America, 1944–1949." *Diplomatic History* 6, no. 3 (summer 1982): 225–43.

Packenham, Robert A. *The Dependency Movement: Scholarship and Politics in Development Studies*. Cambridge, Mass.: Harvard University Press, 1992.

Pastor, Robert A. *Condemned to Repetition: The United States and Nicaragua*. Princeton, N.J.: Princeton University Press, 1987.

———. *Whirlpool: U.S. Foreign Policy toward Latin America and the Caribbean*. Princeton, N.J.: Princeton University Press, 1992.

Peeler, John A. *Latin American Democracies: Colombia, Costa Rica, Venezuela*. Chapel Hill: University of North Carolina Press, 1985.

Pike, Fredrick B. *The Modern History of Peru*. New York: Praeger, 1967.

———. *The Politics of the Miraculous in Peru: Haya de la Torre and the Spiritualist Tradition*. Lincoln: University of Nebraska Press, 1986.

Pipes, Richard. *The Russian Revolution*. New York: Vintage Books, 1991.

———. *Russia under the Bolshevik Regime*. New York: Vintage Books, 1995.

———, ed. *The Unknown Lenin: From the Secret Archive*. New Haven, Conn.: Yale University Press, 1996.

Popper, Karl. *Objective Knowledge: An Evolutionary Approach*. Rev. ed. Oxford: Oxford University Press, 1979.

Potash, Robert A., ed. *Perón y el G.O.U.: Los documentos de una logia secreta*. Buenos Aires: Editorial Sudamericana, 1984.

Quirós, Marcia. "The United States and the Costa Rican Civil War of 1948: The Case against Intervention." Unpublished. 1992.

Rabe, Stephen G. "The Elusive Conference: United States Economic Relations with Latin America, 1945–1952." *Diplomatic History* 2 (summer 1978): 279–94.

———. *The Road to OPEC: United States Relations with Venezuela, 1919–1976*. Austin: University of Texas Press, 1982.

———. *Eisenhower and Latin America: The Foreign Policy of Anticommunism*. Chapel Hill: University of North Carolina Press, 1988.

———. "The Caribbean Triangle: Betancourt, Castro, and Trujillo and U.S. Foreign Policy, 1958–1963." *Diplomatic History* 20 (winter 1996): 55–78.

Radosh, Ronald. *American Labor and United States Foreign Policy*. New York: Random House, 1969.

Rangel, Carlos. *Del buen salvaje al buen revolucionario*. Caracas: Monte Avila, 1976. Published in English as *The Latin Americans: Their Love-Hate Relationship with the United States*. New Brunswick, N.J.: Transaction Books, 1987.

Rawls, Shirley N. "Spruille Braden: A Political Biography." Ph.D. diss., University of New Mexico, 1976.

Robertson, William Spence. *Rise of the Spanish-American Republics: As Told in the Lives of Their Liberators* [1918]. New York: Free Press, 1946.

Robinson, William. *Promoting Polyarchy: Globalization, U.S. Intervention, and Hegemony*. Cambridge, England: Cambridge University Press, 1996.

Roca, Blas. *El triunfo de Grau, la Unidad Nacional, y nuestra actitud*. Havana: Arrow Press, 1944.

Roche, John P. *The History and Impact of Marxist-Leninist Organizational Theory*. Cambridge, Mass.: Institute for Foreign Policy Analysis, 1984.

Rock, David, ed. *Latin America in the 1940s: War and Postwar Transitions*. Berkeley: University of California Press, 1994.

Rodó, José Enrique. *Ariel* [1900]. 9th ed. Montevideo: Librería Cervantes, 1911.

Roerich Museum: A Decade of Activity, 1921–1931. New York: Roerich Museum Press, 1931.

Roerich, Nicholas. "To the Women." *Roerich Museum Bulletin* 1, no. 5 (May 1931): 6.

Roerich Pact: Banner of Peace. 2 vols. New York: Roerich Museum Press, 1934.

Romualdi, Serafino. "Labor and Democracy in Latin America." *Foreign Affairs* 25, no. 3 (April 1947): 477–81.

———. *Presidents and Peons: Recollections of a Labor Ambassador in Latin America*. New York: Funk and Wagnalls, 1967.

Roorda, Eric Paul. "Genocide Next Door: The Good Neighbor Policy, the Trujillo Regime, and the Haitian Massacre of 1937." *Diplomatic History* 20, no. 3 (summer 1996): 301–19.

Roth, Guenther. *The Social Democrats in Imperial Germany* [1963]. New York: Arno, 1979.

Salisbury, Richard V. "The Middle America Exile of Víctor Raúl Haya de la Torre." *The Americas* 40, no. 1 (July 1983): 13–15.

Sánchez, Luis Alberto. *Haya de la Torre y el Apra*. 2d ed. Lima: Editorial Universo, 1980.

———. *Testimonio personal* [1967]. 6 vols. Lima: Mosca Azul Editores, 1987.

Sánchez, Luis Alberto, and Hugo Vallenas. *Sobre la herencia de Haya de la Torre*. Lima: Nova Print, 1994.

Schlesinger, Arthur M., Jr. *A Thousand Days: John F. Kennedy in the White House*. Boston: Houghton Mifflin, 1965.

Schneider, Ronald. *Communism in Guatemala, 1944–1954*. New York: Praeger, 1959.

Schoultz, Lars. *Beneath the United States: A History of U.S. Policy toward Latin America*. Cambridge, Mass.: Harvard University Press, 1998.

Schwartzberg, Steven. "The Lion and the Phoenix: British Policy toward the 'Greek Question,' 1821–1832." *Middle Eastern Studies* 24, nos. 2 and 3 (April and July 1988): 139–77, 287–311.

———. "The 'Soft Peace Boys': Presurrender Planning and Japanese Land Reform." *Journal of American-East Asian Relations* 2, no. 2 (summer 1993): 185–216.

———. "Rómulo Betancourt: From a Communist Anti-Imperialist to a Social Democrat with U.S. Support." *Journal of Latin America Studies* 29, no. 3 (October 1997): 613–65.

Schwarz, Jordan A. *Liberal: Adolf A. Berle and the Vision of an American Era*. New York: Free Press, 1987.

Seoane, Manuel. *Las calumnias contra el aprismo*. Buenos Aires: n.p., 1932.

————. *Nuestra América y la guerra.* Santiago: Ediciones Ercilla, 1940.

Shils, Edward A. *The Torment of Secrecy: The Background and Consequences of American Security Policies.* New York: Free Press, 1956.

————. *The Intellectuals and the Powers and Other Essays.* Chicago: University of Chicago Press, 1972.

————. *Center and Periphery: Essays in Macrosociology.* Chicago: University of Chicago Press, 1975.

————. *Tradition.* Chicago: University of Chicago Press, 1981.

————. "Knowledge and the Sociology of Knowledge." *Knowledge: Creation, Diffusion, Utilization* 4, no. 1 (September 1982): 7–32.

————. "Remembering the Congress for Cultural Freedom." *Encounter* 75, no. 2 (September 1990): 53–65.

————. *The Virtue of Civility.* Indianapolis: Liberty Fund, 1997.

Sieyès, Emmanuel Joseph. *Qu'est-ce que le tiers-etat?* [2d ed., corrigée. Paris?, n.p., 1789]. English transl., London: Pall Mall Press, 1963.

Skidmore, Thomas E. *Politics in Brazil, 1930–1964: An Experiment in Democracy.* New York: Oxford University Press, 1967.

Smith, Gaddis. *American Diplomacy during the Second World War, 1941–1945.* New York: John Wiley and Sons, 1965.

————. *Dean Acheson.* New York: Cooper Square Publishers, 1972.

————. *The Last Years of the Monroe Doctrine, 1945–1993.* New York: Hill and Wang, 1994.

Smith, Peter. *Talons of the Eagle.* Oxford: Oxford University Press, 1996.

Smith, Tony. *America's Mission: The United States and the Worldwide Struggle for Democracy in the Twentieth Century.* Princeton, N.J.: Princeton University Press, 1994.

Stein, Steve. *Populism in Peru: The Emergence of the Masses and the Politics of Social Control.* Madison: University of Wisconsin Press, 1980.

Stephanson, Anders. *Manifest Destiny: American Expansion and the Empire of Right.* New York: Hill and Wang, 1995.

Stiller, Jesse H. *George S. Messersmith: Diplomat of Democracy.* Chapel Hill: University of North Carolina Press, 1987.

Syrquin, Moshe, Lance Taylor, and Larry Westphal. *Economic Structure and Performance: Essays in Honor of Hollis B. Chenery.* New York: Harcourt Brace Jovanovich, 1984.

Taft, Philip. *The A.F. of L. in the Time of Gompers.* New York: Harper and Brothers, 1957.

————. *Defending Freedom: American Labor and Foreign Affairs.* Los Angeles: Nash, 1973.

Thomas, Ann Van Wynen, and A. J. Thomas Jr. *The Organization of American States.* Dallas, Tex.: Southern Methodist University Press, 1963.

Thomas, Hugh. *Cuba: The Pursuit of Freedom.* New York: Harper and Row, 1971.

Tillapaugh, James C. "From War to Cold War: United States Policies toward Latin America, 1943–1948." Ph.D. diss., Northwestern University, 1973.

Townsend Ezcurra, Andres. *Cinquenta años de aprismo: Memorias, ensayos y discursos de un militante.* Lima: n.p., 1989.

Trask, Roger. "Spruille Braden versus George Messersmith: World War II, the Cold War, and Argentine Policy, 1945–1947." *Journal of Inter-American Studies and World Affairs* 26, no. 1 (February 1984): 69–95.

Trotsky, Leon. *Terrorism and Communism: A Reply to Karl Kautsky* [1920]. With an introduction by Max Shachtman. Ann Arbor: University of Michigan Press, 1961.

Troy, Thomas F. *Donovan and the CIA: A History of the Establishment of the Central Intelligence Agency.* Langley, Va.: Central Intelligence Agency, Center for the Study of Intelligence, 1981.

Truman, Harry S. Address to the Governing Board of the Pan American Union, 15 April 1946. Text in *Bulletin of the Pan American Union* 78, no. 69 (June 1946): 309–10.

Unión Panamericana. *Consulta del gobierno del Uruguay y contestaciones de los gobiernos.* Washington, D.C.: Unión Panamericana, 1946.

U.S. Agency for International Development. *U.S. Overseas Loans and Grants.* Washington, D.C.: AID, 1991.

U.S. Department of Commerce. "Indexes of U.S. Trade with Latin America." *World Trade Information Service Statistical Reports*, part 3, no. 55–17. Washington, D.C.: Government Printing Office, 1955.

U.S. Department of State. *Consultation among the American Republics with Respect to the Argentine Situation: Memorandum of the United States Government* (Blue Book). Washington, D.C.: Government Printing Office, 1946.

———. *United States Relations with China: With Special Reference to the Period 1944–1949.* Washington, D.C.: Government Printing Office, 1949.

———. *Foreign Relations of the United States.* Washington, D.C.: Government Printing Office.

———. *Peace in the Americas.* Publication 3964. Washington, D.C.: Government Printing Office, 1950.

———. *Bulletin.* Washington, D.C.: Government Printing Office.

Valenzuela, Arturo. "Paraguay: The Coup That Didn't Happen." *Journal of Democracy* 8, no. 1 (January 1997): 43–55.

Vega, Bernardo. *Los Estados Unidos y Trujillo: Colección de documentos del Departamento de Estado y de las fuerzas armadas norteamericanas* [1945, 1 vol.; 1946 and 1947, 2 vols.]. Santo Domingo: Fundación Cultural Dominicana, 1982–84.

———. *Trujillo y las fuerzas armadas norteamericanas.* Santo Domingo: Fundación Cultural Dominicana, 1992.

Véliz, Claudio. *The New World of the Gothic Fox: Culture and Economy in English and Spanish America.* Berkeley: University of California Press, 1994.

Viner, Jacob. *International Trade and Economic Development.* Glencoe, Ill.: Free Press, 1952.

———. *Essays on the Intellectual History of Economics.* Princeton, N.J.: Princeton University Press, 1991.

Volkogonov, Dmitri. *Lenin: A New Biography.* Translated by Harold Shukman. New York: Free Press, 1994.

Wallace, Henry A. *The Price of Vision: The Diary of Henry A. Wallace, 1942–1946.* Edited by John Morton Blum. Boston: Houghton Mifflin, 1973.

Walter, Knut. *The Regime of Anastasio Somoza, 1936–1956.* Chapel Hill: University of North Carolina Press, 1993.

Warner, Michael, ed. *The CIA under Harry Truman.* Washington, D.C.: Central Intelligence Agency, 1994.

Warren, Harris Gaylord. "Economic Aid for Latin America." *Inter-American Economic Affairs* 5, no. 4 (spring 1952): 92–108.

Weber, Max. *The Methodology of the Social Sciences.* Translated and with an introduction by Edward. A. Shils. New York: Free Press, 1949.

———. *Economy and Society.* Translated and edited by Guenther Roth and Claus Wittich et al. Berkeley: University of California Press, 1978.

———. *From Max Weber: Essays in Sociology.* Translated and edited by H. H. Gerth and C. Wright Mills. New York: Oxford University Press, 1981.

Weil, Martin. *A Pretty Good Club: The Founding Fathers of the U.S. Foreign Service.* New York: W. W. Norton, 1978.

Welles, Sumner. *Naboth's Vineyard: The Dominican Republic, 1844–1924* [1928]. 2 vols. Mamaroneck, N.Y.: Paul Appel, 1966.

Whitaker, Arthur P. *The United States and Argentina.* Cambridge, Mass.: Harvard University Press, 1954.

———, ed. *Latin America and the Enlightenment* [1942]. Ithaca, N.Y.: Cornell University Press, 1961.

White, Graham, and John Maze. *Henry A. Wallace: His Search for a New World Order.* Chapel Hill: University of North Carolina Press, 1995.

Wight, Martin. "International Legitimacy." *International Relations* 4, no. 1 (May 1972).

Wilson, Woodrow. *The Papers of Woodrow Wilson.* 69 vols. Edited by Arthur Link et al. Princeton, N.J.: Princeton University Press, 1966–93.

Windmuller, John P. *American Labor and the International Labor Movement, 1940–1953.* Ithaca, N.Y.: Institute of International Industrial and Labor Relations, 1954.

Wood, Bryce. *The Making of the Good Neighbor Policy.* New York: W. W. Norton, 1967.

———. *The Dismantling of the Good Neighbor Policy.* Austin: University of Texas Press, 1985.

Woytinsky, Emma S., ed. *So Much Alive: The Life and Work of Wladimir S. Woytinsky.* New York: Vanguard, 1962.

Woytinsky, Wladimir S. *The Twelve Who Are to Die.* With a foreword by Karl Kautsky. Berlin: Delegation of the S-R Party Abroad, 1922.

———. *Stormy Passage: A Personal History through Two Russian Revolutions to Democracy and Freedom: 1905–1960.* With a foreword by A. A. Berle Jr. New York: Vanguard, 1961.

Index

Eastern European policy, 25; economy, 26; human rights abuses, 194; in World War II, 23–25, 28–29, 36, 231n24; interest in Balkans, 22–23; movements loyal to, 75; nationalism, 25; Nazi invasion of, 201; obligations under U.N. Charter, 72; policy toward Saudi Arabia, 25; postwar policy, 22–24, 25, 28–29, 29; sphere of influence, 17, 18–19, 25; U.S. military presence in, 24. *See also* Russia; United States (policy toward Soviet Union)

Spain, 91, 225, 239n71; civil war, 9

Stalin, Josef, 1, 27, 129, 258n14

Stettinius, Edward, 26–27, 28

Stockholm Peace petition, 211

Student exchange programs, 191

Suarez Vientimilla, Mariano, 170–71

Suffrage for women, 172, 253n94

Sumner, William Graham, 143–44

Surplus Property Act, 80

Sweden, 73, 121

Tamborini, José P., 57

Thomas, Norman, 94

Thompson, John, 159

Thorpe, Willard L., 238n71

Thurston, Walter, 57

Tito, Josep, 121

Tittman, Harold, 191

Trotsky, Leon, 128, 130, 257n11

Trujillo, Rafael, 10, 33, 90, 127, 158, 176, 219, 224, 269n8; diplomatic recognition of Batista, 211; pro-U.S. politics, 220

Truman, Harry, 29; acceptance of Argentine compliance, 79; arms policy, 80, 84; Cold War liberalism, 196; democratic solidarity policy, 215; diplomatic recognition policy, 187, 193; Gallegos and, 158, 161, 162; government records from administration, 14; nonintervention policy, 187–88, 199; pessimistic about prospects for democracy in Latin America, 198, 203; policy of covert support for Latin America, 15; policy toward Argentina, 52; policy toward Chile, 217, 218, 219; on political and economic sanctions, 189; and strategic goals of U.S., 30

Truman Doctrine, 154

Turkey, 25, 27, 29, 83

Ubico, Jorge, 48, 245n192

Ulate Blanco, Otilio, 174, 176, 178, 179, 180–81, 185

União Democrática Nacional (UDN) (Brazil), 36, 41

Unión Democrática (Argentina), 63, 64

Unión Parlementaria (UP) (Peru), 117

Unión Republicana Democrática (URD) (Venezuela), 152, 153, 156, 159, 198

Unión Revolucionara (UR) (Peru), 114–15

United Fruit, 138

United Nations, 50, 219; charter, 68, 72, 86; Security Council, 18

United States, 58, 125, 127; agrarian movement, 35; anti-imperialism in, 94–95, 107, 247n19; anti-Perón policy, 57, 73; arms policy, 56, 72, 73, 79–85, 81, 82, 87–88, 168, 193, 215, 243n144; Big Stick policy, 53, 54, 100; capitalism, 94, 100, 201; criticism of, 142, 143, 196, 266n146; delatinization of, 92; diplomatic interference policy, 195; diplomatic pressure, 57; diplomatic recognition, 46, 48, 194–96, 266n146, 279n93; diplomatic support of dictatorships, 101–2, 118, 119, 124, 161, 189–90, 191, 193, 199, 224; domestic politics, 223; economy, 20–21, 35; efforts to promote democracy, 63; elections of 1952, 199; exportation of capital, 96; free access policy, 26, 28; global strategy, 17; imperialism, 8–9, 55, 91, 94, 97, 100, 129, 130, 131, 220, 221, 226; inter-American solidarity and, 54, 58, 71, 89; intervention policy, 8–9, 53, 57, 62, 94, 95, 101, 142, 143, 188, 247n18; labor movement, 5, 35; 62; as market for Latin American goods, 139; most-favored nation status and, 28; nonintervention as support of dictatorships, 95, 188–89; nonintervention policy, 31, 35, 53, 54, 57, 75, 125, 165, 168, 189, 197, 198, 199, 201–2, 221; nonintervention policy vs. right to self-defense, 86; oil industry, 165, 261n86; optimism about prospects for democracy in Latin America, 202; policy of covert support, 14–15, 224; policy of democratic solidarity, 219; policy of isolation, 60; policy of paternalism, 200–201; postwar objectives in Eastern Europe and Near East, 17; postwar policy, 24–25, 26, 27–28, 30; as privileged

Steven Schwartzberg has served as visiting assistant professor at the University of Nevada, Las Vegas, and director of undergraduate studies for international studies at Yale. His articles have appeared in the *Journal of Latin American Studies, Middle Eastern Studies,* and the *Journal of American East Asian Relations.*

www.ingramcontent.com/pod-product-compliance
Lightning Source LLC
Chambersburg PA
CBHW020655270326
41928CB00005B/134